河南省"十四五"普通高等教育规划教材
2015年度河南省教育科学研究优秀成果二等奖
2015年度河南省信息技术教育优秀成果二等奖
首届河南省教材建设二等奖

高 等 学 校 计 算 机 专 业 系 列 教 材

基于C#的管理信息系统开发（第3版）

郭基凤 高亮 主编　韩玉民 赵冬 副主编
朱彦松 余雨萍 编著

清华大学出版社
北京

内 容 简 介

本书主要介绍如何使用C#语言进行各类管理信息系统开发，是C#语言学习的实践提高教材。

本书共9章，第1章为管理信息系统概述；第2章介绍数据库高级编程；第3章介绍系统架构；第4章介绍ASP.NET MVC；第5章介绍前端框架Bootstrap；第6～9章介绍实际的MIS案例开发，其中，第6章为图书管理系统案例开发，第7章为超市商品进销存管理系统案例开发，第8章为在线考试系统案例开发，第9章为高校实践课题管理系统案例开发。

本书从实际应用需求引入，对实际案例详解，内容应用性和实践性强，可作为高等院校计算机软件相关专业C#应用程序开发类课程的教材，也可作为软件开发人员的参考用书。

本书封面贴有清华大学出版社防伪标签，无标签者不得销售。
版权所有，侵权必究。举报：010-62782989，beiqinquan@tup.tsinghua.edu.cn。

图书在版编目(CIP)数据

基于C#的管理信息系统开发/郭基凤，高亮主编. —3版. —北京：清华大学出版社，2023.8
高等学校计算机专业系列教材
ISBN 978-7-302-63895-7

Ⅰ.①基… Ⅱ.①郭… ②高… Ⅲ.①管理信息系统－系统开发－高等学校－教材 ②C语言－程序设计－高等学校－教材 Ⅳ.①C931.6 ②TP312.8

中国国家版本馆CIP数据核字(2023)第110361号

责任编辑：龙启铭　薛　阳
封面设计：何凤霞
责任校对：胡伟民
责任印制：沈　露

出版发行：清华大学出版社
　　网　　址：http://www.tup.com.cn, http://www.wqbook.com
　　地　　址：北京清华大学学研大厦A座　　邮　编：100084
　　社 总 机：010-83470000　　邮　购：010-62786544
　　投稿与读者服务：010-62776969, c-service@tup.tsinghua.edu.cn
　　质量反馈：010-62772015, zhiliang@tup.tsinghua.edu.cn
　　课件下载：http://www.tup.com.cn, 010-83470236
印 装 者：三河市铭诚印务有限公司
经　　销：全国新华书店
开　　本：185mm×260mm　　印　张：25　　字　数：628千字
版　　次：2014年6月第1版　2023年9月第3版　　印　次：2023年9月第1次印刷
定　　价：79.00元

产品编号：095458-01

前言

本书第1版自2014年出版以来,先后多次印刷,深受广大读者的欢迎,被多所高等学校选为教材,获得2015年度河南省教育科学研究优秀成果二等奖(豫教〔2015〕04744号)、2015年度河南省信息技术教育优秀成果二等奖(豫教〔2015〕10366号)。本书第2版于2017年出版,2021年获得首届河南省教材建设二等奖(教思政〔2021〕144号)。教材在多年的使用过程中,有不少教师和读者提出了一些很好的意见与建议。为适应技术发展,结合教学实践、读者意见和建议,我们对本教材进行了修订,推出第3版,2020年入选河南省"十四五"普通高等教育规划教材重点建设项目(教高〔2020〕469号)。本次修订保持了前两版的写作风格和特色,侧重MIS开发,采用实用案例,坚持"实际应用需求引入→技术要点分析→关键代码剖析→技术经验总结"的学习路线,突出应用性和实践性。

本版修订的主要内容有:

(1) 升级开发环境与工具。开发环境由第2版的Visual Studio 2012升级为Visual Studio 2019,数据库采用SQL Server 2019,所有案例都是在Visual Studio 2019下完成。

(2) 优化调整了部分章节内容,删减了原第4章RDLC报表、第5章建模工具PowerDesigner,替换为Web开发的必要技术ASP.NET MVC和前端框架Bootstrap,这两部分内容是当下企业人才招聘.NET开发工程师时所必需的技术。

(3) 采用ASP.NET MVC+Bootstrap技术对第9章案例进行了重构。

本书共9章。

第1章,介绍MIS基础知识。

第2~5章,主要介绍C#语言的高级特性和常用前后端框架,其中,第2章介绍利用C#进行数据库操作的高级特性;第3章介绍常用系统架构;第4章简要介绍ASP.NET MVC的基本原理及应用;第5章介绍前端框架Bootstrap典型应用。

第6~9章,为典型的MIS实际案例开发详解,其中,第6章为图书管理系统案例开发;第7章为超市商品进销存管理系统案例开发;第8章为在线考试系统案例开发;第9章为高校实践课题管理系统案例开发。这些实际案例,在解决方案、架构和实现技术上,由浅入深、循序渐进。通过以典型实例为引导,解决实际问题、剖析解决过程、拓展解题思路,结合每章的技术经验总结,可快速提高读者C#应用开发实践能力。

限于篇幅，案例讲解在书中只给出了主要功能的源代码，案例的完整代码和数据库等相关资料可在清华大学出版社网站下载。

本书可作为高等院校计算机软件相关专业C#应用程序开发类课程的教材，也可供软件开发人员参考。相信此次修订后的教材，更适合教师的教学和读者的学习。

本次修订由郭基凤、高亮担任主编，韩玉民、赵冬担任副主编，第1章由韩玉民编写，第2章2.1、2.2节及第5章由赵冬编写，第2章2.3、2.4节、第7章以及第9章由余雨萍编写，第3章由郭基凤编写，第4章和第6章由朱彦松编写，第8章由高亮编写，全书由高亮、余雨萍、赵冬负责统稿。

在本书的修订过程中，得到了中原工学院车战斌教授的指导和帮助，本书的出版得到了河南省"十四五"普通高等教育规划教材建设项目和中原工学院教材建设基金资助，另外也吸取了许多相关专著和文献的优点，在此一并表示感谢。

虽然我们力求完美，但限于水平，不当之处在所难免，敬请广大读者不吝赐教。

作　者
2023年5月

目录

第 1 章 管理信息系统概述 /1

- 1.1 信息、管理、管理信息与系统 ·································· 1
  - 1.1.1 信息与数据 ·································· 1
  - 1.1.2 管理与管理信息 ·································· 3
  - 1.1.3 系统 ·································· 3
- 1.2 信息系统 ·································· 4
  - 1.2.1 信息系统的概念 ·································· 4
  - 1.2.2 信息系统的类型 ·································· 4
  - 1.2.3 信息系统与管理 ·································· 5
- 1.3 管理信息系统 ·································· 5
  - 1.3.1 管理信息系统的概念 ·································· 5
  - 1.3.2 管理信息系统的功能 ·································· 5
  - 1.3.3 管理信息系统的特征 ·································· 6
  - 1.3.4 管理信息系统的类型 ·································· 6
- 1.4 管理信息系统的技术基础 ·································· 7
  - 1.4.1 数据处理技术 ·································· 7
  - 1.4.2 数据库技术 ·································· 8
  - 1.4.3 计算机网络技术 ·································· 8
- 1.5 管理信息系统的开发原则、策略和方法 ·································· 8
  - 1.5.1 管理信息系统的开发原则 ·································· 8
  - 1.5.2 管理信息系统的开发策略 ·································· 9
  - 1.5.3 管理信息系统的开发方法 ·································· 9
- 1.6 管理信息系统的典型案例 ·································· 11
  - 1.6.1 MIS 支持沃尔玛创造商业奇迹 ·································· 11
  - 1.6.2 海尔集团：信息化助力创造世界名牌公司 ·································· 12
- 小结 ·································· 12
- 习题 ·································· 13

第 2 章 数据库高级编程 /14

- 2.1 SQL Server 相关配置 ·································· 14
- 2.2 使用 ADO.NET 访问数据库 ·································· 19

    2.2.1 连接数据库 ·· 19
    2.2.2 对数据库进行添加、修改及删除操作 ·· 20
    2.2.3 查询数据库中的数据 ·· 22
    2.2.4 数据绑定控件 ·· 25
  2.3 Entity Framework 基础知识 ·· 49
    2.3.1 从委托到 Lambda ·· 49
    2.3.2 Entity Framework 架构 ··· 56
  2.4 使用 Entity Framework 访问数据库 ·· 57
    2.4.1 Entity Framework 的安装 ··· 57
    2.4.2 创建数据库及实体对象模型 ·· 57
    2.4.3 数据库增、删、改、查操作 ·· 61
  小结 ··· 66
  习题 ··· 66

第 3 章 系统架构 /67

  3.1 三层架构简介 ··· 67
  3.2 简单三层架构 ··· 69
    3.2.1 数据访问层 ·· 69
    3.2.2 数据访问通用类库 ·· 77
    3.2.3 实体类库 ·· 80
    3.2.4 业务逻辑层 ·· 84
    3.2.5 表示层 ·· 86
  3.3 工厂模式三层架构 ··· 99
    3.3.1 接口类库设计 ·· 100
    3.3.2 工厂类库设计 ·· 102
    3.3.3 其他层的代码修改 ·· 103
  小结 ··· 104
  习题 ··· 105

第 4 章 ASP.NET MVC 模式 /106

  4.1 MVC 模式简介 ·· 106
  4.2 ASP.NET MVC 工作原理 ··· 108
  4.3 ASP.NET MVC 控制器 ·· 112
  4.4 ASP.NET MVC 视图 ·· 115
  4.5 ASP.NET MVC 模型 ·· 119
  小结 ··· 124
  习题 ··· 124

第 5 章　前端框架 Bootstrap　　/125

5.1　Bootstrap 简介 ··· 125
5.1.1　安装 Bootstrap ·· 125
5.1.2　Bootstrap 的主要特性 ··· 127
5.1.3　Bootstrap 在 Visual Studio 2019 中的应用 ························ 128

5.2　Bootstrap 样式 ··· 131
5.2.1　网格系统 ·· 131
5.2.2　排版 ·· 141
5.2.3　表格 ·· 143
5.2.4　表单 ·· 146
5.2.5　按钮 ·· 153
5.2.6　图片 ·· 156

5.3　布局组件 ·· 157
5.3.1　字体图标 ·· 157
5.3.2　下拉菜单 ·· 158
5.3.3　输入框组 ·· 159
5.3.4　导航 ·· 162
5.3.5　其他组件 ·· 164

5.4　JavaScript ·· 164
5.4.1　标签页内容 ·· 165
5.4.2　模态对话框 ·· 168
5.4.3　工具提示和弹出对话框 ··· 171

小结 ·· 173
习题 ·· 173

第 6 章　图书管理系统案例开发　　/174

6.1　项目描述 ·· 174
6.1.1　项目背景 ·· 174
6.1.2　业务描述 ·· 174
6.1.3　用户描述 ·· 175

6.2　系统需求 ·· 175
6.2.1　需求描述 ·· 175
6.2.2　模块设计 ·· 175
6.2.3　数据库设计 ·· 177

6.3　系统实现 ·· 180
6.3.1　技术要点 ·· 180
6.3.2　主要功能模块及界面设计 ··· 180

6.4　程序打包 ·· 193

小结 ·· 199
习题 ·· 199

第 7 章 超市商品进销存管理系统案例开发   /200

7.1 系统需求 ·· 200
7.2 系统设计 ·· 201
7.2.1 模块设计 ·· 201
7.2.2 数据库设计 ·· 201
7.3 系统实现 ·· 202
7.3.1 实体数据模型 ·· 202
7.3.2 主界面模块 ·· 203
7.3.3 商品管理模块 ·· 206
7.3.4 进货管理模块 ·· 211
7.3.5 销售管理模块 ·· 213
7.3.6 库存统计模块 ·· 215
7.4 技术经验总结 ·· 217
7.4.1 技术总结 ·· 217
7.4.2 经验总结 ·· 217

第 8 章 在线考试系统案例开发   /218

8.1 项目概述 ·· 218
8.2 系统需求 ·· 218
8.2.1 业务描述 ·· 218
8.2.2 用户描述 ·· 218
8.2.3 功能分析 ·· 219
8.3 系统分析设计 ·· 220
8.3.1 模块设计 ·· 220
8.3.2 数据库设计 ·· 220
8.4 技术准备 ·· 224
8.4.1 Excel 组件使用 ·· 224
8.4.2 数据库的随机排序方法 ·· 226
8.4.3 API 的使用 ·· 226
8.4.4 注册表的使用 ·· 227
8.4.5 控件的代码生成法 ·· 228
8.5 实体类库实现 ·· 228
8.5.1 Student 类 ·· 229
8.5.2 TestQuestion 类 ·· 230
8.5.3 CreatePaperScheme 类 ·· 232
8.5.4 TestPaper 类 ··· 233

        8.5.5 QuestionTypeScore 类 233
        8.5.6 Questions 类 234
        8.5.7 StudentAnswer 类 235
    8.6 数据访问层实现 237
        8.6.1 DALStudent 类 237
        8.6.2 DALTestQuestion 类 238
        8.6.3 DALCreatePaperScheme 类 240
        8.6.4 DALTestPaper 类 241
        8.6.5 DALQuestionTypeScore 类 241
        8.6.6 DALQuestions 类 242
        8.6.7 DALStudentAnswer 类 243
    8.7 业务逻辑层实现 246
        8.7.1 BLLStudent 类 246
        8.7.2 BLLTestQuestion 类 247
        8.7.3 BLLCreatePaperScheme 类 248
        8.7.4 BLLTestPaper 类 249
        8.7.5 BLLQuestionTypeScore 类 249
        8.7.6 BLLQuestions 类 250
        8.7.7 BLLStudentAnswer 类 251
    8.8 表示层实现 253
        8.8.1 学生信息管理模块——"学生信息管理"窗体 254
        8.8.2 学生信息管理模块——"学生信息编辑"窗体 261
        8.8.3 题库管理模块——"题库管理"窗体 263
        8.8.4 题库管理模块——"题库编辑"窗体 269
        8.8.5 组卷模块 274
        8.8.6 学生端主界面 285
        8.8.7 学生考试模块 288
    8.9 技术经验总结 298
        8.9.1 技术总结 298
        8.9.2 经验总结 298

第 9 章 高校实践课题管理系统案例开发 /299

9.1 项目描述 299
9.2 系统需求分析 300
    9.2.1 总体需求 300
    9.2.2 需求描述 301
9.3 系统设计 308
    9.3.1 总体设计 308
    9.3.2 业务流程建模 309

9.4 数据库设计与实现 ……………………………………………………………… 313
    9.4.1 数据库设计 ……………………………………………………………… 313
    9.4.2 数据库实现 ……………………………………………………………… 314
9.5 系统实现 …………………………………………………………………………… 318
    9.5.1 项目总体实现 …………………………………………………………… 318
    9.5.2 实体及数据访问层实现 ………………………………………………… 320
    9.5.3 管理员模块实现 ………………………………………………………… 324
    9.5.4 教师模块实现 …………………………………………………………… 349
    9.5.5 学生模块实现 …………………………………………………………… 370
9.6 系统测试 …………………………………………………………………………… 379
    9.6.1 学生管理测试用例 ……………………………………………………… 379
    9.6.2 题库管理测试用例 ……………………………………………………… 381
    9.6.3 课题选报测试用例 ……………………………………………………… 385
9.7 技术经验总结 ……………………………………………………………………… 389
    9.7.1 技术总结 ………………………………………………………………… 389
    9.7.2 经验总结 ………………………………………………………………… 389

参考文献 /390

第1章 管理信息系统概述

本章从信息、管理、管理信息、系统、信息系统等概念出发,介绍管理信息系统的基础知识,并介绍建设管理信息系统的技术基础,以及开发管理信息系统的原则、策略和主要开发方法。

1.1 信息、管理、管理信息与系统

管理信息系统是基于管理、信息和系统概念发展起来的,正确理解数据、信息、管理、管理信息和系统的基本含义及其相互关系,对学习和开发管理信息系统具有重要的意义。

1.1.1 信息与数据

1. 什么是数据

数据(Data)是指用来对客观事物的性质、状态以及相互关系等进行记录,并且可以鉴别的物理符号。也就是说,数据是对客观事实的描述,是客观实体属性的值,是可以识别、抽象的符号。例如,描述学生实体的"姓名""性别""学号"和"身高"等。

但计算机系统中所说的数据,其符号形式不仅是数字,还包括字符、文字、图形图像、音频、视频等。

2. 什么是信息

信息(Information)是指反映客观事物运动变化的、能够被人们所接受和理解的、对人类的行为决策有用的各种消息、数据、指令、图像、信号等资料的总称。

信息与数据既有联系又有区别,数据是人们为了反映客观世界而记录下来可以鉴别的符号,信息则是对数据进行提炼、加工的结果,这种结果对管理决策具有现实的或潜在的价值。

例如,学生的课程成绩是原始数据,在评定学年奖学金时需要将平均成绩85分以上的学生先筛选出来,这就需要对原始课程成绩进行加工,算出每个学生的平均成绩,得到的平均成绩及排名就是信息。

数据是和信息互相区别而又紧密联系的两个概念。数据是符号,是物理性的,信息是对数据进行加工处理之后所得到的并对决策产生影响的数据,是逻辑性(观念性)的;数据是信息的表现形式,信息是数据有意义的表示。

数据经过处理后,其表现形式仍然是数据。处理数据的目的是便于更好地解释。只有经过解释,数据才有意义,才成为信息。因此,信息是经过加工以后并对客观世界产生影响的数据。

3. 信息的特征

一般而言,信息的特征主要表现在真实性、价值性、时效性、共享性、传输性、层次性、转换性等方面。

1)真实性

真实性是信息的核心价值,是信息的第一属性。不符合事实的信息不仅没有价值,而且可能价值为负,既害别人,也害自己。虚假信息往往严重误导管理决策,造成重大损失,这在现实中屡见不鲜。

2)价值性

信息是一种重要的资源,具有价值性,即信息对于信息主体是有用的,因而是有价值的。信息的价值性是信息的主要特征。

3)时效性

信息的时效性是指信息资料被提供和利用的时间与信息的使用价值之间存在的比例关系,这种比例关系在大多数情况下表现为一种正比例关系,即信息提供和利用的时间越早,信息的价值就越大;反之,信息的价值就越小。

在信息时代的今天,及时掌握信息、利用信息显得尤为重要,正如著名未来学家托夫勒所说"谁掌握了信息,控制了网络,谁将拥有整个世界。"信息的这一特征,要求在进行信息资源管理时,要不断地更新信息,保持信息资源的使用价值。

4)共享性

信息不同于有形的物质资源,信息是一种无形的资源,具有共享性,即同一条信息可被多个用户完整共享,对于每个用户来说,所获得的都是完整的一条信息。

信息的共享性特征具有积极和消极的两面性,积极的一面是共享信息可提高效率、提高信息利用率;消极的一面是带来信息安全隐患,如被竞争对手"共享"了商业机密信息,则将带来严重后果。

5)传输性

信息可以以多种形式、通过多种渠道进行传输,如可以通过电话、传真、电子邮件、微信、QQ、邮寄等方式进行传输,传输的形式有数字、文字、图形图像、视频、音频等。在网络应用日益广泛的今天,信息的传输性特征更为显著。

6)层次性(等级性)

管理系统在客观上是分等级的(如公司级、工厂级、车间级等)。组织内的管理活动通常可大致分为三个主要层次,即作业级(基层运作层)、战术级(战术管理层)、战略级(战略指挥层)。相应地,管理信息也可划分为基层运作信息、中层控制信息以及高层决策信息三个层次。

7)转换性

信息是可变换的。它可以由不同的方法和不同的载体来承载,可以由一种形态转换成另一种形态。这一特性在多媒体时代尤为重要。

4. 信息的类型

按照不同的分类角度,可以将信息分为不同的类型,表1-1列出了主要的分类角度及其类型。

表 1-1 信息的分类角度及其类型

信息分类角度	信 息 类 型
按产生信息的范围	内部信息、外部信息
按信息的产生领域	社会信息、管理信息、气象信息、地理信息、军事信息等
按信息的加工顺序	原始信息、再生信息
按信息的反映形式	实物信息、声像信息、文本信息等
按信息的管理层次	决策信息、控制信息、作业信息
按信息的发生时间	先导信息、实时信息、滞后信息
按信息的传播方向	纵向信息、横向信息
按信息的发生频率	常规信息、随机信息
按信息的应用领域	社会信息、管理信息、科技信息、军事信息、体育信息等
按信息的确定性	确定性信息、非确定性信息

1.1.2 管理与管理信息

1. 管理的概念

管理是人类各种活动中最重要的活动之一,通俗地讲,管理就是通过他人完成某种任务或某个目标的一切活动,这些活动总体上包括计划、组织、领导和控制等。管理者的主要任务就是利用已有的和可以争取到的各种资源,包括人、财、物等,以最少的投入去获得最大的产出。

2. 管理信息

管理信息是组织在管理活动过程中采集到的、经过加工处理后对管理决策产生影响的各种数据的总称。

管理信息的表现形式:报告、报表、单据、进度图。此外,还有计划书、协议、标准、定额等,类似于报告的形式。

管理信息的作用主要体现如下。

- 是组织进行管理工作的基础和核心。
- 是组织控制管理活动的重要手段,联系各个管理环节的纽带。
- 是提高组织管理效益的关键。

管理信息与信息的关系:管理信息只是信息集中的一个子集,是在管理活动中产生的,经过加工处理后,对管理决策产生影响的各种信息的总称。

1.1.3 系统

系统是指在特定环境下,为实现某一特定功能而由相互联系、相互作用的若干个要素组成的有机整体。或者说,系统是由层次结构和共同目标的相关联的若干元素组成的集合。

这里所说的系统不是指自然系统,而是指人为系统,即有人参与、有目的、有组织的系统。例如,工业企业由人、设备和各种规章制度组成,构成了一个系统。另外,还有人们常说的计算机系统、教育系统、金融系统等。

任何一个系统都包括输入、处理和输出三个基本部分,而输出的结果还会对输入进行反馈,系统和外界环境之间存在一定的边界,系统的模型如图1-1所示。

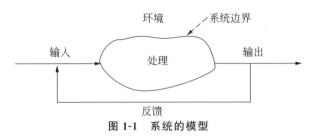

图1-1 系统的模型

从图中可以看出,当一个系统从环境中取得一定的输入内容后,它将按照一定的方法对输入的内容进行加工处理,然后产生一定的输出,这是系统的基本活动方式,这个过程称为处理过程,一般由人和设备分别或共同完成。例如,对于一个生产工厂来说,其输入主要是原材料、能源及市场信息,输出则是它的产品,将原材料加工成产品的过程就是处理过程。

系统的特征主要包括整体性、目的性、层次性、相关性、开放性和环境适应性等,这里不再详述。

1.2 信 息 系 统

伴随人类文明的发展,人类对信息资源的认知深度和重视程度不断提高,如何更有效地获取信息、利用信息,成为越来越多的人思考的焦点。随着系统科学的产生和发展,人们从系统的概念和方法出发,来研究将诸多与信息获取和价值转化相关的要素进行有机组织与管理,集成为"信息系统",信息系统就是对组织中的信息进行综合处理而形成的一个整体。

1.2.1 信息系统的概念

信息系统(Information System,IS)是一个由人、硬件、软件和数据资源组成的系统,其目的是及时、正确地收集、加工、存储、传递和提供信息,实现组织中各项活动的管理、调节和控制。

这里所讲的信息系统主要是指以计算机信息处理为基础的人机一体化的信息系统。在基本构成上,信息系统包括信息处理系统和信息传输系统。其中,信息处理系统对数据进行处理,通过它对输入数据的处理可获得不同形态的新的数据。例如,计算机系统就是一种信息处理系统。信息传输系统用来将数据从一处传到另一处,不改变数据本身,如计算机网络系统。

1.2.2 信息系统的类型

按照处理的对象不同,可把组织的信息系统分为作业信息系统和管理信息系统两大类。

1. 作业信息系统

作业信息系统的任务是处理组织的业务、控制生产过程和支持办公事务。作业信息系统通常由业务处理系统、过程控制系统和办公信息系统三部分组成。

2. 管理信息系统

管理信息系统是对一个组织(单位、企业或部门)进行全面管理的人和计算机相结合的系统,它综合运用计算机技术、信息技术、管理技术和决策技术,结合现代化的管理思想、方法和手段,辅助管理人员进行管理和决策。

管理信息系统不仅是一个技术系统,同时又是一个社会系统。

1.2.3 信息系统与管理

管理的任务在于通过有效地管理好人、财、物等资源来实现组织的目标,而要管理这些资源,需要通过反映这些资源的信息来进行管理。信息是管理上的一项极为重要的资源,其之所以重要在于"管理的实质是决策",决策正确与否决定管理工作的成败,而决策的正确程度则取决于信息的质量。

基于计算机的信息系统,能把生产和流通过程中的巨大数据流收集、组织和控制起来,经过处理,转换为对各部门来说都不可缺少的数据,经过分析,使它变成对各级管理人员做决定具有重要意义的有用信息。

在信息爆炸的今天,只有运用计算机的高速准确的计算能力和海量存储能力、先进的管理理论和方法,才能及时处理繁杂海量的信息,为决策活动提供有效信息。

1.3 管理信息系统

管理信息系统(Management Information System,MIS)的概念是从管理、信息和系统三个概念的基础上发展起来的,是随着管理技术和信息技术的发展而逐步形成的,随着企业的管理过程和信息处理活动产生的。

1.3.1 管理信息系统的概念

管理信息系统是一个由人和计算机等组成的,能进行数据的收集、传输、存储、加工、维护和使用的系统,它具有计划、预测、控制和辅助决策等功能。该定义说明了管理信息系统不仅是一个技术系统,而且要考虑人的行为,是一个社会系统、管理系统,所以说管理信息系统是一个人机系统。

管理信息系统首先是一个系统,其次是一个信息系统,再次是一个用于管理方面的信息系统。

管理信息系统的总体概念如图1-2所示。

1.3.2 管理信息系统的功能

管理信息系统是帮助信息主体实现对管理信息的全生命周期有效管理的系统平台,一个完整的管理信息系统,应该具有下列基本功能。

(1) 数据处理。完成数据的收集、输入、传输、存储、加工处理和输出。
(2) 事务处理。提高管理人员效率。
(3) 预测功能。运用现代数学方法、统计方法或模拟方法,根据现有数据预测未来。
(4) 计划功能。根据现存条件和约束条件,提供各职能部门的计划,如生产计划、财务

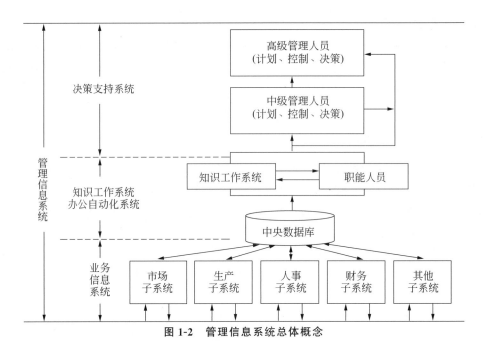

图 1-2 管理信息系统总体概念

计划、采购计划等,并按照不同的管理层次提供相应的计划报告。

(5)控制功能。对计划执行情况进行监督、检查、比较执行与计划的差异、分析差异及产生差异的原因,辅助管理人员及时加以控制。

(6)辅助决策功能。运用相应的数学模型,从大量数据中推导出有关问题的最优解和满意解,辅助管理人员决策。

1.3.3 管理信息系统的特征

管理信息系统作为一般信息系统的实例,具有一般信息系统的全部特征,同时也有其自身的特征。管理信息系统主要有下列特征。

(1)管理信息系统具有"社会-技术"双重属性。管理信息系统不仅是一个技术系统,同时也是一个社会系统、管理系统。

(2)管理信息系统是开放的人机系统。管理信息系统在要素组成上,既包括计算机等设备,还包括系统应用、管理和维护人员。同时具有一般信息系统的开放性特征,确保管理信息系统能够与环境之间进行有效的交互,得到及时调整和改进。

(3)管理信息系统是组织系统的一个子系统。管理信息系统的目标功能是对组织运营管理的各层活动予以支持,是组织系统的一个子系统,需要与组织系统的其他子系统(如人力系统、生产系统、CAD 系统等)有机整合,共同支持组织目标的完成。

(4)管理信息系统是一个集成化系统。管理信息系统要素多、结构复杂,需与其他子系统有机整合。同时管理信息系统是基于管理科学、计算机科学、数学、社会学和系统科学等的一门综合性、交叉性的学科。

1.3.4 管理信息系统的类型

根据管理信息系统的实际应用和面向的服务对象不同,管理信息系统的应用大致有以下几类。

1. 国家经济信息系统

国家经济信息系统是一个统称,是指包括国家各综合统计部门在内的国家级信息系统。其主要功能是处理经济信息,为国家经济部门、各级决策部门提供统计、预测等信息及辅助决策手段,同时也为各级经济部门和企业提供经济信息。

2. 工业企业管理信息系统

工业企业管理信息系统是指工业企业充分利用计算机技术、网络技术和数据库技术等,实现对企业的采购、生产、销售等方面进行全面、系统地科学管理的计算机系统。

3. 商业企业管理信息系统

商业企业管理信息系统是指商业企业充分利用计算机技术、网络技术、数据库技术、RFID和条码技术等,实现对现代化商业企业进行全面、系统地科学管理的计算机系统。

4. 事务管理信息系统

事务管理信息系统是以事业单位为主,主要进行日常事务管理,如学校管理信息系统、医院管理信息系统等。

5. 办公管理信息系统

办公管理信息系统是以国家各级行政机关、企事业单位的行政管理部门为主的管理信息系统,其特点是办公自动化和无纸化。

6. 专业管理信息系统

专业管理信息系统是指从事特定行业或领域的管理信息系统,如房地产管理信息系统、人事管理信息系统、民航信息系统、银行信息系统等。

1.4 管理信息系统的技术基础

现代意义上的管理信息系统是先进管理理念与成熟信息技术相融合的产物,信息技术是管理信息系统的基础,建立管理信息系统的技术基础主要包括数据处理技术、数据库技术和计算机网络技术。

1.4.1 数据处理技术

数据处理是指把来自科学研究、生产实践和社会经济活动等领域中的原始数据,用一定的设备和手段,按一定的使用要求,加工成另一种形式的数据的过程。

数据处理是管理活动的最基本内容,也是管理信息系统的基本功能。数据处理一般不涉及复杂的数学计算,但要求处理的数据量很大。

数据管理先后经历了人工管理、文件系统和数据库系统等阶段。

1. 数据处理的主要目的

数据处理的目的是更好地利用各类信息资源,为管理决策服务。

- 把数据转换成便于观察分析、传送或进一步处理的形式。
- 从大量的原始数据中抽取、推导出对人们有价值的信息,以作为行动和决策的依据。
- 科学地保存和管理已经过处理(如校验、整理等)的大量数据,便于人们充分利用这些信息资源。

2. 数据处理的基本内容

(1) 数据收集。根据用户和系统的需求收集相关的数据。

(2) 数据转换。为了使收集的信息适用于计算机处理,设计各种代码来描述自然界中的各种实际数据,这种将实际数据采用代码表述的方法被称为数据的转换。

(3) 数据的筛选、分组和排序。

(4) 数据的组织。将具有逻辑关系的数据组织起来,按一定的存储表示方式存放在计算机中。目的是使计算机处理时能够符合速度快、占用存储器的容量少、成本低的要求。

(5) 数据的运算。

(6) 数据存储。

(7) 数据检索。

(8) 数据输出。

1.4.2 数据库技术

数据库技术为管理信息系统提供了数据存储、组织、检索、排序、统计分析等技术基础。

数据库是以一定的组织方式存储在一起的相关数据的集合,它能以最佳的方式,最少的数据冗余为多种应用服务,程序与数据具有较高的独立性。

数据库管理系统(DBMS)是一组对数据库进行管理的软件,通常包括数据定义语言及其编译程序、数据操纵语言及其编译程序以及数据管理例行程序。目前主流的 DBMS 都是关系数据库管理系统,主要的 DBMS 有 SQL Server、Oracle、Access、MySQL、IBM DB2 等。

数据库系统是由计算机系统、数据库管理系统、数据库和有关人员组成的具有高度组织的总体。

1.4.3 计算机网络技术

计算机网络是用通信介质把分布在不同地理位置的计算机和其他网络设备连接起来,在网络软件系统的支持下,实现信息互通和资源共享的系统。

计算机网络是管理信息系统的一项基本技术。由于一个企业或组织中的信息处理都是分布式的,分布式信息由分布在不同位置的计算机进行处理,并通过通信网络把分布式信息集成起来,这是管理信息系统的主要运行方式,因此,计算机网络是管理信息系统运行的基础。

计算机网络主要包括局域网(LAN)、广域网(WAN)和城域网(MAN),企业内部一般为局域网。

1.5 管理信息系统的开发原则、策略和方法

1.5.1 管理信息系统的开发原则

管理信息系统开发应遵循下列基本原则。

(1) 领导参加原则,即"一把手"原则。

(2) 适用性与先进性原则。

(3) 四统一原则：统一领导、统一规划、统一目标规范、统一软硬件环境。

(4) 信息工程原则。

(5) 优化与创新原则。

(6) 面向用户原则。

(7) 完整性、相关性、适应性、可靠性、经济性原则。

1.5.2 管理信息系统的开发策略

管理信息系统开发的策略主要有"自下而上"和"自上而下"两种策略。

1. "自下而上"的开发策略

"自下而上"的开发策略是从现行系统的业务需求出发，先实现一个个具体功能，逐步地由低级到高级建立完整的管理信息系统。

"自下而上"开发策略的优点是可以避免大规模系统可能出现运行不协调的危险。其缺点是缺乏从整个系统出发考虑问题，随着系统的进展，往往要做许多重大修改，甚至重新规划、设计。

2. "自上而下"的开发策略

"自上而下"的开发策略是强调从整体上协调与规划，由全面到局部，由长远到近期，从探索合理的信息流出发来开发管理信息系统。

"自上而下"的开发策略的优点是能从整个系统出发考虑问题，使系统具有优良的总体结构。其缺点是要求很强的逻辑性，开发难度较大。

"自下而上"的开发策略通常用于小型系统的设计，适用于缺乏开发工作经验的情况。

对于大型系统，往往把这两者结合起来使用，即先自上而下地做好管理信息系统的战略规划，再自下而上地逐步实现各个系统(子系统)。

1.5.3 管理信息系统的开发方法

管理信息系统作为一种软件系统，其开发方法和过程遵循软件工程规范，主要的开发方法包括结构化系统开发方法、原型法、面向对象方法和CASE方法等。

1. 结构化系统开发方法

结构化系统开发方法(Structured System Development Methodology)是在生命周期法的基础上发展起来的，是目前应用得最广泛的一种开发方法。

结构化系统开发方法的基本思想是：用系统的思想和系统工程的方法，按照用户至上的原则，结构化、模块化、自顶向下地对系统进行分析与设计。

结构化系统开发方法先将整个信息系统开发过程划分为若干个相对独立的阶段，通常包括系统规划、系统分析、系统设计、系统实施、系统运行与维护。在前三个阶段，坚持自顶向下地对系统进行结构化划分：在系统调查和理顺管理业务时，应从最顶层的管理业务入手，逐步深入到最基层；在系统分析，提出目标系统方案和系统设计时，应从宏观整体考虑入手，先考虑系统整体的优化，再考虑局部的优化问题；在系统实施阶段，则坚持自底向上地逐步实施，即组织人员从最基层的模块做起，然后按照系统设计的结构，将模块一个个拼接到一起进行调试，自底向上、逐步地构成整个系统。

结构化系统开发方法具有下列特点。

- 自顶向下整体地进行分析与设计和自底向上逐步实施的系统开发过程。
- 用户至上的原则。
- 符合实际,客观性和科学化。
- 严格区分工作阶段。
- 充分预料可能发生的变化。
- 开发过程工程化等。

结构化系统开发方法适用于大型系统和复杂系统的开发。

2. 原型法

原型(指系统原型)是一个可以实际运行、反复修改、不断完善的系统。

原型法(Prototyping)与结构化开发方法不同,原型法不注重对管理系统进行全面、系统的调查与分析,而是系统开发人员根据对用户需求的理解,先快速实现一个原型系统,然后通过反复修改来实现管理信息系统。

原型法的基本思想是:开发人员首先要对用户提出的问题进行总结,然后开发一个原型系统并运行之。开发人员和用户一起,针对原型系统的运行情况,反复进行改进,直到用户对系统完全满意为止,如图 1-3 所示。

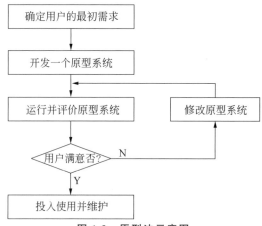

图 1-3 原型法示意图

原型法具有下列特点。
- 遵循了人们认识事物的客观规律,易于掌握和接受。
- 将模拟的手段引入系统分析的初始阶段,强调用户参与、描述、运行、沟通。
- 强调软件工具支持。

原型法适合于开发处理过程明确、业务逻辑简单的小型系统。

3. 面向对象开发方法

客观世界是由各种各样的对象组成的,每种对象都有各自的内部状态和运动规律,不同对象之间的相互作用和联系就构成了各种不同的系统。

在面向对象(Object-Oriented)方法中,使用软件系统中的类与对象来模拟现实世界中的对象及对象类;用对象的属性来表示现实世界中事物在某方面的特征;用对象的方法来模拟现实世界中的对象的行为。将现实系统中的各种事务平滑地过渡到软件系统中的软件要素。

面向对象开发方法的特点包括封装性、抽象性、继承性和动态链接性等。

在大型管理信息系统开发中,面向对象开发方法和结构化方法在系统开发中是相互依存、不可替代的。

4. CASE 方法

CASE(Computer Aided Software Engineering,计算机辅助软件工程)是一种自动化或半自动化的方法,能够全面支持除系统调查外的每一个开发步骤。

目前,CASE 仍是一个发展中的概念,各种 CASE 软件也较多,没有统一的模式和标准。采用 CASE 工具进行系统开发,必须结合一种具体的开发方法,如结构化系统开发方法、面向对象方法或原型化开发方法等,CASE 方法只是为具体的开发方法提供了支持每一过程的专门工具,这些工具既可以单独使用,也可以组合使用。CASE 也正由一种具体的工具逐渐发展成为开发信息系统的方法学。

CASE 方法具有下列特点。

- 解决了从客观对象到软件系统的映射问题,支持系统开发的全过程。
- 提高了软件质量和软件重用性。
- 提高了软件开发效率。
- 简化了软件开发的管理和维护。
- 自动生成开发过程中的各种软件文档。

1.6 管理信息系统的典型案例

在当今信息时代,成功企业无一不是将信息化建设和应用作为其发展战略的重要部分,这里仅以商业巨头沃尔玛和海尔集团为例,说明企业信息化对企业发展的重要性。

1.6.1 MIS 支持沃尔玛创造商业奇迹

沃尔玛公司(Wal-Mart Stores,Inc.)是国际著名的大型零售企业,沃尔玛公司有 8500 家门店,分布于全球 15 个国家,员工超过两百万,是世界上雇员最多的企业。《财富》杂志在 2002 年度公布的世界 500 强企业中,沃尔玛公司以 2198 亿美元的销售额列居榜首,随后连续多年在美国《财富》杂志全球 500 强企业中居首,而所有这一切同其富有远见的信息系统战略应用是分不开的。

沃尔玛公司非常重视信息化应用,把信息技术与经营活动进行密切配合,始终保持领先地位。例如,1969 年沃尔玛最早使用计算机跟踪存货,1974 年全面实现 S.K.U 单品级库存控制,1980 年最早使用条形码,1984 年最早使用 CM 品类管理软件,1985 年最早采用 EDI 系统,1988 年最早使用无线扫描枪。从 1983 年开始,共计投资 4 亿美元发射了一颗商用卫星,实现了全球联网。21 世纪开始,沃尔玛公司又投资 90 亿美元开始实施"互联网统一标准平台"的建设。

沃尔玛公司已建立了全球物流数据处理中心,实现集团内部全球范围内的 24 小时物流动态跟踪与监控,使其采购、库存、订货、配送和销售真正实现了一体化。

沃尔玛公司已实现了全面的信息化管理,典型的信息系统有:自动补货系统、销售时点 POS 与条码应用系统、库存配送控制系统、电子自动订货系统、有效客户反馈系统、快速反应系统、内部供应链管理系统、卫星控制专用通信系统等。限于篇幅,具体功能和应用这里不再详述。

1.6.2 海尔集团:信息化助力创造世界名牌公司

海尔集团成立于1984年,当初是一个亏损147万元的集体企业,目前已发展成为国家特大型企业集团,成为中国家电行业销售额最大、生产的产品品种和规格最多、出口量最大的企业集团。

海尔集团高度重视、运用、推广、发展信息化工作是其成功的秘诀之一。在信息化时代,海尔把全面推进企业信息化建设作为抓住机遇、迎接挑战的有效途径。

海尔集团信息化建设最初主要是建设骨干网络和办公应用,从1997年到现在,海尔集团已经构建了以千兆为骨干的企业内部网,实现数据、视频、IP电话三网合一。

我国加入WTO之后,为了应对激烈的市场竞争和企业内外部的各种挑战,海尔集团开始实施以市场链为纽带的业务流程再造,同时改造海尔集团的信息化应用系统,提高企业的整体管理水平。海尔集团系统地设计和建立了信息化应用框架和系统,配合业务管理的需求,实施了多方面的信息化应用。

海尔集团于2000年专门成立海尔电子商务有限公司,全面开展面向供应商的B2B业务和针对消费者个性化需求的B2C业务。同年,海尔集团在国内率先发布和建立B2C电子商务平台,并实现网上支付,形成以信息流带动物流和资金流的业务应用平台;2000—2001年,建立全球领先的网上协同交易平台(B2B);2000年,建立集成的同步供应链管理平台,在集团范围内实施了销售、生产、采购、仓储、财务与成本等集成应用;2000—2004年,实现生产跟踪与控制系统,在集团各产品事业部实施了MES全程跟踪生产质量;1998—2005年分期建成海尔顾客服务管理系统,实现一站到位的顾客服务;2001—2003年,海尔集团构建了先进的第三方物流管理系统,为海尔及其他知名品牌提供服务。

海尔集团通过电子商务采购平台和定制平台与供应商和销售终端建立起紧密的互联网关系,建立起动态企业联盟,并使企业和供应商、消费者实现互动沟通,使信息增值。在业务流程再造的基础上,海尔形成了"前台一张网,后台一条链"(前台的一张网是海尔客户关系管理网站,后台的一条链是海尔的市场链)的闭环系统,构筑了企业内部供应链系统、ERP系统、物流配送系统、资金流管理结算系统、遍布全国的分销管理系统以及客户服务响应Call Center系统,并形成了以订单信息流为核心的各子系统之间无缝连接的系统集成。

小　　结

本章首先介绍了管理信息系统及其相关基本概念,包括数据、信息、管理、系统、信息系统、管理信息系统等,然后介绍了管理信息系统的技术基础、开发原则、开发策略,并介绍了管理信息系统的主要开发方法,包括结构化系统开发方法、原型法、面向对象方法和CASE方法。最后简要介绍了两家优秀企业的信息化应用。

通过本章学习,了解了管理信息系统的基本知识,为后续管理信息系统的分析、设计和开发打下基础。

习 题

一、名词解释

1. 信息。
2. 管理信息。
3. 信息系统。
4. 管理信息系统。

二、简答题

1. 什么是信息？信息具有哪些特征？
2. 简述信息与数据的关系。
3. 信息系统的含义是什么？信息系统有哪些类型？
4. 什么是管理信息系统？为什么说管理信息系统还是一个社会系统？
5. 管理信息系统的功能有哪些？
6. 简述管理信息系统的技术基础。
7. 简述管理信息系统的开发策略。
8. 简述结构化系统开发方法的基本思想和特点。
9. 简述原型法开发方法的基本思想和特点。

第 2 章 数据库高级编程

ADO.NET 是为.NET 框架而创建的,是对 ADO(ActiveX Data Objects)对象模型的扩充。ADO.NET 提供了一组数据访问服务的类,可用于对 Microsoft SQL Server、Oracle 等数据源的一致访问。ADO.NET 模型分为.NET Data Provider(数据提供程序)和 DataSet 数据集(数据处理的核心)两大主要部分。

ADO.NET 数据提供程序提供了四个核心对象,分别是 Connection、Command、DataReader 和 DataAdapter 对象。功能如表 2-1 所示。

表 2-1 ADO.NET 核心对象

对象	功能
Connection	提供和数据源的连接功能
Command	提供访问数据库命令,执行查询数据或修改数据的功能,例如,运行 SQL 命令和存储过程等
DataReader	从数据源中获取只向前的且只读的数据流
DataAdapter	是 DataSet 对象和数据源间的桥梁。DataAdapter 使用 4 个 Command 对象来运行查询、新建、修改、删除的 SQL 命令,把数据加载到 DataSet,或者把 DataSet 内的数据送回数据源

2.1 SQL Server 相关配置

在使用 C#访问数据库之前,首先创建一个名为"chap2"的数据库,此数据库作为 2.1 节及 2.2 节中例题操作的默认数据库。然后创建数据表 Products,表结构如表 2-2 所示。创建完毕后可录入初始化数据若干条。

表 2-2 Products 表的表结构

序号	列名	字段说明	数据类型	长度	主键	允许空
1	ProductID	商品编号	char	4	主键	否
2	ProductName	商品名称	nvarchar	40		否
3	SupplierName	供应商名称	nvarchar	40		否
4	CategoryName	商品类别名称	nvarchar	40		否
5	UnitPrice	单价	money			否

续表

序号	列名	字段说明	数据类型	长度	主键	允许空
6	UnitsInStock	库存量	smallint		否	
7	Discount	是否折扣	char	1	否	

下面首先介绍几个 SQL Server 2019 的常用操作。这些操作都是初学者在实践环节及上机课的操作中出现问题较多的地方。

1. 身份验证方式

SQL Server 2019 在安装时默认是使用 Windows 验证方式的，但是安装完成后用户可随时修改身份验证方式。

启动 SQL Server Management Studio(本书使用版本号为 V18.9.2)，在"连接到服务器"对话框中选择"Windows 身份验证"连接服务器，连接成功后，在窗体左侧的"对象资源管理器"中右击服务器实例节点，并在弹出的快捷菜单中选择"属性"菜单项，系统将弹出"服务器属性"窗口，切换至"安全性"选项卡，如图 2-1 所示。

图 2-1 "安全性"选项卡

在"服务器身份验证"部分选择"SQL Server 和 Windows 身份验证模式"选项，并单击"确定"按钮。系统将提示需要重新启动 SQL Server 以使配置生效，如图 2-2 所示。

右击"对象资源管理器"的服务器实例节点，在弹出的快捷菜单中选择"重新启动"菜单

图 2-2　系统提示框

项，SQL Server 将重新启动服务，重启成功后即可使用混合验证方式登录 SQL Server 服务器。

2. 添加登录账户

大部分初学者都习惯于使用 SQL Server 的系统管理员账号"sa"来登录数据库服务器，而在实际工作环境中使用 sa 账号登录服务器是不合理的。因为很多情况下系统的数据库是部署在租用的数据库服务器上的，此时数据库设计人员或编程人员都不可能具有 sa 账号的使用权限，因此在将身份验证方式修改为 SQL Server 和 Windows 混合身份验证后，需要为某应用程序创建一个专用的登录账户。其操作步骤描述如下。

图 2-3　"登录名"节点的右键菜单

（1）使用 Windows 身份验证登录 SQL Server，在对象资源管理器中单击"安全性"节点前面的加号"+"，在展开后的"登录名"子节点上单击右键，如图 2-3 所示，并在弹出的快捷菜单中选择"新建登录名"选项。

（2）系统弹出的"登录名-新建"窗口中，如图 2-4 所示。首先在"登录名"输入框中填写需要创建的用户名，此处以"zd"为例；将身份验证方式选为"SQL Server 身份验证"，为新建账户设置密码为"123"，同时取消勾选"强制实施密码策略"和"用户在下次登录时必须更改密码"复选框；最后为账户选择默认数据库"chap2"。

（3）服务器角色节点不予配置。有关 SQL Server 服务器角色请参考相关资料，此处不再详细介绍。

（4）在窗口左侧选择"用户映射"节点，如图 2-5 所示，在"映射到此登录名的用户"列表中，勾选此前创建好的数据库"chap2"，在窗口右下方的"数据库角色成员身份"框里选择 db_owner，即数据库拥有者。

（5）安全对象节点一般不予配置。

（6）在对话框左侧选择"状态"节点，如图 2-6 所示，将"是否允许连接到数据库引擎"选项设为"授予"，同时将"登录名"选项设为"启用"。以上各节点配置完成后单击"确定"按钮，即完成了对账户的创建工作。

（7）新建账户完成后，重新连接 SQL Server，如图 2-7 所示，选择 SQL Server 身份验证方式，输入前面设置的登录名"zd"及密码"123"，单击"连接"按钮，即可完成登录。登录成功后在对象资源管理器中可看到服务器实例名后面显示的登录用户名，如图 2-8 所示。

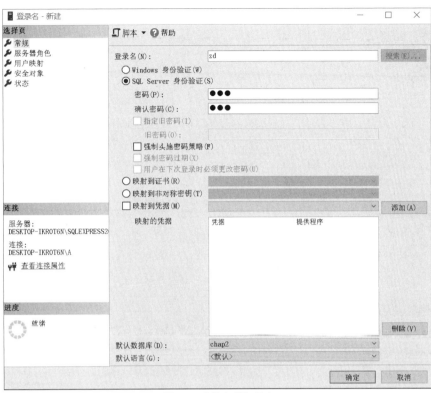

图 2-4 "常规"选项卡

图 2-5 "用户映射"选项卡

图 2-6 "状态"选项卡

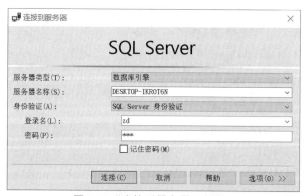

图 2-7 "连接到服务器"对话框

图 2-8 对象资源管理器

2.2 使用 ADO.NET 访问数据库

2.2.1 连接数据库

在对数据源进行操作之前,首先需建立到数据源的连接,可使用 Connection 对象显式创建到数据源的连接。

【例 2-1】 设计一个 Windows 应用程序,能通过"Windows 验证"和"Windows 和 SQL Server 混合验证"两种方式建立与数据库的连接。

实现过程如下。

(1) 新建一个 Windows 窗体应用(.NET Framework)项目(本书创建的所有 Windows 应用程序,均为.NET Framework 项目,下文再描述创建项目类型时会略去.NET Framework 字样),命名为 connection,将创建的默认窗体名更名为 frmConnect,窗体的 Text 属性设置为"连接数据库",界面设计如图 2-9 所示。frmConnect 窗体中的主要控件,按 Tab 键顺序,描述如表 2-3 所示。

图 2-9 "连接数据库"窗体控件 Tab 顺序

表 2-3 "连接数据库"窗体控件及说明

Tab 顺序	控件类型	控件名称	说明	主要属性	
				属性名	属性值
0	Button	btnConnect1	Windows 身份验证方式连接数据库	Text	Windows 验证
1		btnConnect2	混合验证方式连接数据库	Text	混合验证

(2) 主要程序代码。

说明:本节内所有例题代码均需引用 System.Data.SqlClient 命名空间,代码如下。

```
using System.Data.SqlClient;          //添加对 SQL Server 数据访问对象的引用
```

后续例题不再逐一说明。

由于篇幅所限,本节略去了所有例题的异常捕获代码,读者需自行添加获取控件输入及访问数据库等处的异常捕获代码。

双击"Windows 验证"按钮,进入其 Click 事件处理函数,代码如下。

```
//Windows 方式连接数据库
private void btnConnect1_Click(object sender, EventArgs e)
{
    string strConn = "server=(local);database=chap2;integrated security=
              true";                     //连接字符串
```

```
            SqlConnection conn = new SqlConnection(strConn);    //创建连接对象
            conn.Open();                                         //打开连接
            //如连接成功则弹出消息框提示
            MessageBox.Show("数据库已通过集成验证方式连接成功","连接状态对话框");
            conn.Close();                                        //使用完毕后关闭数据库连接
        }
```

双击"混合验证"按钮,进入其 Click 事件处理函数,代码如下。

```
        //SQL Server + Windows 方式连接数据库
        private void btnConnect2_Click(object sender, EventArgs e)
        {
            string strConn = "server=(local);database=chap2;uid=zd;pwd=123";
                                                                 //连接字符串
            SqlConnection conn = new SqlConnection(strConn);    //创建连接对象
            conn.Open();                                         //打开连接
            //如连接成功则弹出消息框提示
            MessageBox.Show("数据库已通过混合验证方式连接成功","连接状态对话框");
            conn.Close();                                        //使用完毕后关闭数据库连接
        }
```

数据库连接字符串包含要连接的数据库的信息,如 server 属性指定数据库服务器名称,database 属性指定数据库名称,使用 Windows 身份验证方式只需要给出 server 和 database 两个属性的值,并使用"integrated security=true"指定身份验证方式为 Windows 验证;当使用混合验证时则需要使用 uid 属性指定数据库账户、pwd 属性指定该账号的密码。

说明:例 2-1 中的连接字符串中的用户名"zd"和密码"123",是以 2.1 节"添加登录账户"的方式创建的,读者可自行修改为自己计算机的 SQLServer 登录名及密码。

运行程序,分别单击"Windows 验证"和"混合验证"两个按钮,如连接成功,将分别弹出不同的连接状态对话框,如图 2-10 所示。

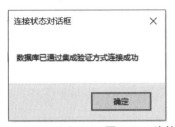

图 2-10 连接成功状态对话框

2.2.2 对数据库进行添加、修改及删除操作

在创建好到数据库的连接之后,可以使用 Command 对象对数据库进行更新操作。

【例 2-2】 设计一个 Windows 应用程序,实现对数据库表的添加、修改及删除操作。实现过程如下。

(1) 新建一个 Windows 应用程序,命名为 operateData,将创建的默认窗体名更名为 frmCommand,窗体的 Text 属性设置为"对数据库执行添加、修改及删除操作",界面设计如图 2-11 所示。frmCommand 窗体中的主要控件,按 Tab 键顺序,描述如表 2-4 所示。

图 2-11 "对数据库执行添加、修改及删除操作"窗体 Tab 顺序视图

表 2-4 "对数据库执行添加、修改及删除操作"窗体控件及说明

Tab 顺序	控件类型	控件名称	说明	主要属性	
				属性名	属性值
0	Button	btnInsert	向数据库表添加一条记录	Text	添加
1		btnUpdate	修改数据库表中的记录	Text	修改
2		btnDelete	删除数据库表中的记录	Text	删除

(2) 主要程序代码。

双击"添加"按钮，进入其 Click 事件处理函数，代码如下。

```
//"添加"按钮单击事件处理函数
private void btnInsert_Click(object sender, EventArgs e)
{
    string strConn = "server=(local);database=chap2;integrated security=
        true";                                    //连接字符串
    SqlConnection conn = new SqlConnection(strConn);   //声明并创建连接对象
    conn.Open();                                  //打开数据库连接
    //向商品表插入一条新记录
    string strSql="insert into Products values('0012','双层蒸锅','苏泊尔集团',
        '厨具',129.9,100,'false')";
    SqlCommand comm = new SqlCommand(strSql, conn);    //声明并创建命令对象
    int row = comm.ExecuteNonQuery();             //执行 SQL 语句，并获取受影响的行数
    if (row > 0)                                  //如果记录插入成功，则弹出消息框提示
    {
        MessageBox.Show("插入数据成功", "操作状态对话框");
    }
    conn.Close();                                 //关闭数据库连接
}
```

双击"修改"按钮，进入其 Click 事件处理函数，代码如下。

```
//"修改"按钮单击事件处理函数
private void btnUpdate_Click(object sender, EventArgs e)
{
    string strConn = "server=(local);database=chap2;integrated security=
        true";
    SqlConnection conn = new SqlConnection(strConn);
    conn.Open();
    //修改商品表中的一条记录
    string strSql = "update Products set UnitsInStock=500 where ProductID='0012'";
```

```
        SqlCommand comm = new SqlCommand(strSql, conn);
        int row = comm.ExecuteNonQuery();
        if (row > 0)
        {
            MessageBox.Show("修改数据成功","操作状态对话框");
        }
        conn.Close();
    }
```

双击"删除"按钮,进入其 Click 事件处理函数,代码如下。

```
//"删除"按钮单击事件处理函数
private void btnDelete_Click(object sender, EventArgs e)
{
    string strConn = "server=(local);database=chap2;integrated security=
        true";
    SqlConnection conn = new SqlConnection(strConn);
    conn.Open();
    //删除商品表中的一条记录
    string strSql = "delete from Products where ProductID='0012'";
    SqlCommand comm = new SqlCommand(strSql, conn);
    int row = comm.ExecuteNonQuery();
    if (row > 0)
    {
        MessageBox.Show("删除数据成功","操作状态对话框");
    }
    conn.Close();
}
```

运行程序,分别单击"添加""修改"和"删除"按钮,如操作成功,将分别弹出不同的操作状态对话框,如图 2-12 所示。对于数据库记录的修改情况,读者可同时从 SQL Server 管理控制台访问数据库 chap2 的 Products 表进行验证。

图 2-12 操作成功状态对话框

2.2.3 查询数据库中的数据

【例 2-3】 设计一个 Windows 应用程序,使用 DataReader 查询数据库中的信息并加载到 ComboBox 控件的选项中。

实现过程如下。

(1) 新建一个 Windows 应用程序,命名为 testDataReader,将创建的默认窗体名更名为 frmProducts,窗体的 Text 属性设置为"商品类别及名称",界面设计如图 2-13 所示。frmProducts 窗体中的主要控件,按 Tab 键顺序,描述如表 2-5 所示。

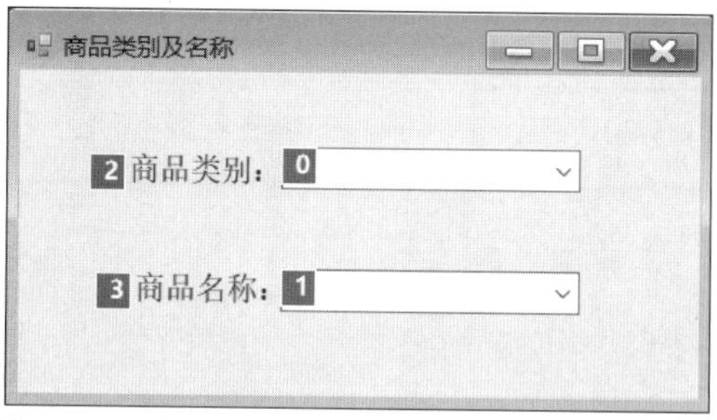

图 2-13 "商品类别及名称"窗体 Tab 键顺序视图

表 2-5 "商品类别及名称"窗体控件及说明

Tab 顺序	控件类型	控件名称	说明	主要属性	
				属性名	属性值
0	ComboBox	comboCategory	所有商品类别名称	DropDownStyle	DropDownList
1		comboProducts	某商品类别下的商品名称	DropDownStyle	DropDownList

说明：界面中不参与编程的 Label 控件不再进行说明，以下各例题均同样处理。

(2) 主要程序代码。

双击窗体标题栏，进入 Load 事件处理函数，编写代码：访问数据库，为"商品类别"下拉框加载数据，代码如下。

```
//窗体加载事件处理函数,为"商品类别"下拉框加载所有的商品类别数据
private void frmProducts_Load(object sender, EventArgs e)
{
    string strConn = "server=(local);database=chap2;integrated security=
        true";                                           //连接字符串
    SqlConnection conn = new SqlConnection(strConn);    //声明并创建连接对象
    conn.Open();                                         //打开数据库连接
    string strSql = "select distinct CategoryName from Products";    //查询
    SqlCommand comm = new SqlCommand(strSql, conn);
    SqlDataReader dr = comm.ExecuteReader();
    while (dr.Read())
        comboCategory.Items.Add(dr[0]);                 //依次加载数据项至 ComboBox
    dr.Close();
    conn.Close();
}
```

双击"商品类别"下拉框，进入其 SelectedIndexChanged 事件处理函数，根据其选项为"商品名称"下拉框加载数据，代码如下。

```
//"商品类别"下拉框选项索引变化事件处理函数
//根据"商品类别"下拉框中的选项加载该类别下的所有的商品名称
private void comboCategory_SelectedIndexChanged(object sender, EventArgs e)
{
    comboProducts.Items.Clear();
    string strConn = "server=(local);database=chap2;integrated security=
        true";
    SqlConnection conn = new SqlConnection(strConn);
    conn.Open();
```

```
        string strSql = "select ProductName from Products where CategoryName='"+
            comboCategory.Text+"'";
        SqlCommand comm = new SqlCommand(strSql, conn);
        SqlDataReader dr = comm.ExecuteReader();
        while (dr.Read())
            comboProducts.Items.Add(dr[0]);
        dr.Close();
        conn.Close();
    }
```

运行程序,窗体加载后单击"商品类别"下拉框,已加载不重复的商品分类数据,选择某个类别后单击"商品名称"下拉框,已加载该类别下的商品名称,如图 2-14 所示。

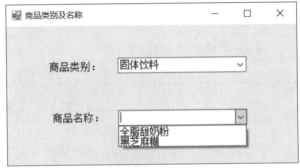

图 2-14 "商品类别及名称"窗口运行效果

【例 2-4】 使用 DataAdaper 和 DataSet 对象查询数据库中的信息并加载到 ComboBox 控件的选项中。

实现过程如下。

(1) 新建一个 Windows 应用程序,命名为 testDataSet,将创建的默认窗体名更名为 frmProducts,窗体及各主要控件的属性设置同例 2-3。

(2) 主要程序代码。

双击窗体标题栏,进入其 Load 事件处理函数,编写代码:访问数据库,为"商品类别"下拉框加载数据,代码如下。

```
//窗体加载事件处理函数,为"商品类别"下拉框加载所有的商品分类数据
private void frmProducts_Load(object sender, EventArgs e)
{
    string strConn = "server=(local);database=chap2;integrated security=
        true";                                         //连接字符串
    SqlConnection conn = new SqlConnection(strConn);
                                                      //声明并创建连接对象
    string strSql = "select distinct CategoryName from Products";
                                                      //查询不重复的商品类别名称
    SqlDataAdapter da = new SqlDataAdapter(strSql, conn);
                                                      //声明并创建数据适配器对象
    DataSet ds = new DataSet();                       //声明并创建数据集对象
    da.Fill(ds);                                      //使用数据适配器填充数据集
    comboCategory.DataSource = ds.Tables[0];          //设置"商品类别"下拉数据源
    comboCategory.DisplayMember = "CategoryName";     //设置"商品类别"下拉框的显示属性
}
```

双击"商品类别"下拉框，进入其 SelectedIndexChanged 事件处理函数，根据其选中项为"商品名称"下拉框加载数据，代码如下。

```
//"商品类别"下拉框选项索引变化事件处理函数
//根据"商品类别"下拉框中的选项加载该类别下的所有的商品名称
private void comboCatagory_SelectedIndexChanged(object sender, EventArgs e)
{
    string strConn = "server=(local);database=chap2;integrated security=true";
    SqlConnection conn = new SqlConnection(strConn);
    //根据"商品类别"下拉框中的选项查询商品名称
    string strSql="select ProductName from Products where CategoryName='"+
            comboCategory.Text+"'";
    SqlDataAdapter da = new SqlDataAdapter(strSql, conn);
    DataSet ds = new DataSet();
    da.Fill(ds);
    comboProducts.DataSource = ds.Tables[0];        //设置"商品名称"下拉框的数据源
    comboProducts.DisplayMember = "ProductName";    //设置"商品名称"下拉框的显示属性
}
```

思考：细心的同学会发现，例 2-3 和例 2-4 虽然运行界面完全相同，但是窗体加载之后列表框中选项的情况是有区别的。那么，区别在哪儿？原因又是什么呢？

2.2.4 数据绑定控件

【例 2-5】 设计一个 Windows 应用程序，实现商品信息的维护。本例题中，程序要读取数据库中的数据，加载数据至 ListBox 和 ComboBox 控件，并根据用户在 ListBox 控件中选择的数据项再次访问数据库，获取相关记录。另外，本例题还实现了对商品表 Products 的增加、修改及删除操作。

实现过程如下。

（1）新建一 Windows 应用程序，命名为 products，将创建的默认窗体名更名为 frmProducts，窗体的 Text 属性设置为"商品信息管理"，界面设计如图 2-15 所示。frmProducts 窗体中的主要控件，按 Tab 键顺序，描述如表 2-6 所示。

图 2-15 "商品信息管理"窗体 Tab 键顺序视图

表 2-6 "商品信息管理"窗体控件及说明

Tab 顺序	控件类型	控件名称	说明	主要属性 属性名	主要属性 属性值
0	TextBox	txtID	输入和显示商品编号	Readonly	True
1	TextBox	txtName	输入和显示商品名称	Readonly	True
2	TextBox	txtSupplier	输入和显示供应商名称	Readonly	True
3	ComboBox	comboCategory	输入和显示商品类别	Enabled	False
4	TextBox	txtUnitPrice	输入和显示商品单价	Readonly	True
5	TextBox	txtUnitsInStock	输入和显示库存数量	Readonly	True
6	CheckBox	chkDisc	输入和显示是否打折	Enabled	False
7	Button	btnInsert	添加商品	Enabled	True
8	Button	btnUpdate	修改商品	Enabled	True
9	Button	btnSave	保存数据	Enabled	False
10	Button	btnCancle	取消编辑	Enabled	False
11	Button	btnDelete	删除数据	Enabled	True
12	ListBox	lstProducts	商品名称列表	Enabled	True

（2）主要程序代码。

首先要为该程序添加两个成员变量，代码如下。

```
string strConn = "server=(local);database=chap2;integrated security=true";
                                    //连接字符串
string insertORupdate = "";         //标识变量，用来记录要保存的是添加还是修改操作
```

自定义方法 DataLoad()，访问数据库，加载商品类别列表及商品名称列表，代码如下。

```
///<summary>
///访问数据库,加载商品类别列表及商品名称列表
///</summary>
void DataLoad()
{
    //以下代码使用 DataReader 访问数据库
    SqlConnection conn = new SqlConnection(strConn);    //创建连接对象
    conn.Open();                                         //打开连接
    string strSql = "select distinct CategoryName from Products";
                                                         //查询不重复的商品类别名
    SqlCommand comm = new SqlCommand(strSql, conn);      //声明并创建命令对象
    SqlDataReader dr = comm.ExecuteReader();             //执行查询,用 DataReader 存放数据
    while (dr.Read())                                    //如果查询到数据
        comboCategory.Items.Add(dr[0]);                  //逐项加载商品类别名至 ComboBox
    dr.Close();                                          //关闭 dataReader
    //以下代码使用 DataAdapter 和 DataSet 访问数据库
    strSql = "select ProductName,ProductID from Products";
                                                         //查询商品名称及商品编号
```

```
    SqlDataAdapter da = new SqlDataAdapter(strSql, conn);
                                                    //声明并创建数据适配器对象
    DataSet ds = new DataSet();                     //声明并创建数据集对象
    da.Fill(ds);                                    //填充数据集
    lstProducts.DataSource = ds.Tables[0];          //设置商品名称列表的数据源
    lstProducts.DisplayMember = "ProductName";      //设置显示值属性
    lstProducts.ValueMember = "ProductID";          //设置实际值属性
    conn.Close();                                   //关闭连接
    lstProducts.SelectedIndex = -1;                 //使商品名称列表没有选中项
}
```

商品管理窗体的 Load 事件处理函数,就是调用 DataLoad()方法,代码如下。

```
//窗体加载事件处理函数
private void frmProducts_Load(object sender, EventArgs e)
{
    DataLoad();
}
```

声明自定义方法 controlEnabled(),控制各个输入控件在"查看"和"编辑"操作时的可用性,代码如下。

```
//自定义方法,控制控件的可用性,将控件可用性分为"查看"和"编辑"两种状态
public void controlEnabled(string status)
{
    if (status == "show")                    //当前为查看数据状态,控件都不可编辑
    {
        btnInsert.Enabled = true;
        btnUpdate.Enabled = true;
        btnSave.Enabled = false;
        btnCancle.Enabled = false;
        btnDelete.Enabled = true;
        chkDisc.Enabled = false;
        comboCategory.Enabled = false;
        foreach (Control c in this.Controls)
        {
            if (c is TextBox)
            {
                TextBox txtb = ((TextBox)c);
                txtb.ReadOnly = true;
            }
        }
    }
    else                                     //当前为编辑数据状态,控件可用
    {
        btnInsert.Enabled = false;
        btnUpdate.Enabled = false;
        btnSave.Enabled = true;
        btnCancle.Enabled = true;
        btnDelete.Enabled = false;
        chkDisc.Enabled = true;
        comboCategory.Enabled = true;
        foreach (Control c in this.Controls)
```

```csharp
        {
            if (c is TextBox)
            {
                TextBox txtb = ((TextBox)c);
                txtb.ReadOnly = false;
            }
        }
    }
}
```

双击 lstProducts 控件,进入其选项索引变化事件处理函数,根据选择的商品,查询该商品其他信息,并为界面其他控件赋值,代码如下。

```csharp
//商品名称列表选项索引变化事件,根据选择的商品名称加载商品其他信息
private void lstProducts_SelectedIndexChanged(object sender, EventArgs e)
{
    //用来判断用户是否选中了有效的选项,且保证是数据加载后用户进行的操作
    if ((lstProducts.SelectedIndex != -1)
        &&(lstProducts.SelectedValue.ToString()!=
            "System.Data.DataRowView"))
    {
        string proId = lstProducts.SelectedValue.ToString();
                                    //获取当前选中商品的商品编号
        SqlConnection conn=new SqlConnection(strConn);
                                    //声明并创建连接对象
        conn.Open();                //打开数据库连接
        //由商品编号查询该商品其他信息
        string strSql="select * from Products where ProductId='"+proId+"'";
        SqlCommand comm=new SqlCommand(strSql,conn);  //声明并创建命令对象
        SqlDataReader dr = comm.ExecuteReader(); //使用 DataReader 获取查询结果
        if (dr.Read()) //如果查询到数据,就将该商品各字段的值赋予窗体各控件用以显示
        {
            txtID.Text = dr["ProductID"].ToString();
            txtName.Text=dr["ProductName"].ToString();
            txtSupplier.Text=dr["SupplierName"].ToString();
            comboCategory.Text = dr["CategoryName"].ToString();
            txtUnitPrice.Text=dr["UnitPrice"].ToString();
            txtUnitsInStock.Text=dr["UnitsInStock"].ToString();
            chkDisc.Checked = (dr["Discount"].ToString())=="True"?true:false;
        }
        dr.Close();                         //关闭 DataReader
        conn.Close();                       //关闭连接
        controlEnabled("show");             //将控件设置为查看状态
    }
}
```

说明:由于为 ListBox 控件加载选项时会触发 SelectedIndexChanged 事件,此时获取到的 ListBox.SelectedValue.ToString() 值为"System.Data.DataRowView",而不是经用户选择过的商品编号,程序需过滤掉这种情况。只有完成 ListBox 控件的选项加载后,经用户选择某条商品数据时,程序才进行后续操作,如下代码即可实现这种过滤功能。

```
if ((lstProducts.SelectedIndex != -1)&&
    (lstProducts.SelectedValue.ToString()!="System.Data.DataRowView"))
```

双击 btnInsert 按钮，进入其 Click 事件处理函数，清空所有输入控件并使其为可编辑状态，设置编辑状态为 insert，真正的插入操作是在 btnSave 的 Click 事件处理函数中进行。代码如下。

```
//"添加"按钮单击事件处理函数
private void btnInsert_Click(object sender, EventArgs e)
{
    insertORupdate = "insert";              //设置标识变量为添加操作
    controlEnabled("edit");                 //将控件设置为编辑状态
    //清空所有控件
    foreach (Control c in this.Controls)
    {
        if (c is TextBox)
        {
            TextBox txtb = ((TextBox)c);
            txtb.Text = "";
        }
    }
    comboCategory.SelectedIndex = -1;
    chkDisc.Checked = false;
}
```

双击 btnUpdate 按钮，进入其 Click 事件处理函数，使各输入控件为可编辑状态，设置编辑状态为 update，真正的修改操作是在 btnSave 的 Click 事件处理函数中进行。代码如下。

```
//"修改"按钮单击事件处理函数
private void btnUpdate_Click(object sender, EventArgs e)
{
    controlEnabled("edit");
    txtID.ReadOnly = true;                  //商品编号不能修改
    insertORupdate = "update";              //设置标志变量为修改操作
}
```

双击 btnSave 按钮，进入其 Click 事件处理函数，根据编辑状态对数据库进行 insert 或 update 操作，代码如下。

```
//"保存"按钮单击事件处理函数，完成添加和修改操作
private void btnSave_Click(object sender, EventArgs e)
{
    SqlConnection conn = new SqlConnection(strConn);   //声明并创建连接对象
    conn.Open();                                        //打开数据库连接
    //下面一段代码将保存添加的商品数据
    if (insertORupdate == "insert")
    {
        string strSql = "insert into Products values(@ProductID,@ProductName
        ,@SupplierName,@CategoryName,@UnitPrice,@UnitsInStock,@Discount)";
        SqlCommand comm = new SqlCommand(strSql, conn);
        comm.Parameters.Add(new SqlParameter("@ProductID", txtID.Text));
        comm.Parameters.Add(new SqlParameter("@ProductName", txtName.Text));
```

```csharp
        comm.Parameters.Add(new SqlParameter("@SupplierName",
            txtSupplier.Text));
        comm.Parameters.Add(new SqlParameter("@CategoryName",
            comboCategory.Text));
        comm.Parameters.Add(new SqlParameter("@UnitPrice",
            float.Parse(txtUnitPrice.Text)));
        comm.Parameters.Add(new SqlParameter("@UnitsInStock",
            float.Parse(txtUnitsInStock.Text)));
        comm.Parameters.Add(new SqlParameter("@Discount", (chkDisc.Checked ==
            true ?"1" : "0")));
        if (comm.ExecuteNonQuery() > 0)
            MessageBox.Show("添加商品信息成功!");
        else
            MessageBox.Show("添加商品信息失败!");
    }
    //下面一段代码将保存修改的商品数据
    else
    {
        string strSql = "update Products set ProductName=@ProductName,
            SupplierName=@SupplierName,CategoryName=@CategoryName,UnitPrice=
            @UnitPrice,UnitsInStock=@UnitsInStock,
            Discount=@Discount where ProductID=@ProductID";
        SqlCommand comm = new SqlCommand(strSql, conn);
        comm.Parameters.Add(new SqlParameter("@ProductID", txtID.Text));
        comm.Parameters.Add(new SqlParameter("@ProductName", txtName.Text));
        comm.Parameters.Add(new SqlParameter("@SupplierName",
            txtSupplier.Text));
        comm.Parameters.Add(new SqlParameter("@CategoryName",
            comboCategory.Text));
        comm.Parameters.Add(new SqlParameter("@UnitPrice",
            float.Parse(txtUnitPrice.Text)));
        comm.Parameters.Add(new SqlParameter("@UnitsInStock",
            float.Parse(txtUnitsInStock.Text)));
        comm.Parameters.Add(new SqlParameter("@Discount", (chkDisc.Checked ==
            true ?"1" : "0")));
        if (comm.ExecuteNonQuery() > 0)
            MessageBox.Show("更新商品信息成功!");
        else
            MessageBox.Show("更新商品信息失败!");
    }
    conn.Close();                           //关闭数据库连接
    DataLoad();                             //重新访问数据库,刷新界面显示的商品信息
    controlEnabled("show");                 //将控件设置为查看状态
}
```

说明：代码中出现的 SqlParameter 类为 SQL 命令参数类。命令对象可使用参数来将值传递给 SQL 语句或存储过程,提供类型检查和验证。与命令文本不同,参数输入被视为文本值,而不是可执行代码,这样可帮助抵御"SQL 注入"攻击,这种攻击的攻击者会将命令插入 SQL 语句,从而危及服务器的安全。一般来说,在更新 DataTable 或 DataSet 时,如果不采用 SqlParameter,那么当输入的 SQL 语句出现歧义时,如字符串中含有单引号,程序就会发生错误,并且他人可以轻易地通过拼接 SQL 语句来进行注入攻击。

参数化命令还可提高查询执行性能,因为它们可帮助数据库服务器将传入命令与适当的缓存查询计划进行准确匹配。除具备安全和性能优势外,参数化命令还提供一种用于组织传递到数据源的值的便捷方法。

双击 btnCancel 按钮单击事件处理函数,控制各输入控件的可编辑状态,恢复查看状态,代码如下。

```
//"取消"按钮单击事件处理函数,退出编辑状态
private void btnCancle_Click(object sender, EventArgs e)
{
    controlEnabled("show");                  //将控件设置为查看状态
}
```

双击 btnDelete 按钮,进入 Click 事件处理函数,根据选择商品的编号删除该商品信息,代码如下。

```
//"删除"按钮单击事件处理函数
private void btnDelete_Click(object sender, EventArgs e)
{
    SqlConnection conn = new SqlConnection(strConn);
    conn.Open();
    string strSql = "delete from Products where ProductID=@ProductID";
    SqlCommand comm = new SqlCommand(strSql, conn);
    comm.Parameters.Add(new SqlParameter("@ProductID", txtID.Text));
    if (comm.ExecuteNonQuery() > 0)
        MessageBox.Show("删除商品信息成功!");
    else
        MessageBox.Show("删除商品信息失败!");
    conn.Close();                    //关闭数据库连接
    DataLoad();                      //重新访问数据库,刷新界面显示的商品信息
    controlEnabled("show");          //将控件设置为查看状态
}
```

运行程序,显示"商品信息管理"界面,如图 2-16 所示。界面左侧的商品名称列表中加载了所有的商品名称,单击任一商品名称,右侧商品详细信息区域的各控件中将加载该商品记录的其他字段,"添加""修改"及"删除"按钮可用,"保存"及"取消"按钮不可用。

单击"添加"按钮后,右侧控件全部清空,"保存"及"取消"按钮可用,同时"修改"及"删除"按钮不可用。如单击"修改"按钮,则右侧控件均为可编辑状态(ReadOnly 属性为 False,商品类别及折扣控件 Enabled 属性为 True),按钮可用性同上。

【例 2-6】 设计一个 Windows 应用程序,实现对个人年龄及爱好的维护功能。

本例题中,程序要构造一个数据集(DataSet),添加一个数据表(DataTable)并插入数据,将构造好的 DataSet 设置为 DataGridView 控件的数据源。另外,还实现了对数据表的增加、修改及删除操作。

实现过程如下。

(1) 新建一个 Windows 应用程序,命名为 operateDataSet,将创建的默认窗体名更名为 frmDataSet,窗体的 Text 属性设置为"DataSet 操作",界面设计如图 2-17 所示。frmDataSet 窗体中的主要控件,按 Tab 键顺序,描述如表 2-7 所示。

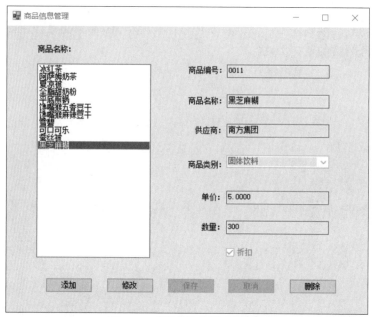

图 2-16 "商品信息管理"界面

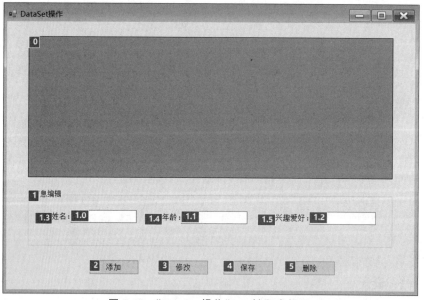

图 2-17 "DataSet 操作"Tab 键顺序视图

表 2-7 "DataSet 操作"窗体控件及说明

Tab 顺序	控件类型	控件名称	说　　明	主　要　属　性	
				属性名	属性值
0	DataGridView	dgvHobby	显示个人年龄及爱好	SelectionMode	FullRowSelect
1	GroupBox	groupBoxEdit	输入和显示商品类别	Text	信息编辑

续表

Tab 顺序	控件类型	控件名称	说明	主要属性	
				属性名	属性值
1.0	TextBox	txtName	输入和显示姓名	Readonly	True
1.1		txtAge	输入和显示年龄	Readonly	True
1.2		txtHobby	输入和显示兴趣爱好	Readonly	True
2	Button	btnInsert	添加信息	Enabled	True
3		btnUpdate	修改信息	Enabled	True
4		btnSave	保存信息	Enabled	False
5		btnDelete	删除信息	Enabled	True

(2) 主要程序代码。

首先要为该程序添加四个成员变量,代码如下。

```
//声明数据集、数据表及数据行对象
DataSet myds = new DataSet();
DataTable mydt;
DataRow mydr;
string insertORupdate;                          //标识符变量,值为"添加"或"修改"
```

双击窗体标题栏,进入其 Load 事件处理函数,编写代码:构造数据集、添加数据表并插入初始数据,最终作为数据源显示在 dgvHobby 中,代码如下。

```
private void frmDataSet_Load(object sender, EventArgs e)
{
    mydt = new DataTable("hobby");                    //创建数据表对象
    //定义表结构
    mydt.Columns.Add(new DataColumn("姓名", typeof(string)));
    mydt.Columns.Add(new DataColumn("年龄", typeof(Int32)));
    mydt.Columns.Add(new DataColumn("爱好", typeof(string)));
    //为数据表设置主键是为了在删除的时候可以定位到要删除的记录
    mydt.PrimaryKey = new DataColumn[] { mydt.Columns["姓名"] };
    //新建一行数据
    mydr = mydt.NewRow();
    mydr[0] = "张三";
    mydr[1] = 21;
    mydr[2] = "看电视";
    mydt.Rows.Add(mydr);
    //新建第二行数据
    mydr = mydt.NewRow();
    mydr[0] = "李四";
    mydr[1] = 22;
    mydr[2] = "打篮球";
    mydt.Rows.Add(mydr);
    myds.Tables.Add(mydt);                            //加入生成的表到数据集
    dgvHobby.DataSource = myds.Tables["hobby"].DefaultView;
                                                      //将数据显示到数据绑定控件
}
```

此处要补充说明的是 DataTable.PrimaryKey 属性，获取或设置充当数据表主键的列的数组。因为主键可由多列组成，所以 PrimaryKey 属性由 DataColumn 对象的数组组成。如 DataTable 对象不设置 PrimaryKey 属性，则删除时将不能通过 DataTable.Rows.Find() 方法找到需要删除的数据行。

双击 btnInsert 按钮，进入其 Click 事件处理函数，主要功能是控制按钮及各输入控件的可用性，真正的添加和修改操作都是在 btnSave 按钮中完成的，代码如下。

```csharp
//"添加"按钮单击事件处理函数
private void btnInsert_Click(object sender, EventArgs e)
{
    txtName.ReadOnly = false;            //清空输入控件并使之可编辑
    txtName.Text = "";
    txtAge.ReadOnly = false;
    txtAge.Text = "";
    txtHobby.ReadOnly = false;
    txtHobby.Text = "";
    insertORupdate = "insert";           //设置标识变量
    btnInsert.Enabled = false;           //控制按钮可用性
    btnUpdate.Enabled = false;
    btnSave.Enabled = true;
}
```

双击 btnUpdate 按钮，进入其 Click 事件处理函数，主要功能是控制按钮及各输入控件的可用性，真正的添加和修改操作都是在 btnSave 按钮中完成的，代码如下。

```csharp
//"修改"按钮单击事件处理函数
private void btnUpdate_Click(object sender, EventArgs e)
{
    txtName.ReadOnly = false;            //使输入控件可编辑
    txtAge.ReadOnly = false;
    txtHobby.ReadOnly = false;
    insertORupdate = "update";           //设置标识变量
    btnUpdate.Enabled = false;           //控制按钮可用性
    btnInsert.Enabled = false;
    btnSave.Enabled = true;
}
```

双击 btnSave 按钮，进入 Click 事件处理函数，主要功能是实现对 DataSet 的添加及修改，并控制按钮及输入控件的可用性，代码如下。

```csharp
//"保存"按钮单击事件处理函数
private void btnSave_Click(object sender, EventArgs e)
{
    if (insertORupdate == "insert")              //如要保存的是添加的结果
    {
        //新建一行数据
        mydr = mydt.NewRow();
        mydr[0] = txtName.Text.Trim();
        mydr[1] = Int32.Parse(txtAge.Text.Trim());
        mydr[2] = txtHobby.Text.Trim();
        mydt.Rows.Add(mydr);
    }
```

```
        else                                              //如要保存的是修改的结果
        {
            //修改一行数据
            int rowNumber = dgvHobby.CurrentRow.Index;    //获取当前行索引
            mydt.Rows[rowNumber][0] = txtName.Text.Trim();
            mydt.Rows[rowNumber][1] = Int32.Parse(txtAge.Text.Trim());
            mydt.Rows[rowNumber][2] = txtHobby.Text.Trim();
        }
        btnInsert.Enabled = true;                         //控制按钮可用性
        btnUpdate.Enabled = true;
        btnSave.Enabled = false;
}
```

双击 btnDelete 按钮，进入其 Click 事件处理函数，首先从 dgvHobby 控件中获取选中行中的"姓名"属性值，然后使用 DataTable.Rows.Find() 方法通过数据表的主键"姓名"找到指定数据行，最后从数据表的行集合中移除指定行。代码如下。

```
//"删除"按钮单击事件处理函数
private void btnDelete_Click(object sender, EventArgs e)
{
    //获取选中行的主键，即"姓名"的值
    string name = dgvHobby.SelectedRows[0].Cells[0].Value.ToString();
    DataRow drow = mydt.Rows.Find(name);                  //获取由主键指定的数据行
    mydt.Rows.Remove(drow);                               //移除指定的数据行
}
```

选择 dgvHobby 控件，并从事件列表中进入其 CellClick 事件处理函数，其功能为当单击一条数据时，在各输入控件中加载相应字段的值，代码如下。

```
//DataGridView单击单元格事件处理函数，将选中数据加载至控件并控制控件可编辑性
private void dgvHobby_CellClick(object sender, DataGridViewCellEventArgs e)
{
    if (e.RowIndex <= (mydt.Rows.Count - 1))
    {
        txtName.ReadOnly = true;
        txtAge.ReadOnly = true;
        txtHobby.ReadOnly = true;
        btnInsert.Enabled = true;
        btnUpdate.Enabled = true;
        btnSave.Enabled = false;
        int rowNumber = e.RowIndex;
        txtName.Text = mydt.Rows[rowNumber][0].ToString();
        txtAge.Text = mydt.Rows[rowNumber][1].ToString();
        txtHobby.Text = mydt.Rows[rowNumber][2].ToString();
    }
}
```

程序运行界面如图 2-18 所示。

程序操作流程不再描述。本例题所有数据都在内存中处理，没有连接数据库。读者也可改造例题为操作从数据库填充的数据集。

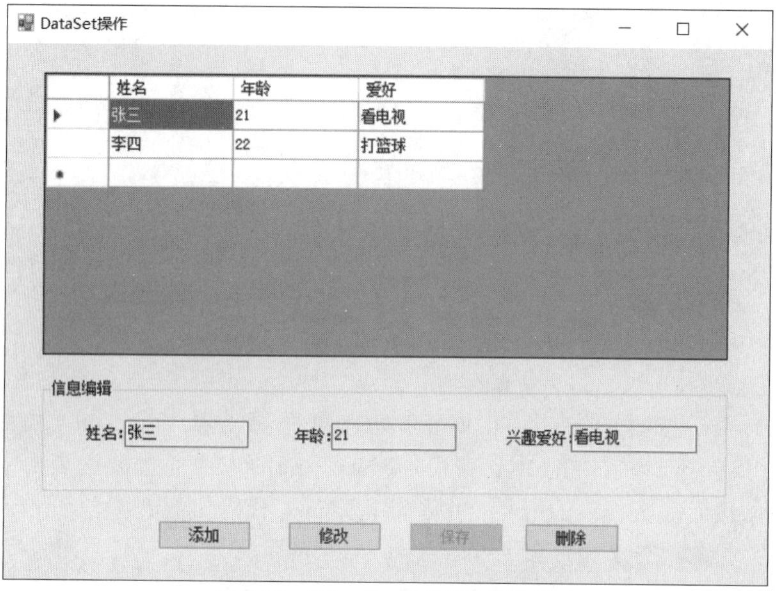

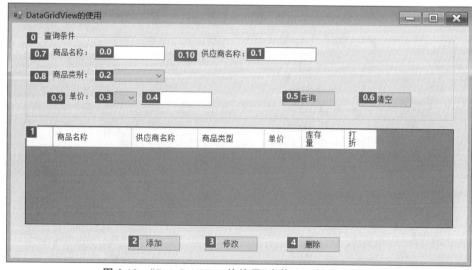

图 2-18 "DataSet 操作"运行效果

【例 2-7】 设计一个 Windows 应用程序，实现商品信息维护。本例题中，要实现使用 DataGridView 控件显示数据库中的数据，并提供组合条件的查询及对数据的添加、删除及修改功能。

实现过程如下。

（1）新建一个 Windows 应用程序，命名为 DataGridView，将创建的默认窗体名更名为 frmProducts，窗体的 Text 属性设置为"DataGridView 的使用"，界面设计如图 2-19 所示。frmProducts 窗体中的主要控件，按 Tab 键顺序，描述如表 2-8 所示。

图 2-19 "DataGridView 的使用"窗体 Tab 键顺序视图

表 2-8 "DataGridView 的使用"窗体控件及说明

Tab 顺序	控件类型	控件名称	说　明	主要属性	
				属性名	属性值
0	GroupBox	groupBoxQuery	商品信息查询条件的容器	Text	查询条件
0.0	TextBox	txtProName	输入商品名称	Text	""
0.1		txtSupName	输入供应商名称	Text	""
0.2	ComboBox	comboCategory	显示所有商品类别	DropDownStyle	DropDownList
0.3		comboOperator	选择商品单价的比较运算符	Items	请选择 < <= = > >=
0.4	TextBox	txtUnitPrice	输入商品单价查询数额	Enabled	False
0.5	Button	btnSelect	查询符合条件的商品记录	Text	查询
0.6		btnClear	清空所有查询条件	Text	清空
1	DataGridView	dGVProducts	显示商品信息	SelectionMode	FullRowSelect
2	Button	btnInsert	添加信息	Text	添加
3		btnUpdate	修改信息	Text	修改
4		btnDelete	删除信息	Text	删除

（2）对于控件 dGVProducts，需要对列进行编辑，为每列指定属性 DataPropertyName 为对应的数据表字段，为每列指定 HeaderText 为中文列头，如图 2-20 所示。其中，"商品编号"列不需要显示，因此其 Visible 属性设置为 False，其他字段都默认设置为 True。

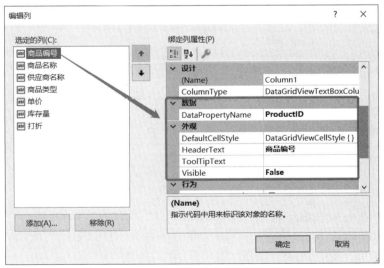

图 2-20　dGVProducts 的"编辑列"对话框

dGVProducts 中各列的属性设置如表 2-9 所示。

表 2-9　dGVProducts 中各列的属性设置

列头文本	属性名	属性值
商品编号	DataPropertyName	ProductID
	Visible	False
商品名称	DataPropertyName	ProductName
供应商名称	DataPropertyName	SupplierName
商品类型	DataPropertyName	CategoryName
单价	DataPropertyName	UnitPrice
库存量	DataPropertyName	UnitsInStock
打折	DataPropertyName	Discount

（3）添加一个 Windows 窗体，修改名称为 frmDetails，并设计界面如图 2-21 所示。frmDetails 窗体中的主要控件，按 Tab 键顺序，描述如表 2-10 所示。

图 2-21　"商品详细信息"窗体 Tab 键顺序视图

表 2-10　"商品详细信息"窗体控件及说明

Tab 顺序	控件类型	控件名称	说明	主要属性	
				属性名	属性值
0	TextBox	txtID	输入和显示商品编号	Text	""
1		txtName	输入和显示商品名称	Text	""
2		txtSupplier	输入和显示供应商	Text	""
3	ComboBox	comboCategory	用于选择商品类别	DropDownStyle	DropDownList

续表

Tab 顺序	控件类型	控件名称	说明	主要属性	
				属性名	属性值
4	TextBox	txtUnitPrice	输入和显示单价	Text	""
5		txtUnitsInStock	输入和显示库存数量	Text	""
6	Check	chkDisc	勾选是否有折扣	Text	折扣
				Checked	False
7	Button	btnOperate	操作按钮，用于添加或修改		

（4）商品信息管理窗体(frmProducts)的主要代码。

首先要为该程序添加3个成员变量，代码如下。

```
string strConn = "server=(local);database=chap2;integrated security=true";
                                                //连接字符串
SqlConnection conn;                             //声明连接对象为全局变量
string strSql;                                  //声明字符串变量，用来存储 SQL 语句
```

双击窗体，进入其窗体加载事件处理函数，连接数据库并查询 Products 表，为"商品类别"下拉框加载所有的商品类别。代码如下。

```
//窗体加载事件处理函数，为"商品类别"下拉框加载数据
private void frmProducts_Load(object sender, EventArgs e)
{
    string strSql = "select distinct CategoryName from Products";
    conn = new SqlConnection(strConn);
    SqlDataAdapter da = new SqlDataAdapter(strSql, conn);
    DataSet ds = new DataSet();
    da.Fill(ds);
    comboCategory.DataSource = ds.Tables[0];
    comboCategory.DisplayMember = "CategoryName";
}
```

输入及显示单价的文本框控件 txtUnitPrice 在窗体加载时为不可用，在用户选择过比较运算符之后才可输入单价。双击比较运算符下拉框，进入其选项索引变化事件处理函数，代码如下。

```
//当单价的比较条件被选择时，后面的文本框才可以输入数字
private void comboOperator_SelectedIndexChanged(object sender, EventArgs e)
{
    if (comboOperator.SelectedIndex != -1)
        txtUnitPrice.Enabled = true;
    else
        txtUnitPrice.Enabled = false;
}
```

定义方法 Query()，按用户在"查询条件"分组框各个控件中输入的查询条件对商品信息实现组合条件查询。

```csharp
//自定义方法,用于查询
private void Query()
{
    //此处省略了在获取每个控件的值时的异常捕获代码
    string strSql = "select * from Products where 1=1";
    if (txtProName.Text != "")              //如果"商品名称"不为空,则加入查询条件
        strSql += " and ProductName like '%" + txtProName.Text.Trim() + "%'";
    if (txtSupName.Text != "")              //如果"供应商名称"不为空,则加入查询条件
        strSql += " and SupplierName like '%" + txtSupName.Text.Trim() + "%'";
    if (txtUnitPrice.Text != "")            //如果"单价"不为空,则将比较运算符和单价
                                            //加入查询条件
        strSql += " and UnitPrice " + comboOperator.Text +
            txtUnitPrice.Text.Trim();
    if (comboCategory.SelectedIndex > -1)   //如果"商品类别"不为空,则加入查询条件
        strSql += "and CategoryName='" + comboCategory.Text + "'";
    conn = new SqlConnection(strConn);
    SqlDataAdapter da = new SqlDataAdapter(strSql, conn);
    DataSet ds = new DataSet();
    da.Fill(ds);
    dGVProducts.DataSource = ds.Tables[0];
}
```

说明：组合条件查询的实现技巧在于"where"子句的构造。由于事先无法判断用户会在哪个控件中输入查询条件,所以在"where"子句中先构造一个永真的条件,如本例中的"1=1",然后依次判断各个查询条件的输入控件是否有值,如用户有输入,则将该条件连接在"where"子句后面。

双击 btnSelect 按钮,进入其 Click 事件处理函数,调用 Query()方法,代码如下。

```csharp
//"查询"按钮单击事件处理函数,实现组合查询
private void btnSelect_Click(object sender, EventArgs e)
{
    Query();
}
```

双击 btnClear 按钮,进入其 Click 事件处理函数,清空查询条件,代码如下。

```csharp
//"清空"按钮单击事件处理函数,清空所有查询条件及结果
private void btnClear_Click(object sender, EventArgs e)
{
    //清空所有控件中的查询条件
    foreach (Control c in groupBoxQuery.Controls)
    {
        if (c is TextBox)
            ((TextBox)c).Text = "";
        if(c is ComboBox)
            ((ComboBox)c).SelectedIndex=-1;
    }
    //清空 DataGridView 中的数据
    DataTable dt = (DataTable)dGVProducts.DataSource;
    dt.Rows.Clear();
    dGVProducts.DataSource = dt;
}
```

说明：要清空 DataGridView 中的数据，使用 datagridview.DataSource=null 是不行的，因为这样会使编辑过的列头消失，使用 datagridview.Columns.Clear() 的效果也一样。如果使用 datagridview.Rows.Clear() 则会显示"不能清除此列表"。因此，想清空 DataGridView 中的数据又不影响列头就需要使用 DataTable 对象，如上述代码所示。

双击 btnInsert 按钮，进入 Click 事件处理函数，弹出商品详细信息窗体（frmDetails）。同时需传入商品详细信息窗体如下几个变量。

- 操作状态（insert），以确定在商品详细信息窗体中需进行的相关操作。
- dGVProducts 控件的引用，以在添加完毕后刷新 frmProducts 窗体中的 dGVProducts 控件中的数据。代码如下。

```csharp
//"添加"按钮单击事件处理函数
private void btnInsert_Click(object sender, EventArgs e)
{
    frmDetails frm = new frmDetails();
    frm.insertORupdate = "insert";      //以 insert 方式打开详细信息窗体
    frm.dgv = dGVProducts;              //将 DataGridView 的引用传入详细信息编辑窗体
    frm.Show();
}
```

说明：上述代码中向 frmDetails 窗体传值，在编写这段代码之前需要先在 frmDetail 窗体的代码中声明相应字段，请参阅后面的代码。

双击 btnUpdate 按钮，进入 Click 事件处理函数，弹出商品详细信息窗体（frmDetails）。同时需传入商品详细信息窗体如下几个变量。

- 操作状态（update），以确定在商品详细信息窗体中需进行的相关操作。
- dGVProducts 控件的引用，以在修改完毕后刷新 frmProducts 窗体中的 dGVProducts 控件中的数据。
- 用户在商品信息列表中选择的商品的编号，以在商品详细信息窗体中加载该商品的所有字段值。代码如下。

```csharp
//"修改"按钮单击事件处理函数
private void btnUpdate_Click(object sender, EventArgs e)
{
    frmDetails frm = new frmDetails();
    frm.insertORupdate = "update";      //以 update 方式打开详细信息窗体
    frm.dgv = dGVProducts;              //将 DataGridView 的引用传入详细信息窗体
    //取当前行的商品编号字段传入详细信息窗体
    frm.pId = dGVProducts.CurrentRow.Cells[0].Value.ToString();
    frm.Show();
}
```

双击 btnDelete 按钮，进入 Click 事件处理函数，删除所选行的记录，并刷新商品信息列表。

```csharp
//"删除"按钮单击事件处理函数
private void btnDelete_Click(object sender, EventArgs e)
{
    conn = new SqlConnection(strConn);
    conn.Open();
```

```
string strSql = "delete from Products where ProductID=@ProductID";
SqlCommand comm = new SqlCommand(strSql, conn);
comm.Parameters.Add(new SqlParameter("@ProductID",
    dGVProducts.CurrentRow.Cells[0].Value.ToString()));
if (comm.ExecuteNonQuery() > 0)         //如该命令影响的记录行数>0
    MessageBox.Show("删除商品信息成功!");
else
    MessageBox.Show("删除商品信息失败!");
conn.Close();
Query();                                //重新访问数据库,刷新界面显示的商品信息
}
```

(5) 商品详细信息窗体(frmDetails)主要代码。

首先声明如下几个变量:

```
public string insertORupdate = "";    //标识变量,记录是由添加还是修改进入当前窗体的
public DataGridView dgv;              //存放商品列表窗体中的 DataGridView 控件引用
public string pId = "";               //待修改的商品编号
string strConn = "server=(local);database=chap2;integrated security=true";
                                      //连接字符串
string strSql;                        //全局变量,用来存放待执行的 SQL 语句
```

双击窗体标题栏,进入其 Load 事件处理函数,首先从数据库表中查询出不重复的商品类别名称并加载至"商品类别"下拉框(ComboCategory),然后根据标识变量的值确定后续要执行的代码。

- 如是 insert,则将 btnOperate 的 Text 属性设置为"添加"。
- 如是 update,则将 btnOperate 的 Text 属性设置为"修改",然后根据从 frmProducts 传过来的待修改商品编号 pId 访问数据库,查询该商品的其他字段,为界面其他控件赋值。代码如下。

```
//窗体加载事件处理函数
private void frmDetails_Load(object sender, EventArgs e)
{
    //为"商品类别"下拉框加载数据
    SqlConnection conn = new SqlConnection(strConn);   //创建连接对象
    string strSql = "select distinct CategoryName from Products";
                                                       //查询不重复的商品类别名
    SqlDataAdapter da = new SqlDataAdapter(strSql, conn);
                                                       //声明并创建数据适配器对象
    DataSet ds = new DataSet();                        //声明并创建数据集
    da.Fill(ds);                                       //填充数据集
    comboCategory.DataSource = ds.Tables[0];           //设置数据源
    comboCategory.DisplayMember="CategoryName";
    //根据标识变量的值确定按钮上的文字
    if (insertORupdate == "insert")
    {
        btnOperate.Text = "添加";
    }
    else
    {
        btnOperate.Text = "修改";
```

```csharp
        txtID.ReadOnly = true;
        conn = new SqlConnection(strConn);           //创建连接对象
        conn.Open();                                  //打开连接
        strSql = "select * from Products where ProductID='" + pId + "'";
                                                      //查询指定商品的所有字段
        SqlCommand comm = new SqlCommand(strSql, conn);
                                                      //声明并创建命令对象
        SqlDataReader dr = comm.ExecuteReader();      //执行查询,用 DataReader 存放数据
        if (dr.Read())                                //如果查询到数据
        {
            //为各控件加载数据
            txtID.Text = pId;
            txtName.Text = dr["ProductName"].ToString();
            txtSupplier.Text=dr["SupplierName"].ToString();
            comboCategory.Text = dr["CategoryName"].ToString();
            txtUnitPrice.Text = dr["UnitPrice"].ToString();
            txtUnitsInStock.Text = dr["UnitsInStock"].ToString();
            chkDisc.Checked = (dr["Discount"].ToString() == "True");
        }
        dr.Close();                                   //关闭 DataReader
        conn.Close();                                 //关闭数据库连接
    }
}
```

双击 btnOperate 按钮,进入其 Click 事件处理函数,根据从列表窗体传过来的操作类别(insert 或 update)对数据库执行添加或修改操作,代码如下。

```csharp
//操作按钮单击事件处理函数,根据从列表窗体传过来的操作类别访问数据库
private void btnOperate_Click(object sender, EventArgs e)
{
    SqlConnection conn = new SqlConnection(strConn);   //声明并创建连接对象
    conn.Open();                                        //打开数据库连接
    //下面一段代码将保存添加的商品数据
    if (insertORupdate == "insert")
    {
        strSql = "insert into Products values(@ProductID, @ProductName,
            @SupplierName, @CategoryName, @UnitPrice, @UnitsInStock, @Discount)";
        SqlCommand comm = new SqlCommand(strSql, conn);
        comm.Parameters.Add(new SqlParameter("@ProductID", txtID.Text));
        comm.Parameters.Add(new SqlParameter("@ProductName", txtName.Text));
        comm.Parameters.Add(new SqlParameter("@SupplierName",
            txtSupplier.Text));
        comm.Parameters.Add(new SqlParameter("@CategoryName",
            comboCategory.Text));
        comm.Parameters.Add(new SqlParameter("@UnitPrice",
            float.Parse(txtUnitPrice.Text)));
        comm.Parameters.Add(new SqlParameter("@UnitsInStock",
            float.Parse(txtUnitsInStock.Text)));
        comm.Parameters.Add(new SqlParameter("@Discount", (chkDisc.Checked ==
            true ?"1" : "0")));
        if (comm.ExecuteNonQuery() > 0)
            MessageBox.Show("添加商品信息成功!");
```

```csharp
        else
            MessageBox.Show("添加商品信息失败!");
    }
    //下面一段代码将保存修改的商品数据
    else
    {
        strSql = "update Products set ProductName=@ProductName,
            SupplierName=@SupplierName,CategoryName=@CategoryName,UnitPrice=
            @UnitPrice, UnitsInStock=@UnitsInStock, Discount=@Discount where
            ProductID=@ProductID";
        SqlCommand comm = new SqlCommand(strSql, conn);
        comm.Parameters.Add(new SqlParameter("@ProductID", txtID.Text));
        comm.Parameters.Add(new SqlParameter("@ProductName", txtName.Text));
        comm.Parameters.Add(new SqlParameter("@SupplierName",
            txtSupplier.Text));
        comm.Parameters.Add(new SqlParameter("@CategoryName",
            comboCategory.Text));
        comm.Parameters.Add(new SqlParameter("@UnitPrice",
            float.Parse(txtUnitPrice.Text)));
        comm.Parameters.Add(new SqlParameter("@UnitsInStock",
            float.Parse(txtUnitsInStock.Text)));
        comm.Parameters.Add(new SqlParameter("@Discount", (chkDisc.Checked ==
            true ?"1" : "0")));
        if (comm.ExecuteNonQuery() > 0)
            MessageBox.Show("更新商品信息成功!");
        else
            MessageBox.Show("更新商品信息失败!");
    }
    //刷新商品列表界面的DataGridView控件
    strSql = "select * from Products";
    SqlDataAdapter da = new SqlDataAdapter(strSql, conn);
    DataSet ds = new DataSet();
    da.Fill(ds);
    dgv.DataSource = ds.Tables[0];
    conn.Close();
}
```

运行程序,显示"DataGridView 的使用"界面,可输入查询条件对商品进行查询,如图 2-22 所示。

选择一条记录,单击"修改"按钮,弹出"商品详细信息"界面,加载选中商品所有字段,如图 2-23 所示。

总结:本例题是一个综合性较强的题目,其中包含组合条件查询、DataGridView 控件的数据绑定、对数据库的增加、删除及修改操作,还包括窗体之间传递控件引用等知识点。读者可结合自己要做的习题要求,使用本例题中讲解的代码。

图 2-22 DataGridView 的使用

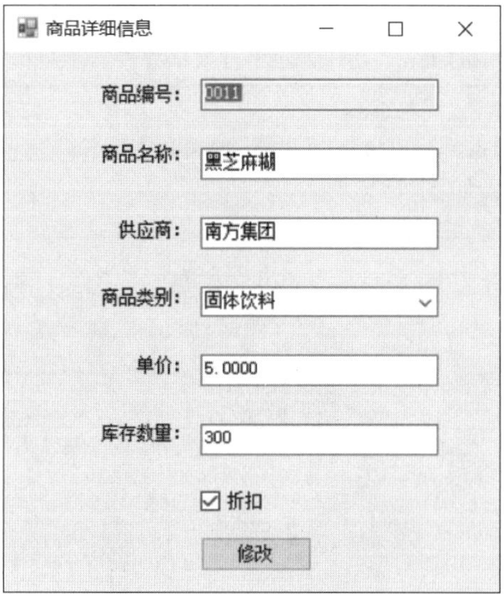

图 2-23 商品详细信息

【例 2-8】 设计一个 Windows 应用程序，实现商品信息的增加、删除、修改。本例题中，仅使用 DataGridView 完成对数据的显示及编辑操作，实现面向无连接的数据加载、批量添加、修改及删除操作。代码中需要使用 DataAdapter、DataSet 和 CommandBuilder 对象。

实现过程如下。

(1) 新建一个 Windows 应用程序，命名为 CommandBuilder，将创建的默认窗体名更名为 frmProducts，窗体的 Text 属性设置为"DataGridView 直接编辑数据"，界面设计如图 2-24 所示。frmProducts 窗体中的主要控件，按 Tab 键顺序，描述如表 2-11 所示。

图 2-24 "DataGridView 直接编辑数据"窗体 Tab 键顺序视图

表 2-11 "DataGridView 直接编辑数据"窗体控件及说明

Tab 顺序	控件类型	控件名称	说　　明	主要属性	
				属性名	属性值
0	DataGridView	dgvProducts	显示及编辑商品详细信息		需要编辑列
1	Button	btnUpdate	将添加和修改提交至数据源	Text	更新
2		btnDelete	删除多行数据并提交至数据源	Text	删除

其中,dgvProducts 控件编辑列时,"打折"列的 ColumnType 设计为 DataGridViewCheckBoxColumn,对其"数据"部分的属性设置如图 2-25 所示。

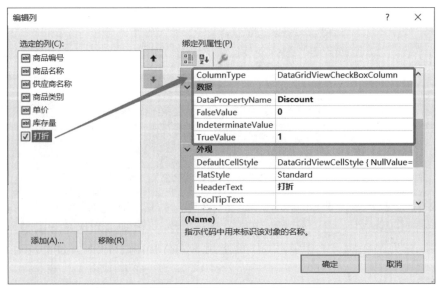

图 2-25 "编辑列"对话框中对 CheckBox 列的设置

dgvProducts 中各列的属性设置如表 2-12 所示。

表 2-12 dgvProducts 中各列的属性设置

列头文本	属性名	属性值
商品编号	DataPropertyName	ProductID
	Visible	False
商品名称	DataPropertyName	ProductName
供应商名称	DataPropertyName	SupplierName
商品类型	DataPropertyName	CategoryName
单价	DataPropertyName	UnitPrice
库存量	DataPropertyName	UnitsInStock
打折	ColumnType	DataGridViewCheckBoxColumn
	DataPropertyName	Discount
	FalseValue	0
	TrueValue	1

(2) 主要程序代码。

声明 3 个成员变量，代码如下。

```
//声明连接字符串为全局变量
string strConn = "server=(local);database=chap2;integrated security=true";
SqlDataAdapter da;                        //数据适配器对象
DataSet ds;                               //数据集对象
```

双击窗体标题栏，进入其 Load 事件处理函数，编写代码：读取商品表的全部数据，并加载至 DataGridView 控件中显示。

```
//窗体加载事件处理函数,读取数据并加载至 DataGridView
private void frmProducts_Load(object sender, EventArgs e)
{
    SqlConnection conn = new SqlConnection(strConn);
    string strSql = "select * from Products";
    da = new SqlDataAdapter(strSql, conn);
    ds = new DataSet();
    da.Fill(ds);
    ds.Tables[0].PrimaryKey = new DataColumn[] {
        ds.Tables[0].Columns["ProductId"] };
    dgvProducts.DataSource = ds.Tables[0];
}
```

双击 btnUpdate 按钮，进入其 Click 事件处理函数，为 DataAdapter 创建 CommandBuilder 对象，并将对 DataSet 所进行的更改提交至数据库。

```
//提交修改至数据源
private void btnUpdate_Click(object sender, EventArgs e)
{
    //为数据适配器创建 SqlCommandBuilder 对象
    SqlCommandBuilder mBuilder = new SqlCommandBuilder(da);
```

```
            if (ds.HasChanges())                        //如数据集发生更改
            {
                da.Update(ds);                          //将更改提交至数据库
            }
        }
```

SqlCommandBuilder 类的对象可自动生成单表命令,用于将对 DataSet 所做的更改与关联的 SQL Server 数据库的更改相同步。

双击 btnDelete 按钮,进入其 Click 事件处理函数,循环删除所有选中行,并将对数据集的更新提交至数据源。

```
//"删除"按钮单击事件处理函数,删除选中行并提交至数据库
private void btnDelete_Click(object sender, EventArgs e)
{
    //声明变量存储在 DataGridView 中的选中行
    DataGridViewSelectedRowCollection rows=dgvProducts.SelectedRows;
    int count = rows.Count;                         //计算选中的行数
    //循环删除选中行
    for (int i = 0; i < count; i++)
    {
        string id = rows[i].Cells[0].Value.ToString();
        DataRow drow = ds.Tables["products"].Rows.Find(id);
        drow.Delete();
    }
    //为数据适配器创建 SqlCommandBuilder 对象
    SqlCommandBuilder mBuilder = new SqlCommandBuilder(da);
    da.Update(ds, "products");                      //将更改提交至数据库
}
```

程序运行效果如图 2-26 所示。

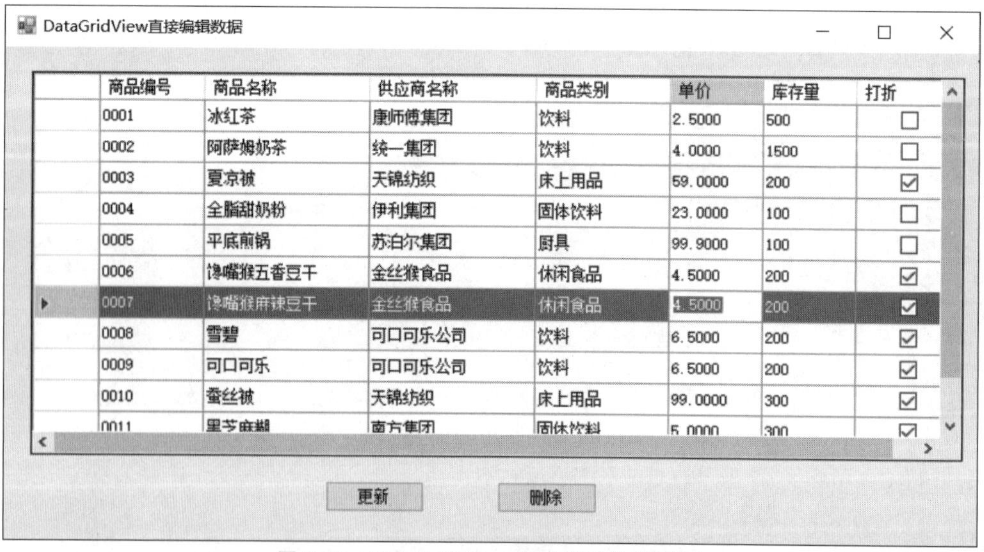

图 2-26 DataGridView 直接编辑数据界面

在数据列表中单击任一单元格,对数据进行修改,然后单击"更新"按钮,即可修改数据集并同时将修改提交至数据源。选择一行数据后单击"删除"按钮,即可删除该条记录。

说明：在例 2-6 中，从 DataSet 删除行使用的是 DataRow.Remove()方法，该方法是直接在 DataTable 中将 Row 删除，本例的删除代码中使用了 DataRow.Delete()方法，该方法标记 ROW 为删除，在调用 DataAdapter.Update()方法的时候才会真正从 DataTable 中删除。

2.3 Entity Framework 基础知识

Entity Framework（简称 EF）是微软官方提供的 ORM（Object Relational Mapping，对象关系映射）工具，ORM 让开发人员节省开发数据库访问代码的时间，将更多的时间放到业务逻辑层代码上。EF 提供变更跟踪、唯一性约束、惰性加载、查询事务等。

2.3.1 从委托到 Lambda

在 2.0 之前的 C# 版本中，声明委托的唯一方法是使用命名方法。C# 2.0 引入了匿名方法，而在 C# 3.0 及更高版本中，Lambda 表达式取代了匿名方法，成为编写内联代码的首选方式。Lambda 表达式在对匿名委托的处理上提供了更清晰的实现方式，对于编写 LINQ to Entities 查询表达式特别有用。

1. 委托

为便于解释委托，现以一个例子说明。定义一个处理用户订单的购物车 ShoppingCart 类，经理决定根据数量、价格等给客人折扣。他们已经实现了处理订单时要考虑的其他方面，作为其中的一部分，现在需要简单声明一个变量来保存"有吸引力的折扣"（magicDiscount），然后实现逻辑部分。

```csharp
class Program
{
    static void Main(string[] args)
    {
        //购物车处理逻辑
        new ShoppingCart().Process();
    }
}
class ShoppingCart
{
    public void Process()
    {
        //有吸引力的折扣
        int magicDiscount = 5;
    }
}
```

第二天，异想天开的经理决定根据购买时间调整折扣：如果在 12 点之前购买，折扣为 10。这个很简单，仅需要加一段代码。

```csharp
public void Process()
{
    //有吸引力的折扣
    int magicDiscount = 5;
```

```
//根据购买时间调整折扣
if (DateTime.Now.Hour < 12)
{
    magicDiscount = 10;
}
}
```

接下来一段时间内,经理又反复添加更多折扣方面的逻辑。那么该怎么做才能把这些无聊的逻辑从代码中剥离出去,让该处理的人去处理呢?这时要做的是移交或者委派这些任务给相应职能的人。幸运的是,.NET 为此提供了一种称为"委托"的机制。

如果读者了解 C/C++ 编程语言,描述委托最好的方法是"函数指针"。对所有人来说,可以认为把委托传递给方法与把值或对象传递给方法是一样的,比如下面三行代码就表现出这样的原理。

```
//给方法 Process 传递一个整型值
Process(5);
//给方法 Process 传递一个 ArrayList 的引用
Process(new ArrayList());
//给方法 Process 传递一个方法的引用
Process(discountDelegate);
```

discountDelegate 是什么?如何创建?Process 方法该如何使用?首先如同声明一个类一样,声明一个委托类型。

```
delegate int DiscountDelegate();
```

这行代码声明一个名称为 DiscountDelegate 的委托类型,可以像使用类、结构体等一样使用它。它不需要传入参数,但返回一个整型值。像类一样,必须创建一个它的实例它才有意义,创建一个委托实例实质上是创建一个方法的引用。创建实例时关键是要明白 DiscountDelegate 没有任何构造方法,它有一个隐式的构造函数来构造一个与它相同签名的方法(没有传入参数,返回一个整数)。

```
DiscountDelegate discount = new DiscountDelegate(class.method);
```

在深入学习之前,先回到刚才的例子,重构一下代码。添加一个 Calculator 类来帮助处理折扣逻辑部分,并给委托提供一些方法。

```
//声明委托类型
delegate int DiscountDelegate();
class Program
{
    static void Main(string[] args)
    {
        //实例化计算对象
        Calculator calc = new Calculator();
        //声明委托引用
        DiscountDelegate discount = null;
        if (DateTime.Now.Hour < 12)
        {
            //把 calc.Morning 方法委托给委托引用
```

```csharp
                discount = new DiscountDelegate(calc.Morning);
            }
            else if (DateTime.Now.Hour < 20)
            {
                //把 calc.Afternoon 方法委托给委托引用
                discount = new DiscountDelegate(calc.Afternoon);
            }
            else
            {
                //把 calc.Night 方法委托给委托引用
                discount = new DiscountDelegate(calc.Night);
            }
        //购物车处理逻辑
        new ShoppingCart().Process(discount);
        }
}
//计算折扣类
class Calculator
{
    //不同的时间返回不同的折扣
    public int Morning()
    {
        return 5;
    }
    public int Afternoon()
    {
        return 10;
    }
    public int Night()
    {
        return 15;
    }
}
class ShoppingCart
{
    //把委托引用作为参数
    public void Process(DiscountDelegate discount)
    {
        //把委托引用的方法的运行结果赋给 magicDiscount 变量
        int magicDiscount = discount();
    }
}
```

在 Calculator 类中,为每个逻辑分支创建了一个方法。在 Main 方法中,创建一个 Calculator 实例和一个 DiscountDelegate 实例,并按照所期望的把它们整合在一起。

现在不用再担心 Process 方法中的逻辑,只需要简单回调定义的委托。不用关心委托是如何创建的,就像调用其他方法一样调用它。另一种理解委托的方法是,它延迟执行一个方法。Calculator 方法作为参数被传递,但不会执行,直到开始调用 discount() 的时候才执行。现在看看完成的解决方案,这里仍然存在一些丑陋的代码。在 Calculator 类中,可以用一个方法来返回替代所有有返回值的方法吗? 答案是肯定的,现在将这些乱糟糟的代码合并起来。

```csharp
//定义委托类型
delegate int DiscountDelegate();
class Program
{
    static void Main(string[] args)
    {
        //购物车处理逻辑
        new ShoppingCart().Process(new DiscountDelegate(Calculator.Calculate));
    }
}
//计算类
class Calculator
{
    public static int Calculate()
    {
        //不同的时间返回不同的折扣
        int discount = 0;
        if (DateTime.Now.Hour < 12)
        {
            discount = 5;
        }
        else if (DateTime.Now.Hour < 20)
        {
            discount = 10;
        }
        else
        {
            discount = 15;
        }
        return discount;
    }
}
class ShoppingCart
{
    //把委托引用作为参数
    public void Process(DiscountDelegate discount)
    {
        //把委托引用的方法的运行结果赋给 magicDiscount 变量
        int magicDiscount = discount();
    }
}
```

这样代码看起来要好一些,用一个静态的 Calculate 方法替换了所有原来的方法,在 Main 方法中也不用费心维护一个指向 DiscountDelegate 的引用。

2. 泛型委托

微软在.NET 2.0 中引入了泛型,并提供了一个泛型委托:Action<T>,后来在.NET 3.5 中,它提供了一个 Func 通用委托,扩展了 Action。二者唯一的区别在于 Func 型有一个返回值,而 Action 型没有。

这意味着开发者不需要声明自己的 DiscountDelegate,可以用 Func<int>替代。为了说明 Func 委托是如何工作的,假设经理又一次改变了逻辑,需要提供一些特殊的折扣。实施起来很简单,给 Calculate 方法传入一个 bool 类型值就可以实现。

现在委托签名变成 Func<bool,int>。注意 Calculate 方法现在包含一个 bool 型参数，用一个 bool 值调用 discount()。

```csharp
class Program
{
    static void Main(string[] args)
    {
        //购物车处理逻辑,把 Calculator.Calculate 方法委托给一个 Func 引用
        //并把该引用作为参数传递给 Process()方法。
        new ShoppingCart().Process(new Func<bool, int>(Calculator.Calculate));
    }
}
//计算类
class Calculator
{
    //根据时间和 special 的值返回折扣
    public static int Calculate(bool special)
    {
        int discount = 0;
        if (DateTime.Now.Hour < 12)
        {
            discount = 5;
        }
        else if (DateTime.Now.Hour < 20)
        {
            discount = 10;
        }
        //special 为 true 时,discount=20
        else if (special)
        {
            discount = 20;
        }
        else
        {
            discount = 15;
        }
        return discount;
    }
}
class ShoppingCart
{
    //把 Func 型委托引用作为参数,并传递两个参数
    public void Process(Func<bool, int> discount)
    {
        //把 bool 类型的值作为参数传递给委托引用
        //并把返回的值赋给变量 magicDiscount
        int magicDiscount = discount(false);
        int magicDiscount2 = discount(true);
    }
}
```

好像还算不错,省了一行代码,这样算结束了吗？当然没有,还可以省掉类型判断。只要传递的方法有严格签名的委托,.NET 允许完全忽略掉显式创建 Func<bool,int>。

```
//因为Process期望的方法有一个bool型输入参数和返回一个int值,所以下面这句话是正
//确的
new ShoppingCart().Process(Calculator.Calculate);
```

至此,首先忽略自定义委托,然后忽略显式创建Func委托。还能继续压缩代码吗?答案显然是可以的,好戏才刚刚开始。

3. 匿名方法

匿名方法能够声明一个方法体而不需要给它指定一个名字。在接下来的场景里,它们以一个"普通的"方法存在,但是代码中没有任何方法显式调用它。匿名方法只能在使用委托的时候创建,而且它们只能通过delegate关键字创建。

```
static void Main(string[] args)
{
    new ShoppingCart().Process(new Func<bool, int>(delegate(bool x) { return x ? 10 : 5; }));
}
```

如上所示,代码完全没有Calculator类的出现。可以在大括号中添加任何其他方法中的逻辑。如果这段代码理解起来比较困难,可以把delegate(bool x)看作一个方法签名,而不是一个关键字。设想这段代码在一个类里,delegate(bool x){return 5;}是一个完整的合法方法声明(确实有一个返回值),恰好delegate是一个保留字,在这里它让这个方法匿名。

至此,确信现在这里甚至能压缩更多的代码。顺理成章地,能忽略显式声明Func委托的需要,.NET让使用delegate关键字更加方便。

```
class Program
{
    static void Main(string[] args)
    {
        new ShoppingCart().Process(delegate(bool x) { return x ? 10 : 5; });
    }
}
```

当.NET把方法作为委托参数处理时,就能看到匿名方法的真正用处。之前,已经为所关注的所有可能行为创建了一个方法,现在仅需以内联的方式创建它们,这样可以避免污染命名空间。

```
//创建一个匿名比对方法
custs.Sort(delegate(Customer c1, Customer c2) { return Comparer<int>.Default.Compare(c1.ID, c2.ID); });
//创建一个匿名事件
button1.Click += delegate(object o, EventArgs e) { MessageBox.Show("Click!"); };
```

4. Lambda表达式

"Lambda表达式"是一个匿名函数,它可以包含表达式和语句,并且可用于创建委托或表达式树类型。下面说明如何使用Lambda表达式替换匿名方法和Lambda表达式的其他特性。回顾刚才的例子,如下代码所示,已经在一行代码里压缩了处理整个折扣算法的逻辑。

```csharp
class Program
{
    static void Main(string[] args)
    {
        new ShoppingCart().Process(delegate(bool x) { return x ? 10 : 5; });
    }
}
```

能够让上面的代码更短吗？Lambda 表达式用"=>"运算符表明什么参数传递给表达式。编译器进一步处理，允许忽略类型并自动推断这些类型。如果有两个或更多个参数，需要用圆括号：(x,y)=>。如果只有一个，需要设置成这样：x=>。

```csharp
static void Main(string[] args)
{
    Func<bool, int> del = x => x ? 10 : 5;
    new ShoppingCart().Process(del);
}
//更短了…
static void Main(string[] args)
{
    new ShoppingCart().Process(x => x ? 10 : 5);
}
```

如此，x 被推断为 bool 型，并且有返回值，因为 Process 接收了一个 Func<bool,int> 委托。如果想实现像之前那样的完整代码块，只需要加上大括号。

```csharp
class ShoppingCart
{
    public void Process(Func<bool, int> discount)
    {
        int magicDiscount = discount(false);
        int magicDiscount2 = discount(true);
    }
}
class Program
{
    static void Main(string[] args)
    {
        new ShoppingCart().Process(x =>
        {
            int discount = 0;
            if (DateTime.Now.Hour < 12)
            {
                discount = 5;
            }
            else if (DateTime.Now.Hour < 20)
            {
                discount = 10;
            }
            else if (x)
            {
                discount = 20;
            }
```

```
            else
            {
                discount = 15;
            }
            return discount;
        });
    }
}
```

5. var 关键字

从 .NET Framework 3.0 开始,在方法范围中声明的变量可以具有隐式类型 var,可以使用 var 关键字来避免使用泛型语法。隐式类型的本地变量是强类型变量,但由编译器确定类型。下面代码中的两个 i 声明在功能上是等效的。

```
var i = 10;                                          //隐式声明
int i = 10;                                          //显式声明
```

2.3.2 Entity Framework 架构

Entity Framework(EF)有三种使用场景:从数据库生成类、由实体类生成数据库表结构、通过数据库可视化设计器设计数据库并同时生成实体类。EF 的架构如图 2-27 所示。

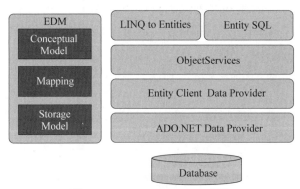

图 2-27 Entity Framework 架构

Entity Data Model(EDM)是类和数据库之间的映射模型,它包含概念模型、映射和存储模型。概念模型包含模型类和它们之间的关系,独立于数据库表的设计。映射包含有关如何将概念模型映射到存储模型的信息。存储模型是数据库设计模型,包括表、视图、存储过程和它们的关系和键。

LINQ to Entities 和 Entity SQL 是查询对象模型的两种语言。LINQ to Entities 是一种用于编写针对对象模型查询的查询语言,它返回在概念模型中定义的实体。Entity SQL 是类似于 SQL 的与存储无关的查询语言。通过 Entity SQL,可以将实体数据作为对象或以表格形式进行查询。

对象服务层在执行查询时将查询转换为一个命令树,并将这个命令树传递给 Entity Client;在返回结果时将 Entity Client 层获取的数据转换为对象,同时它也负责管理对象状态,跟踪对象的改变。

Entity Client Data Provider 层又称为 Entity Client,主要将 LINQ to Entities 和 Entity

SQL的查询转换为SQL语句,同时将数据库表格式数据转换为对象表格式数据,并传递给Object Services层。它使用ADO.NET向数据库发送数据或获取数据。

2.4 使用Entity Framework访问数据库

LINQ to Entities是LINQ中最吸引人的部分,可以使用标准的C#对象与数据库的结构和数据打交道,使用LINQ to Entities时,LINQ查询在后台转换为SQL查询语句并在需要数据的时候执行。

2.4.1 Entity Framework的安装

1. EF Tools for Visual Studio

Entity Framework 6 Tools已经包含在Visual Studio 2019中,如果使用的Visual Studio低于2013版,需要自行安装。

2. EF Runtime

(1)打开Visual Studio 2019。
(2)单击工具栏中的"工具"→"NuGet包管理器"→"程序包管理器控制台"。
(3)在程序包管理器控制台中,输入"Install-Package EntityFramework",安装EF。

2.4.2 创建数据库及实体对象模型

手工创建数据库表之间的关系烦琐又容易出错,在下面例子中将展示如何通过EF设计器生成对象模型并完成简单的查询功能。

1. 创建数据库test

(1)客户表(Customers)。客户表表结构如表2-13所示,用来保存客户的基本信息。

表2-13 客户表(Customers)

列名	数据类型	是否主键	是否外键	是否允许空	说明
CustomerID	int	是	否	否	客户ID
City	nvarchar(255)	否	否	是	客户城市

(2)订单表(Orders)。订单表表结构如表2-14所示,用来保存订单信息。

表2-14 订单表(Orders)

列名	数据类型	是否主键	是否外键	是否允许空	说明
OrderID	int	是	否	否	订单ID
CustomerID	int	否	是	是	客户ID

2. 添加ADO.NET实体数据模型文件

(1)启动Visual Studio 2019。
(2)在Visual Studio中,单击"创建新项目"。
(3)在"创建新项目"对话框中,选择C#、Windows和"控制台"过滤条件,选择"控制台应用(.NET Framework)",单击"下一步"按钮。

（4）在"项目名称"中,输入"EFTest",为项目起个名字。

（5）单击"创建"按钮。

（6）在 Visual Studio 环境中,单击"项目"→"添加新项"菜单项。

（7）在模板框中,选中"ADO.NET 实体数据模型"。

（8）在"名称"文本框中输入"BookStoreModel",单击"添加"按钮,如图 2-28 所示。

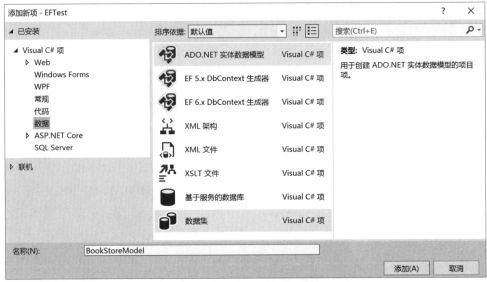

图 2-28　添加 ADO.NET 实体数据模型文件

（9）在打开的"实体数据模型向导"中,选择"来自数据库的 Code First",单击"下一步"按钮,如图 2-29 所示。

图 2-29　选择模型类型

（10）在打开的"实体数据模型向导"中,选择建好的数据库连接（如果没有,就新建一个),勾选"将 App.Config 中的连接设置另存为"复选框,输入"BookStoreModel",单击"下一步"按钮,如图 2-30 所示。

图 2-30　保存连接

(11) 在打开的实体数据模型向导中,选择 Customers 表和 Orders 表,勾选"确定所生成对象名称的单复数形式"复选框,如图 2-31 所示,单击"完成"按钮。

图 2-31　选择实体对象

3. 相关文件说明

ADO.NET 实体数据模型添加以后，项目会添加与 EF 相关的引用和文件。

(1) 打开解决方案资源管理器，会看到如图 2-32 所示的文件结构。每个实体数据模型生成一个 context 类，数据库每个表生成一个 entity 类，如 BookStoreModel 类、Customer 类和 Order 类。

图 2-32 项目文件结构

(2) 在项目的 app.config 中会自动添加如下内容。

```xml
<?xml version="1.0" encoding="utf-8"?>
<configuration>
  <configSections>
    <section name="entityFramework" type =
            "System.Data.Entity.Internal.ConfigFile.EntityFrameworkSection,
            EntityFramework, Version=6.0.0.0, Culture=neutral,
            PublicKeyToken=b77a5c561934e089" requirePermission="false" />
  </configSections>
  <startup>
    <supportedRuntime version="v4.0" sku=".NETFramework,Version=v4.7.2" />
  </startup>
  <entityFramework>
    <defaultConnectionFactory type=
            "System.Data.Entity.Infrastructure.LocalDbConnectionFactory,
            EntityFramework">
      <parameters>
        <parameter value="mssqllocaldb" />
      </parameters>
    </defaultConnectionFactory>
    <providers>
      <provider invariantName="System.Data.SqlClient" type =
            "System.Data.Entity.SqlServer.SqlProviderServices,
            EntityFramework.SqlServer" />
    </providers>
  </entityFramework>
  <connectionStrings>
    <add name=" BookStoreModel" connectionString="data source=.;
            initial catalog=test;
            integrated security=True;MultipleActiveResultSets=True;
            App=EntityFramework" providerName="System.Data.SqlClient" />
  </connectionStrings>
</configuration>
```

(3) 项目中自动添加 packages.config 文件，从该文件里面可以看出所引用的包的信息以及版本，内容如下。

```xml
<?xml version="1.0" encoding="utf-8"?>
<packages>
    <package id="EntityFramework" version="6.2.0" targetFramework="net472" />
    <package id="EntityFramework.zh-Hans" version="6.2.0"
        targetFramework="net472" />
</packages>
```

2.4.3 数据库增、删、改、查操作

实体数据模型生成 BookStoreModel 类,该类从 System.Data.Entity.DbContext 类继承。DbContext 主要负责以下活动。

- EntitySet：DbContext 包含所有映射到表的 entities。
- Querying：将 Linq-To-Entities 转译为 SQL 语句并发送到数据库。
- Change Tracking：从数据库获取 entities 后保留并跟踪实体数据变化。
- Persisting Data：根据 entity 状态执行 insert、update、delete 命令。
- Caching：DbContext 的默认第一级缓存,在上下文中的生命周期中存储 entity。
- Manage Relationship：DbContext 在 DbFirst 模式中使用 CSDL、MSL、SSDL 管理对象关系,Code First 中使用 fluent api 管理关系。
- Object Materialization：DbContext 将物理表转成 entity 实例对象。

1. 查询数据

修改 Main 方法,使用自动生成的数据库对象模型,创建一个简单查询：根据客户的地址是"Zhengzhou",返回所有客户的 ID 和他们的订单数量。

```
static void Main(string[] args)
{
    //DbContext 实例化
    using (BookStoreModel content = new BookStoreModel())
    {
        //使用 content 实例进行条件查询
        var customers = content.Customers.Where
            //Lambda 表达式
            (c => c.City == "zhengzhou");
        //循环输出客户的信息
        foreach (var customer in customers)
        {
            Console.WriteLine("ID={0}, Qty={1}",
                customer.CustomerID,           //客户的 ID
                customer.Orders.Count);        //客户的订单的数量
        }
    }
}
```

运行程序,结果如图 2-33 所示。

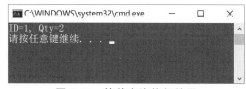

图 2-33 简单查询执行结果

2. 添加数据

(1) 创建一个新的实体对象,和创建普通的对象一样,像 Customers 和 Orders 对象都可以通过 new 运算符来创建对象。当然需要注意,该对象外键的依赖性检查要通过才行。

（2）修改 Main 方法，创建一个新的 Customers 对象。

```csharp
static void Main(string[] args)
{
    //DbContext 实例化
    using (BookStoreModel content = new BookStoreModel())
    {
        Console.WriteLine("\n更新之前的数据。");
        //构建查询表达式,返回所有客户
        var customers = content.Customers;
        //输出客户 ID,城市,客户订单数
        foreach (var c in customers)
        {
            Console.WriteLine("{0}, {1}, {2}", c.CustomerID, c.City, c.Orders.Count);
        }
        //创建新的 Customer 对象
        Customer customer = new Customer();
        customer.City = "zhumadian";
        customer.CustomerID = 2;
        //把新对象添加到 Customer 表中
        content.Customers.Add(customer);
        Console.WriteLine("\n插入之后的数据。");
        //输出客户 ID,城市,客户订单数
        foreach (var c in customers)
        {
            Console.WriteLine("{0}, {1}, {2}", c.CustomerID, c.City,
                c.Orders.Count);
        }
    }
}
```

（3）运行程序，结果如图 2-34 所示。

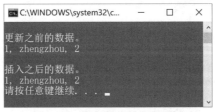

图 2-34　添加数据执行结果 1

注意：返回结果中并没有得到新插入的数据，通过上述结果可以看出，数据其实没有添加到数据库中。

（4）修改代码，在代码 content.Customers.Add(customer);下插入下列一行代码。

```csharp
content.SaveChanges();
```

（5）再运行程序，已经得到正确结果，如图 2-35 所示。

3．更新数据

（1）当得到一个实体对象的引用后，可以和修改其他对象的属性一样修改该对象的属性。

图 2-35　添加数据执行结果 2

（2）修改 Main 方法，实现对返回的第一个对象修改 City 属性。

```
static void Main(string[] args)
{
    //DbContext 实例化
    using (BookStoreModel content = new BookStoreModel())
    {
        Console.WriteLine("\n更新之前的数据。");
        //构建查询表达式,返回城市 ID 等于 1 的客户
        var customers = content.Customers.Where(c => c.CustomerID==1);
        //输出客户 ID,城市,客户订单数
        foreach (var c in customers)
        {
            Console.WriteLine("{0}, {1}, {2}", c.CustomerID, c.City,
                c.Orders.Count);
        }
        //获取第一个 Customer 对象
        Customer customer = customers.First();
        customer.City = "luoyang";
        //把更新的状态保存到数据库
        content.SaveChanges();
        Console.WriteLine("\n更新之后的数据。");
        //输出客户 ID,城市,客户订单数
        foreach (var c in customers)
        {
            Console.WriteLine("{0}, {1}, {2}", c.CustomerID, c.City,
                c.Orders.Count);
        }
    }
}
```

运行程序，结果如图 2-36 所示。

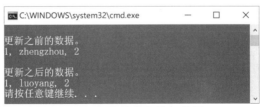

图 2-36　修改数据执行结果

4．删除数据

（1）得到一个 Customer 对象，删除对应的 Order 对象。

(2) 下面的代码演示如何从数据库中删除一行数据。

```csharp
static void Main(string[] args)
{
    //DbContext 实例化
    using (BookStoreModel content = new BookStoreModel())
    {
        Console.WriteLine("\n删除之前的数据。");
        //构建查询表达式,返回 ID 等于 1 的客户列表
        var customers = content.Customers.Where(c => c.CustomerID==1);
        //输出客户 ID,城市,客户订单数
        foreach (var c in customers)
        {
            Console.WriteLine("{0}, {1}, {2}", c.CustomerID, c.City,
                c.Orders.Count);
        }
        //获取客户列表中第一个客户的第一个订单
        Order order = customers.First().Orders.First();
        //删除该订单
        customers.First().Orders.Remove(order);
        //把更新的状态保存到数据库
        content.SaveChanges();
        Console.WriteLine("\n删除之后的数据。");
        //输出客户 ID,城市,客户订单数
        foreach (var c in customers)
        {
            Console.WriteLine("{0}, {1}, {2}", c.CustomerID, c.City,
                c.Orders.Count);
        }
    }
}
```

运行程序,结果如图 2-37 所示。

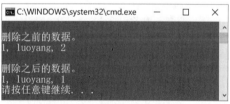

图 2-37 删除数据执行结果

5. 使用事务

(1) 添加对 System.Transactions 的引用,在 porgram.cs 文件上方,添加如下声明。

```
using System.Transactions;
```

(2) 在 Main 方法中添加如下代码,把添加操作放到事务中,模拟事务没有完成前出错的情景。

```csharp
static void Main(string[] args)
{
```

```
            Console.WriteLine("\n执行事务之前的数据。");
            display();
            ts();
            Console.WriteLine("\n执行事务之后的数据。");
            display();
        }
        static void ts()
        {
            using (BookStoreModel content = new BookStoreModel())
            {
                //TransactionScope 实例化
                using (TransactionScope ts = new TransactionScope())
                {
                    //创建新的 Customer 对象
                    Customer customer1 = new Customer();
                    customer1.City = "shangqiu";
                    customer1.CustomerID = 3;
                    //把新对象添加到 Customer 表中
                    content.Customers.Add(customer1);
                    content.SaveChanges();
                    //函数将返回,模拟出错
                    return;
                    //事务完成函数 Complete 得不到执行,整个事务的操作会回滚到执行之前的状态
                    ts.Complete();
                }
            }
        }
        static void display()
        {
            using (BookStoreModel content = new BookStoreModel())
            {
                //构建查询表达式
                var customers = content.Customers;
                //输出客户 ID,城市,客户订单数
                foreach (var c in customers)
                {
                    Console.WriteLine("{0}, {1}", c.CustomerID, c.City);
                }
            }
        }
```

(3) 运行程序,观察输出结果,第一条数据并没有插入,说明事务已经回滚,如图 2-38 所示。

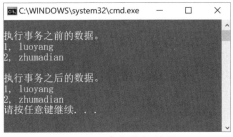

图 2-38 事务执行结果

小　　结

通过本章的学习,应掌握 ADO.NET 访问数据库的基础知识,包括连接数据库,对数据库进行添加、修改及删除操作,查询数据库中的数据及数据绑定控件的使用。还应掌握 LINQ 的基础知识,包括委托到 Lambda,LINQ 常用关键字及 EF 基础知识,最后应掌握使用 EF 访问数据库的方法,包括创建数据库对象模型,查询数据库的数据及修改数据库中的数据。

为了能正常访问数据库,2.1 节先对 SQL Server 2019 中的常用操作进行了简单介绍。本章的难点在于委托和 Lambda 表达式理解和使用。通过本章的学习,读者应能通过 ADO.NET 或 EF 熟练访问数据库,并结合实际业务设计出界面美观实用、操作方便、功能明确、代码简洁的数据库应用程序。

习　　题

1. 仿照例 2-6,设计一张订单表及一张订单详情表,实现在一张订单里添加多种商品,暂存在数据集里,最终提交时再生成完整订单。

2. 在例 2-7 基础上增加供应商管理及商品类别管理界面,并补充代码。

3. 用 EF 实现例 2-7。

第 3 章 系统架构

在进行具有一定规模的数据库应用系统开发时,如果仍采用传统的代码编写方式,将一个功能模块的所有代码都写在 Form 中的做法是非常不合适的。因为以这种方式编写的代码,在面临需求变更时,所引发的修改往往是灾难性的。即使是一个数据库 IP 地址的变更都可能会导致数十甚至上百处的代码变化(每个涉及连接数据库的代码都要修改连接字符串)。所有的代码堆砌在一个窗体内,职责繁杂造成代码可读性、可维护性、可移植性差,违反了单一职责原则;在面临需求变更时,必须通读所有代码,再在合适的位置做修改,违反了对修改关闭、对扩展开放的开放-关闭原则;所有代码没有任何抽象,不对接口编程,代码耦合度太高,无法适应较大的需求变更,违反了依赖倒转原则。

例如,第 8 章的在线考试系统属于中小型应用系统,该系统分为两个子系统:教师端子系统和学生端子系统。首先,两个子系统都访问同一个数据库,其中有许多访问数据库的操作及业务逻辑都是相同的,如果再像传统的编写方式一样将代码都放在各个 Form 中,那就无法实现代码的复用,必然造成大量的冗余,为后续扩展和维护带来麻烦。此外,本在线考试系统面对的客户不同,其对于软件产品的经济投入也会不同,必然涉及不同的用户采用不同类型数据库的情况,如果代码不做到充分解耦,在面对数据库类型变更时,几乎要把所有访问数据库的代码修改一遍,显然是不现实的。

采用一些典型架构开发软件,其目的就是为了使软件代码更具可维护性、可扩展性、可复用性,从而令系统更为灵活,可以适应任何合理的需求变更。

3.1 三层架构简介

在软件体系架构设计中,分层式结构是最常见也是最重要的一种结构,微软推荐的分层式结构一般分为三层,即三层架构(3-Tier Application),这三层从下至上分别为:数据访问层(Data Access Layer,DAL)、业务逻辑层(Business Logic Layer,BLL)以及表示层(User Interface,UI),如图 3-1 所示。

1. 数据访问层

数据访问层又称持久层,该层负责访问数据库,通俗点讲就是该层负责实现对数据库各表的增、删、改、查操作,当然数据存储方式不一定是数据库,也可能是文本文件、XML 文档等。该层不负责任何业务逻辑的处理,更不涉及任何界面元素。

2. 业务逻辑层

业务逻辑层又称领域层。该层是整个系统的核心,负责处理所有的业务流程,从简单的数据有效性验证到复杂的对一整条业务链的处理。例如,商城购物,从查询商品到添加购物

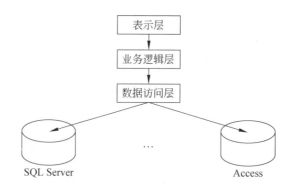

图 3-1　三层架构示意图

车,再到下订单,直至付款结束等过程。当然,不排除个别软件项目业务逻辑简单,导致业务逻辑层代码较少的情况。例如,本章由于篇幅所限,所提供的示例业务逻辑简单,就会出现业务逻辑层"瘦小"的现象。当业务逻辑层需要访问数据库时,它会通过调用数据访问层来实现,而不直接访问数据库。这样可以使业务逻辑层的实现与具体数据库无关,从而有效解耦。业务逻辑层同样不涉及任何界面元素。

3. 表示层

表示层即用户界面,表示层可以是 WinForm、WebForm 甚至是控制台,该层负责用户与系统的交互,接收用户的输入及事件触发。理想状态下,该层不应包含系统的业务逻辑,即使有逻辑代码,也应只与界面元素有关。例如,根据用户的身份控制按钮的可用性等。具体的业务逻辑可通过调用业务逻辑层来完成,该层不能直接调用数据访问层,更不能直接访问数据库。

如此分层具有以下优点。

(1) 分散关注:开发人员可以只关注自己所负责一层的技术实现。例如,负责数据访问层的开发人员,可以不需要关心系统的任何业务逻辑,更不用关心界面的设计。只需要关心所访问的数据库类型及表结构,最大限度地实现对各数据表的增、删、改、查操作即可。如此,对于开发人员的技术要求可以降到最低,项目经理也可以根据团队成员的专长,合理为其分配擅长的领域工作。

(2) 松散耦合:三层之间呈线性调用,业务逻辑层的实现不依赖于数据访问层的具体实现,表示层的实现同样不依赖于业务逻辑层的具体实现,可以很容易用新的实现来替换原有层次的实现,而不会对其他层造成影响。

(3) 逻辑复用:个别层代码所生成的组件(动态链接库文件 DLL)可以直接被其他项目所使用。例如,某系统最初只有 WinForm 版本,随着业务扩展,逐渐有了 Web 版、手机版等需求,但各版本功能一致,业务逻辑相同。这样在新建 Web 版和手机版项目时,只需将原 WinForm 版项目中的业务逻辑层和数据访问层组件引用到新项目中,直接使用即可,无须再重写代码。

当然,在获得优点的同时,分层也不可避免地会付出一些"代价",其缺点如下。

(1) 降低了系统性能:原本在不采用分层的情况下,UI 可以直接访问数据库,但现在要通过层层调用才能达到同样的目的,必然会在运行效率上有所降低。

（2）容易导致级联修改：用户某些需求的变化，如用户觉得某个功能模块目前所维护的信息不够，需要再加入一些信息，势必导致 UI 的变化，为了存储这些数据也会导致相应数据表字段的增加，从而数据访问层和业务逻辑层都会受到影响，这就是级联修改。

3.2 简单三层架构

简单三层架构即基本三层架构，其结构如图 3-1 所示。现以一个小示例介绍简单三层架构的代码编写方式。

示例所用数据库及业务需求如下。

要求设计一个通讯录软件，实现对联系人类型的定制以及联系人的管理，即实现对联系人类型和联系人的增、删、改、查功能。

数据库名为 MyDb，其中有两个数据表，名为 LinkmanType（联系人类型）表和 Linkmen（联系人）表，表结构分别如表 3-1 和表 3-2 所示。

表 3-1 LinkmanType（联系人类型）表结构

字段名	数据类型	长度	主键	含义
typeId	nvarchar	20	是	联系人类型编号
typeName	nvarchar	20	否	联系人类型名称

表 3-2 Linkmen（联系人）表结构

字段名	数据类型	长度	主键	含义
lkmId	int	4	是	联系人编号（自动加 1）
lkmName	nvarchar	10	否	联系人姓名
lkmMPNum	nvarchar	12	否	联系人移动电话
lkmOPNum	nvarchar	20	否	联系人办公室电话
lkmEmail	nvarchar	30	否	联系人电子邮箱
lkmCompName	nvarchar	50	否	联系人单位名称
typeId	nvarchar	20	否	联系人类型编号

3.2.1 数据访问层

1. 创建一个空解决方案

打开 Visual Studio 2019，单击"创建新项目"，在弹出的"创建新项目"对话框中的"搜索模板"搜索框内输入"空白解决方案"，查询"空白解决方案"模板，如图 3-2 所示。选择查询到的"空白解决方案"模板，单击"下一步"按钮，打开"配置新项目"窗口，修改项目名称为"ThreeLayer"，选择好位置，单击"创建"按钮，完成空解决方案的创建，如图 3-3 所示。

2. 创建数据访问层项目 DAL

在图 3-3 中右侧的"解决方案资源管理器"子窗口中的"解决方案 ThreeLayer"节点上单

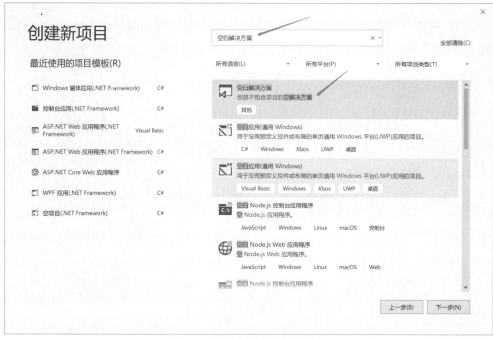

图 3-2 "创建新项目"对话框

图 3-3 创建后的空解决方案

击鼠标右键,选择"添加"→"新建项目",会再次弹出类似图 3-2 的"添加新项目"对话框,在其中搜索"类库"模板,选择"类库(.NET Framework)"模板,单击"下一步"按钮,将项目名称改为"DAL",单击"创建"按钮,此时,图 3-3 的解决方案会变成如图 3-4 所示状态。

3. 编写数据访问层代码

右击 DAL 项目中的 Class1.cs 文件,在弹出菜单中选择"删除"命令,将 DAL 默认创建的 Class1.cs 文件删除。右击 DAL 项目,在弹出菜单中选择"添加"→"类",弹出如图 3-5 所

图 3-4 创建 DAL 项目之后的解决方案

示的"添加新项"对话框。

图 3-5 "添加新项"对话框

在图 3-5 中,将名称命名为"LinkmanType.cs",单击"添加"按钮,在 DAL 项目中,会出现名为"LinkmanType.cs"的类文件。

在 3.1 节提到数据访问层的任务就是实现对数据库的操作，实现对各数据表数据的增加、删除、修改、查询。作为 LinkmanType 类，其功能就是要实现对 LinkmanType 数据表的增加、删除、修改、查询操作。

DAL 项目中的 LinkmanType.cs 文件代码如下。

```csharp
namespace DAL            //需要手动引用 System.Data 和 System.Data.SqlClient 命名空间
{
    //LinkmanType 类默认无访问修饰符,此处必须声明为 public,因 BLL 在调用 DAL 中该类时,
    //属于跨项目访问,只有声明为 public 才能够被 BLL 所访问。
    public class LinkmanType
    {
        ///<summary>
        ///数据库连接字符串,server 为数据库服务器的名字或 IP 地址,database 为数据库的名字,
        ///uid 为数据库用户名,pwd 为该用户的密码
        ///</summary>
        public string connString = "server=(local);database=mydb;uid=test;pwd=test";
        ///<summary>
        ///插入数据的方法
        ///</summary>
        ///<param name="typeId">要插入的联系人类型编号</param>
        ///<param name="typeName">要插入的联系人类型名称</param>
        ///<returns>插入成功返回 true,插入失败返回 false</returns>
        public bool insert(string typeId, string typeName)
        {
            try
            {
                SqlConnection conn = new SqlConnection();
                conn.ConnectionString = connString;
                conn.Open();
                SqlCommand cmd = new SqlCommand();
                cmd.Connection = conn;
                cmd.CommandText = "insert into linkmantype(typeid,typename)
                                   values(@typeid,@typename)";   //参数形式的 SQL 语句
                //以下两句为 SQL 参数赋值
                cmd.Parameters.Add(new SqlParameter("@typeid", typeId));
                cmd.Parameters.Add(new SqlParameter("@typename", typeName));
                cmd.ExecuteNonQuery();
                conn.Close();
                return true;
            }
            catch
            {
                return false;
            }
        }
        ///<summary>
        ///修改数据的方法
        ///</summary>
        ///<param name="typeId">要修改的联系人类型新编号</param>
        ///<param name="typeName">要修改的联系人类型新名称</param>
        ///<param name="oldTypeId">要修改的联系人类型原编号</param>
```

///<returns>修改成功返回 true,修改失败返回 false</returns>
public bool update(string typeId,string typeName,string oldTypeId)
{
    try
    {
        SqlConnection conn = new SqlConnection();
        conn.ConnectionString = connString;
        conn.Open();
        SqlCommand cmd = new SqlCommand();
        cmd.Connection = conn;
        cmd.CommandText="update linkmantype set typeid=@typeid,
                        typename=@typename where typeid=@oldTypeId";
        cmd.Parameters.Add(new SqlParameter("@typeid", typeId));
        cmd.Parameters.Add(new SqlParameter("@typename", typeName));
        cmd.Parameters.Add(new SqlParameter("@oldTypeId", oldTypeId));
        cmd.ExecuteNonQuery();
        conn.Close();
        return true;
    }
    catch
    {
        return false;
    }
}
///<summary>
///删除数据的方法
///</summary>
///<param name="typeId">要删除的联系人类型编号</param>
///<returns>删除成功返回 true,删除失败返回 false</returns>
public bool delete(string typeId)
{
    try
    {
        SqlConnection conn = new SqlConnection();
        conn.ConnectionString = connString;
        conn.Open();
        SqlCommand cmd = new SqlCommand();
        cmd.Connection = conn;
        cmd.CommandText = "delete from linkmantype where typeid=@typeid";
        cmd.Parameters.Add(new SqlParameter("typeid", typeId));
        cmd.ExecuteNonQuery();
        conn.Close();
        return true;
    }
    catch
    {
        return false;
    }
}
///<summary>
///查询数据的方法
///</summary>
///<param name="strWhere">strWhere 为空字符串时,代表查询表中所有数据

```
        ///为非空时应传入查询依据,即 where 子句的内容,如"typeName='朋友'"等</param>
        ///<returns>返回 null 代表查询失败,返回非 null 代表查询成功
        ///且结果存于返回的 DataTable 中</returns>
        public DataTable select(string strWhere)
        {
            try
            {
                string sql = "select * from linkmantype";
                if (strWhere != "")
                {
                    sql += " where " + strWhere;
                }
                SqlConnection conn = new SqlConnection();
                conn.ConnectionString = connString;
                SqlDataAdapter da = new SqlDataAdapter(sql, conn);
                DataSet ds = new DataSet();
                da.Fill(ds);
                return ds.Tables[0];
            }
            catch
            {
                return null;
            }
        }
    }
}
```

接下来实现 Linkmen 表的数据访问层代码。采用与创建 LinkmanType.cs 类文件同样的方法,在 DAL 项目中创建 Linkmen.cs 类文件。在其中编写对 Linkmen 表的访问代码如下。

```
namespace DAL          //需要手动引用 System.Data 和 System.Data.SqlClient 命名空间
{
    public class Linkmen
    {
        public string connString = "server=(local);database=mydb;uid=test;
            pwd=test";
        ///<summary>
        ///插入数据的方法
        ///</summary>
        ///<param name="lkmName">姓名</param>
        ///<param name="lkmMPNum">移动电话</param>
        ///<param name="lkmOPNum">固定电话</param>
        ///<param name="lkmEmail">电子邮箱</param>
        ///<param name="lkmCompName">单位名称</param>
        ///<param name="typeId">联系人类型编号</param>
        ///<returns>插入成功返回 true,插入失败返回 false</returns>
        public bool insert(string lkmName, string lkmMPNum, string lkmOPNum,
                    string lkmEmail, string lkmCompName, string typeId)
        {
            try
            {
                SqlConnection conn = new SqlConnection();
```

```csharp
            conn.ConnectionString = connString;
            conn.Open();
            SqlCommand cmd = new SqlCommand();
            cmd.Connection = conn;
            cmd.CommandText = "insert into linkmen(lkmname, lkmMPNum, lkmOPNum,
                     lkmEmail, lkmCompName, typeId) values(@lkmname,
                     @lkmMPNum, @lkmOPNum, @lkmEmail, @lkmCompName,
                     @typeId)";
            cmd.Parameters.Add(new SqlParameter("@lkmname", lkmName));
            cmd.Parameters.Add(new SqlParameter("@lkmMPNum", lkmMPNum));
            cmd.Parameters.Add(new SqlParameter("@lkmOPNum", lkmOPNum));
            cmd.Parameters.Add(new SqlParameter("@lkmEmail", lkmEmail));
            cmd.Parameters.Add(new SqlParameter("@lkmCompName", lkmCompName));
            cmd.Parameters.Add(new SqlParameter("@typeId", typeId));
            cmd.ExecuteNonQuery();
            conn.Close();
            return true;
        }
        catch
        {
            return false;
        }
    }
    ///<summary>
    ///修改数据的方法
    ///</summary>
    ///<param name="lkmId">联系人编号</param>
    ///<param name="lkmName">姓名</param>
    ///<param name="lkmMPNum">移动电话</param>
    ///<param name="lkmOPNum">固定电话</param>
    ///<param name="lkmEmail">电子邮箱</param>
    ///<param name="lkmCompName">单位名称</param>
    ///<param name="typeId">联系人类型编号</param>
    ///<returns>修改成功返回 true,修改失败返回 false</returns>
    public bool update(string lkmId, string lkmName, string lkmMPNum,
        string lkmOPNum, string lkmEmail, string lkmCompName, string typeId)
    {
        try
        {
            SqlConnection conn = new SqlConnection();
            conn.ConnectionString = connString;
            conn.Open();
            SqlCommand cmd = new SqlCommand();
            cmd.Connection = conn;
            cmd.CommandText = "update linkmen set lkmname=@lkmname,
                     lkmMPNum=@lkmMPNum, lkmOPNum=@lkmOPNum,
                     lkmEmail=@lkmEmail, lkmCompName=@lkmCompName,
                     typeId=@typeId where lkmid=@lkmid";
            cmd.Parameters.Add(new SqlParameter("@lkmname", lkmName));
            cmd.Parameters.Add(new SqlParameter("@lkmMPNum", lkmMPNum));
            cmd.Parameters.Add(new SqlParameter("@lkmOPNum", lkmOPNum));
            cmd.Parameters.Add(new SqlParameter("@lkmEmail", lkmEmail));
```

```csharp
            cmd.Parameters.Add(new SqlParameter("@lkmCompName", lkmCompName));
            cmd.Parameters.Add(new SqlParameter("@typeId", typeId));
            cmd.Parameters.Add(new SqlParameter("@lkmid", lkmId));
            cmd.ExecuteNonQuery();
            conn.Close();
            return true;
        }
        catch
        {
            return false;
        }
    }
    ///<summary>
    ///删除数据的方法
    ///</summary>
    ///<param name="lkmId">要删除的联系人的编号</param>
    ///<returns>删除成功返回 true,删除失败返回 false</returns>
    public bool delete(string lkmId)
    {
        try
        {
            SqlConnection conn = new SqlConnection();
            conn.ConnectionString = connString;
            conn.Open();
            SqlCommand cmd = new SqlCommand();
            cmd.Connection = conn;
            cmd.CommandText = "delete from linkmen where lkmid=@lkmid";
            cmd.Parameters.Add(new SqlParameter("@lkmid", lkmId));
            cmd.ExecuteNonQuery();
            conn.Close();
            return true;
        }
        catch
        {
            return false;
        }
    }
    ///<summary>
    ///查询数据的方法
    ///</summary>
    ///<param name="strWhere">strWhere 为空字符串时,代表查询表中所有数据
    ///为非空时应传入查询依据,即 where 子句的内容,如"lkmName='张三'"等</param>
    ///<returns>返回 null 代表查询失败,返回非 null 代表查询成功
    ///且结果存于返回的 DataTable 中</returns>
    public DataTable select(string strWhere)
    {
        try
        {
            string sql = "select linkmen.typeid as typeid, typename, lkmname,
                lkmid,lkmMPNum, lkmOPNum, lkmEmail, lkmCompName from linkmen
                left join linkmantype on linkmen.typeid=linkmantype.typeid";
            if (strWhere != "")
```

```
                {
                    sql += " where " + strWhere;
                }
                SqlConnection conn = new SqlConnection();
                conn.ConnectionString = connString;
                SqlDataAdapter da = new SqlDataAdapter(sql, conn);
                DataSet ds = new DataSet();
                da.Fill(ds);
                return ds.Tables[0];
            }
            catch
            {
                return null;
            }
        }
    }
}
```

上述代码为数据访问层的最基本实现,但还存在如下诸多不足。

(1)增加、删除、修改功能的代码基本类似,存在大量的冗余。事实上,除了所执行的 SQL 语句以及所传递的 SQL 参数不同外,其他代码是一样的。此外,各类的查询功能实现也极其相似,只是 Select 语句不同罢了。再者,每个类中都维护着同一个数据库连接字符串,不但冗余,更会给数据库迁移带来莫大的灾难,每次数据库迁移,都要修改每个类的连接字符串,何其麻烦! 因此,完全可以对这些冗余的代码进行精简。

(2)以各类的 insert 函数为例,操作联系人类型表的 LinkmanType 类中的 insert 函数有两个形参:typeId 和 typeName,分别代表要插入类型的两个字段,而操作联系人表的 Linkmen 类中的 insert 函数则有 6 个参数:lkmName、lkmMPNum、lkmOPNum、lkmEmail、lkmCompName 和 typeId,可见,函数的形参个数与数据表的字段数是成正比的,如果一个数据表的字段数过多,势必导致相关函数的形参数过于冗长,非常不利于调用和规范化管理。

3.2.2 数据访问通用类库

解决以上第一个不足,精简冗余的数据库访问代码,可考虑再创建一个数据库访问辅助类库,将重复的代码进行封装。

1. 创建数据访问通用类库 DBUtility

右击解决方案,单击"添加"→"新建项目",创建一个名为"DBUtility"的类库项目。添加项目之后的解决方案列表如图 3-6 所示。

2. 编写数据访问通用类库中的类代码

在图 3-6 中,删除 DBUtitlity 项目中的 Class1.cs 类文件,新建一个名为 "DbHelperSQL.cs" 的类文件,DbHelperSQL.cs 类代码如下。

图 3-6 添加 DBUtility 类库后的解决方案

```csharp
namespace DBUtility    //需要手动引用命名空间 System.Data 和 System.Data.SqlClient
{
    public class DbHelperSQL
    {
        public static string connString = "server=(local);database=mydb;
            uid=test;pwd=test";
        ///<summary>
        ///数据增、删、改要调用的通用方法
        ///</summary>
        ///<param name="sql">要执行的 SQL 语句</param>
        ///<param name="sqlParams">所有要传给 SQL 语句的参数集合</param>
        ///<returns>返回 true 表示执行成功,false 为执行失败</returns>
        public static bool ExecuteSql(string sql,List<SqlParameter> sqlParams)
        {
            try
            {
                SqlConnection conn = new SqlConnection();
                conn.ConnectionString = connString;
                conn.Open();
                SqlCommand cmd = new SqlCommand();
                cmd.Connection = conn;
                cmd.CommandText = sql;
                //遍历传过来的 SQL 参数集合,将其逐一加到 SqlCommand 对象的参数集合中
                for(int i=0;i<sqlParams.Count ;i++)
                    cmd.Parameters.Add(sqlParams[i]);
                cmd.ExecuteNonQuery();
                conn.Close();
                return true;
            }
            catch
            {
                return false;
            }
        }
        ///<summary>
        ///查询数据的通用方法
        ///</summary>
        ///<param name="sql">select 语句</param>
        ///<returns>返回 null 代表查询失败,返回非 null 代表查询成功
        ///且结果存于返回的 DataTable 中</returns>
        public static DataTable Query(string sql)
        {
            try
            {
                SqlConnection conn = new SqlConnection();
                conn.ConnectionString = connString;
                SqlDataAdapter da = new SqlDataAdapter(sql, conn);
                DataSet ds = new DataSet();
                da.Fill(ds);        //将 sql 语句的查询结果填充到 ds 中
                return ds.Tables[0];
            }
            catch
            {
```

```
                return null;
            }
        }
    }
}
```

如此一来,数据访问层 DAL 项目中的各函数,只需要调用 DBUtility 中的函数即可实现对数据库的访问。

3. 为数据访问层项目 DAL 添加引用

要在 DAL 中调用 DBUtility 中的类和函数,需将 DBUtility 项目引入到 DAL 项目中:右击 DAL 项目节点下的"引用"节点,在弹出式菜单中选择"添加引用"命令,会弹出如图 3-7 所示的"引用管理器"对话框。

图 3-7 "引用管理器"对话框

在图 3-7 中,选择"项目"→"解决方案"选项,勾选 DBUtility 项目,单击"确定"按钮,会发现 DAL 项目的引用列表中,多出一个名为"DBUtility"的引用,如图 3-8 所示。

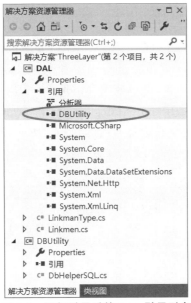

图 3-8 添加引用后的 DAL 引用列表

4. 修改 3.2.1 节中的数据访问层代码

现在，可以在 DAL 项目中调用 DBUtility 中所有公开（public）的类和函数。以 Linkmen 类的 insert 函数为例，此时，insert 函数可通过调用 DBUtility 的 DbHelperSQL 类中的 ExecuteSql 函数来实现数据的插入，而无须书写重复冗余的代码，修改后的 insert 函数如下。

```csharp
public bool insert(string lkmName,string lkmMPNum,string lkmOPNum,
        string lkmEmail,string lkmCompName,string typeId)
{
    string sql = "insert into linkmen(lkmname,lkmMPNum,lkmOPNum,lkmEmail,
            lkmCompName, typeId)values(@lkmname, @lkmMPNum, @lkmOPNum,
            @lkmEmail, @lkmCompName, @typeId)";
    List<SqlParameter> sqlParams = new List<SqlParameter>();
    //以下六句代码把要传给 SQL 语句的参数存入集合，以便传递给函数
    sqlParams.Add(new SqlParameter("@lkmname", lkmName));
    sqlParams.Add(new SqlParameter("@lkmMPNum", lkmMPNum));
    sqlParams.Add(new SqlParameter("@lkmOPNum", lkmOPNum));
    sqlParams.Add(new SqlParameter("@lkmEmail", lkmEmail));
    sqlParams.Add(new SqlParameter("@lkmCompName", lkmCompName));
    sqlParams.Add(new SqlParameter("@typeId", typeId));
    //调用通用类库中的 ExecuteSql 方法执行 SQL 语句
    return DBUtility.DbHelperSQL.ExecuteSql(sql, sqlParams);
}
```

由上述代码可见，在 insert 函数中，已无须再编写 SqlConnection、SqlCommand 对象的创建和属性赋值、方法调用等代码。同样，update、delete 等函数也不必再写这些重复代码，代码复用度更高。此外，由于连接字符串已写在了 DbHelperSQL 类中，不会在其他类中出现，对于数据库迁移所造成的修改量降到了最低——只需修改 DbHelperSQL 中的连接字符串即可。完整的数据访问层代码将在解决第二个不足之后给出。

3.2.3 实体类库

针对第二个不足——函数参数个数因数据表字段过多而变得复杂的问题，可以利用面向对象的思想，将数据表封装成类。如对于 LinkmanType 表，可以定义 Model.LinkmanType 类，其中包括两个成员变量 typeId 和 typeName，分别对应 LinkmanType 表的两个字段。而对于 Linkmen 表，可以定义 Model.Linkmen 类，其中包含 7 个成员变量 lkmId、lkmName、lkmMPNum、lkmOPNum、lkmEmail、lkmCompName 和 typeId，分别对应 Linkmen 表的 7 个字段。这样在设计对应的 insert 和 update 函数时，可以用对应的类类型来作为形参，例如 Linkmen 类的 insert 函数，只需用以下方式定义即可。

```csharp
public bool insert(Model.Linkmen mLKM);
```

如此大大缩减了形参数量，简化了函数结构。

可以创建一个专门的类库，用于设计这些针对数据表结构而产生的类，我们称为实体（Model）类库。

1. 创建实体类库 Model

右击解决方案，单击"添加"→"新建项目"，创建一个名为"Model"的类库项目。添加项

目之后的解决方案列表如图 3-9 所示。

图 3-9　添加 Model 之后的解决方案资源管理器

2．编写实体类库中的类代码

在图 3-9 中，删除 Model 项目中的 Class1.cs 类文件，新建两个分别名为"LinkmanType.cs"和"Linkmen.cs"的类文件，各自代码如下。

LinkmanType.cs 类代码如下。

```
namespace Model
{
    public class LinkmanType
    {
        public string typeId;
        public string typeName;
    }
}
```

Linkmen.cs 类代码如下。

```
namespace Model
{
    public class Linkmen
    {
        public string lkmId;
        public string lkmName;
        public string lkmMPNum;
        public string lkmOPNum;
        public string lkmEmail;
        public string lkmCompName;
        public string typeId;
    }
}
```

3．修改数据访问层代码

首先，与引用 DBUtility 项目相同的方法，将 Model 项目引入到 DAL 项目中。

修改 LinkmanType.cs 类文件如下。

```csharp
namespace DAL                    //需要引入System.Data和System.Data.SqlClient命名空间
{
    public class LinkmanType
    {
        public bool insert(Model.LinkmanType mLKMT)
        {
            string sql= "insert into linkmantype(typeid,typename) values
                (@typeid, @typename)";
            List<SqlParameter> sqlParams=new List<SqlParameter>();
            sqlParams.Add(new SqlParameter("@typeid",   mLKMT.typeId));
            sqlParams.Add(new SqlParameter("@typename", mLKMT.typeName));
            return DBUtility.DbHelperSQL.ExecuteSql(sql, sqlParams);
        }
        public bool update(Model.LinkmanType mLKMT,string oldTypeId)
        {
            string sql= "update linkmantype set typeid=@typeid,
                    typename=@typename where typeid=@oldTypeId";
            List<SqlParameter> sqlParams=new List<SqlParameter>();
            sqlParams.Add(new SqlParameter("@typeid", mLKMT.typeId));
            sqlParams.Add(new SqlParameter("@typename", mLKMT.typeName));
            sqlParams.Add(new SqlParameter("@oldTypeId", oldTypeId));
            return DBUtility.DbHelperSQL.ExecuteSql(sql, sqlParams);
        }
        public bool delete(string typeId)
        {
            string sql= "delete from linkmantype where typeid=@typeid";
            List<SqlParameter> sqlParams=new List<SqlParameter>();
            sqlParams.Add(new SqlParameter("typeid",typeId));
            return DBUtility.DbHelperSQL.ExecuteSql(sql, sqlParams);
        }
        public DataTable select(string strWhere)
        {
            string sql = "select * from linkmantype";
            if (strWhere != "")
            {
                sql += " where " + strWhere;
            }
            return DBUtility.DbHelperSQL.Query(sql);
        }
    }
}
```

修改 Linkmen 类文件如下。

```csharp
namespace DAL
{
    public class Linkmen
    {
        public bool insert(Model.Linkmen mLKM)
        {
            string sql = "insert into linkmen(lkmname,lkmMPNum,lkmOPNum,
                lkmEmail, lkmCompName, typeId) values(@lkmname, @lkmMPNum, @lkmOPNum,
```

```csharp
                    @lkmEmail,@lkmCompName,@typeId)";
            List<SqlParameter> sqlParams = new List<SqlParameter>();
            sqlParams.Add(new SqlParameter("@lkmname", mLKM.lkmName));
            sqlParams.Add(new SqlParameter("@lkmMPNum", mLKM.lkmMPNum));
            sqlParams.Add(new SqlParameter("@lkmOPNum", mLKM.lkmOPNum));
            sqlParams.Add(new SqlParameter("@lkmEmail", mLKM.lkmEmail));
            sqlParams.Add(new SqlParameter("@lkmCompName", mLKM.lkmCompName));
            sqlParams.Add(new SqlParameter("@typeId", mLKM.typeId));
            return DBUtility.DbHelperSQL.ExecuteSql(sql, sqlParams);
        }
        public bool update(Model.Linkmen mLKM)
        {
            string sql = "update linkmen set lkmname=@lkmname,
                lkmMPNum=@lkmMPNum,lkmOPNum=@lkmOPNum,lkmEmail=@lkmEmail,
                lkmCompName=@lkmCompName,typeId=@typeId where lkmid=@lkmid";
            List<SqlParameter> sqlParams = new List<SqlParameter>();
            sqlParams.Add(new SqlParameter("@lkmname", mLKM.lkmName));
            sqlParams.Add(new SqlParameter("@lkmMPNum", mLKM.lkmMPNum));
            sqlParams.Add(new SqlParameter("@lkmOPNum", mLKM.lkmOPNum));
            sqlParams.Add(new SqlParameter("@lkmEmail", mLKM.lkmEmail));
            sqlParams.Add(new SqlParameter("@lkmCompName", mLKM.lkmCompName));
            sqlParams.Add(new SqlParameter("@typeId", mLKM.typeId));
            sqlParams.Add(new SqlParameter("@lkmid", mLKM.lkmId));
            return DBUtility.DbHelperSQL.ExecuteSql(sql, sqlParams);
        }
        public bool delete(string lkmId)
        {
            string sql= "delete from linkmen where lkmid=@lkmid";
            List<SqlParameter> sqlParams = new List<SqlParameter>();
            sqlParams.Add(new SqlParameter("@lkmid", lkmId));
            return DBUtility.DbHelperSQL.ExecuteSql(sql, sqlParams);
        }
        public DataTable select(string strWhere)
        {
            string sql = "select linkmen.typeid as typeid,typename,lkmname,
                lkmid,lkmMPNum, lkmOPNum,lkmEmail,lkmCompName from linkmen
                    left join linkmantype on linkmen.typeid=linkmantype.typeid";
            if (strWhere != "")
            {
                sql += " where " + strWhere;
            }
            return DBUtility.DbHelperSQL.Query(sql);
        }
    }
}
```

上述 LinkmanType 类和 Linkmen 类，明显较上一版本要精简得多，函数实现得到精简，函数参数也得到了精简。此代码为本书简单三层架构终态的数据访问层代码结构。其中，DAL 调用了 DBUtility 项目的代码，但 DBUtility 类库不能称为一层，它的存在只是提供一套通用的访问数据库的方法。而 Model 类库更不能称为一层，在后面章节中可以看到，Model 实际上是贯穿了数据访问层、业务逻辑层和表示层这三层的，因为三层均要调用 Model 中的类。

3.2.4 业务逻辑层

1. 创建业务逻辑层项目 BLL

右击解决方案，单击"添加"→"新建项目"，创建一个名为"BLL"的类库项目。添加项目之后的解决方案列表如图 3-10 所示。

2. 编写业务逻辑层代码

先引用 DAL 和 Model 项目，删除 BLL 项目中的 Class1.cs 文件，然后新建名为"LinkmanType.cs"的类文件，以实现联系人类型管理的业务逻辑。联系人类型管理的业务逻辑非常简单，只有基本的对联系人类型的增加、删除、修改、查询功能。因此，BLL 的 LinkmanType 类中的代码也只是简单地调用 DAL 中的 LinkmanType 类来实现这些功能。

图 3-10 添加 BLL 之后的解决方案资源管理器

LinkmanType.cs 类文件代码如下。

```csharp
namespace BLL
{
    public class LinkmanType
    {
        DAL.LinkmanType dLKMT = new DAL.LinkmanType();
        public bool insert(Model.LinkmanType mLKMT)
        {
            return dLKMT.insert(mLKMT);
        }
        public bool update(Model.LinkmanType mLKMT, string oldTypeId)
        {
            return dLKMT.update(mLKMT, oldTypeId);
        }
        public bool delete(string typeId)
        {
            return dLKMT.delete(typeId); ;
        }
        public DataTable select(string strWhere)
        {
            return dLKMT.select(strWhere);
        }
    }
}
```

现在来实现联系人管理的业务逻辑层代码，与联系人类型管理的业务逻辑相比，在实现联系人增加、删除、修改、查询功能之外，还需实现随机抽取一名联系人的功能，这就是一种业务逻辑，需在业务逻辑层实现。

在 BLL 项目中新建名为"Linkmen.cs"的类文件，添加代码如下。

```csharp
namespace BLL
{
    public class Linkmen
    {
        DAL.Linkmen dLKM = new DAL.Linkmen();
        public bool insert(Model.Linkmen mLKM)
        {
            return dLKM.insert(mLKM);
        }
        public bool update(Model.Linkmen mLKM)
        {
            return dLKM.update(mLKM);
        }
        public bool delete(string stuId)
        {
            return dLKM.delete(stuId);
        }
        public DataTable select(string strWhere)
        {
            return dLKM.select(strWhere);
        }
        ///<summary>
        ///随机抽取一名联系人
        ///</summary>
        ///<returns>返回抽取到的联系人对象</returns>
        public Model.Linkmen randomFriend()
        {
            DataTable dt=select("");
            if (dt.Rows.Count > 0)
            {
                Random random = new Random();
                int currNum = random.Next(0, dt.Rows.Count);
                Model.Linkmen mLKM = new Model.Linkmen();
                mLKM.lkmId = dt.Rows[currNum]["lkmid"].ToString();
                mLKM.lkmName = dt.Rows[currNum]["lkmname"].ToString();
                mLKM.lkmMPNum = dt.Rows[currNum]["lkmmpnum"].ToString();
                mLKM.lkmOPNum = dt.Rows[currNum]["lkmopnum"].ToString();
                mLKM.lkmEmail= dt.Rows[currNum]["lkmemail"].ToString();
                mLKM.lkmCompName = dt.Rows[currNum]["lkmcompname"].ToString();
                mLKM.typeId = dt.Rows[currNum]["typeid"].ToString();
                return mLKM;
            }
            else
            {
                return null;
            }
        }
    }
}
```

可见随着业务逻辑的复杂度增加,业务逻辑层代码也会相应增加。

3.2.5 表示层

1. 创建表示层项目 UI

3.1 节提到表示层其实就是用户界面层,所以表示层的项目类型不是 DAL、BLL 这样的类库,而是 Windows 窗体应用程序。

右击解决方案,选择"添加"→"新建项目"命令,打开"添加新项目"对话框,搜索"Windows 窗体应用"模板,选择"Windows 窗体应用(.NET Framework)"模板,单击"下一步"按钮,将项目名称改为"UI",单击"创建"按钮。此时,解决方案资源管理器中的项目结构如图 3-11 所示。

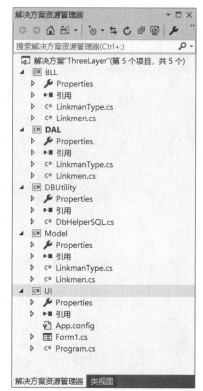

图 3-11 添加 UI 之后的解决方案资源管理器

2. 编写表示层代码

表示层需要引用 BLL 和 Model 项目,无须引用 DAL。删除 UI 项目中的 Form1.cs 窗体文件后,右击 UI 项目,在弹出式菜单中选择"添加"→"窗体(Windows 窗体)"命令,在弹出的"添加新项"窗体中,将名称改为 MainForm.cs,单击"添加"按钮完成窗体的添加。用同样的方法再添加四个 Windows 窗体,分别命名为 LinkmanTypeManage.cs、LinkmanTypeEdit.cs、LinkmenManage.cs 以及 LinkmenEdit.cs。各窗体的作用如表 3-3 所示。

表 3-3 各窗体作用

窗 体 名	作 用
MainForm	入口主窗体,程序的 MDI 父窗体
LinkmanTypeManage	联系人类型管理窗体,显示联系人类型列表并且是编辑入口
LinkmanTypeEdit	联系人类型编辑窗体
LinkmenManage	联系人管理窗体,显示联系人列表并且是编辑入口
LinkmenEdit	联系人编辑窗体

将 UI 项目中的 Program.cs 文件的 Main 方法中的 Application.Run(new Form1())语句改为 Application.Run(new MainForm()),指明应用程序运行时首先运行 MainForm 窗体。

接下来设置 MainForm 窗体的若干属性及其值,如表 3-4 所示。

表 3-4 MainForm 属性设置表

属 性 名	属 性 值	作 用
Text	通讯录管理系统	设置窗体的标题文本
WindowState	Maximized	令窗体最大化
IsMdiContainer	True	设置该窗体为 MDI 父窗体

从工具箱中拖动一个 MenuStrip 控件到 MainForm 上,将该 MenuStrip 的 Name 属性更改为 menuMain,设计菜单样式如图 3-12 所示。

图 3-12 MainForm 窗体上的菜单样式

双击"联系人类型管理"菜单项,进入该菜单项的 Click 事件处理函数。填写代码如下。

```
LinkmanTypeManage frm = new LinkmanTypeManage();    //创建联系人类型管理窗体对象
frm.MdiParent = this;    //指定联系人类型管理窗体的 MDI 父窗体是 this,即 MainForm
frm.Show();    //显示联系人类型管理窗体
```

双击"联系人管理"菜单项,进入该菜单项的 Click 事件处理函数。填写代码如下。

```
LinkmenManage frm = new LinkmenManage();    //创建联系人管理窗体对象
frm.MdiParent = this;
frm.Show();
```

LinkmanTypeManage 窗体设计如图 3-13 所示。

图 3-13 LinkmanTypeManage 窗体设计

对于 LinkmanTypeManage 窗体的属性设置如表 3-5 所示。

表 3-5 LinkmanTypeManage 窗体属性设置表

属 性 名	属 性 值	作 用
Text	联系人类型管理	设置窗体的标题文本

LinkmanTypeManage 窗体中的主要控件，按 Tab 顺序，描述如表 3-6 所示。

表 3-6 LinkmanTypeManage 窗体中的主要控件

Tab 顺序	控 件 类 型	属 性 名	属 性 值
1	TextBox	Name	txtTypeName
2	Button	Name	btnSearch
		Text	查询
3	DataGridView	Name	dgvTypeList
		AllowUserToAddRows	False
4	Button	Name	btnAdd
		Text	添加
5	Button	Name	btnUpdate
		Text	修改
6	Button	Name	btnDelete
		Text	删除

为 DataGridView 控件 dgvTypeList 添加列。右击该控件，在弹出式菜单中单击"添加列"命令，弹出如图 3-14 所示"添加列"对话框。

图 3-14 "添加列"对话框

在图 3-14 中，输入页眉文本为"联系人类型编号"，单击"添加"按钮，会看到 dgvTypeList

中已经添加了一个页眉为"联系人类型编号"的列。用同样方法再添加一个页眉文本为"联系人类型名称"的列。dgvTypeList 结果样式如图 3-15 所示。

图 3-15　dgvTypeList 控件结果样式

接下来为每一列绑定要显示的数据字段名。再次右击 dgvTypeList，在弹出式菜单中单击"编辑列"命令，弹出如图 3-16 所示的"编辑列"对话框。

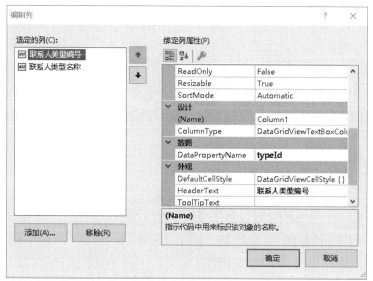

图 3-16　"编辑列"对话框

在图 3-16 的左侧选中"联系人类型编号"列，在右侧将 DataPropertyName 的值设置为"typeId"，即绑定该列将会显示数据源中的 typeId 字段的数据。同样方法将"联系人类型名称"列的 DataPropertyName 属性值设置为"typeName"。之后，单击"确定"按钮，完成 dgvTypeList 的设计。

接着设计 LinkmanTypeEdit 窗体，如图 3-17 所示。

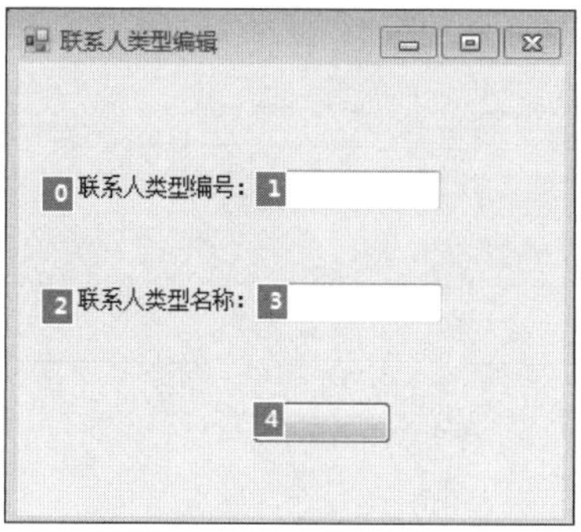

图 3-17　LinkmanTypeEdit 窗体设计

对于 LinkmanTypeEdit 窗体的属性设置如表 3-7 所示。

表 3-7 LinkmanTypeEdit 窗体属性设置表

属 性 名	属 性 值	作 用
Text	联系人类型编辑	设置窗体的标题文本

LinkmanTypeEdit 窗体中的主要控件，按 Tab 顺序，描述如表 3-8 所示。

表 3-8 LinkmanTypeEdit 窗体中的主要控件

Tab 顺序	控 件 类 型	属 性 名	属 性 值
1	TextBox	Name	txtTypeId
3	TextBox	Name	txtTypeName
4	Button	Name	btnSubmit
		Text	

LinkmanTypeManage 窗体和 LinkmanTypeEdit 窗体共同完成对联系人类型的增加、删除、修改、查询操作。首先，LinkmanTypeManage 窗体加载时，dgvTypeList 中显示数据表 LinkmanType 中所有的联系人类别。在 LinkmanTypeManage 窗体的 txtTypeName 中输入一个联系人类别名称，单击"查询"按钮，可以进行模糊查询，并将结果显示在 dgvTypeList 中。单击"添加"按钮，弹出 LinkmanTypeEdit 窗体，并且 LinkmanTypeEdit 窗体中的 btnSubmit 按钮在该窗体加载时 Text 属性变为"添加"，在 LinkmanTypeEdit 窗体中输入要添加的联系人类型编号和名称后，单击"添加"按钮实现数据的添加，并刷新 LinkmanTypeManage 窗体中的 dgvTypeList。在 dgvTypeList 中选中一个联系人类型，单击"修改"按钮，同样弹出 LinkmanTypeEdit 窗体，但会在 LinkmanTypeEdit 窗体加载时呈现在 dgvTypeList 选中的这个联系人类型的详细信息，并将 btnSubmit 的 Text 属性变为"修改"，输入新的联系人类型编号和名称，单击"修改"按钮，实现数据的修改，且刷新 LinkmanTypeManage 窗体中的 dgvTypeList。在 dgvTypeList 中选中一个联系人类型，单击"删除"按钮，会弹出确认对话框，询问用户是否确认删除这个联系人类型，如果单击确认对话框中的"是"按钮，则执行删除，并刷新 dgvTypeList，如果单击"否"按钮则什么都不做。

在 UI 项目中，引入 BLL 和 Model 项目，编写 LinkmanTypeManage.cs 代码如下。

```
namespace UI
{
    public partial class LinkmanTypeManage : Form
    {
        ///<summary>
        ///实例化业务逻辑层 LinkmanType 对象
        ///</summary>
        BLL.LinkmanType bLKMT = new BLL.LinkmanType();
        ///<summary>
        ///当前查询条件,如果为空字符串,代表查询全部
        ///否则为指定查询条件,如 typename like '%朋友%'
        ///</summary>
```

```csharp
string currSearchContent = "";
public LinkmanTypeManage()
{
    InitializeComponent();
}
private void DepartmentManage_Load(object sender, EventArgs e)
                                                    //窗体 Load 事件
{
    dgvTypeList.AutoGenerateColumns = false;
                                       //禁止 dgvTypeList 自动创建列
    bindGridView();
}
///<summary>
///为 dgvTypeList 绑定数据源
///</summary>
public void bindGridView()
{
    dgvTypeList.DataSource = bLKMT.select(currSearchContent);
}
private void btnSearch_Click(object sender, EventArgs e)
                                                    //"查询"按钮事件
{
    currSearchContent = "typename like '%" + txtTypeName.Text + "%'";
                                                    //设定查询条件
    bindGridView();
}
private void btnDelete_Click(object sender, EventArgs e)
                                                    //"删除"按钮事件
{
    DialogResult dr = MessageBox.Show("确认删除该联系人类型吗?",
            "删除确认", MessageBoxButtons.YesNo);
                                                    //弹出确认对话框
    if (dr == DialogResult.Yes)                     //如果选"是"
    {
        //执行删除,dgvTypeList.CurrentRow.Cells[0].Value 可以取得
        //dgvTypeList 当前选中行的第一个单元格内容,即联系人类型编号
        bLKMT.delete(dgvTypeList.CurrentRow.Cells[0].Value.ToString());
        bindGridView();
    }
}
private void btnUpdate_Click(object sender, EventArgs e)
                                                    //"修改"按钮事件
{
    LinkmanTypeEdit frm = new LinkmanTypeEdit();
                                       //实例化 LinkmanTypeEdit 窗体对象
    //将当前选中行的联系人类型编号赋给 frm 窗体对象的 typeId 成员变量
    frm.typeId = dgvTypeList.CurrentRow.Cells[0].Value.ToString();
    frm.status = "修改";                //将当前的 frm 窗体对象标记为修改状态
    frm.MdiParent = this.MdiParent;    //设置 frm 窗体对象的 Mdi 父窗体
    //将当前 LinkmanTypeManage 窗体对象传递给 frm 对象,以便在 frm 对象中
    //调用当前 LinkmanTypeManage 对象的 bindGridView 函数,完成列表更新
    frm.myParentFrm = this;
    frm.Show();                        //显示 LinkmanTypeEdit 窗体
```

```csharp
        }
        private void btnAdd_Click(object sender, EventArgs e)    //"添加"按钮事件
        {
            LinkmanTypeEdit frm = new LinkmanTypeEdit();
            frm.status = "添加";
            frm.MdiParent = this.MdiParent;
            frm.myParentFrm = this;
            frm.Show();
        }
    }
}
```

编写 LinkmanTypeEdit.cs 代码如下。

```csharp
namespace UI
{
    public partial class LinkmanTypeEdit : Form
    {
        //用于接收从 LinkmanTypeManage 窗体传递过来的要修改的联系人类型的编号
        public string typeId;
        //用于接收从 LinkmanTypeManage 窗体传递过来的当前操作状态是添加还是修改
        public string status;
        //用于接收传递过来的 LinkmanTypeManage 窗体,
        //以便调用 LinkmanTypeMange 窗体对象的 bindGridView 方法
        public LinkmanTypeManage myParentFrm;
        public LinkmanTypeEdit()
        {
            InitializeComponent();
        }
        BLL.LinkmanType bLKMT = new BLL.LinkmanType();
        Model.LinkmanType mLKMT = new Model.LinkmanType();
                                    //实例化 LinkmanType 实体类
        private void DepartmentEdit_Load(object sender, EventArgs e)
        {
            btnSubmit.Text = status;      //设置 btnSubmit 当前文本为"添加"或"修改"
            if (status == "修改")         //如果是修改,将当前的联系人类型原信息首先
                                          //呈现在各文本框内
            {
                DataTable dt = bLKMT.select("typeid='" + typeId + "'");
                txtTypeId.Text = dt.Rows[0]["typeid"].ToString();
                txtTypeName.Text = dt.Rows[0]["typename"].ToString();
            }
        }
        private void btnSubmit_Click(object sender, EventArgs e)
                                                //添加或修改事件代码
        {
            mLKMT.typeId = txtTypeId.Text ;
            mLKMT.typeName = txtTypeName.Text;    //为实体类对象赋属性值
            bool result = false;                  //标记是否添加或修改成功
            switch (status)
            {
                case "修改":
                    result=bLKMT.update(mLKMT, typeId);   //执行修改
```

```
                break;
            case "添加":
                result=bLKMT.insert(mLKMT);          //执行添加
                break;
        }
        if (result)                                  //如果操作成功
        {
            //调用LinkmanTypeManage窗体的bindGridView函数,完成列表的刷新
            myParentFrm.bindGridView();
            MessageBox.Show(status+ "成功!");
        }
        else
            MessageBox.Show(status + "失败!");
    }
}
```

LinkmenManage 窗体设计如图 3-18 所示。

图 3-18 LinkmenManage 窗体设计

对于 LinkmenManage 窗体的属性设置如表 3-9 所示。

表 3-9 LinkmenManage 窗体属性设置表

属 性 名	属 性 值	作 用
Text	联系人管理	设置窗体的标题文本

LinkmenManage 窗体中的主要控件,按 Tab 顺序,描述如表 3-10 所示。

表 3-10 LinkmenManage 窗体中的主要控件

Tab 顺序	控 件 类 型	属 性 名	属 性 值
1	ComboBox	Name	cmbSearchField
		DropDownStyle	DropDownList
2	ComboBox	Name	cmbOperator
		DropDownStyle	DropDownList
3	TextBox	Name	txtSearchContent

续表

Tab 顺序	控件类型	属性名	属性值
4	Button	Name	btnSearch
		Text	查询
5	DataGridView	Name	dgvLinkmenList
		AllowUserToAddRows	False
6	Button	Name	btnAdd
		Text	添加
7	Button	Name	btnUpdate
		Text	修改
8	Button	Name	btnDelete
		Text	删除
9	Button	Name	btnRandom
		Text	随机抽取联系人

为 DataGridView 控件 dgvLinkmenList 添加列,如表 3-11 所示。

表 3-11 dgvLinkmenList 列设置表

列头名	DataPropertyName 属性值	Visible 属性值
编号	lkmId	False
姓名	lkmName	True
移动电话	lkmMPNum	True
办公电话	lkmOPNum	True
电子邮箱	lkmEmail	True
工作单位	lkmCompName	True
联系人类型	typeName	True

接着设计 LinkmenEdit 窗体,如图 3-19 所示。

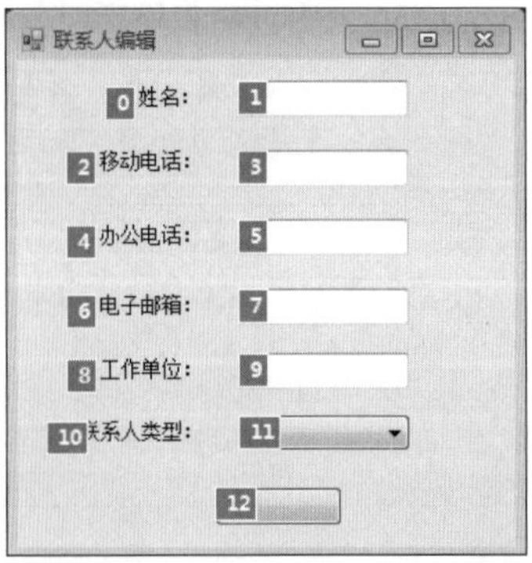

图 3-19 LinkmenEdit 窗体设计

对于 LinkmenEdit 窗体的属性设置如表 3-12 所示。

表 3-12 LinkmenEdit 窗体属性设置表

属 性 名	属 性 值	作 用
Text	联系人编辑	设置窗体的标题文本

LinkmenEdit 窗体中的主要控件，按 Tab 顺序，描述如表 3-13 所示。

表 3-13 LinkmenEdit 窗体中的主要控件

Tab 顺序	控 件 类 型	属 性 名	属 性 值
1	TextBox	Name	txtName
3	TextBox	Name	txtMPNum
5	TextBox	Name	txtOPNum
7	TextBox	Name	txtEMail
9	TextBox	Name	txtCompName
11	ComboBox	Name	cmbTypeName
		DropDownStyle	DropDownList
12	Button	Name	btnSubmit
		Text	

LinkmenManage 窗体和 LinkmenEdit 窗体共同完成对联系人的增加、删除、修改、查询操作。首先，LinkmenManage 窗体加载时，dgvLinkmenList 中显示数据表 Linkmen 中所有的联系人信息。在 LinkmenManage 窗体的 cmbSearchField 中选择要查询的字段，如"姓名"；在 cmbOperator 中选择一个比较运算符，如"等于"；在 txtSearchContent 中输入要查询的数据，如"张三"；单击"查询"按钮，可以进行相应查询，并将结果显示在 dgvLinkmenList 中。单击"添加"按钮，弹出 LinkmenEdit 窗体，并且 LinkmenEdit 窗体中的 btnSubmit 按钮在该窗体加载时 Text 属性变为"添加"，在 LinkmenEdit 窗体中输入要添加的联系人信息，单击"添加"按钮实现数据的添加，并刷新 LinkmenManage 窗体中的 dgvLinkmenList。在 dgvLinkmenList 中选中一条联系人信息，单击"修改"按钮，同样弹出 LinkmenEdit 窗体，但会在 LinkmenEdit 窗体加载时呈现在 dgvLinkmenList 选中的这条联系人现有信息，并将 btnSubmit 的 Text 属性变为"修改"，输入新的联系人信息，单击"修改"按钮，实现数据的修改，且刷新 LinkmenManage 窗体中的 dgvLinkmenList。在 dgvLinkmenList 中选中一条联系人信息，单击"删除"按钮，会弹出确认对话框，询问用户是否确认删除这个联系人，如果单击确认对话框中的"是"按钮，则执行删除，并刷新 dgvLinkmenList；如果单击"否"按钮，则什么都不做。单击"随机抽取联系人"按钮，弹出 MessageBox 显示抽取到的联系人基本信息。

编写 LinkmenManage.cs 代码如下。

```
namespace UI
{
    public partial class LinkmenManage : Form
```

```csharp
{
    BLL.Linkmen bLKM = new BLL.Linkmen();
    string currSearchContent = "";
    public LinkmenManage()
    {
        InitializeComponent();
    }
    private void StudentManage_Load(object sender, EventArgs e)
    {
        //以下6句,向cmbSearchField中添加可选项
        cmbSearchField.Items.Add("姓名");
        cmbSearchField.Items.Add("移动电话");
        cmbSearchField.Items.Add("办公电话");
        cmbSearchField.Items.Add("电子邮箱");
        cmbSearchField.Items.Add("工作单位");
        cmbSearchField.Items.Add("所属类别");
        //以下2句,向cmbOperator中添加可选项
        cmbOperator.Items.Add("等于");
        cmbOperator.Items.Add("类似于");
        dgvLinkmenList.AutoGenerateColumns = false;
        bindGridView();
    }
    public void bindGridView()
    {
        dgvLinkmenList.DataSource = bLKM.select(currSearchContent);
    }
    private void btnSearch_Click(object sender, EventArgs e)
    {
        string searchField = "";
        //将cmbSearchField中选中的项转换成对应的数据表字段名
        switch (cmbSearchField.SelectedItem.ToString())
        {
            case "姓名":
                searchField = "lkmname";
                break;
            case "移动电话":
                searchField = "lkmmpnum";
                break;
            case "固定电话":
                searchField = "lkmopnum";
                break;
            case "电子邮箱":
                searchField = "lkmemail";
                break;
            case "工作单位":
                searchField = "lkmcompname";
                break;
            case "所属类别":
                searchField = "typename";
                break;
        }
        if (cmbOperator.SelectedItem.ToString()!="类似于")//组建查询子句
```

```
                    currSearchContent = searchField + cmbOperator.SelectedItem.
                         ToString() + "'"+ txtSearchContent.Text + "'";
            else
                currSearchContent = searchField+" like '%" + txtSearchContent.
Text + "%'";
            bindGridView();
        }
        private void btnDelete_Click(object sender, EventArgs e)
        {
            DialogResult dr = MessageBox.Show("确认删除该联系人吗?",
                        "删除确认", MessageBoxButtons.YesNo);
            if (dr == DialogResult.Yes)
            {
                bLKM.delete(dgvLinkmenList.CurrentRow.Cells[0].Value.ToString());
                bindGridView();
            }
        }
        private void btnUpdate_Click(object sender, EventArgs e)
        {
            LinkmenEdit frm = new LinkmenEdit();
            frm.lkmId = dgvLinkmenList.CurrentRow.Cells[0].Value.ToString();
            frm.status = "修改";
            frm.MdiParent = this.MdiParent;
            frm.myParentFrm = this;
            frm.Show();
        }
        private void btnAdd_Click(object sender, EventArgs e)
        {
            LinkmenEdit frm = new LinkmenEdit();
            frm.status = "添加";
            frm.MdiParent = this.MdiParent;
            frm.myParentFrm = this;
            frm.Show();
        }
        private void btnRandom_Click(object sender, EventArgs e)
                                    //随机抽取联系人事件
        {
            Model.Linkmen mLKM = bLKM.randomFriend();
                                    //调用业务逻辑层随机抽取函数
            MessageBox.Show("抽取到的联系人:姓名" + mLKM.lkmName+ ",联系电话"
                    + mLKM.lkmMPNum + ",固定电话"
                    + mLKM.lkmOPNum);   //显示抽到的联系人主要信息
        }
    }
}
```

编写 LinkmenEdit.cs 代码如下。

```
namespace UI
{
    public partial class LinkmenEdit : Form
    {
        public string lkmId;
```

```csharp
public string status;
public LinkmenManage myParentFrm;
public LinkmenEdit()
{
    InitializeComponent();
}
BLL.Linkmen bLKM = new BLL.Linkmen();
Model.Linkmen mLKM = new Model.Linkmen();
private void StudentEdit_Load(object sender, EventArgs e)
{
    btnSubmit.Text = status;
    //以下 4 句,将联系人类型信息从联系人类型表取出,绑定到 cmbTypeName 中
    DataTable dtLKMT = new BLL.LinkmanType().select("");
    cmbTypeName.DataSource = dtLKMT;
    cmbTypeName.DisplayMember = "typename";
    cmbTypeName.ValueMember = "typeid";
    if (status == "修改")
    {
        DataTable dt = bLKM.select("lkmid='" + lkmId + "'");
        txtName.Text = dt.Rows[0]["lkmname"].ToString();
        txtMPNum.Text = dt.Rows[0]["lkmmpnum"].ToString();
        txtOPNum.Text = dt.Rows[0]["lkmopnum"].ToString();
        txtEMail.Text = dt.Rows[0]["lkmemail"].ToString();
        txtCompName.Text = dt.Rows[0]["lkmcompname"].ToString();
        cmbTypeName.SelectedValue = dt.Rows[0]["typeid"].ToString();
    }
}
private void btnSubmit_Click(object sender, EventArgs e)
{
    mLKM.lkmName = txtName.Text;
    mLKM.lkmMPNum = txtMPNum.Text;
    mLKM.lkmOPNum=txtOPNum.Text;
    mLKM.lkmEmail=txtEMail.Text;
    mLKM.lkmCompName = txtCompName.Text;
    mLKM.typeId = cmbTypeName.SelectedValue.ToString();
    bool result = false;
    switch (status)
    {
        case "修改":
            mLKM.lkmId = lkmId;
            result = bLKM.update(mLKM);
            break;
        case "添加":
            result = bLKM.insert(mLKM);
            break;
    }
    if (result)
    {
        myParentFrm.bindGridView();
        MessageBox.Show(status + "成功!");
    }
```

```
            else
                MessageBox.Show(status + "失败!");
        }
    }
}
```

3.3　工厂模式三层架构

在上述简单三层架构的通讯录管理软件中,数据访问层是针对 SQL Server 数据库实现的,如果用户需求变更,不再打算使用 SQL Server 作为数据库,而改用 Access 数据库,需要做哪些变更呢?

以上需求变更,可能会有两种结果:其一,用户打算永久将数据库变更为 Access 而不再变回 SQL Server;其二,用户也不确定是否会再次变回 SQL Server。

面对第一种需求变更,只需将 DBUtility 中的 DbHelperSQL 类,以及数据访问层 DAL 中 LinkmanType 类和 Linkmen 类中的访问 SQL Server 数据库相关的类对象彻底更换成访问 Access 数据库的类对象即可,无须修改其他层的代码。而面对第二种需求变更,由于用户需求变更的不确定性,不但要为其实现访问 Access 数据库,还要为其保留现有的访问 SQL Server 实现。即,应保留 DBUtility 中的 DbHelperSQL 类,以及 DAL 中的所有类,并创建新的访问 Access 数据库的数据访问层实现。前面提到 DBUtility 是一个为简化数据库访问代码提供的通用类库,既然其中的 DbHelperSQL 类是访问 SQL Server 的通用类,那么现在可再创建一个名为 DbHelperAccess 的类作为访问 Access 的通用类。而 DAL 项目的所有实现都是针对 SQL Server 的数据访问层实现。访问 Access 的数据访问层实现已不适合放在 DAL 中,应创建单独的名为 AccessDAL 的类库作为新的访问 Access 数据库的数据访问层实现,其中的各类,同样名为 LinkmanType 和 Linkmen。如此一来,请读者考虑,基于 3.2 节中简单三层架构的代码结构,在进行数据库访问实现的切换时,是不是还需要涉及变更其他层呢?以 BLL 的 LinkmanType 类为例,数据库的切换,也就是数据访问层 DAL 与 AccessDAL 的切换。BLL 的 LinkmanType 类当前调用数据访问层是通过 DAL.LinkmanType dLKMT = new DAL.LinkmanType()来实例化数据访问层对象的。如果要切换到调用 AccessDAL 中的 LinkmanType 类,需要改写上述代码为 AccessDAL.LinkmanType dLKMT = new AccessDAL.LinkmanType()。可见,简单三层架构在面临这种需求变更时,耦合度还是偏高,需要继续解耦,尝试在数据访问层被替换时,不会影响业务逻辑层的变动。

上述问题可分为两个部分:第一,如何使业务逻辑层中定义数据访问层对象引用的类型保持不变;第二,如何使业务逻辑层中实例化数据访问层对象的代码保持不变。

解决第一个问题,可以为 DAL.LinkmanType 和 AccessDAL.LinkmanType 类创建一个公共接口 IDal.ILinkmanType。在定义数据访问层对象引用时,可以使用该接口来定义,这样该引用可以指向任何实现该接口的类的实例对象。

解决第二个问题,可以使用 C# 中的一种称为"反射"的机制来实现。所谓反射,即是审查元数据并收集关于它的类型信息的能力。元数据(编译以后的最基本数据单元)就是一套表,当编译程序集或者模块时,编译器会创建一个类定义表、一个字段定义表和一个方法定义表。System.Reflection 命名空间包括的几个类,允许反射(解析)这些元数据表的代码。通俗点讲,通过反射可以根据字符串形式的程序集和类名,实例化该类的对象。例如:

```
Assembly.Load("DAL").CreateInstance("DAL.LinkmanType");
```

以上代码可实现加载"DAL"程序集,并实例化该程序集中"DAL.LinkmanType"类的对象。由此可见,用反射机制创建数据访问层对象的方法,在需要更换不同的数据访问层实现时,只需将"DAL"字符串改为"AccessDAL"即可。而字符串完全可以存到文本文件或者配置文件 App.Config 中。经过这样的变更,数据访问层可完全与业务逻辑层解耦。

基于以上实现,可在现有简单三层架构基础上,再添加一个用于存放数据访问层各类接口的接口类库,以及一个专门用于实例化数据访问层各类对象的类库,此类库即是所谓的"工厂",生产数据访问层类对象的工厂。改造后的三层架构就是工厂模式三层架构。其基本结构如图 3-20 所示。

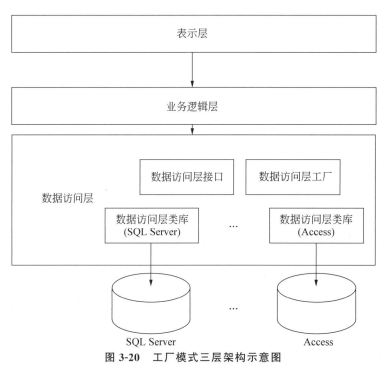

图 3-20 工厂模式三层架构示意图

3.3.1 接口类库设计

接下来,将 3.2 节中的简单三层架构项目 ThreeLayer 改写为工厂模式三层架构。

1. 创建数据访问层接口类库 IDAL

右击解决方案,选择"添加"→"新建项目"命令,创建一个名为"IDAL"的类库项目。添加项目之后的解决方案列表如图 3-21 所示。

2. 编写 IDAL 中数据访问层各接口

先引用 Model 项目,删除 IDAL 项目中的 Class1.cs 文件,然后右击 IDAL 项目,选择

图 3-21　添加 IDAL 之后的解决方案资源管理器

"添加"→"新建项"命令,弹出"添加新项"对话框,在中间的列表中选择"接口",将名称改为"ILinkmanType.cs",单击"添加"按钮,完成 ILinkmanType 接口的添加。再以同样方法创建一个名为"ILinkmen.cs"的接口文件。

编写 ILinkmanType.cs 代码如下。

```
namespace IDAL
{
    public interface ILinkmanType
    {
        bool insert(Model.LinkmanType mDep);
        bool update(Model.LinkmanType mDep, string oldTypeId);
        bool delete(string typeId);
        DataTable select(string strWhere);
    }
}
```

编写 ILinkmen.cs 代码如下。

```
namespace IDAL
{
    public interface ILinkmen
    {
        bool insert(Model.Linkmen mStu);
        bool update(Model.Linkmen mStu);
        bool delete(string lkmId);
        DataTable select(string strWhere);
    }
}
```

3.3.2 工厂类库设计

1. 创建数据访问层的工厂类库 DalFactory

右击解决方案,单击"添加"→"新建项目"命令,创建一个名为"DalFactory"的类库项目。添加项目之后的解决方案列表如图 3-22 所示。

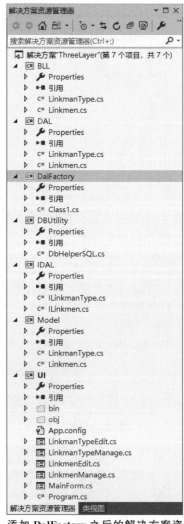

图 3-22 添加 DalFactory 之后的解决方案资源管理器

2. 编写 DalFactory 中生产数据访问层各类对象的代码

先引用 Model 项目和 IDAL 项目，删除 DalFactory 项目中的 Class1.cs 文件，然后添加一个名为"DataAccess.cs"的类文件。

编写 DataAccess.cs 代码如下。

```csharp
using System.Configuration;          //ConfigurationSettings 所在命名空间
using System.Reflection;             //Assembly 类所在命名空间
namespace DalFactory
{
    public class DataAccess
    {
        ///<summary>
        ///DAL 程序集名称，从 App.config 配置文件的 AppSettiings 节中
        ///读取 key 为 DalAssemblyName 的值
        ///</summary>
        static readonly string AssemblyName = ConfigurationSettings.AppSettings
            ["DalAssemblyName"];
        ///<summary>
        ///创建 LinkmanType 数据访问层对象
        ///</summary>
        public static IDAL.ILinkmanType CreateLinkmanType()
        {
            string ClassNamespace = AssemblyName + ".LinkmanType";
            object objType = Assembly.Load(AssemblyName).CreateInstance
                (ClassNamespace);
            return (IDAL.ILinkmanType)objType;
        }
        ///<summary>
        ///创建 Linkmen 数据访问层对象
        ///</summary>
        public static IDAL.ILinkmen CreateLinkmen()
        {
            string ClassNamespace = AssemblyName + ".Linkmen";
            object objType = Assembly.Load(AssemblyName).CreateInstance
                (ClassNamespace);
            return (IDAL.ILinkmen)objType;
        }
    }
}
```

3.3.3 其他层的代码修改

1. 改写 DAL

首先，引用 IDAL 项目。然后，修改 DAL 中的 LinkmanType 类，令其实现 IDAL.ILinkmanType 接口：public class LinkmanType：IDAL.ILinkmanType。接着，修改 Linkmen 类，令其实现 IDAL.ILinkmen 接口：public class Linkmen：IDAL.ILinkmen。

2. 改写 BLL

首先，删除对 DAL 的引用，加入对 IDAL 和 DalFactory 项目的引用。然后修改 BLL 中的 LinkmanType 类中的 DAL.LinkmanType dLKMT = new DAL.LinkmanType()语句为：IDAL.ILinkmanType dLKMT = DalFactory.DataAccess.CreateLinkmanType()，修改

Linkmen 类中的 DAL.Linkmen dLKM = new DAL.Linkmen()语句为：IDAL.ILinkmen dLKM = DalFactory.DataAccess.CreateLinkmen()。

3. 改写 UI

首先，加入对 DAL 项目的引用。然后，右击 UI 项目，选择"添加"→"新建项"命令，弹出"添加新项"对话框，在中间的列表中选择"应用程序配置文件"，单击"添加"按钮，添加 App.config 配置文件，改写 App.config 文件内容如下。

```xml
<?xml version="1.0" encoding="utf-8" ?>
<configuration>
    <appSettings>
        <add key="DalAssemblyName" value="DAL"/>
    </appSettings>
</configuration>
```

再次面对上述数据库迁移的需求变更时，除需要编写访问对应数据库的数据访问层项目外（如访问 Access 数据库的 AccessDAL 项目，访问 Oracle 数据库的 OracleDAL 项目），只需修改 App.config 中的 DalAccemblyName 的 value 为"AccessDAL"或"OracleDAL"即可，而无须改动其他层的代码。真正做到了抽屉式的代码替换，耦合度降到了最低。

通过上述 IDAL 和 DalFactory，只能使业务逻辑层和数据访问层得到最大解耦，若要使表示层和业务逻辑层也能够完全解耦，又该如何实现？读者可自行思考。

此外，对于 DBUtility.DbHelperSQL 类中的数据库连接字符串 connString 的值，也可存放于 App.config 中，这样更有利于数据库迁移，在数据库连接信息变更时，可以不用重新编译程序，直接修改 App.config 即可。

修改 App.config 配置文件如下。

```xml
<?xml version="1.0" encoding="utf-8" ?>
<configuration>
    <appSettings>
        <add key="DalAssemblyName" value="DAL"/>
        <add key="connString" value="server=(local);database=mydb;uid=test;
            pwd=test"/>
    </appSettings>
</configuration>
```

修改 DBUtility.DbHelperSQL 类中初始化静态成员变量 connString 的代码如下。

```
public static string connString = System.Configuration.ConfigurationSettings.
AppSettings["connString"];
```

当然，对于 Windows 应用程序，从安全考虑，应将 App.Config 中 connString 的 value 进行加密，读者可自行完成。

小　　结

通过本章的学习，应基本掌握三层架构的设计思想，能够利用 C#语言在 Visual Studio 集成开发环境下，熟练地进行简单三层架构和工厂模式三层架构的项目开发。能够理解分层目的和解耦的原理，并能够尝试自行创造满足项目实际需求变更的软件体系架构。

本章的难点在于对于三层架构设计思想的理解、对于降低程序耦合度原理的理解以及对于反射机制的理解,读者应结合实际示例多加揣摩。学习三层架构的目的不是学会三层架构下代码分层的"形",而是要理解其"神"——分层的目的是降低程序耦合度,耦合度越低,代码复用度就越高,且面临需求变更时,代码的修改量就会越小。三层架构只是"一式剑招",它不一定适用于任何需求的变更,应做到面对不同的项目、不同的需求变更点,真正做到"见招拆招""无招胜有招",只要能做到面对需求变更,代码修改量最小化即是好招。所以,真正在项目开发中,完全可以创造自己的架构。

习 题

1. 用简单三层架构实现一个简易学生信息管理系统。
2. 将上述简单三层架构的学生信息管理系统改造成工厂模式三层架构。

第 4 章 ASP.NET MVC 模式

本章讲解 MVC 模式、ASP.NET MVC 框架的基本原理和应用。现阶段，使用.NET 作为 Web 开发技术的互联网企业大多采用 ASP.NET MVC 框架，传统的 Web Form 项目已基本退出主流技术舞台。应用 ASP.NET MVC 框架开发 Web 应用程序，具有低耦合、高性能的特点，一方面，方便项目后期的维护和扩展；另一方面，ASP.NET MVC 项目的性能表现也比 Web Form 项目有明显的优势。

通过本章的学习，读者应该重点掌握 MVC 模式的基本原理和 ASP.NET MVC 框架的工作原理以及基本应用，能够应用 ASP.NET MVC 框架开发基本的 Web 应用项目。

4.1 MVC 模式简介

MVC(Model-View-Controller)模式是软件工程中的一种软件设计模式，把软件系统分为三个基本部分：模型(Model)、视图(View)和控制器(Controller)。MVC 模式最早由 Trygve Reenskaug 提出。MVC 模式本身并不引入新的功能，只是用来指导开发者改善应用程序的架构，使得应用的模型和视图相分离，从而得到更好的开发和维护效率。

模型：负责封装应用的状态，并实现应用的功能。通常又分为数据模型和业务逻辑模型，数据模型用来存放业务数据，如订单信息、用户信息等；而业务逻辑模型包含应用的业务操作，如订单的添加或者修改等。

视图：用来将模型的内容展现给用户，用户可以通过视图来请求模型进行更新。视图从模型获得要展示的数据，然后用自己的方式展现给用户，相当于提供界面来与用户进行人机交互；用户在界面上操作或者填写完成后，会单击"提交"按钮或是以其他触发事件的方式，来向控制器发出请求。

控制器：用来控制应用程序的流程和处理视图所发出的请求。当控制器接收到用户的请求后，会将用户的数据和模型的更新相映射，也就是调用模型来实现用户请求的功能；然后控制器会选择用于响应的视图，把模型更新后的数据展示给用户。

在 MVC 中，模型和视图是分离的，通常视图里面不会有任何逻辑实现；而模型也不依赖于视图，同一个模型可能会有很多种不同的展示方式，也就是同一个模型可以对应多种不同的视图。例如，在 Windows 操作系统上浏览文件夹时，对于同一文件夹及其内部的文件，可以有大图标、小图标、详细信息等多种展示方式。模型负责输出的内容，视图负责输出的形式。

MVC 的组件关系如图 4-1 所示。

一次完整的交互过程如下。

(1) 首先是展示视图给用户，用户在该视图上进行操作，并填写一些业务数据。

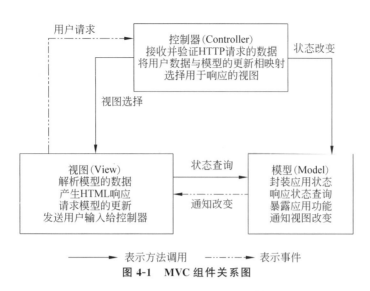

图 4-1 MVC 组件关系图

(2) 用户单击"提交"按钮(或触发其他提交事件),向控制器发出请求,将输入的数据提交给控制器。

(3) 控制器接到用户请求,把请求中的数据进行封装,选择并调用合适的模型,请求模型进行状态更新,然后选择接下来要展示给用户的视图。

(4) 模型处理用户请求的业务功能,同时进行模型状态的维护和更新。

(5) 当模型状态发生改变的时候,模型会通知相应的视图,告诉视图它的状态发生了改变。

(6) 视图接到模型的通知后,会向模型进行状态查询,获取需要展示的数据,然后按照视图本身的展示方式,把这些数据展示出来。

MVC 模式具有以下优点。

(1) 低耦合性:视图和模型分离,这样就允许更改视图层代码而不用重新编译模型和控制器代码。同样,一个应用的业务流程或者业务规则的改变只需要改动模型即可,因为模型与控制器和视图相分离,所以很容易改变应用程序的数据模型和业务规则。

(2) 高重用性和可适用性:允许使用各种不同样式的视图来访问同一个服务器端的代码。例如,很多电商平台既有 Web 端,又有移动 APP 端,还有小程序端,虽然表现形式不同,但它们的业务逻辑、需要访问的数据模型基本相同,在开发这样的应用时,至少模型层可以通用。

(3) 快速的部署:使用 MVC 模式使开发时间得到相当大的缩减,它使程序员(服务器端开发人员)可以集中精力于业务逻辑,前端程序员(网页开发人员或移动端界面开发人员)集中精力于表现形式上。

(4) 可维护性高:分离视图层和业务层也使得应用系统更便于维护和修改。

(5) 有利于软件工程化管理:由于不同的层各司其职,每一层不同的应用具有某些相同的特征,有利于通过工程化、工具化管理程序代码。

MVC 也存在如下一些缺点。

(1) 增加了系统结构和实现的复杂性:对于简单的小项目,严格遵循 MVC,使模型、视图与控制器分离,会增加结构的复杂性,并可能产生过多的更新操作,一定程度上降低了运行效率。

（2）视图与控制器过于紧密的连接：视图与控制器虽相互分离，但仍存在着紧密的联系，视图没有控制器的存在，其应用是很有限的，反之亦然，这样就妨碍了它们的独立重用。

（3）视图对模型数据的低效率访问：依据模型操作接口的不同，视图可能需要多次调用才能获得足够的显示数据。对未变化数据的不必要的频繁访问，也会损害操作性能。

4.2　ASP.NET MVC 工作原理

通过 4.1 节的学习，读者已经对 MVC 模式有了一个基本的认知，ASP.NET MVC 是微软官方提供的以 MVC 模式为基础的 ASP.NET Web 应用程序（Web Application）框架。那么 ASP.NET MVC 项目和大家熟悉的 WebForm 项目有什么不同呢？其各个部分又是怎样分工的呢？

首先，来看一下普通的 WebForm 项目下，假如用户请求一个例如 http：/localhost/Views/Home/Index.aspx 的 URL，那么 WebForm 程序会到网站根目录下去寻找 Views 目录下的 Home 目录下的 Index.aspx 文件，然后由 Index.aspx 页面的 CodeBehind 文件（.CS 文件）进行逻辑处理，其中或许也包括到数据库去取出数据（其中经过怎样的 BLL 到 DAL 这里就不谈了），然后再由 Index.aspx 页面来呈现给用户。简单的示意图如图 4-2 所示。

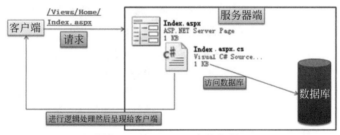

图 4-2　WebForm 程序执行状况

一个 URL 请求的是服务器上该 URL 对应路径上的物理文件（ASPX 文件或其他），然后由该文件来处理这个请求并返回结果给客户端。但是，对于 ASP.NET MVC 项目，这是怎样的一个过程呢？

首先来建一个 ASP.NET MVC 的项目，打开 Visual Studio 2019，单击"创建新项目"，在弹出的"创建新项目"窗口中的"搜索模板"搜索框内输入"MVC"，找到"ASP.NET Web 应用程序(.NET Framework)"模板，如图 4-3 所示，单击"下一步"按钮，打开"配置新项目"窗口，单击"创建"按钮，打开"创建新的 ASP.NET Web 应用程序"对话框，如图 4-4 所示。选择 MVC 模板，单击"创建"按钮，完成 ASP.NET Web 应用程序创建，创建后的项目解决方案如图 4-5 所示。

按照前面说的 WebForm 项目的程序执行方法，这里可以在解决方案资源管理器中找到 Views\Home\Index.cshtml 文件，运行该地址可以看到如图 4-6 所示的程序错误提示。

路径是对的，文件也存在，但为什么会是"404"错误，提示找不到文件呢？如果不是直接访问存在的物理文件，那么 ASP.NET MVC 又是怎样工作的呢？ASP.NET MVC 项目的工作过程如图 4-7 所示。

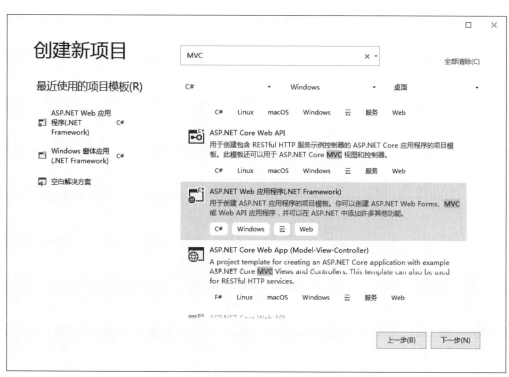

图 4-3 "创建新项目"窗口

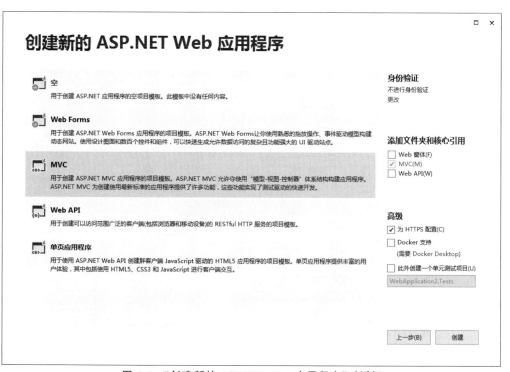

图 4-4 "创建新的 ASP.NET Web 应用程序"对话框

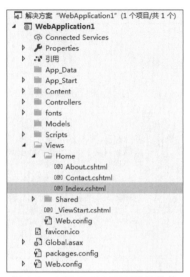

图 4-5　ASP.NET MVC 项目结构

图 4-6　直接运行 Index.cshtml 文件的错误提示

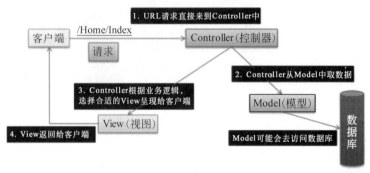

图 4-7　MVC 项目文件请求处理过程

在 ASP.NET MVC 中，客户端所请求的 URL 是被映射到相应的 Controller 去，然后由 Controller 来处理业务逻辑，比如从 Model 中取数据，然后再由 Controller 选择合适的 View 返回给客户端。例如前面要运行的 ASP.NET MVC 程序访问的 http://localhost：44338/Home/Index 这个 URL，它访问的其实是 HomeController 中的 Index() 方法，如图 4-8 所示。

```
namespace WebApplication1.Controllers
{
    0 个引用
    public class HomeController : Controller
    {
        0 个引用
        public ActionResult Index()
        {
            return View();
        }
    }
}
```

图 4-8　HomeController 中的 Index() 方法

其中，public ActionResult Index() 方法称为 Controller 的 Action，它返回的是 ActionResult 类型。一个 Controller 可以有多个 Action。那么一个 URL 是怎样被定位到 Controller 中来的呢？这里就需要查看 App_Start 目录下的路由配置文件 RouteConfig.cs 中的配置，如图 4-9 所示。

```
namespace WebApplication1
{
    0 个引用
    public class RouteConfig
    {
        0 个引用
        public static void RegisterRoutes(RouteCollection routes)
        {
            //忽略对.axd文件的Route, 也就是和WebForm一样直接去访问.axd文件
            routes.IgnoreRoute("{resource}.axd/{*pathInfo}");

            routes.MapRoute(
                //Route的名称
                name: "Default",
                //URL的地址格式, 第一部分为Controller的名字, 第二部分为Action的名字,
                //第三部分为可选参数(可以没有参数)
                url: "{controller}/{action}/{id}",
                //默认参数
                defaults: new { controller = "Home", action = "Index", id = UrlParameter.Optional }
            );
        }
    }
}
```

图 4-9　路由配置文件

可以看到这里定义了一个名为"Default"的 Route，并定义了 URL 的地址格式，还定义了默认的参数。默认参数的意义在于，当访问例如 http://localhost：44338/ 的 URL 的时候，它会将不存在的参数用默认的参数补上，也就是相当于访问 http://localhost：44338/Home/Index 一样。

已经明白了一个 URL 是怎样定位到相应的 Controller 中的，那么 View 又是怎么被返回给客户端的呢？从图 4-8 可见，Controller 中的 Action 方法中有个 return View() 的方法。默认情况下，它会返回与 Action 同名的 View。在 ASP.NET MVC 默认的视图引擎（WebFormViewEngine）下，View 是按如下路径访问的。

/Views/{Controller}/{Action}.cshtml

也就是说，对于 http://localhost：44338/Home/Index 这个路径，在默认情况下，在

Index 这个 Action 中用 return View() 来返回 View 的时候,会去寻找\Views\Home\Index.cshtml 文件,如果找不到这个文件,就会去 Share 目录中寻找\Views\Share\Index.cshtml,如果都找不到,就会抛出找不到 View 的异常。return View(视图名称)来指定要返回哪一个 View,如 return View("About");可以返回\Views\Home\About.cshtml 这个视图。

那么为什么前面直接访问 Views\Home\Index.cshtml 文件的时候会出现"404"错误呢?因为在 ASP.NET MVC 项目中,不建议直接去访问 View:Views 目录下有一个默认的 Web.config 配置文件,该文件配置有以下信息:

```
<system.webServer>
    <handlers>
    <remove name="BlockViewHandler"/>
    <add name="BlockViewHandler" path="*" verb="*"
        preCondition="integratedMode"
        type="System.Web.HttpNotFoundHandler" />
    </handlers>
</system.webServer>
```

该配置信息控制着如果想直接访问 Views 目录下的任何文件都会由 System.Web.HttpNotFoundHandler 来处理,所以请不要将资源文件(CSS、JS、图片等)放到 Views 目录中。如果一定要放到 Views 目录下的话,请修改 Views\Web.config 文件。

4.3 ASP.NET MVC 控制器

在 ASP.NET MVC 框架项目中,控制器的作用非常重要,它可以接收用户请求的参数、处理数据,可以与 Model 层连接并获取数据,然后根据业务逻辑把数据传输到视图。在渲染视图上,控制层并不是只能返回对应的视图,也可以自定义返回其他视图,甚至仅返回一串字符。下面来介绍如何创建一个控制器。

在解决方案资源管理器中,右击 Controllers 目录节点,然后选择"添加"→"控制器"命令,如图 4-10 所示。

单击"控制器"菜单项后,进入如图 4-11 所示的"添加已搭建基架的新项"界面。

这里的对于 MVC 5 专用的基架,在添加控制器时可以指定 3 类控制器基架,分别如下。

(1) MVC 5 控制器-空:最为干净的基架,创建完成后只有控制器和一个 Index() 操作方法。

(2) 包含读/写操作的 MVC 5 控制器:创建完成后会有控制器,以及读数据的操作方法和写数据的操作方法。

(3) 包含视图的 MVC 5 控制器(使用 Entity Framework):基于 EF ORM 框架生成控制器。

1. 以"MVC 5 控制器-空"基架创建控制器

在图 4-11 中选择"MVC 5 控制器-空"基架,单击"添加"按钮,会弹出如图 4-12 所示"添加控制器"界面,要求输入控制器名称。在这里只需要将"Controller"字符串前面的内容改为合适的控制器名称即可,例如,把默认的"Default1"改为"Login",单击"添加"按钮,正式

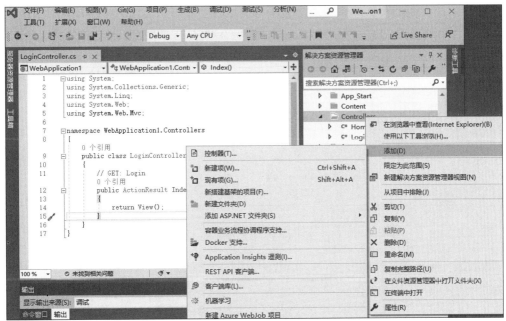

图 4-10　添加控制器

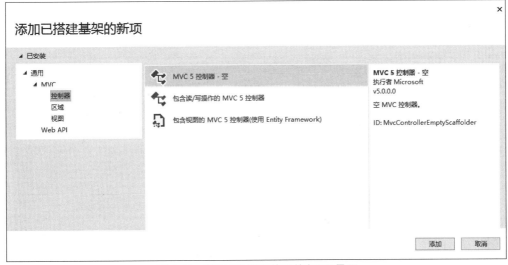

图 4-11　"添加已搭建基架的新项"界面

创建控制器,创建后的解决方案资源管理器及自动生成的 Login 控制器代码如图 4-13 所示。

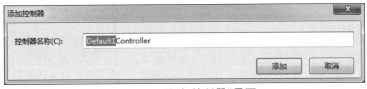

图 4-12　"添加控制器"界面

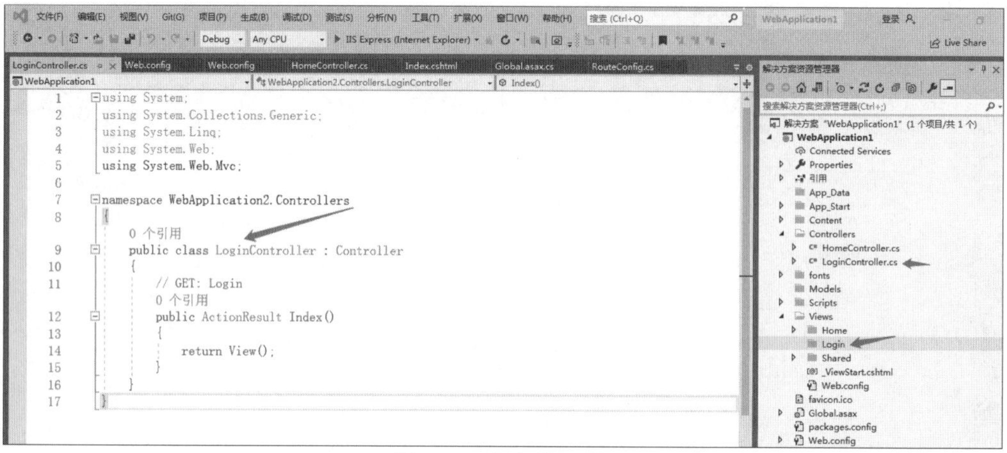

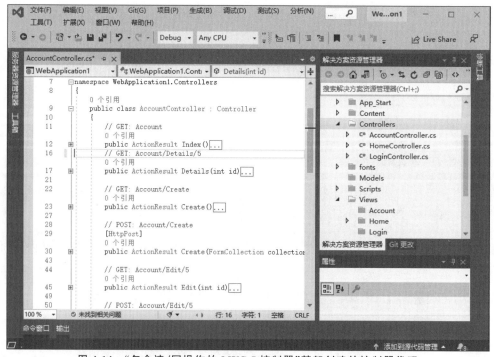

图 4-13 添加控制器

从解决方案资源管理器可见,在 Controller 目录下创建了一个名为 LoginController.cs 的控制器类文件,同时在 Views 目录下创建了一个名为 Login 的空子目录,这个目录用来存放 Login 控制器所对应的视图。而在 LoginController 类中,自动生成了一个名为 Index 的 Action 方法。

2. 包含读/写操作的 MVC 5 控制器

如果在图 4-11 中选择的是"包含读/写操作的 MVC 5 控制器"基架,则生成的代码会多一些,适合进行 CRUD 操作的应用程序,如图 4-14 所示。

图 4-14 "包含读/写操作的 MVC 5 控制器"基架创建的控制器代码

它会生成 Create、Edit、Details、Index 操作的样板代码,没有实际逻辑,需要开发人员去根据业务需求编写。

3. 包含视图的 MVC 5 控制器（使用 Entity Framework）

此基架是根据微软的 ORM 工具 Entity Framework 生成的，需要指定模型和上下文对象，而且可以选择自动生成对应的视图，生成的方式如图 4-15 所示。关于生成基于 EF 的 MVC 5 控制器的具体步骤，请参看 9.5.3 节。

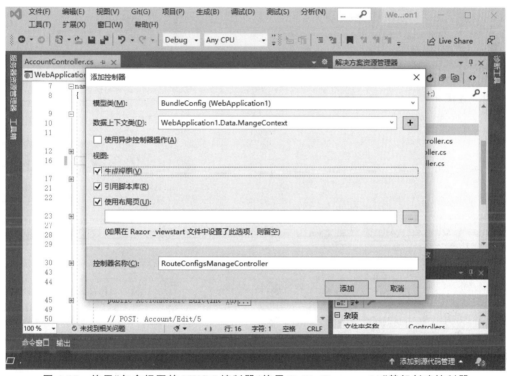

图 4-15　使用"包含视图的 MVC 5 控制器（使用 Entity Framework）"基架创建控制器

4.4　ASP.NET MVC 视图

在 4.3 节中创建了 LoginController 控制类，接下来将介绍如何创建对应的视图。ASP.NET MVC 5 所使用的视图是 Razor 视图引擎，Razor 视图模板文件使用.cshtml 文件扩展名，并提供了一个优雅的方式来使用 C♯语言创建所要输出的 HTML。用 Razor 编写一个视图模板文件时，将所需的字符和按键数量降到了最低，并实现了快速、流畅的编码工作流程。

在 LoginController 的代码中，右击 Index()方法，如图 4-16 所示，在弹出的上下文菜单中选择"添加视图"命令，在弹出的"添加已搭建基架的新项"窗口中选择默认的"MVC 5 视图"并单击"添加"按钮，可以完成 Index 这个 Action 所对应的视图创建，即图 4-17 中解决方案资源管理器的 Views\Login\Index.cshtml 文件。

修改该视图文件，在<h2>标签后面添加 HTML：<p>这是一个 MVC 框架程序</p>，代码如下。

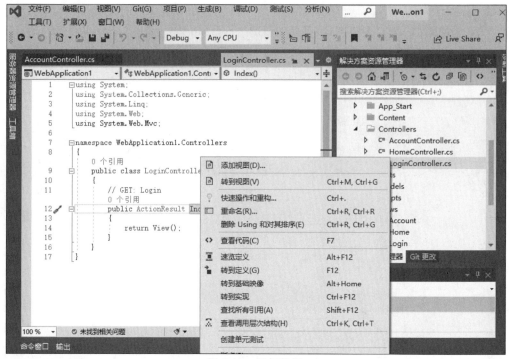

图 4-16　添加视图

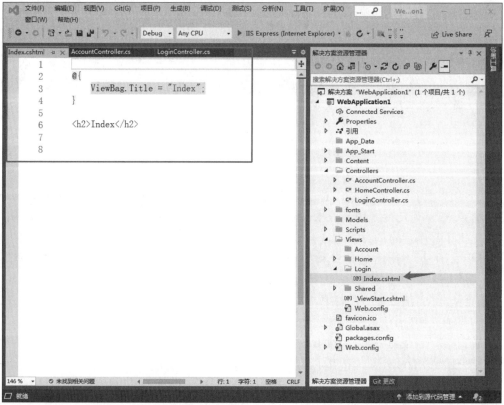

图 4-17　添加视图之后的解决方案资源管理器及新建视图代码

```
@{
    ViewBag.Title = "Index";
}
<h2>Index</h2>
<p>这是一个 MVC 架构程序</p>
```

输入"http：//localhost：44338/Login/Index"运行程序，效果如图 4-18 所示。

图 4-18 新视图运行效果

在控制器的 Index 方法中并没有做太多的工作，它只是执行了 return View()，该方法指定使用一个视图模板文件来 Render 返回给浏览器的 HTML。因为没有明确指定使用哪个视图模板文件，ASP.NET MVC 会默认使用\Views\Login 文件夹下与 Index 这个 Action 同名的 Index.cshtml 视图文件。但是这里的页面显示最左上角的"应用程序名称"几个字并不在 Index.cshtml 中，它是在一个公共布局页面中，即\Views\Shared 文件夹下的 _Layout.cshtml 文件，所有的子页面都共享使用这个布局页面，如图 4-19 所示。

图 4-19 公共布局页面 _Layout.cshtml

布局模板允许在一个位置放置占位所需的 HTML 容器，然后将其应用到网站中所有的网页布局。所有视图页面都会被"包装"在布局页面的@RenderBody()位置来显示，RenderBody 只是个占位符。例如，如果单击"关于（About）"链接，Views\Home\About.cshtml 视图会在@RenderBody()位置进行 Render。在图 4-19 中把 Html.ActionLink 方法的第一个参数从"应用程序名称"改为"我爱软件开发"，运行结果如图 4-20 所示。

图 4-20　修改公共布局页面后的运行效果

可以通过控制器向视图传递数据，修改\Views\Login\Index.cshtml 文件如下。

```
@{
    ViewBag.Title = "Index";
}
<h2>Index</h2>
<p>这是一个 MVC 架构程序</p>
<h1>@ViewBag.msg</h1>
```

修改 LoginController 类，代码如下。

```
public class LoginController : Controller
{
    //GET: Login
    public ActionResult Index()
    {
        ViewBag.msg = "这里是要传递的数据";
        return View();
    }
}
```

运行效果如图 4-21 所示。

本例中 ViewBag.msg 是控制层向视图层传输数据的一种方式，当然还有 ViewData 等其他传值方式。

图 4-21 通过控制层向视图层传值

4.5 ASP.NET MVC 模型

为了理解模型,这里在 ASP.NET MVC 项目中创建数据模型以便于展示数据查询的结果,首先需要在 SQL Server 2019 中创建一个数据库名为 usermanage,并在其中创建一个用户信息表 t_Users,表结构如表 4-1 所示。

表 4-1 用户信息表 t_Users 表结构

字 段 名	数据类型	长 度	主 键	含 义
Id	int		是	编号
UserName	nvarchar	50	否	用户名
Password	nvarchar	50	否	密码

数据操作过程就是把每一个用户信息封装成一个用户信息对象,存于一个用户信息类型的 List 集合中,然后循环遍历该集合,在视图中展示数据。

首先,在解决方案资源管理器右击 Models 目录,在弹出的上下文菜单中依次选择"添加"→"类"命令,如图 4-22 所示。

新建一个 userinfo 用户信息类,用来封装用户信息,代码如下。

```
namespace WebApplication1.Models
{
    public class userinfo
    {
        public int Id { set; get; }
        public string UserName { set; get; }
        public string Password { set; get; }
    }
}
```

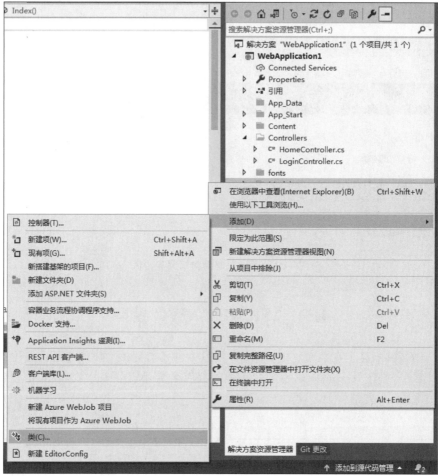

图 4-22　新建模型类

在 Models 目录下再新建一个用于操作用户信息表的业务类 DBOP，代码如下。

```
namespace WebApplication1.Models
{
    public class DBOP
    {
        public static string SqlCon =
            Convert.ToString(System.Configuration.ConfigurationManager.
            AppSettings["sqlcon"]);
        ///<summary>
        ///查询所有用户
        ///</summary>
        ///<returns>用户类集合</returns>
        public List<userinfo> UserList()
        {
            using (SqlConnection conn = new SqlConnection(SqlCon))
            {
                SqlCommand cmd = new SqlCommand();         //新建数据库操作类
                cmd.Connection = conn;                     //设置数据连接
                cmd.CommandText = "SELECT * FROM t_Users"; //设置查询语句
```

```csharp
            conn.Open();                                  //打开数据库连接
            SqlDataReader dr = cmd.ExecuteReader();       //执行 Reader 查询,存入 dr
            List<userinfo> u1 = new List<userinfo>();     //新建一个 User 类的集合
            while (dr.Read())                             //遍历 dr
            {
                userinfo u0 = new userinfo();             //临时 User 类变量 u0
                //把查询的当前记录各字段值赋值给对应的 u0 的属性
                u0.UserName = dr["UserName"].ToString();
                u0.Password = dr["Password"].ToString();
                u0.Id = int.Parse(dr["Id"].ToString());
                u1.Add(u0);                               //把有数据的 u0 加入 User 类的集合
            }
            dr.Close();
            conn.Close();
            //循环结束后,每一个用户数据都会被加入用户类集合 u1,最后返回 u1
            return u1;
        }
    }
}
```

在 LoginController 类中添加名为 LLview 的 Action,用于从 Model 获取用户信息列表,并返回视图。修改后的 LoginController 代码如下。

```csharp
public class LoginController : Controller
{
    //GET: Login
    public ActionResult Index()
    {
        @ViewBag.msg = "这里是要传递的数据";
        return View("Index");
    }
    public ActionResult LLview()
    {
        //从 Model 获取用户信息列表,通过 ViewData 传递给视图
        ViewData["UserList"] =
                new WebApplication1.Models.DBOP().UserList();
        return View();
    }
}
```

在 LoginController 类中,右击 LLview 方法名,创建相应的视图,视图文件名为 "LLview.cshtml",其代码如下。

```csharp
@{
    ViewBag.Title = "用户管理";
    List<WebApplication1.Models.userinfo> userlst =
            (List<WebApplication1.Models.userinfo>)ViewData["UserList"];
}
<table class="table" border="1">
    <tr>
        <th>
            用户名:
```

```
            </th>
            <th>
                密码：
            </th>
            <th></th>
        </tr>

        @foreach (var item in userlst)
        {
            <tr>
                <td>
                    @Html.DisplayFor(modelItem => item.UserName)
                </td>
                <td>
                    @Html.DisplayFor(modelItem => item.Password)
                </td>
                <td>
                    @Html.ActionLink("编辑", "Edit", new { id = item.Id }) |
                    @Html.ActionLink("详情", "Details", new { id = item.Id }) |
                    @Html.ActionLink("删除", "Delete", new { id = item.Id })
                </td>
            </tr>
        }
</table>
```

最终运行效果如图 4-23 所示。

图 4-23　最终数据显示效果

以上演示了创建模型，实现数据查询以及显示的具体实现。作为 Web 项目，还应该有一个重要的技术点就是表单数据的提交以及获取。

在解决方案资源管理器中项目节点 WebApplication1 上右击，添加一个名为 Form 的 HTML 页，设计文件 Form.html 的代码如下。

```
<html>
```

```html
<head>
    <meta charset="utf-8" />
    <title></title>
</head>
<body>
    <form action="Login/Jumpm" method="get">
        参数1:<input type="text" name="name1" />
        <br />
        参数2:<input type="text" name="name2" />
        <br /><br />
        <input type="submit" value="Submit" />
    </form>
</body>
</html>
```

表单提交时,会将表单中的数据提交给 form 的 action 属性指向的"Login/Jumpm",也就是控制器。

在 LoginController 类中创建一个名为 Jumpm 的 action 方法,用来接收从 Form.html 页面传递过来的参数值,代码如下。

```
public ActionResult Jumpm()
{
    string q1 = Request.QueryString["name1"];   //接收表单中名为 name1 的文本框的值
    string q2 = Request.QueryString["name2"];   //接收表单中名为 name2 的文本框的值
    @ViewBag.msg = q1 + "<br>" + q2;            //构造给显示页面 DetailView 传递的数据
    return View("DetailView");                  //跳转到视图 DetailView
}
```

右击解决方案资源管理器 Views\Login 目录节点,创建一个视图 DetailView,用于显示接收到的数据,设计 Views\Login\DetailView.cshtml 文件的代码如下。

```
@{
    ViewBag.Title = "传递过来的值是";
}

<h2>传递过来的值是</h2>
<h1>@ViewBag.msg</h1>
```

最终运行效果如图 4-24 和图 4-25 所示。

图 4-24　Form.html 页面运行效果

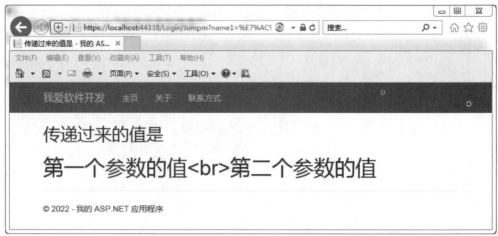

图 4-25 单击 Submit 按钮后，跳转视图运行效果

如果 Form 使用 Post 方式提交，需要将 Jumpm 方法中的 Request.QueryString["参数名"] 改成 Request.Form["参数名"]，代码如下。

```
public ActionResult Jumpm()
{
    string q1 = Request.Form["name1"];
    string q2 = Request.Form["name2"];
    @ViewBag.msg = q1 + "<br>" + q2;
    return View("DetailView");
}
```

此外，如果在 Action 方法上方加上[HttpPost]或[HttpGet]，那么该方法会被限制只能接收 Post 或 Get 的一种传值方式，如果强制使用另一种方法执行程序则会报错，如果不加任何限制，则两种传值方式都可以执行。

小 结

通过本章的学习，读者应初步掌握如何在 Visual Studio 2019 环境下运用 ASP.NET MVC 框架进行 Web 项目开发。限于篇幅，本章只对 ASP.NET MVC 框架进行了基本的介绍，有关 ASP.NET MVC 更深入的内容请读者自行学习。

本章的难点在于理解 MVC 模式的基本原理，掌握模型、控制器和视图之间的交互关系，并能够将 MVC 模式应用于恰当的开发场景。

习 题

新建一个 ASP.NET MVC 项目，实现用户的注册和登录。

第 5 章 前端框架 Bootstrap

5.1 Bootstrap 简介

Bootstrap 是美国 Twitter 公司推出的基于 HTML、CSS、JavaScript 开发的前端开发框架。Bootstrap 用于快速开发 Web 应用程序和网站,是由 Twitter 的 Mark Otto 和 Jacob Thornton 开发的。Bootstrap 使用简洁灵活且完全开源,是目前广受欢迎的前端框架。

5.1.1 安装 Bootstrap

1. Bootstrap 的下载

可以通过 https://v3.bootcss.com/下载本节所使用的 Bootstrap 的 v3.4.1 版本,Bootstrap 中文文档页面如图 5-1 所示。注意:Visual Studio 2019 已经内嵌了 Bootstrap v3.4.1 版本,无须再下载安装。

图 5-1 Bootstrap v3.4.1 中文文档首页

单击"下载 Bootstrap"按钮,将会看到如图 5-2 所示的三种下载方式。

为了更好地理解和更方便地使用,本节中使用 Bootstrap 的预编译版本,即使用第一种方式进行 Bootstrap 环境的安装。

图 5-2　Bootstrap 的下载方式

2. 预编译版

Bootstrap 提供了两种形式的压缩包,在下载的压缩包内可以看到以下目录和文件,这些文件按照类别放到了不同的目录内,并且提供了压缩与未压缩两种版本。

下载压缩包之后,将其解压缩到任意目录即可看到如图 5-3 所示的目录结构。

图 5-3　解压缩后的目录结构

图 5-3 展示的是 Bootstrap 的基本文件结构:可以看到已编译好的 CSS 和 JS (bootstrap.*) 文件,还有经过压缩的 CSS 和 JS (bootstrap.min.*) 文件。同时还提供了 CSS 源码映射表 (bootstrap.*.map),可以在某些浏览器的开发工具中使用。还有来自 Glyphicons 的图标字体,在附带的 Bootstrap 主题中使用到了这些图标。

预编译文件可以直接应用到任何 Web 项目中。

3. Bootstrap 源码

Bootstrap 源码包含预先编译的 CSS、JS 和图标字体文件,并且还有 LESS、JavaScript 和文档的源码。

less\js\和 fonts\目录分别包含 CSS、JS 和字体图标的源码。dist\目录包含上面所说的预编译 Bootstrap 包内的所有文件。docs\包含所有文档的源码文件,examples\目录是 Bootstrap 官方提供的实例工程。除了这些,其他文件还包含 Bootstrap 安装包的定义文件、许可证文件和编译脚本等。

5.1.2 Bootstrap 的主要特性

1. HTML 5 文档类型

Bootstrap 使用到的某些 HTML 元素和 CSS 属性需要将页面设置为 HTML 5 文档类型。在项目中的每个页面都要参照下面的格式进行设置。

```
<!doctype html>
<html lang="en">
    ...
</html>
```

2. 移动设备优先

移动设备优先是 Bootstrap v.3.4.1 的最显著的变化。在之前的 Bootstrap 版本中(直到 2.x)，需要手动引用另一个 CSS，才能让整个项目支持移动设备。而 Bootstrap v.3.4.1 默认的 CSS 本身就对移动设备优先支持，然后才是桌面设备(PC 显示器)。

为了让 Bootstrap 开发的网站对移动设备友好，确保适当的绘制和触屏缩放，需要在 ＜head＞之中添加视口(viewport)元数据标签，代码如下。

```
<meta name="viewport" content="width=device-width, initial-scale=1">
```

说明：

(1) width 属性控制设备的宽度。假设开发的网站将面向不同屏幕分辨率的设备浏览，那么将它设置为 device-width 可以确保它能正确呈现在不同设备上。

(2) initial-scale=1 确保网页加载时，以 1∶1 的比例呈现，不会有任何的缩放。

(3) 在移动设备浏览器上，通过为视口设置 meta 属性为 user-scalable=no 可以禁用其缩放(zooming)功能。禁用缩放功能后，用户只能滚动屏幕，使网站看上去更像原生 App。

```
<meta name="viewport" content="width=device-width, initial-scale=1,
        maximum-scale=1, user-scalable=no">
```

3. 排版与链接

Bootstrap 的排版链接样式均设置了基本的全局样式，分别描述如下。

(1) 为 body 元素设置背景色为♯fff。

(2) 使用@font-family-base、@font-size-base 和@line-height-base 变量作为排版的基本参数。

(3) 为所有链接设置了基本颜色@link-color，并且当链接处于悬停状态时才添加下画线。

这些样式都能在 scaffolding.less 文件中找到对应的源码。

4. Normalize.css

为了增强跨浏览器渲染的一致性，Bootstrap 使用了 Normalize.css，这是由 Nicolas Gallagher 和 Jonathan Neal 维护的一个 CSS 重置样式库，在 HTML 元素的默认样式中提供了更好的跨浏览器一致性。

5. 布局容器

Bootstrap 需要为页面内容和网格系统包裹一个 container 容器。Bootstrap 提供了两个类。

(1) container 类用于固定宽度并支持响应式布局的容器。

```
<div class="container">
  ...
</div>
```

(2) container-fluid 类用于 100% 宽度，占据全部视口的容器。

```
<div class="container-fluid">
  ...
</div>
```

注意，由于 padding 等属性的原因，这两种容器类不能互相嵌套。

5.1.3　Bootstrap 在 Visual Studio 2019 中的应用

Bootstrap 可用任何 Web 开发环境进行编写，本节实例使用 Visual Studio 2019 进行编写。下面给出第一个例子的实现步骤。

【例 5-1】　第一个实例 Hello BootStrap。

(1) 启动 Visual Studio 2019，新建一"ASP.NET Web 应用程序(.NET Framework)"，单击"下一步"按钮，如图 5-4 所示。

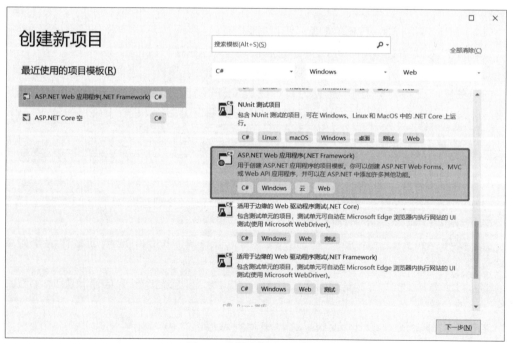

图 5-4　"创建新项目"窗口

(2) 在"配置新项目"对话框中输入项目名称并选择保存位置后单击"创建"按钮，如图 5-5 所示。

(3) 在"创建新的 ASP.NET Web 应用程序"对话框中选择项目类型——Web Forms 选项，然后单击"创建"按钮，完成项目创建，如图 5-6 所示。

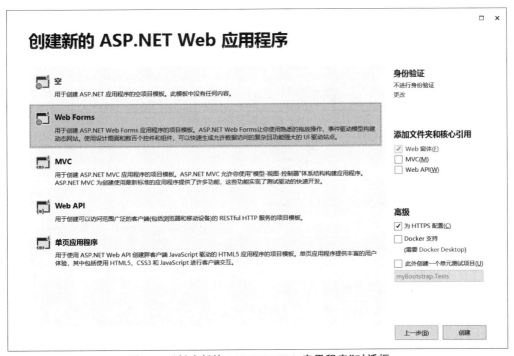

图 5-5 "配置新项目"对话框

图 5-6 "创建新的 ASP.NET Web 应用程序"对话框

（4）在"解决方案资源管理器"中可以看到，VS2019 中已添加了 Bootstrap 核心文件，如图 5-7 所示。

（5）右击项目，在弹出的右键菜单中依次选择"添加"→"Web 窗体"命令，在弹出的"指

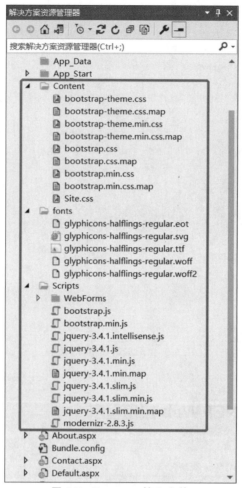

图 5-7　Bootstrap 核心文件

定项名称"对话框中输入项名称,如图 5-8 所示。

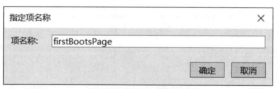

图 5-8　指定项名称

(6) 在文件中增加两个 meta 标签,代码如下。

```
<!-- 用以声明当前页面用最新的 IE 版本模式来渲染-->
<meta http-equiv="X-UA-Compatible" content="IE=edge" />
<!-- 让 Bootstrap 开发的网站对移动设备友好,确保适当的绘制和触屏缩放-->
<meta name="viewport" content="width=device-width, initial-scale=1.0" />
```

(7) 导入 Bootstrap 主样式,代码如下。

```
<!-- 导入 bootstrap 的主样式-->
<link rel="stylesheet" href="Content/bootstrap.min.css" type="text/css" />
```

注意：如自定义文件夹与本节代码不同，请将路径修改为自己命名的文件夹。

在文件的＜body＞标签中添加代码如下。

```
<h1>Hello,Bootstrap!</h1>
```

即完成第一个例子，如图 5-9 所示。

图 5-9　第一个例子

右击 firstBootsPage，可直接在浏览器中查看页面运行效果，如图 5-10 所示。

图 5-10　在浏览器中查看页面

后续例子均可在该项目下新建 HTML 文件运行。

5.2　Bootstrap 样式

本节将讲述 Bootstrap 底层结构的关键部分，包括网格系统、排版、表格、表单及按钮等。

5.2.1　网格系统

1. 简介

Bootstrap 提供了一套响应式、移动设备优先的流式网格系统，随着屏幕或视口尺寸的增加，系统会自动分为最多 12 列。它包含易于使用的预定义类，还有强大的 mixin 用于生成更具语义的布局。

2. 工作原理

网格（也称栅格）系统用于通过一系列的行（row）与列（column）的组合来创建页面布局，而网页的内容就可以放入这些创建好的布局中。以下介绍 Bootstrap 网格系统的工作原理。

（1）"行"必须包含在固定宽度的容器（container）或 container-fluid（100% 宽度）中，以便为其赋予合适的对齐（alignment）和内边距（padding）。

（2）通过"行"在水平方向创建一组"列"。内容应当放置于"列"内，并且，只有"列"可以作为"行"的直接子元素。

（3）类似 row 和 col-xs-4 这种预定义的类，可以用来快速创建网格布局。Bootstrap 源码中定义的 mixin 也可以用来创建语义化的布局。

（4）通过为"列"设置内边距属性，从而创建列与列之间的间隔（gutter）。通过为"行"元素设置负值边距（margin）从而抵消掉为 container 元素设置的内边距，也就间接为"行"所包含的"列"抵消掉了内边距。

（5）负值的边距可以使得页面元素向外突出。在网格列中的内容排成一行。

（6）网格系统中的列是通过指定 1～12 的值来表示其跨越的范围。例如，三个等宽的列可以使用三个 col-**-4 来创建。

（7）如果一"行"中包含的"列"大于 12，多余的"列"所在的元素将被作为一个整体另起一行排列。

（8）网格类适用于屏幕宽度大于或等于分界点大小的设备，并且针对小屏幕设备覆盖网格类。因此，在元素上应用任何 col-md-* 网格类适用于屏幕宽度大于或等于分界点大小的设备，并且针对小屏幕设备覆盖网格类。

3. 媒体类型查询

在网格系统中，使用媒体类型查询来创建关键的分界点阈值，代码如下。

```
/* 超小屏幕(手机,小于 768px) */
/* 没有任何相关的代码,因为这在 Bootstrap 中是默认的(Bootstrap 是移动设备优先) */
/* 小屏幕(平板,大于或等于 768px) */
@media (min-width: @screen-sm-min) { … }
/* 中等屏幕(桌面显示器,大于或等于 992px) */
@media (min-width: @screen-md-min) { … }
/* 大屏幕(大桌面显示器,大于或等于 1200px) */
@media (min-width: @screen-lg-min) { … }
```

我们偶尔也会在媒体类型查询代码中包含 max-width 从而将 CSS 的影响限制在更小范围的屏幕大小之内，如下。

```
@media (max-width: @screen-xs-max) { … }
@media (min-width: @screen-sm-min) and (max-width: @screen-sm-max) { … }
@media (min-width: @screen-md-min) and (max-width: @screen-md-max) { … }
@media (min-width: @screen-lg-min) { … }
```

4. 网格参数

Bootstrap 的网格系统在多种屏幕设备上工作的方式，如表 5-1 所示。

表 5-1 网格系统在各种屏幕上工作的方式

屏幕类型属性	网格系统行为	.container 最大宽度	类前缀	最大列宽
超小屏幕(手机)(＜768px)	总是水平排列	None(自动)	col-xs-	自动
小屏幕(平板)(≥768px)	开始是堆叠在一起的,当大于这些阈值时将变为水平排列	750px	col-sm-	～62px
中等屏幕(桌面显示器)(≥992px)		970px	col-md-	～81px
大屏幕(大桌面显示器)(≥1200px)		1170px	col-lg-	～97px

另外,对于各种类型的屏幕,其最大列数均为 12,间隔(gutter)宽均为 30px,可嵌套、有偏移且按列排序。

注意：后续文字描述中均以超小屏幕指代手机屏幕,小屏幕指代平板屏幕,中等屏幕指代桌面显示器,大屏幕指代大桌面显示器。

5. 基本的网格结构

基本的网格结构代码如下。

```
<div class="container">
    <div class="row">
        <div class="col-*-*"></div>
        <div class="col-*-*"></div>
    </div>
    <div class="row">…</div>
</div>
```

即为每一个列元素指定类。例 5-2 给出一个基本网格系统的例子。

说明：由于 Bootstrap 代码量较大,本节例题在正文中均只给出关键代码(省略部分由"…"开头的斜体文字说明),以读者能理解其结构及作用为主,完整代码请参考配套资料中的例题。

【**例 5-2**】 网格系统从堆叠到水平排列。

使用单一的一组 col-md-* 网格类,就可以创建一个基本的网格系统,在超小屏幕和小屏幕设备上是堆叠在一起的,在中等屏幕设备上就会变成水平排列的。所有列必须放在行内。

```
<div class="container">
    <div class="row">
        <div class="col-md-1">内容 1</div>
        <div class="col-md-1">内容 2</div>
        …省略 3~11 列部分代码
        <div class="col-md-1">内容 12</div>
    </div>
    <div class="row">
        <div class="col-md-4">内容 1</div>
        <div class="col-md-4">内容 2</div>
        <div class="col-md-4">内容 3</div>
    </div>
    <div class="row">
```

```
        <div class="col-md-6">内容1</div>
        <div class="col-md-6">内容2</div>
    </div>
    <div class="row">
        <div class="col-md-12">内容1</div>
    </div>
</div>
```

保存代码并运行,在超小屏幕及小屏幕上显示效果如图5-11所示。

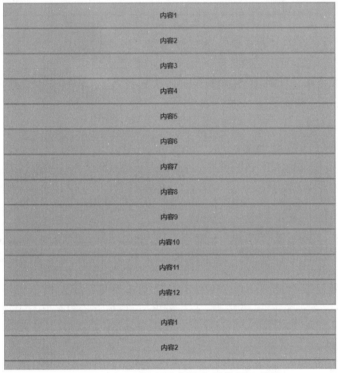

图5-11 例5-2 超小屏幕及小屏幕显示效果

在中等屏幕上显示效果如图5-12所示。

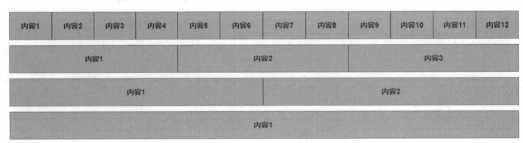

图5-12 例5-2 中等屏幕显示效果

说明:

(1) 为了呈现更好的效果方便观看,为网格系统(除例5-8嵌套列)的例子均设置了如下样式。

```
<style type="text/css">
.row {
    font-weight: bold;
    padding-top: 10px;
    line-height: 50px;
}
.row div{
    background: #c0c0c0;
    border: 1px solid rgba(101, 101, 102, 0.68);
    text-align: center;
}
</style>
```

以例 5-2 为例设置前效果如图 5-13 所示。

内容1	内容2	内容3	内容4	内容5	内容6	内容7	内容8	内容9	内容10	内容11	内容12
内容1				内容2				内容3			
内容1						内容2					
内容1											

图 5-13 未设置样式的显示效果

设置后效果如图 5-14 所示。

图 5-14 设置样式后的显示效果

(2) 在浏览器上进行不同屏幕显示效果的仿真。

编写好代码后,选择浏览器运行(以谷歌浏览器为例),此时显示的效果是在大屏幕上的显示效果。

若要显示小屏幕的显示效果或者中等屏幕的显示效果,可以使用快捷键 Ctrl+Shift+I 进入开发者工具仿真,单击如图 5-15 所示图标或者使用快捷键 Ctrl+Shift+M 进行设备切换。可以在如图 5-15 所示位置调整屏幕宽度,来进行不同屏幕显示效果的模拟。

图 5-15 中屏幕宽度为 992px,是中等屏幕,所以网格系统是水平显示。当更改屏幕宽度为 991px 时,该宽度属于小屏幕,所以网格系统是堆叠显示的,如图 5-16 所示。

如果不希望在小屏幕设备上所有列都堆叠在一起,可以使用针对超小屏幕和中等屏幕设备所定义的类,即 col-xs-* 和 col-md-*。例 5-3 给出了超小屏幕和中等屏幕的水平排列效果对比。

【例 5-3】 在超小屏幕和中等屏幕的水平排列。

如想要在超小屏幕上也可以实现水平排列而不是堆叠排列,可以使用.col-xs-* 来定义想要实现的排列效果。

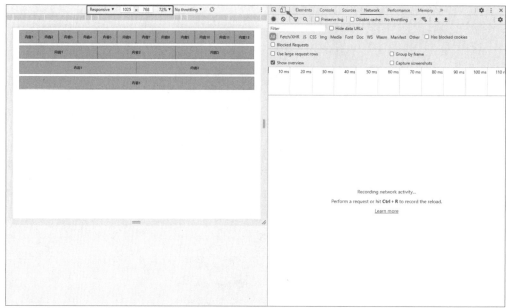

图 5-15　谷歌浏览器开发者工具-设备仿真

图 5-16　在小屏幕上堆叠显示

```
<div class="row">
    <div class="col-xs-12 col-md-8">.col-xs-12 .col-md-8</div>
    <div class="col-xs-6 col-md-4">.col-xs-6 .col-md-4</div>
</div>
<div class="row">
    <div class="col-xs-6 col-md-4">.col-xs-6 .col-md-4</div>
    <div class="col-xs-6 col-md-4">.col-xs-6 .col-md-4</div>
    <div class="col-xs-6 col-md-4">.col-xs-6 .col-md-4</div>
</div>
<!-- Columns are always 50% wide, on mobile and desktop -->
<div class="row">
    <div class="col-xs-6">.col-xs-6</div>
    <div class="col-xs-6">.col-xs-6</div>
</div>
```

代码中使用了超小屏幕 12 和中等屏幕 8 的 div，在超小屏幕中占据一行，而在中等屏幕中则与第二个 div 共同占据一行。此代码未定义 col-sm-*，那么在小屏幕上的排列效果和超小屏幕的排列效果是一致的。

保存代码并运行,超小屏幕显示效果如图 5-17 所示。

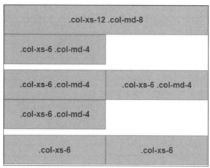

图 5-17 例 5-3 超小屏幕显示效果

中等屏幕显示效果如图 5-18 所示。

图 5-18 例 5-3 中等屏幕显示效果

【例 5-4】 在超小屏幕、小屏幕、中等屏幕呈现不同效果。

在前两个例子的基础上,通过使用针对小屏幕的 col-sm-＊ 类,可以创建更加强大的布局。

```
<div class="row">
    <div class="col-xs-12 col-sm-6 col-md-8">.col-xs-12 .col-sm-6 .col-md-8
</div>
    <div class="col-xs-6 col-md-4">.col-xs-6 .col-md-4</div>
</div>
<div class="row">
    <div class="col-xs-6 col-sm-4">.col-xs-6 .col-sm-4</div>
    <div class="col-xs-6 col-sm-4">.col-xs-6 .col-sm-4</div>
    <!-- Optional: clear the XS cols if their content doesn't match in height -->
    <div class="clearfix visible-xs-block"></div>
    <div class="col-xs-6 col-sm-4">.col-xs-6 .col-sm-4</div>
</div>
```

超小屏幕显示效果如图 5-19 所示。

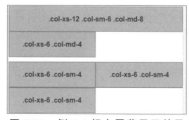

图 5-19 例 5-4 超小屏幕显示效果

小屏幕显示效果如图 5-20 所示。

图 5-20　例 5-4 小屏幕显示效果

中等屏幕显示效果如图 5-21 所示。

图 5-21　例 5-4 中等屏幕显示效果

【例 5-5】 多余的列(column)将另起一行排列。

如果在一个 .row 内包含的列数(column)大于 12，多余列的元素将作为一个整体单元被另起一行排列。

```
<div class="row">
    <div class="col-xs-9">.col-xs-9</div>
    <div class="col-xs-4">.col-xs-4<br>因为 9+4=13>12,所以多余的这些要另起一行排列</div>
    <div class="col-xs-6">.col-xs-6<br>后续 div 将沿着新行继续</div>
</div>
```

保存代码并运行，效果如图 5-22 所示。

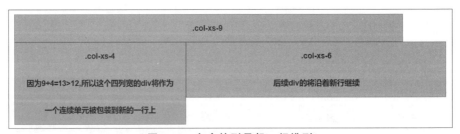

图 5-22　多余的列另起一行排列

6. 响应式列重置

在某些阈值时，某些列可能会出现比别的列高的情况，导致实际的效果并不是自己想要的。例 5-6 想要达到的效果是在超小屏幕上内容以四部分呈现（两行两列的效果），但是实际呈现的效果却是由于第二～四部分的高度不够，使得这几部分堆叠在了一起。为了克服这一问题，可以使用 clearfix visible-xs 类进行响应式列重置。

【例 5-6】 进行响应式列重置。

```
<div class="row" >
    <div class="col-xs-6 col-sm-3">
        <p>
            第一部分,想要显示在第一行第一列<br>
```

```
        …省略文字部分代码
        </p>
    </div>
    <div class="col-xs-6 col-sm-3">
        <p>
            第二部分,想要显示在第一行第二列<br>
            Bootstrap 是目前最受欢迎的前端框架。
        </p>
    </div>
    <!-- <div class="clearfix visible-xs"></div>   该行代码可进行响应式列重置-->
    <div class="col-xs-6 col-sm-3">
        <p>
            第三部分,想要显示在第二行第一列<br>
            可以通过 https://v3.bootcss.com/ 下载 Bootstrap。
        </p>
    </div>
    <div class="col-xs-6 col-sm-3">
        <p>
            第四部分,想要显示在第二行第二列<br>
            目前基本上所有的 Web 系统前端都在使用该框架。
        </p>
    </div>
</div>
```

保存代码并运行,未使用 clearfix 响应式列重置时页面效果如图 5-23 所示。

图 5-23 未进行响应式列重置效果

将代码中粗体部分注释符号去掉,即使用响应式列重置,运行效果如图 5-24 所示。

7. 列偏移

使用 col-md-offset-* 类可以将列向右侧偏移。这些类实际是通过使用 * 选择器为当前元素增加了左侧的边距。例如,col-md-offset-4 类将 col-md-4 元素向右侧偏移了 4 个列的宽度。

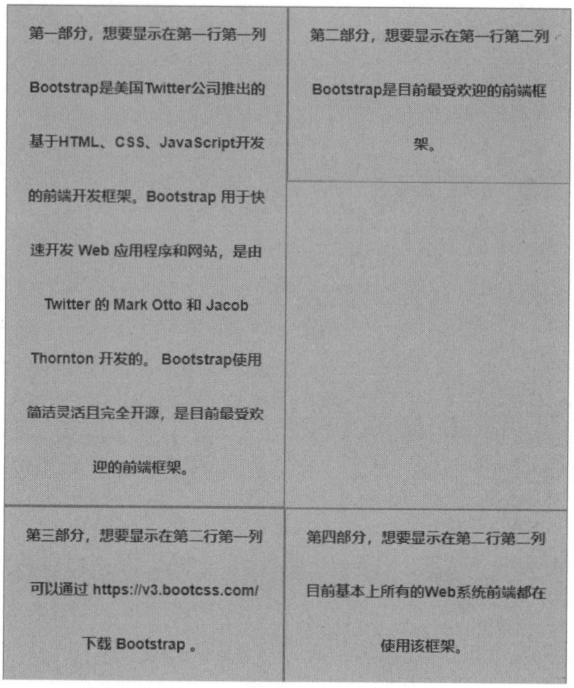

图 5-24　进行了响应式列重置效果

【例 5-7】 列偏移。

```
<div class="row">
    <div class="col-md-4">.col-md-4</div>
    <div class="col-md-4 col-md-offset-4">.col-md-4 .col-md-offset-4</div>
</div>
<div class="row">
    <div class="col-md-3 col-md-offset-3">.col-md-3 .col-md-offset-3</div>
    <div class="col-md-3 col-md-offset-3">.col-md-3 .col-md-offset-3</div>
</div>
<div class="row">
    <div class="col-md-6 col-md-offset-3">.col-md-6 .col-md-offset-3</div>
</div>
```

效果如图 5-25 所示。

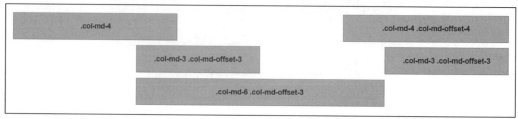

图 5-25　列偏移显示效果（中等屏幕）

8. 嵌套列

网格系统内还可以嵌套其他内容,可以通过添加一个新的 row 元素和一系列 col-sm-* 元素到已存在的 col-sm-* 元素内实现。被嵌套的行所包含的列不能超过 12 列。例 5-8

给出了嵌套列的效果。

【例 5-8】 嵌套列。

```
<div class="row">
    <div class="col-sm-9" style="background: #c0c0c0">
        第一层,占 9 列
        <div class="row">
            <div class="col-xs-6 col-sm-6" style="background: #b89b98">
                第 2 层,占 6 列
            </div>
            <div class="col-xs-4 col-sm-5" style="background: #b89b98">
                第 2 层,超小屏幕 4 列,小屏幕 5 列
            </div>
        </div>
    </div>
</div>
```

小屏幕上显示效果如图 5-26 所示。

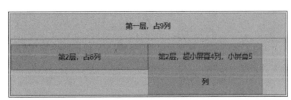

图 5-26　嵌套列在小屏幕上的显示效果

9. 列排序

通过使用 col-md-push-* 和 col-md-pull-* 类可以很容易改变列的顺序。其中,col-md-push-* 可以指定向右推的列数,col-md-pull-* 可以指定向左拉的列数。例 5-9 给出了改变列顺序的效果。

【例 5-9】 改变列顺序。

```
<div class="row">
    <div class="col-md-9 col-md-push-3">中等屏幕,占 9 列,向右推三列</div>
    <div class="col-md-3 col-md-pull-9">中等屏幕,占 3 列,向左拉三列</div>
</div>
```

效果如图 5-27 所示。

图 5-27　改变列顺序在中等屏幕上的显示效果

5.2.2　排版

1. 标题

HTML 中的所有标题标签即＜h1＞～＜h6＞均可使用。另外,还提供了 h1～h6 类,为行内(inline)属性的文本赋予标题的样式。

如果需要向任何标题添加一个行内子标题,只需要简单地在标题内添加 ＜small＞ 标签或赋予 small 类的元素,就能得到一个字号更小且颜色更浅的文本。例 5-10 给出了标题

的效果。

【例 5-10】 标题及<small>标签。

```
<h1>h1. Bootstrap heading <small>Secondary text</small></h1>
    …省略标题代码
<h6>h6. Bootstrap heading <small>Secondary text</small></h6>
```

保存代码并运行，效果如图 5-28 所示。

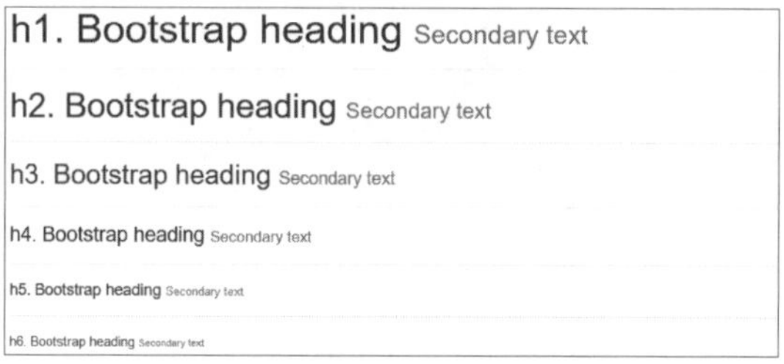

图 5-28　标题及<small>标签

2. 页面主体

Bootstrap 将全局 font-size 设置为 14px，line-height 设置为 1.428。这些属性直接赋予<body>元素和所有段落元素。另外，<p>元素还被设置了等于 1/2 行高（即 10px）的底部外边距。

3. 中心内容

通过添加 class="lead"可以让段落突出显示，得到更大更粗、行高更高的文本。例 5-11 给出了段落突出显示的效果。

【例 5-11】 段落突出显示。

```
<div>未添加 class="lead"的效果。</div>
<div class="lead">
    添加 class="lead"后的效果，可以让段落突出显示，得到更大更粗、行高更高的文本。
</div>
```

运行结果如图 5-29 所示。

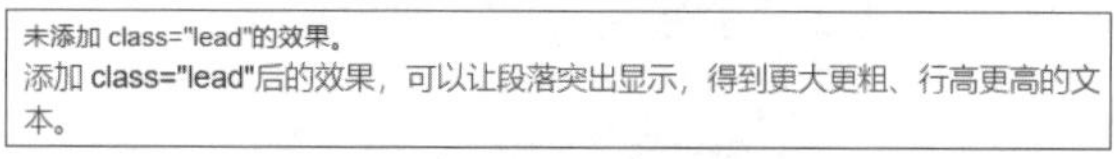

图 5-29　段落突出显示效果

4. 文本元素

对于文本元素，常用的效果包括删除线、下画线、强调效果（高亮显示）等，例 5-12 给出了各种标签对应的效果。

【例 5-12】 文本元素标签对应效果。

```
<div>这是<del>被删除的文本</del>,使用了 del 标签</div>
<div>这是<mark>想要强调的文本</mark>,使用了 mark 标签</div>
<div>这是<s>没用的文本</s>,使用了 s 标签</div>
<div>这是<ins>额外插入的文本</ins>,使用了 ins 标签</div>
<div>这是<u>为文本添加下画线</u>,使用了 u 标签</div>
```

```
<div>这是<strong>文本加粗显示</strong>,使用了 strong 标签</div>
<div>这是<em>用斜体强调一段文本</em>,使用了 em 标签</div>
```

保存代码并运行,结果如图 5-30 所示。

图 5-30 文本元素标签对应效果

5.2.3 表格

1. 表格元素

Bootstrap 提供了一个清晰的创建表格的布局。Bootstrap 支持的一些表格元素如表 5-2 所示。

表 5-2 表格元素及描述

标　　签	描　　述
<table>	为表格添加基础样式
<thead>	表格标题行的容器元素,用来标识表格列
<tbody>	表格主体中的表格行的容器元素
<tr>	一组出现在单行上的表格单元格的容器元素
<td>	默认的表格单元格
<th>	特殊的表格单元格,用来标识列或行(取决于范围和位置) 必须在 <thead> 内使用
<caption>	关于表格存储内容的描述或总结

利用这些元素可以很简单地创建一个基本表,如例 5-13 所示。

【例 5-13】 一个只带有内边距和水平分隔的基本表。

```
<!--通过添加 table 可以生成默认的表格样式-->
<table class="table">
    <caption>只带有内边距和水平分隔的基本表</caption>
    <thead>
    <tr>
        <th>表头 1</th>
        <th>表头 2</th>
        <th>表头 3</th>
    </tr>
    </thead>
    <tbody>
    <tr>
        <td>单元格 1</td>
        <td>单元格 2</td>
```

```
        <td>单元格 3</td>
    </tr>
    …省略第 2、3 行代码
    </tbody>
</table>
```

效果如图 5-31 所示。

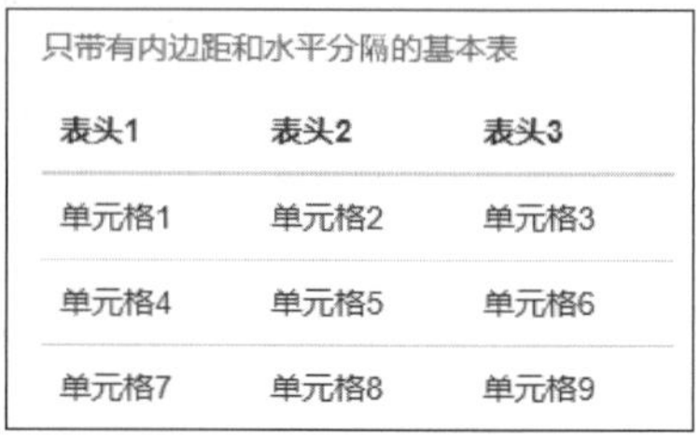

2. 表格样式类

Bootstrap 提供了丰富的表格样式类，如条纹状表格、带边框的表格、鼠标悬停效果的表格等。

（1）条纹状表格。

通过 table-striped 类可以给<tbody>之内的每一行增加斑马条纹样式，即隔行样式。修改例 5-13 中<table>标签的 class 为"table table-striped"，即可得到斑马条纹样式的表格。

（2）带边框的表格。

通过添加 table-bordered 类为表格和其中的每个单元格增加边框。修改例 5-13 中<table>标签的 class 为"table table-bordered"，即可得到带边框的表格。

（3）表格的鼠标悬停效果。

通过添加 table-hover 类可以让<tbody>中的每一行对鼠标悬停状态做出响应。修改例 5-13 中<table>标签的 class 为"table table-hover"，即可得到有鼠标悬停效果的表格。

（4）紧缩表格。

通过添加 table-condensed 类可以让表格更加紧凑，单元格中的内边距均会减半。修改例 5-13 中<table>标签的 class 为"table table-condensed table-bordered"，即可得到紧缩的表格。

3. 通过设置状态类设置颜色

通过表 5-3 的状态类可以为行或单元格设置颜色，例如，active 是浅灰色、success 是浅绿色等。例 5-14 给出了不同状态类对应的颜色。

图 5-31 只带有内边距和水平分隔的基本表

表 5-3 状态类及描述

状 态 类	描 述
active	鼠标悬停在行或单元格上时所设置的颜色
success	标识成功或积极的动作
info	标识普通的提示信息或动作
warning	标识警告或需要用户注意
danger	标识危险或潜在地带来负面影响的动作

【例 5-14】 为不同的行设置状态类。

```
<table class="table">
    <caption>为不同行设置不同状态类</caption>
```

```html
<thead>
    <tr>
        <th>状态类</th>
        <th>描述</th>
    </tr>
</thead>
<tbody>
<tr class="active">
    <td>.active</td>
    <td>鼠标悬停在行或单元格上时所设置的颜色(浅灰色)</td>
</tr>
…省略行状态类部分代码
</tbody>
</table>
```

保存并运行代码，效果如图 5-32 所示。

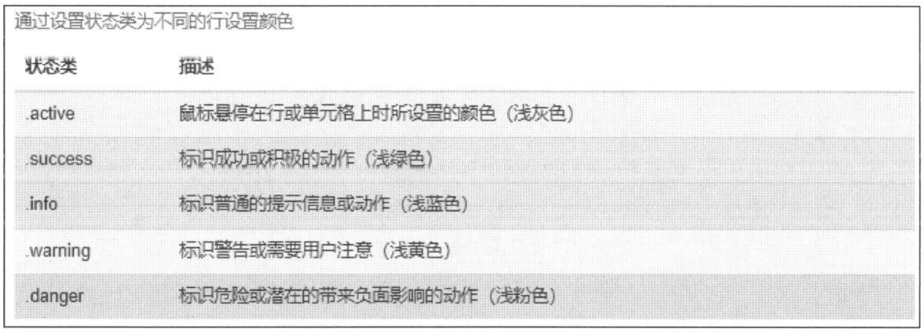

状态类	描述
通过设置状态类为不同的行设置颜色	
.active	鼠标悬停在行或单元格上时所设置的颜色（浅灰色）
.success	标识成功或积极的动作（浅绿色）
.info	标识普通的提示信息或动作（浅蓝色）
.warning	标识警告或需要用户注意（浅黄色）
.danger	标识危险或潜在的带来负面影响的动作（浅粉色）

图 5-32　添加不同状态类的显示效果

4. 响应式表格

通过把任意的.table 元素嵌套在.table-responsive 元素内，即可创建响应式表格。响应式表格的临界宽度值是 767，即表格内容宽度超过 767 时，一进入小屏幕模式即会出现水平滚动条。如果表格内容宽度低于 767，则会在屏幕宽度小于表格内容宽度时自动出现水平滚动条。

【例 5-15】　响应式表格。

```html
<div class="table-responsive">
    <table class="table">
        <caption>一个响应式表格</caption>
        <thead>
            <tr>
                <th>表头 1</th>
                <th>表头 2</th>
                    …省略表头部分代码
                <th>表头 6</th>
            </tr>
        </thead>
        <tbody>
            …省略表格内容部分代码
        </tbody>
    </table>
</div>
```

5.2.4 表单

1. 垂直表单

单独的表单控件会被自动赋予一些全局样式。例如，所有设置了 form-control 类的 <input>、<textarea> 和 <select> 元素宽度都将被设置为 100%，并设置了其他相应的样式如高度、行高、边距等，以保证控件水平宽度一致。而将 label 元素和表单控件嵌套在 form-group 中可以增大两组 form-group 之间的间距，使得布局更加美观。

【例 5-16】 一个垂直布局表单。

```html
<form action="#" name="myform01" method="get">
    <div class="form-group">
        <label for="example01">用户名:</label>
        <input type="text" class="form-control" id="example01" placeholder="请
            输入用户名">
    </div>
    <div class="form-group">
        <label for="example02">文件</label>
        <!--file 控件不使用 form-control 类,否则会变形-->
        <input type="file" placeholder="单击选择文件">
        <p class="help-block">请选择合适的文件上传</p>
    </div>
        <!--单选以及复选控件不使用 form-group 类以及 form-control 类,否则控件会
            变形-->
    <div class="radio">
        性别:<label><input type="radio" value="male">男</label>
             <label><input type="radio" value="female">女</label>
    </div>
    <button type="submit" class="btn btn-default">单击提交</button>
</form>
```

效果如图 5-33 所示。

2. 行内表单

行内表单是用来控制控件在一行中显示。为 <form> 标签添加 form-inline 类可使其内容左对齐并且表现为 inline-block 的控件，即该表单中的元素中间不换行。只适用于视口大于或等于 768px 宽度时(视口宽度再小的话就会使表单折叠)。例 5-17 给出了一个隐藏了 label 内容行内表单的例子。

图 5-33 垂直表单

【例 5-17】 一个隐藏了 label 内容的行内表单。

```html
<form action="#" name="myform01" method="get" class="form-inline">
    <div class="form-group">
        <label for="example01" class="sr-only">用户名:</label>
        <input type="text" class="form-control" id="example01" placeholder="请
            输入用户名">
    </div>
    <div class="form-group">
        <label for="example02"class="sr-only">密码:</label>
```

```
        <input type="password" class="form-control" id="example02" placeholder=
            "请输入密码">
    </div>
    <button type="submit" class="btn btn-default">单击提交</button>
</form>
```

结果如图 5-34 所示。

图 5-34 隐藏 label 内容的行内表单

注意：

（1）可能需要手动设置宽度。

在 Bootstrap 中，＜input＞、＜textarea＞和＜select＞元素宽度都默认设置为 width：100%，而在行内表单中，将这些元素的宽度设置为 width：auto；，多个控件就可以排列在同一行。

（2）一定要添加 label 标签。

如果没有为每个输入控件设置 label 标签，屏幕阅读器将无法正确识别。对于这些行内表单，可以通过为 label 设置.sr-only 类将其隐藏。还有一些辅助技术提供 label 标签的替代方案，如 aria-label、aria-labelledby 或 title 属性。如果这些都不存在，屏幕阅读器会采取使用 placeholder 属性，如果存在，则使用占位符来替代其他的标记。

3. 水平表单

水平表单与其他表单不仅标记的数量不同，表单的呈现形式也不同。如需创建一个水平布局的表单，需要向父＜form＞元素添加 form-horizontal 类，把 label 标签和控件放在一个带有 form-group 类的＜div＞中，为 label 标签添加 control-label 类，同时需要使用网格布局。例 5-18 给出一个水平表单。

【例 5-18】 一个水平表单。

```
<div class="container">
    <form action="#" class="form-horizontal">
        <div class="form-group">
            <!-- 还需要使用网格布局使得表单呈水平。-->
            <!-- 注意要给 input 一个父元素，使得 input 能够继承父元素的布局效果。-->
            <label class="control-label col-md-1">用户名</label>
            <div class="col-md-6">
                <input type="text" placeholder="请输入用户名" class=
                    "form-control">
            </div>
        </div>
        <div class="form-group">
            <label class="control-label col-md-1">密码</label>
            <div class="col-md-6">
                <input type="text" placeholder="请输入密码" class=
                    "form-control">
            </div>
        </div>
```

```html
            <div class="form-group ">
                <div class="col-md-offset-1 col-md-4">
                    <div class="checkbox ">
                        <label><input type="checkbox">记住我</label>
                    </div>
                </div>
            </div>
            <div class="form-group">
                <div class="col-md-offset-1 col-md-4">
                    <button class="btn btn-success" type="submit">提交</button>
                </div>
            </div>
    </form>
</div>
```

在中等屏幕上显示效果如图 5-35 所示。

图 5-35　水平表单(中等屏幕)

在小屏幕上显示效果如图 5-36 所示。

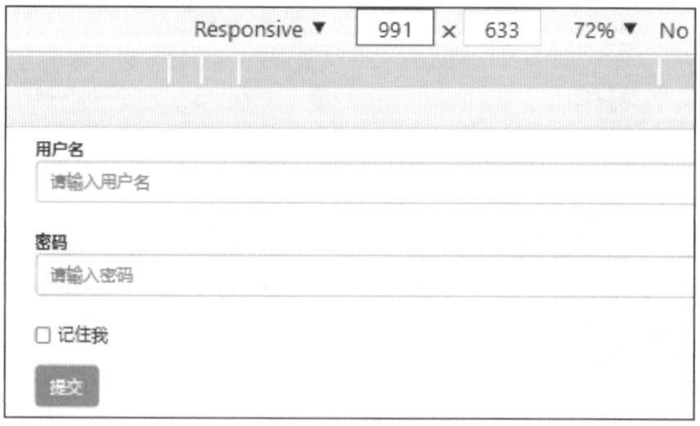

图 5-36　水平表单(小屏幕)

4．支持的表单控件

Bootstrap 支持大部分表单控件、文本输入域控件，还支持所有 HTML 5 类型的输入控件，包括 text、password、datetime、datetime-local、date、month、time、week、number、email、url、search、tel 和 color 等。只有正确设置了 type 属性的输入控件才能被赋予正确的样式。

(1) 输入框(input)：代码及效果参考例 5-16。

(2) 文本域(textarea)：Bootstrap 支持多行文本的表单控件。可根据需要改变 rows 属性。

【例 5-19】 一个文本域。

```
<form>
    <div class="form-group">
        <label for="name">文本框</label>
        <textarea class="form-control" rows="3"></textarea>
    </div>
</form>
```

效果如图 5-37 所示。

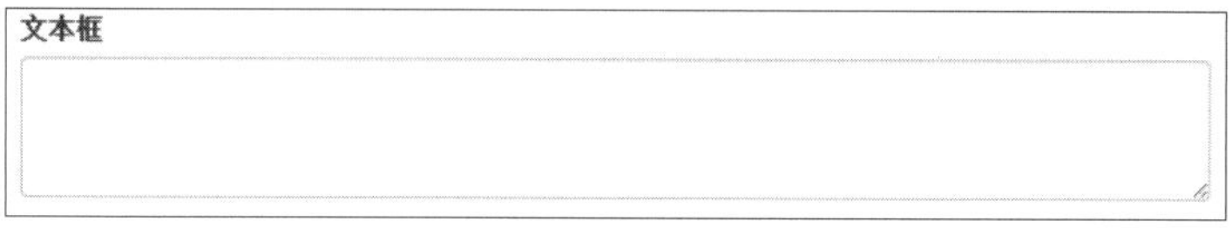

图 5-37 文本域

（3）复选框（checkbox）和单选按钮（radio）。

复选框（checkbox）用于选择列表中的一个或多个选项，而单选按钮（radio）用于从多个选项中只选择一个。默认显示会堆叠在一起，呈竖直排列。

【例 5-20】 一个默认显示的复选框和单选按钮。

```
<label for="name">默认的复选框和单选按钮的实例</label>
<div class="checkbox">
    <label><input type="checkbox" value="" name="optioncheckbox">选项 1
        </label>
</div>
    …省略选项 2 部分代码
<div class="radio">
    <label>
        <input type="radio" name="optionsRadios" id="optionsRadios1"
            value="option1" checked> 选项 1,有 checked,页面加载时该选项被预先
            选定
    </label>
</div>
    …省略选项 2 部分代码
```

效果如图 5-38 所示。

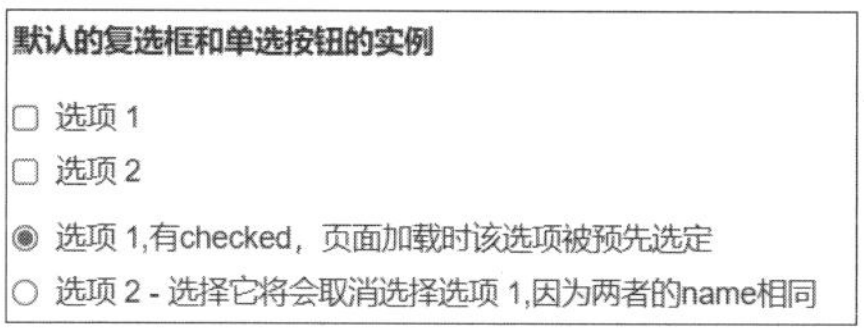

图 5-38 复选框和单选按钮

通过将 checkbox-inline 或 radio-inline 类应用到一系列的多选框或单选按钮控件上，可以使这些控件排列在一行。请读者自行修改代码查看效果。

（4）下拉列表（select）。

select 控件默认情况下只显示一项，下拉后可选择其他选项。但标记了 multiple 属性的 <select> 控件，默认显示多选项。例 5-21 给出了普通下拉列表和显示多项的下拉列表

对比。

【例 5-21】 下拉列表。

```html
<form>
    <div class="form-group">
        <label>普通下拉列表</label>
        <select class="form-control">
            <option value="">选项 1</option>
            …省略选项 2、3、4 部分代码
        </select>
    </div>
    <div class="form-group">
        <label>显示多项的下拉列表</label>
        <select class="form-control" multiple>
            <option value="">选项 1</option>
            …省略选项 2、3、4 部分代码
        </select>
    </div>
</form>
```

保存代码并运行,效果如图 5-39 所示。

图 5-39 下拉列表

(5) 静态控件。

当需要在一个 label 元素的后面放置纯文本时,为<p>元素添加 form-control-static 类即可。

【例 5-22】 包含静态控件的水平表单。

```html
<form class="form-horizontal">
    <div class="form-group">
        <label class="col-sm-2 control-label">Email</label>
        <div class="col-sm-10">
        <p class="form-control-static">email@example.com</p>
        </div>
    </div>
    <div class="form-group">
        <label for="inputPassword" class="col-sm-2 control-label">Password
            </label>
        <div class="col-sm-10">
            <input type="password" class="form-control" id="inputPassword">
        </div>
    </div>
</form>
```

效果如图 5-40 所示。

图 5-40　包含静态控件的水平表单

5. 表单控件状态

用户单击 input 或使用 Tab 键聚焦到 input 控件上时,可以使用 focus 选择器,Bootstrap 还为禁用的输入框定义了样式,并提供了表单验证的类。

(1) 输入框焦点。

当输入框获得焦点时,将某些表单控件的默认 outline 样式移除,然后对 focus 状态赋予 box-shadow 属性,如图 5-41 所示。

图 5-41　输入框焦点

(2) 禁用和只读输入框。

为输入框设置 disabled 属性,可以禁止其与用户有任何交互(获取焦点、输入等)。被禁用的输入框颜色更浅,并且还添加了 not-allowed 鼠标状态。为输入框设置 readonly 属性可以禁止用户修改输入框中的内容。处于只读状态的输入框颜色更浅(就像被禁用的输入框一样),但是仍然保留标准的鼠标状态。

【例 5-23】　禁用和只读输入框。

```
<input class="form-control" id="disabledInput" type="text" placeholder=
    "该输入框禁止输入" disabled>
<input class="form - control" type="text" placeholder="只读状态的输入框"
    readonly>
```

效果如图 5-42 所示。

图 5-42　禁用和只读输入框

(3) 禁用的控件集 fieldset。

为控件集设置 disabled 属性,可以禁用<fieldset>中包含的所有控件。

【例 5-24】　禁用控件集。

```
<form>
    <fieldset disabled>
        …省略控件集部分代码
    </fieldset>
</form>
```

效果如图 5-43 所示。

(4) 验证状态。

表单验证状态是在输入组件父 div 中添加 has-warning、has-error 及 has-success 等类,但是在 Bootstrap 4 中不再生效。

图 5-43　禁用的控件集

【例 5-25】　输入框的三种验证状态。

```
<form class="form-horizontal">
    <div class="form-group has-success">
        <label class="control-label col-md-2">输入成功</label>
        <div class="col-md-10"><input type="text" class="form-control" value=
            "边框及文字为绿色"></div>
    </div>
    <div class="form-group has-error">
        <label class="control-label col-md-2">输入错误</label>
        <div class="col-md-10"><input type="text" class="form-control" value=
            "边框及文字为红色"></div>
    </div>
    <div class="form-group has-warning">
        <label class="control-label col-md-2">输入警告</label>
        <div class="col-md-10"><input type="text" class="form-control" value=
            "边框及文字为棕色"></div>
    </div>
</form>
```

保存代码并运行，结果如图 5-44 所示。

图 5-44　输入框的验证状态

6. 表单控件尺寸

（1）高度。

可以使用 input-lg 使 input、textarea 和 select 控件比正常更大，而使用 input-sm 让控件比正常更小，但是都需要同时使用 form-control 类维持基本样式。

【例 5-26】　不同高度的表单控件。

```
<input class="form-control input-lg" type="text" placeholder="更大的输入框">
<input class="form-control" type="text" placeholder="默认的输入框">
<input class="form-control input-sm" type="text" placeholder="更小的输入框">
```

（2）宽度。

用网格系统中的列嵌套输入框或其父元素，都可以很容易地为控件设置宽度。

【例 5-27】 不同宽度的表单。

```
<div class="row">
    <div class="col-xs-2"><input type="text" class="form-control"
        placeholder=".col-xs-2"></div>
    <div class="col-xs-3"><input type="text" class="form-control"
        placeholder=".col-xs-3"></div>
    <div class="col-xs-4"><input type="text" class="form-control"
        placeholder=".col-xs-4"></div>
</div>
```

（3）水平排列的表单组的尺寸。

可以通过为水平排列的 label 元素和表单控件添加 form-group-lg 或 form-group-sm 类快速设置其尺寸。

【例 5-28】 水平排列的不同尺寸的表单组。

```
<form class="form-horizontal">
    <div class="form-group form-group-lg">
        …省略表单部分代码
    </div>
    <div class="form-group form-group-sm">
        …省略表单部分代码
    </div>
</form>
```

5.2.5 按钮

为<a>、<button>或<input>元素添加按钮类(button class)即可使用 Bootstrap 提供的样式。

1. 预定义样式

Bootstrap 提供了一系列可用于<a>、<button>或 <input> 元素上的预定义样式的按钮样式类，如表 5-4 所示。

表 5-4 可创建带有预定义样式的按钮的类及其描述

类	描 述
.btn	为按钮添加基本样式
.btn-default	默认/标准按钮
.btn-primary	原始按钮样式(未被操作)
.btn-success	表示成功的动作
.btn-info	该样式可用于要弹出信息的按钮
.btn-warning	表示需要谨慎操作的按钮
.btn-danger	表示一个危险动作的按钮操作
.btn-link	让按钮看起来像个链接（仍然保留按钮行为）

【例5-29】 创建一个带有预定义样式的按钮。

```
<!-- 标准的按钮 -->
<button type="button" class="btn btn-default">默认按钮</button>
<!-- 提供额外的视觉效果,标识一组按钮中的原始动作 -->
<button type="button" class="btn btn-primary">原始按钮</button>
…省略按钮部分代码
```

效果如图5-45所示。

图 5-45　各种按钮样式

注意：

（1）虽然按钮类可以应用到＜a＞和＜button＞元素上，但是导航和导航条组件只支持＜button＞元素。

（2）如果＜a＞元素被作为按钮使用，并用于在当前页面触发某些功能，而不是用于链接其他页面或链接当前页面中的其他部分，则必须为其设置role＝"button"属性。

2. 按钮大小

使用btn-lg、btn-sm或btn-xs就可以获得不同尺寸的按钮，而btn-block会创建块级的按钮，可以将其拉伸至父元素100％的宽度。

【例5-30】 创建不同尺寸的按钮。

```
<button type="button" class="btn btn-default btn-lg">大的默认按钮</button>
<button type="button" class="btn btn-primary btn-sm">小的原始按钮</button>
<button type="button" class="btn btn-success btn-xs">特别小的成功按钮</button>
<button type="button" class="btn btn-info">默认大小的信息按钮</button>
```

效果如图5-46所示。

图 5-46　按钮的各个尺寸对比

3. 按钮状态

Bootstrap提供了激活、禁用等按钮状态的类。

（1）激活状态。

按钮在激活时将呈现为被按压的外观(深色的背景、深色的边框、阴影)。

对于＜button＞元素，是通过active状态实现的，因此无须额外添加，但是在需要让其表现出同样外观的时候可以添加active类。对于＜a＞元素，是通过active类实现的。

【例5-31】 激活状态的按钮。

```
<p>
    <button type="button" class="btn btn-default btn-lg ">默认按钮</button>
    <button type="button" class="btn btn-default btn-lg active">激活按钮
        </button>
</p>
<p>
```

```
        <button type="button" class="btn btn-primary btn-lg ">原始按钮</button>
        <button type="button" class="btn btn-primary btn-lg active">激活的原始按钮
</button>
</p>
<p>
    <a href="#" class="btn btn-primary btn-lg active" role="button">激活原始链
        接</a>
    <a href="#" class="btn btn-default btn-lg active" role="button">激活的默认
        链接</a>
</p>
```

保存代码并运行,效果如图 5-47 所示。

(2) 禁用状态。

当禁用一个按钮时,它的颜色会变淡 50%,并呈现无法单击的效果。为<button>元素添加 disabled 属性,为基于<a>元素创建的按钮添加 disabled 类,都可使其表现出禁用状态。

4. 按钮标签

在<a>、<button>或<input>元素上都可以使用按钮类。但是建议在<button>元素上使用按钮 class,避免跨浏览器的不一致性问题。

【例 5-32】 不同元素上使用按钮类。

```
<a class="btn btn-default" href="#" role="button">链接</a>
<button class="btn btn-default" type="submit">按钮</button>
<input class="btn btn-default" type="button" value="输入">
<input class="btn btn-default" type="submit" value="提交">
```

效果如图 5-48 所示。

图 5-47 按钮的激活状态

图 5-48 各种元素应用按钮类的效果

5. 按钮组

(1) 按钮组的创建。

在 div 中直接使用 btn-group 可以创建按钮组,可以使用.btn-group-lg | sm | xs 来控制按钮组的大小。

【例 5-33】 创建不同大小的按钮组。

```
<div class="btn-group btn-group-lg">
    <button type="button" class="btn btn-default">大按钮 A</button>
    <button type="button" class="btn btn-default">大按钮 B</button>
    <button type="button" class="btn btn-default">大按钮 C</button>
```

```
</div>
<div class="btn-group btn-group-sm">
    …省略按钮代码
</div>
<div class="btn-group btn-group-xs">
    …省略按钮代码
</div>
```

效果如图 5-49 所示。

(2) 垂直方向按钮组。

要设置垂直方向的按钮可以通过 btn-group-vertical 类来设置。

【例 5-34】 一个垂直方向的<a>元素按钮组。

```
<div class="btn-group-vertical" role="group">
    <a href="#" class="btn" role="button">按钮 1</a>
    <a href="#" class="btn" role="button">按钮 2</a>
    <a href="#" class="btn" role="button">按钮 3</a>
</div>
```

(3) 自适应按钮组。

可以通过 btn-group-justified 类来设置根据屏幕大小进行自适应的按钮组。修改例 5-34 中 div 的 class 为"btn-group btn-group-justified",即可得到自适应的按钮组效果。

5.2.6 图片

Bootstrap 提供了三个可对图片应用简单样式的类。

(1) img-rounded：添加 border-radius：6px 来获得图片圆角。

(2) img-circle：添加 border-radius：50% 来让整个图片变成圆形。

(3) img-thumbnail：添加一些内边距和一个灰色的边框。

【例 5-35】 带有图片的按钮组。

```
<img src="/wp-content/uploads/2014/06/download.png" class="img-rounded">
<img src="/wp-content/uploads/2014/06/download.png" class="img-circle">
<img src="/wp-content/uploads/2014/06/download.png" class="img-thumbnail">
```

效果如图 5-50 所示。

图 5-49　按钮组的尺寸对比

图 5-50　图片按钮组

5.3 布 局 组 件

组件贯穿整个 Bootstrap 框架,可以通过一些变量来设置其属性默认值。

5.3.1 字体图标

在 Web 项目中经常要使用字体图标。虽然使用字体图标需要商业许可,但是可以通过基于项目的 Bootstrap 来免费使用这些图标。Bootstrap 捆绑了二百多种字体格式的字形,本节将通过实例讲解其使用。

1. 字体图标的获取

在下载的 Bootstrap 源文件 fonts 文件夹内可以找到字体图标,它包含下列这些文件。

(1) glyphicons-halflings-regular.eot。

(2) glyphicons-halflings-regular.svg。

(3) glyphicons-halflings-regular.ttf。

(4) glyphicons-halflings-regular.woff。

相关的 CSS 规则可在 dist|css 文件夹内的 bootstrap.css 和 bootstrap min.css 文件中查看。

2. 用法

如果需使用图标,只需要简单地使用下面的代码即可。

```
<span class="glyphicon glyphicon- * "></span>
```

其中,*表示具体图标内容。

3. 定制字体图标

对字体图标可以定制字体尺寸、颜色及文本阴影等。

【例 5-36】 定制字体图标。

```
<button type="button" class="btn btn-primary btn-lg">
    <span class="glyphicon glyphicon-user"></span> 默认状态
</button>
<button type="button" class="btn btn-primary btn-lg" style="font-size: 60px">
    <span class="glyphicon glyphicon-user"></span> 大号字
</button>
<button type="button" class="btn btn-primary btn-lg" style="color: rgb(212, 106, 64);">
    <span class="glyphicon glyphicon-user"></span> 定制颜色
</button>
<button type="button" class="btn btn-primary btn-lg" style="text-shadow: black 5px 3px 3px;">
    <span class="glyphicon glyphicon-user"></span> 文本阴影
</button>
```

保存代码并运行,结果如图 5-51 所示。

图 5-51 定制字体图标

5.3.2 下拉菜单

下拉菜单是可切换的,是以列表格式显示链接的上下文菜单,可以通过与下拉菜单 JavaScript 插件(Dropdown)的互动来实现,请注意,本节所有例题均需在页面的头部引入 js 文件,代码如下。

```
<!-- bootstrap 的核心 js 文件 -->
<script src="scripts/jquery-3.4.1.min.js"></script>
<script src="scripts/bootstrap.min.js"></script>
```

注意:如自定义文件夹与本节代码不同,请将路径修改为自己命名的文件夹。

1. 下拉菜单的创建

dropdown-menu 类用于创建下拉菜单,divider 类用于 li 标签中产生分隔线。

【例 5-37】 一个下拉菜单。

```
<div class="dropdown">
    <button type="button" class="btn dropdown-toggle" id="dropdownMenu1"
        data-toggle="dropdown">主题<span class="caret"></span>
    </button>
    <ul class="dropdown-menu" role="menu" aria-labelledby="dropdownMenu1">
        <li role="presentation"><a role="menuitem" tabindex="-1" href="#">
            Java</a></li>
        <li role="presentation"><a role="menuitem" tabindex="-1" href="#">
            数据挖掘</a></li>
        <li role="presentation"><a role="menuitem" tabindex="-1" href="#">
            数据通信/网络</a></li>
        <li role="presentation" class="divider"></li>
        <li role="presentation"><a role="menuitem" tabindex="-1" href="#">
            分离的链接</a></li>
    </ul>
</div>
```

结果如图 5-52 所示。

图 5-52 下拉菜单

2. 向上弹出的下拉菜单

可以用 dropup 类指定一个向上的下拉菜单。

【例 5-38】 一个向上弹出的下拉菜单。

```
<div class="dropup">
    <button class="btn btn-default dropdown-toggle" type="button" id="menu1"
        data-toggle="dropdown">教程 <span class="caret"></span></button>
    <ul class="dropdown-menu" role="menu" aria-labelledby="menu1">
```

```
            <li role="presentation"><a role="menuitem" tabindex="-1" href="#">HTML
</a></li>
            …省略菜单项代码
        </ul>
    </div>
```

保存代码并运行,效果如图 5-53 所示。

5.3.3 输入框组

从表单控件可以扩展出输入框组。可以通过为文本输入框 <input> 添加前缀或后缀实现对表单控件的扩展。为输入框组赋予 input-group-addon 或 input-group-btn 类,可以为 form-control 的前面或后面添加附加的元素。输入框组只支持文本输入框 <input>,不支持 <select> 和 <textarea>。

图 5-53 向上弹出的下拉菜单

1. 基本的输入框组

在输入框的任意一侧可以添加附加元素或按钮。还可以在输入框的两侧同时添加附加元素。

【例 5-39】 一个基本的输入框组。

```
<div style="padding: 100px 100px 10px;">
    <form class="bs-example bs-example-form" role="form">
        <div class="input-group">
            <span class="input-group-addon">@</span>
            <input type="text" class="form-control"
                placeholder="twitterhandle">
        </div>
        <br>
        <div class="input-group">
            <input type="text" class="form-control">
            <span class="input-group-addon">.00</span>
        </div>
        <br>
        <div class="input-group">
            <span class="input-group-addon">$</span>
            <input type="text" class="form-control">
            <span class="input-group-addon">.00</span>
        </div>
    </form>
</div>
```

保存代码并运行,效果如图 5-54 所示。

图 5-54 基本的输入框组

注意：不支持在输入框的一侧同时添加多个元素。不支持在单个输入框组中添加多个表单控件。

2. 输入框组的大小

为 input-group 添加相应的尺寸类（如 input-group-lg、input-group-sm），其内部包含的元素将自动调整自身的尺寸。不需要为输入框组中的每个元素重复地添加控制尺寸的类。

【例 5-40】 不同尺寸的输入框组。

```html
<div style="padding: 100px 100px 10px;">
    <form class="bs-example bs-example-form" role="form">
        <div class="input-group input-group-lg">
            <span class="input-group-addon">@</span>
            <input type="text" class="form-control" placeholder="Username">
        </div><br>
        …省略默认尺寸和小尺寸输入控件部分代码
    </form>
</div>
```

保存代码并运行，效果如图 5-55 所示。

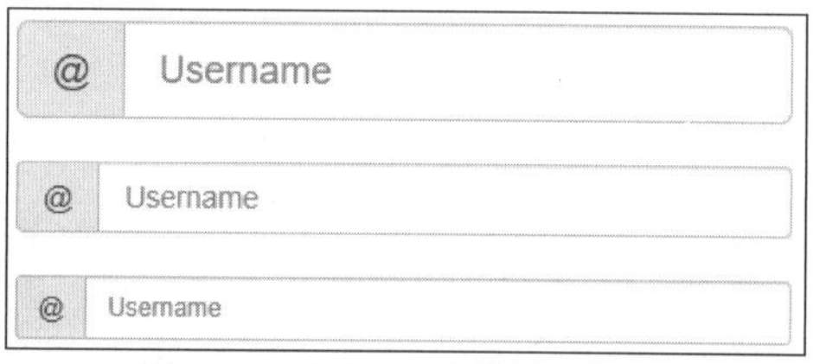

图 5-55 不同尺寸的输入框组

3. 作为附加元素的复选框和单选框

可以将复选框或单选框作为附加元素添加到输入框组中。

【例 5-41】 含复选框和单选框的输入框组。

```html
<div class="row">
    <div class="col-lg-6">
        <div class="input-group">
            <span class="input-group-addon"><input type="checkbox" aria-label=
                "..."></span>
            <input type="text" class="form-control" aria-label="...">
        </div><!-- /input-group -->
    </div><!-- /.col-lg-6 -->
    <div class="col-lg-6">
        <div class="input-group">
            <span class="input-group-addon"><input type="radio" aria-label=
                "..."></span>
            <input type="text" class="form-control" aria-label="...">
        </div><!-- /input-group -->
    </div><!-- /.col-lg-6 -->
</div><!-- /.row -->
```

效果如图 5-56 所示。

注意：本例效果要去除<head></head>中的自定义样式。

图 5-56　含复选框和单选框的输入框组

4. 作为附加元素的按钮

为输入框组添加按钮需要增加一层 input-group-btn 类来嵌套按钮元素。

【例 5-42】　含按钮的输入框组。

```
<div class="row">
    <div class="col-lg-6">
        <div class="input-group">
            <span class="input-group-btn"><button class="btn btn-default"
                type="button">Go!</button></span>
            <input type="text" class="form-control" placeholder="Search
                for...">
        </div><!-- /input-group -->
    </div><!-- /.col-lg-6 -->
    <div class="col-lg-6">
        <div class="input-group">
            <input type="text" class="form-control" placeholder="Search
                for...">
            <span class="input-group-btn"><button class="btn btn-default"
                type="button">Go!</button></span>
        </div><!-- /input-group -->
    </div><!-- /.col-lg-6 -->
</div><!-- /.row -->
```

效果如图 5-57 所示。

图 5-57　含按钮的输入框组

5. 作为附加元素的按钮式下拉菜单

在输入框组中添加带有下拉菜单的按钮，只需要简单地在一个 input-group-btn 类中嵌套按钮和下拉菜单即可。

【例 5-43】　含按钮式下拉菜单的输入框组。

```
<div class="row">
    <div class="col-lg-6">
        <div class="input-group">
            <div class="input-group-btn">
                <button type="button" class="btn btn-default dropdown-toggle"
                    data-toggle="dropdown" aria-haspopup="true" aria-
                    expanded="false">
                    Action <span class="caret"></span></button>
                <ul class="dropdown-menu">
                    <li><a href="#">Action</a></li>
                    …省略菜单项代码
                </ul>
            </div><!-- /btn-group -->
```

```
            <input type="text" class="form-control" aria-label="...">
        </div><!-- /input-group -->
    </div><!-- /.col-lg-6 -->
    <div class="col-lg-6">
        <div class="input-group">
            <input type="text" class="form-control" aria-label="...">
            …省略按钮式下拉菜单代码
        </div><!-- /.col-lg-6 -->
</div><!-- /.row -->
```

效果如图 5-58 所示。

图 5-58　含按钮式下拉菜单的输入框组

5.3.4　导航

Bootstrap 中的导航组件都依赖同一个 nav 类，状态类也是共用的。改变修饰类可以改变样式。

1. 标签式的导航菜单

以一个带有类 nav 的无序列表开始，添加类 nav-tabs，可实现标签式导航菜单。

【例 5-44】　一个标签式的导航菜单。

```
<ul class="nav nav-tabs">
    <li class="active"><a href="#">Home</a></li>
    <li><a href="#">SVN</a></li>
        …省略菜单项代码
</ul>
```

结果如图 5-59 所示。

图 5-59　标签式的导航菜单

2. 胶囊式的导航菜单

（1）基本的胶囊式导航菜单。

如果需要把标签改成胶囊的样式，只要将例 5-44 中＜ul＞标签的 class 替换为"nav nav-pills"即可。修改后的运行效果如图 5-60 所示。

图 5-60　基本的胶囊式导航菜单

（2）垂直的胶囊式导航菜单。

在使用class .nav、.nav-pills的同时使用类nav-stacked,可以让胶囊垂直堆叠。将例5-44中＜ul＞标签的class替换为"nav nav-pills nav-stacked"即可。

3. 两端对齐的导航

在屏幕宽度大于768px时,通过在分别使用nav、nav-tabs或nav、nav-pills的同时使用nav-justified,让标签式或胶囊式导航菜单与父元素等宽。在小屏幕上,导航链接会出现堆叠。

【例5-45】 两端对齐的胶囊式导航菜单和标签式导航菜单。

```
<ul class="nav nav-pills nav-justified">
    <li class="active"><a href="#">Home</a></li>
        <li><a href="#">SVN</a></li>
    …省略菜单项代码
</ul><br><br><br>
<ul class="nav nav-tabs nav-justified">
    <li class="active"><a href="#">Home</a></li>
        <li><a href="#">SVN</a></li>
    …省略菜单项代码
</ul>
```

中等屏幕上的效果如图5-61所示。

图5-61 中等屏幕显示两端对齐的导航菜单

4. 带有下拉菜单的标签导航

导航菜单与下拉菜单使用相似的语法。默认情况下,列表项的超链接与一些数据属性配合可以触发带有dropdown-menu类的无序列表。

向标签添加下拉菜单的步骤如下。

（1）以一个带有nav类的无序列表开始。

（2）添加nav-tabs类。

（3）添加带有dropdown-menu类的无序列表。

【例5-46】 带有下拉菜单的标签式导航菜单。

```
<ul class="nav nav-tabs">
    <li class="active"><a href="#">Home</a></li>
    …省略菜单项代码
    <li class="dropdown">
      <a class="dropdown-toggle" data-toggle="dropdown" href="#">
      Java <span class="caret"></span></a>
      <ul class="dropdown-menu">
          …省略菜单项代码
      </ul>
```

```
          </li>
          <li><a href="#">PHP</a></li>
</ul>
```

结果如图 5-62 所示。

图 5-62　带有下拉菜单的标签导航

5.3.5　其他组件

除了上述布局组件，Bootstrap 还提供了很多其他组件，包括导航栏、分页、标签、徽章、页面标题、缩略图等。限于篇幅，本教材无法给出所有组件的实例，但是其他组件的使用方式和本节给出的组件是一致的，只是对应不同的 Bootstrap 类而已，请读者自行查阅官方文档。

5.4　JavaScript

JavaScript 插件可以单个引入（使用 Bootstrap 提供的单个 *.js 文件），或者一次性全部引入（使用 bootstrap.js 或压缩版的 bootstrap.min.js）。所有的插件依赖于 jQuery。所以必须在插件文件之前引用 jQuery。

在 VS2019 中创建的 ASP.NET Web 应用程序已默认引用了一系列 js 文件，可在项目资源管理器中 App_start 文件夹下的 BundleConfig.cs 文件中进行查看，如图 5-63 所示。

图 5-63　VS 中对 js 文件的引用

在该文件中加入如下代码。

```
//jQuery js
bundles.Add(new ScriptBundle("~/bundles/jquery").Include("~/Scripts
    /jquery-{version}.js"));
//jQuery validate
bundles.Add(new ScriptBundle("~/bundles/jqueryval").Include("~/Scripts
    /jquery.validate*"));
//bootstrap js
bundles.Add(new ScriptBundle("~/bundles/bootstrap").Include("~/Scripts
    /bootstrap.js"));
bundles.Add(new ScriptBundle("~/bundles/adminlte").Include("~/Scripts
    /adminlte.js"));
//css
bundles.Add(new StyleBundle("~/Content/css").Include("~/Content/bootstrap.css",
    "~/Content/AdminLTE.css"));
```

即可引用 Bootstrap 中的 js 文件。

5.4.1 标签页内容

可以通过结合一些 data 属性,轻松地创建一个标签页,而不需要自己编写 JavaScript 代码,这是 Bootstrap 中的一等 API,也应该是设计页面的首选方式。通过这个插件可以把内容放置在标签页或者是胶囊式标签页甚至是下拉菜单标签页中。

1. 启动标签页的方法

可以通过设置 data 属性和使用 js 两种方式启动标签页。

(1) 设置 data 属性方式需要添加 data-toggle="tab"或 data-toggle="pill"到文本超链接中。添加 nav 和 nav-tabs 类到 ul 中,将会应用 Bootstrap 标签样式;添加 nav 和 nav-pills 类到 ul 中,将会应用 Bootstrap 胶囊样式。

```
<ul class="nav nav-tabs">
    <li><a href="#identifier" data-toggle="tab">Home</a></li>
    ...
</ul>
```

(2) 通过 JavaScript 来启动标签页。

```
$('#myTab a').click(function (e) {
    e.preventDefault()
    $(this).tab('show')
}
```

2. 设置 data 属性方式实现标签页

如果需要为标签页设置淡入淡出效果,请添加 fade 到每个 tab-pane 后面。第一个标签页必须添加 in 类,以便淡入显示初始内容,代码如下。

```
<div class="tab-content">
    <div class="tab-pane fade in active" id="home">...</div>
    <div class="tab-pane fade" id="svn">...</div>
    <div class="tab-pane fade" id="ios">...</div>
    <div class="tab-pane fade" id="java">...</div>
</div>
```

【例 5-47】 一个有淡入淡出效果的标签页。

```html
<ul id="myTab" class="nav nav-tabs">
    <li class="active">
        <a href="#home" data-toggle="tab">
            Bootstrap
        </a>
    </li>
    <li><a href="#ios" data-toggle="tab">iOS</a></li>
    <li class="dropdown">
        <a href="#" id="myTabDrop1" class="dropdown-toggle"
          data-toggle="dropdown">Java
            <b class="caret"></b>
        </a>
        <ul class="dropdown-menu" role="menu" aria-labelledby="myTabDrop1">
            <li><a href="#jmeter" tabindex="-1" data-toggle="tab">
                jmeter</a></li>
            <li><a href="#ejb" tabindex="-1" data-toggle="tab">ejb</a></li>
        </ul>
    </li>
</ul>
<div id="myTabContent" class="tab-content">
    <div class="tab-pane fade in active" id="home">
        <p>Bootstrap 是一个用于快速开发 Web 应用程序和网站的前端框架,是基于 HTML、
           CSS、JavaScript 的。Bootstrap 是由 Twitter 的 Mark Otto 和 JacobThornton
           开发的。</p>
    </div>
    <div class="tab-pane fade" id="ios">
        <p>iOS 是一个由苹果公司开发和发布的手机操作系统。</p>
    </div>
    <div class="tab-pane fade" id="jmeter">
        <p>jMeter 是一款开源的测试软件。</p>
    </div>
    <div class="tab-pane fade" id="ejb">
        <p>Enterprise Java Beans(EJB)是一个创建高度可扩展性和强大企业级应用程序的
            开发架构。
        </p>
    </div>
</div>
```

结果如图 5-64 所示。可以看出,第一个标签页被激活。

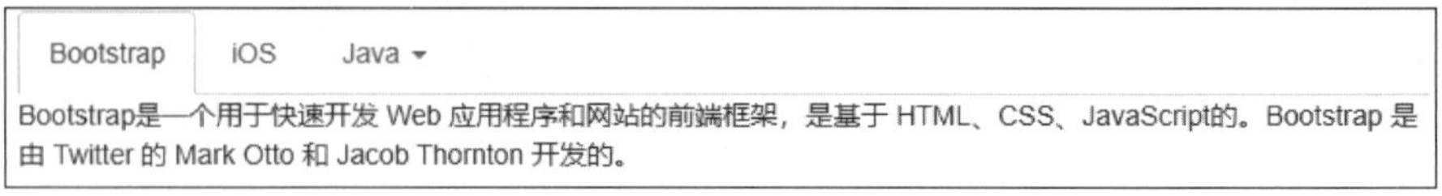

图 5-64 淡入淡出效果

3. 使用 JavaScript 方式实现标签页

使用 $().tab 方法可以激活标签页元素和内容容器。标签页需要用一个 data-target 或者一个指向 DOM 中容器节点的 href,代码如下。

```
//通过名称选取标签页
$('#myTab a[href="#profile"]').tab('show')
//选取第一个标签页
$('#myTab a:first').tab('show')
//选取最后一个标签页
$('#myTab a:last').tab('show')
//选取第三个标签页(从 0 开始索引)
$('#myTab li:eq(2) a').tab('show')
```

修改例 5-47 的代码,在页面头部增加以下 JavaScript 代码,可激活第二个标签页。

```
<script>
    $(function () {
        $('#myTab li:eq(1) a').tab('show');    //索引从 0 开始
    });
</script>
```

4. 事件

标签页(Tab)插件中要用到的事件如表 5-5 所示。

表 5-5 标签页(Tab)插件常用事件及其描述

事 件	描 述
show.bs.tab	该事件在标签页显示时触发,但是必须在新标签页被显示之前。分别使用 event.target 和 event.relatedTarget 来定位到激活的标签页和前一个激活的标签页
shown.bs.tab	该事件在标签页显示时触发,但是必须在某个标签页已经显示之后。分别使用 event.target 和 event.relatedTarget 来定位到激活的标签页和前一个激活的标签页

继续修改例 5-47 的代码,在标签页前面增加如下代码,用来显示结果。

```
<hr>
<p class="active-tab"><strong>激活的标签页</strong>:<span></span></p>
<p class="previous-tab"><strong>前一个激活的标签页</strong>:<span></span></p>
<hr>
<!--复制例 5-47 代码-->
…省略例 5-47 代码
```

同时在页面头部增加以下 JavaScript 代码,用来获取当前激活标签页和上一个激活标签页。

```
<script>
    $(function(){
        $('a[data-toggle="tab"]').on('shown.bs.tab', function (e) {
            //获取已激活的标签页的名称
            var activeTab = $(e.target).text();
            //获取前一个激活的标签页的名称
            var previousTab = $(e.relatedTarget).text();
            $(".active-tab span").html(activeTab);
            $(".previous-tab span").html(previousTab);
        });
    });
</script>
```

保存并运行后，默认激活的是第一个标签页，单击切换到第二个标签页，结果如图 5-65 所示。

图 5-65　获取正在激活以及前一个激活页面

5.4.2　模态对话框

模态对话框（Modal），简称模态框，是覆盖在父窗体上的子窗体。通常，目的是显示一个独立的页面，可以在不离开父窗体的情况下有一些互动。子窗体可提供信息交互等。如果想要单独引用该插件的功能，可以单独引用 modal.js，如已引用 bootstrap.js 或压缩版的 bootstrap.min.js 则不用重复引用。

1. 创建模态对话框的方法

可以通过设置 data 属性和使用 JavaScript 两种方式创建模态对话框。

（1）设置 data 属性方式在控制器元素（如按钮或者链接）上设置属性 data-toggle="modal"，同时设置 data-target="#identifier" 或 href="#identifier" 来指定要切换的特定的模态框（带有 id="identifier"）。

（2）使用 JavaScript 创建模态对话框，只需要简单的一行 JavaScript 来调用带有 id="identifier" 的模态框，代码如下。

```
$('#identifier').modal(options)
```

2. 设置 data 属性创建模态框

【例 5-48】　通过设置 data 属性创建一个按钮触发的模态框。

```html
<h2>创建模态框(Modal)</h2>
<!-- 按钮触发模态框 -->
<button class="btn btn-primary btn-lg" 
        data-toggle="modal" data-target="#myModal">开始演示模态框</button>
<!-- 模态框(Modal) -->
<div class="modal fade" id="myModal" tabindex="-1" role="dialog"
        aria-labelledby="myModalLabel" aria-hidden="true">
    <div class="modal-dialog">
        <div class="modal-content">
            <div class="modal-header">
                <button type="button" class="close" data-dismiss="modal"
                        aria-hidden="true">&times;</button>
                <h4 class="modal-title" id="myModalLabel">模态框(Modal)标题</h4>
            </div>
            <div class="modal-body">在这里添加一些文本</div>
```

```
            <div class="modal-footer">
                <button type="button" class="btn btn-default" data-dismiss=
                    "modal">关闭</button>
                <button type="button" class="btn btn-primary">提交更改</button>
            </div>
        </div><!-- /.modal-content -->
    </div><!-- /.modal -->
</div>
```

保存后运行页面,结果如图 5-66 所示。

图 5-66　基本模态框

说明:
- aria-labelledby="myModalLabel",该属性引用模态框的标题。
- 属性 aria-hidden="true" 用于保持模态窗口不可见,直到触发器被触发为止(如单击在相关的按钮上)。
- ＜div class="modal-header"＞,modal-header 是为模态窗口的头部定义样式的类。
- class="close",close 是一个 CSS 类,用于为模态窗口的"关闭"按钮设置样式。
- data-dismiss="modal",是一个自定义的 HTML 5 data 属性。在这里它被用于关闭模态窗口。
- class="modal-body" 和 class="modal-footer" 是 Bootstrap CSS 的一个样式类,用于为模态窗口的主体和底部设置样式。

有一些选项可以用来定制模态窗口(Modal Window)的外观和感观,它们是通过 data 属性或 JavaScript 来传递的。这些选项如表 5-6 所示。

表 5-6　用来定制模态框外观和感观的一些选项

选项名称	类型/默认值	Data 属性名称	描　　述
backdrop	boolean 或 string 'static'默认值: true	data-backdrop	指定一个静态的背景,当用户单击模态框外部时不会关闭模态框
keyboard	boolean 默认值: true	data-keyboard	当按下 Esc 键时关闭模态框,设置为 false 时则按键无效
show	boolean 默认值: true	data-show	当初始化时显示模态框
remote	path 默认值: false	data-remote	使用 jQuery.load 方法,为模态框的主体注入内容。如果添加了一个带有有效 URL 的 href,则会加载其中的内容

可与 modal() 一起使用的一些有用的方法如表 5-7 所示。

表 5-7　可与 modal() 一起使用的一些有用的方法

方　　法	描　　述
Options：.modal(options)	把内容作为模态框激活。接收一个可选的选项对象
Toggle：.modal('toggle')	手动切换模态框
Show：.modal('show')	手动打开模态框
Hide：.modal('hide')	手动隐藏模态框

3. 事件

模态框中要用到的事件如表 5-8 所示。这些事件可在函数中当钩子使用。

表 5-8　模态框中要用到的事件

事　　件	描　　述
show.bs.modal	在调用 show 方法后触发
shown.bs.modal	当模态框对用户可见时触发（将等待 CSS 过渡效果完成）
hide.bs.modal	当调用 hide 实例方法时触发
hidden.bs.modal	当模态框完全对用户隐藏时触发

修改例 5-48 中的代码，增加如下 JavaScript 代码，可实现调用 hide 实例时显示模态框。

```
<script>
    $(function() {
        $('#myModal').modal('hide')
    });
</script>
<script>
    $(function() {
        $('#myModal').on('hide.bs.modal',
        function() {
            alert('嘿,我听说您喜欢模态框...');
        })
    });
</script>
```

保存代码并运行，在单击模态对话框的"关闭"按钮时将触发 hide 事件，弹出消息框，结果如图 5-67 所示。

图 5-67　hide 事件触发模态框

5.4.3 工具提示和弹出对话框

1. 工具提示

如果想要单独引用该插件的功能，可以单独引用 tooltip.js，如已引用 bootstrap.js 或压缩版的 bootstrap.min.js 则不用重复引用。

可以通过设置 data 属性和使用 JavaScript 两种方式添加提示工具（tooltip）。

（1）设置 data 属性方式只需在一个超链接中添加 data-toggle="tooltip" 即可。超链接的 title 即为提示工具的文本。默认情况下，插件把提示工具设置在顶部，代码如下。

```
<a href="#" data-toggle="tooltip" title="Example tooltip">请悬停在上面</a>
```

（2）通过 JavaScript 触发提示工具，代码如下。

```
$('#identifier').tooltip(options)
```

注意：工具提示插件不像下拉菜单及其他插件，它不是纯 CSS 插件。如需使用该插件，必须使用 jQuery 激活它（读取 JavaScript）。使用下面的脚本来启用页面中的所有的提示工具（tooltip）：

```
$(function () { $("[data-toggle='tooltip']").tooltip(); });
```

【例 5-49】 通过 data 属性为超链接和按钮添加工具提示。

```
<h4>工具提示(Tooltip)插件 - 超链接</h4>
    这是一个 <a href="#" class="tooltip-test" data-toggle="tooltip"
            title="默认 Tooltip">默认 Tooltip</a>
    这是一个 <a href="#" class="tooltip-test" data-toggle="tooltip" data-
            placement="left"
            title="左侧 Tooltip">左侧 Tooltip</a>
    …省略顶部、底部和右侧 Tooltip 代码
<br>
<h4>提工具示(Tooltip)插件 - 按钮</h4>
<button type="button" class="btn btn-default" data-toggle="tooltip" title="默
    认 Tooltip">默认 Tooltip</button>
<button type="button" class="btn btn-default" data-toggle="tooltip" data-
    placement="left"
        title="左侧 Tooltip">左侧 Tooltip</button>
    …省略顶部、底部和右侧 Tooltip 代码
```

添加脚本如下。

```
<script>
    $(function () { $("[data-toggle='tooltip']").tooltip(); });
</script>
```

结果如图 5-68 所示。

工具提示插件还有一些属性、方法和事件，可增强各种效果，这里不再详述。

2. 弹出对话框用法

弹出框（Popover）与工具提示类似，提供了一个扩展的视图。如需激活弹出框，用户只需把鼠标悬停在元素上即可。弹出框的内容完全可使用 Bootstrap 数据 API 来填充。该方法依赖于工具提示。如果想要单独引用该插件的功能，可以单独引用 popover.js，它依赖于

图 5-68　超链接和按钮的工具提示

工具提示插件,如已引用 bootstrap.js 或压缩版的 bootstrap.min.js 则不用重复引用。

弹出框插件根据需求生成内容和标记,默认情况下是把弹出框放在其触发元素后面。可以通过设置 data 属性和使用 JavaScript 两种方式添加弹出框。

(1) 可以通过设置 data 属性在一个超链接或按钮标签中添加 data-toggle="popover" 即可,超链接的 title 即为弹出框的文本。

(2) 通过 JavaScript 启用弹出框,代码如下。

```
$('#identifier').popover(options)
```

注意:弹出框插件不像之前所讨论的下拉菜单及其他插件那样,它不是纯 CSS 插件。如需使用该插件,必须使用 jQuery 进行激活(读取 JavaScript)。使用下面的脚本来启用页面中的所有的弹出框,代码如下。

```
$(function () { $("[data-toggle='popover']").popover(); });
```

【例 5-50】　通过 data 属性添加弹出框。

```
<div class="container" style="padding: 100px 50px 10px;" >
    <button type="button" class="btn btn-default" title="Popover title"
        data-container="body" data-toggle="popover" data-placement="left"
        data-content="左侧 Popover 内容">左侧 Popover
    </button>
    <button type="button" class="btn btn-primary" title="Popover title"
        data-container="body" data-toggle="popover" data-placement="top"
        data-content="顶部 Popover 内容">顶部的 Popover
    </button>
    <button type="button" class="btn btn-success" title="Popover title"
        data-container="body" data-toggle="popover" data-placement="bottom"
        data-content="底部 Popover 内容">底部的 Popover
    </button>
    <button type="button" class="btn btn-warning" title="Popover title"
        data-container="body" data-toggle="popover" data-placement="right"
        data-content="右侧 Popover 内容">右侧的 Popover
    </button>
</div>
    <script>
        $(function (){
            $("[data-toggle='popover']").popover();
        });
    </script>
</div>
```

保存代码并运行,依次单击每个按钮,效果如图 5-69 所示。

弹出对话框还有一些属性、方法和事件,可为弹出对话框增加各种效果,这里不再详述。

图 5-69　按钮触发的弹出框

小　　结

Bootstrap 是基于 HTML、CSS、JavaScript 的，它简洁灵活，使得 Web 开发更加快捷，具有移动优先的特点。

本章讲解 Bootstrap 框架的基础，通过学习这些内容，读者可以轻松地创建 Web 项目。教程被分为 Bootstrap 基本结构、Bootstrap 样式、布局组件等几个部分，每个部分都包含与该主题相关的简单有用的实例。

习　　题

1. 制作一个垂直表单，要求包含如图 5-70 所示表单控件。

图 5-70　垂直表单

2. 将题 1 表单中填写的内容提交给后端，并保存于数据库。

第 6 章 图书管理系统案例开发

本章将讲解利用 C♯ 语言开发简单但完整的管理信息系统，主要以图书信息管理系统的系统管理、图书管理、读者管理、用户管理、图书借还管理等模块为主线进行管理信息系统开发的描述。

通过本章的学习，读者应该重点掌握简单管理信息系统开发的需求分析、设计和实现过程。

6.1 项目描述

随着社会信息量的与日俱增，图书馆的规模和存书量都比以往大得多，因此，图书管理部门就需要使用一种方便、有效的管理方式来管理图书馆的书籍。在计算机日益普及的今天，对图书管理部门而言，以前单一的手工检索已不能满足人们的需求，为了便于图书资料的管理，就需要有效的图书管理软件，这也是图书管理系统开发的目的和意义。

6.1.1 项目背景

图书管理系统主要完成图书信息维护、读者借出和归还图书等工作，而这些工作又是比较繁杂的，若采用低级的手工操作往往需要耗费大量的人力、物力，而且效率低，很容易出错。提高图书馆的管理效率，对图书馆来说是一个很大的问题。而图书管理系统的开发，解决了这样的问题，通过图书管理系统的使用，不需要太多的人力，只需要在图书管理系统的帮助下，就能掌控图书馆的管理，既方便又经济。

6.1.2 业务描述

图书管理系统主要业务如下。

1. 图书入库

图书入库主要是采购员将图书采购回来后，由采编人员编目，然后将这些新书添加到系统中。在添加新书时，采购员可能添加同类的书籍，对于已经录入到系统中的书籍，可以修改部分信息；还有可能删除录入的书籍，如新录入的错误的书籍，以及过时的、丢失的书籍等。

2. 借出图书

当读者需要借书时，工作人员进入到借书管理的界面，输入读者借书证号和图书号，系统会将相应的图书信息及读者信息显示在界面上，设定借出时间即可以单击"借出"按钮来完成借书，并且也可以将读者所有借书信息显示出来。

3. 归还图书

当读者还书的时候,工作人员进入还书管理的界面,输入读者借书证号和图书号,调出读者的借阅信息,判断该书是否有超期,是否需要做罚款处理;如果读者丢失了所借阅的图书,读者要赔偿一定的金额;读者也可以续借图书,系统还可以提示借书者是否还有其他已到期未还的书。

6.1.3 用户描述

图书管理系统开发的总体任务是实现图书的借阅和管理信息化,因此系统中既有面向读者的图书及个人信息查询接口,也有面向管理员的系统管理接口。

对于读者来说,所关心的问题主要包括以下几个。

(1) 如何方便地查询到图书馆中的书籍?

(2) 如何知道自己借阅过什么样的书籍?

(3) 如何确定自己所借的书籍是否到期,是否有罚款的记录等?

而对于图书管理员来说,所关心的问题主要有以下几个。

(1) 图书馆有哪些书?可不可以被借阅?不同类型的书都放在哪儿?图书入库的时候有没有相同的图书类型?

(2) 如何管理不同类型的读者?不同类型的读者分别可以借阅哪些书?每次的借书量和借书的期限是多长?

(3) 如何确定这些借书证是否可用?借书的归还期限如何?

6.2 系统需求

6.2.1 需求描述

图书馆是高等院校的重要组成部门,是教师和学生获取知识的重要场所。一直以来,传统图书管理的特点是,中小型书店、中小学的小型图书馆及各高校图书馆和资料室使用传统的人工方式管理图书档案、会员档案。这种管理方式存在着诸多缺点,如手续烦琐、效率低下、出错率高等,对大量资料的查询、更新及维护都带来不少困难。

随着计算机技术的飞速发展,利用计算机来获得和处理信息是当今信息管理的一大特点。伴随计算机硬件的快速发展,有关信息管理的软件——数据库系统软件也在迅猛发展着。所以将计算机信息技术应用到图书管理当中是当前时代发展的需要。本系统是结合实际情况开发的图书资料管理系统。系统开发的主要任务是针对原来管理办公的时效性、数据的正确性、操作的方便性上的不足,解决图书流通上的问题,实现图书信息管理的系统化、规范化和自动化,以最大限度提高操作人员的办公效率。

6.2.2 模块设计

1. 系统管理模块

系统管理模块的设计,主要是为了管理系统的用户,主要包括添加用户、浏览用户功能,为了保证系统的安全性,只有管理员才具有管理用户的权限,在该模块管理员可以添加、删除用户的信息。该模块共有三级权限,只有管理员才有最高权限,不同的权限管理的功能不同。有三级权限的是最高管理员,拥有所有的权限;其次是拥有两级权限的管理员,只能管理借书、还书以及图书查询和修改密码的操作;最低权限的管理员只具有查询和修改密码的功能。为了保证用户信息的安全性,该系统设计中管理员不具有修改用户信息的功能。

2. 图书管理模块

图书管理模块,设计了对图书的管理,主要包括图书分类和浏览图书的功能,以便于实现对图书的管理,拥有该模块管理权限的管理人员是最高管理员。为了方便图书的管理,把图书分为不同的类型,除了设计图书类型的总界面外,还有添加、修改图书类型的界面,管理员可以添加新的图书类型,删除错误的图书类型,也可以修改图书的类型和浏览所有图书的图书类型。对图书的管理同图书类型相似,可以对图书的信息进行添加、删除、修改和浏览所有图书的信息。

3. 读者管理模块

该模块主要负责对读者的管理,主要包括浏览身份和浏览读者功能,以实现对读者类型和读者基本信息的管理。不同类型的读者对应不同的借书规则,如最长借阅时间、最大借书量等;这样除了限制不同读者具有不同的图书借阅量外,也帮助了不同身份的读者合理地利用了时间。特别对学生而言,不会使学生过度沉溺于课外书。在对读者类型的管理中,可以添加、修改、删除读者的类型信息。

读者的信息管理,设计了浏览信息的界面,具有增加、修改、删除读者信息的操作,同时也设计了添加读者、修改读者的界面。在浏览信息界面可显示读者的借书证号、姓名、身份证号等详细信息,界面的设计在后面的章节中可以看到。

4. 用户登录模块

用户登录模块的设计主要是为了方便用户使用该系统。主要包括修改密码和重新登录功能,以便于实现对不同用户的登录相关操作,当用户登录时如果发生错误,可以重新登录该系统,方便了用户对该系统的使用。该模块中,除了方便用户登录系统外,用户也可以在该模块修改自己的密码。

5. 借还管理模块

该模块是该系统中最重要的部分,主要包括借书和还书功能,本系统为了方便用户的使用,设计了基于快捷键的模式,当读者要借书时,工作人员只需要输入读者的借书证号,按Enter键就可以查看到读者的信息,当然,前提是读者的信息已经注册到图书馆;同时输入图书号,按 Enter 键,读者所借阅的图书的信息就会显示在操作界面上,此时可以看到读者借阅图书的数量;单击"借书"按钮,就完成了读者借书的过程。这种操作方式不仅减少了工作人员烦琐的工作,也提高了工作效率。同样,当读者还书的时候,工作人员只需要输入图书号和读者的借书证号,单击"还书"按钮,即可完成还书操作。

6. 查询操作模块

设计该模块的目的主要是实现读者对图书借阅相关信息的检索,包括图书查询和借阅功能,以便于读者查询借阅图书,不需要麻烦管理人员,读者就可以自己登录系统,通过查询操作来查看图书馆的图书信息,同时也可以看到自己已借阅的图书信息和自己借书的详细信息,是否被罚款等;在读者查询图书时可以输入图书号,若读者不知道图书号,也可以输入书名或作者进行查询,实现了系统的人性化;管理员也可以通过此界面查询图书馆的图书信息。当图书馆需要添加图书而不确定该本书是否已经存在时,可以通过该模块来查询相关的图书信息。

系统功能结构如图 6-1 所示。

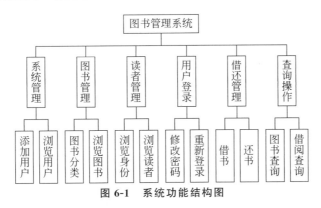

图 6-1 系统功能结构图

6.2.3 数据库设计

1. E-R 图

通过对数据库设计的分析得到该图书管理系统的局部 E-R 图,如图 6-2 所示。

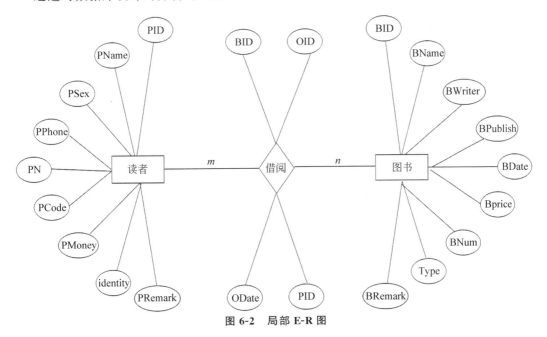

图 6-2 局部 E-R 图

2. 数据库关系表的设计

(1) 读者信息表(person)。读者信息表主要存放读者的基本信息,表结构如表 6-1 所示。

表 6-1 读者信息表

序号	字段名	数据类型	长度	主键	可否为空	备注
1	PID	varchar	50	YES	NO	读者编号
2	PName	varchar	10	NO	NO	姓名
3	PSex	varchar	4	NO	YES	性别
4	PPhone	varchar	11	NO	YES	电话
5	PN	varchar	20	NO	NO	识别码
6	PCode	varchar	20	NO	NO	密码
7	PMoney	float		NO	YES	罚款
8	identity	varchar	50	NO	YES	身份
9	PRemark	varchar	100	NO	YES	备注

(2) 管理员信息表(manage)。管理员信息表主要是存储管理员的信息,如用户名、密码、是否管理员等,如表 6-2 所示。

表 6-2 管理员信息表

序号	字段名	数据类型	长度	主键	可否为空	备注
1	MName	varchar	10	NO	NO	姓名
2	Password	varchar	10	NO	NO	密码
3	MCode	varchar	20	YES	NO	编号
4	manage	varchar	10	NO	YES	是否管理员
5	work	varchar	10	NO	YES	是否工作人员
6	query	varchar	10	NO	YES	是否查询人员

(3) 图书信息表(book)。图书信息表用于存放图书馆图书的基本信息,如书号、书名、作者、出版社、书价、类型、数量等,如表 6-3 所示。

表 6-3 图书信息表

序号	字段名	数据类型	长度	主键	可否为空	备注
1	BID	varchar	50	YES	NO	书号
2	BName	varchar	10	NO	YES	书名
3	BWriter	varchar	50	NO	YES	作者
4	BPublish	varchar	50	NO	YES	出版社
5	BDate	varchar	50	NO	YES	出版日期

续表

序号	字段名	数据类型	长度	主键	可否为空	备注
6	BPrice	float		NO	YES	书价
7	BNum	varchar	50	NO	YES	数量
8	Type	varchar	10	NO	YES	类型
9	BRemark	varchar	100	NO	YES	备注

（4）借出图书信息表（bookout）。该表存储借出书籍的信息，如图书编号、读者编号、借出日期等，如表 6-4 所示。

表 6-4　借出图书信息表

序号	字段名	数据类型	长度	主键	可否为空	备注
1	OID	varchar	50	YES	NO	借阅序号
2	BID	varchar	50	YES	NO	图书编号
3	PID	varchar	50	YES	NO	读者编号
4	ODate	varchar	50	NO	YES	借出日期

（5）书籍类型表（type）。书籍类型表存放图书的类型，如表 6-5 所示。

表 6-5　书籍类型表

序号	字段名	数据类型	长度	主键	可否为空	备注
1	TID	varchar	50	YES	NO	读者编号
2	Type	varchar	10	NO	YES	类别
3	tRemark	varchar	50	NO	YES	备注

（6）读者借阅类型表（identityinfo）。读者借阅类型表存放读者的身份标识、借阅时间和数量，如表 6-6 所示。

表 6-6　读者借阅类型表

序号	字段名	数据类型	长度	主键	可否为空	备注
1	identity	varchar	50	YES	NO	身份标识
2	longTime	varchar	50	NO	YES	借阅时间
3	bigNum	varchar	50	NO	YES	数量

（7）数据库关系图。通过使用 PowerDesigner 设计工具得到的图书管理信息系统的数据库关系图，如图 6-3 所示。

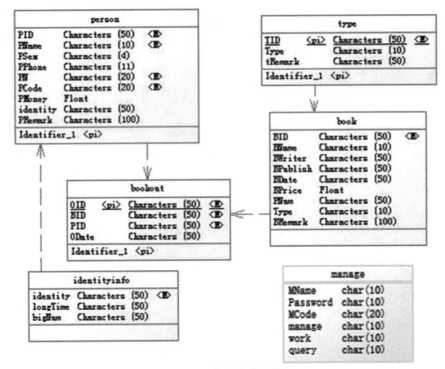

图 6-3　数据库关系图

6.3　系 统 实 现

6.3.1　技术要点

1. 开发环境

（1）系统开发环境：Visual Studio 2019。

（2）系统开发语言：C♯。

（3）运行平台：Windows 10。

（4）数据库：SQL Server 2019。

2. 程序界面

为便于操作，本程序在开发过程中应当选择父子窗体的样式，即所有窗体都应该在父窗体内显示。在开发过程当中应注意父子窗体的程序设计方式。

3. 程序设计

为便于数据查询及打印，在数据统计界面当中使用 RDLC 报表技术。鉴于程序复杂程度，本程序架构采用一般的程序开发结构，并未对其进行分层。

6.3.2　主要功能模块及界面设计

1. 主要模块

（1）用户管理模块：只有管理员才有权限对用户信息进行管理，浏览用户管理模块主要是实现对用户信息的浏览和删除功能。

(2)图书书目管理模块:该模块中,主要实现了管理员对图书书目进行添加、删除、修改和浏览的功能。

(3)读者信息管理模块:管理员对读者的基本信息进行添加、删除、修改、查询等操作。

(4)借还管理模块:该模块的管理者是工作人员,工作人员通过该模块实现对读者借书和还书的操作。

(5)查询操作模块:该模块主要实现读者对自己借阅图书的查询功能。

2. 功能实现

(1)浏览用户信息界面的设计:图书管理员登录后跳转至管理员主界面,在该界面管理员可以对系统、图书、读者、登录用户等进行管理,单击"系统管理"下拉列表,可以看到对用户的管理功能,主界面的详细设计如图 6-4 所示。

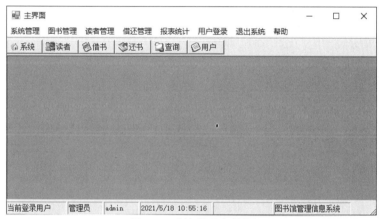

图 6-4　系统管理主界面

在图 6-4 中单击"系统管理"→"浏览用户",就会弹出浏览用户界面,如图 6-5 所示。该界面会显示所有用户的信息,在其中还可以实现对用户权限删除的操作,如果发现有信息错误或者已经失效等,可以选中该信息,单击"删除"按钮,被选中的信息就会被删除。单击"退出"按钮,系统跳至主界面。

图 6-5　浏览用户信息界面

当前窗体的初始化代码如下。

```
DataSet ds;
private void User_Load(object sender, System.EventArgs e)
{
    oleConnection1.Open();
    string sql = "select MName as 用户名,MCode as 密码,manage as 权限1,work as 权限2,
        query as 权限3 from manager";
    SqlDataAdapter adp = new SqlDataAdapter(sql,oleConnection1);
    ds = new DataSet();
    ds.Clear();
    adp.Fill(ds,"user");
    dataGrid1.DataSource = ds.Tables["user"].DefaultView;
    dataGrid1.CaptionText = "共有"+ds.Tables["user"].Rows.Count+"条记录";
    oleConnection1.Close();
}
```

在"修改"按钮的事件代码中添加如下代码。

```
ModifyUser modifyUser;
private void btModify_Click(object sender, System.EventArgs e)
{
    if (dataGrid1.CurrentRowIndex>=0&&dataGrid1.DataSource !=
        null&&dataGrid1[dataGrid1.CurrentCell]!=null)
    {
        modifyUser = new ModifyUser();
        modifyUser.textName.Text =
            ds.Tables[0].Rows[dataGrid1.CurrentCell.RowNumber][0].ToString().
            Trim();
        modifyUser.ShowDialog();
    }
}
```

在"删除"按钮的事件代码中添加如下代码。

```
private void btDel_Click(object sender, System.EventArgs e)
{
    if (dataGrid1.CurrentRowIndex>=0&&dataGrid1.DataSource !=
        null&&dataGrid1[dataGrid1.CurrentCell]!=null)
    {
        oleConnection1.Open();
        string sql="delete * from manager where MName =
            '"+ds.Tables["user"].Rows[dataGrid1.CurrentCell.RowNumber][0].
            ToString().Trim()+"'";
        SqlCommand cmd = new SqlCommand(sql,oleConnection1);
        cmd.ExecuteNonQuery();
        MessageBox.Show("删除用户'"
            +ds.Tables[0].Rows[dataGrid1.CurrentCell.RowNumber][0].
            ToString().Trim()
            +"'成功!","提示");
        oleConnection1.Close();
    }
    else
        return;
}
```

（2）图书书目管理。只有图书管理员才有权限管理图书书目信息，管理员登录成功后，直接跳至管理员主界面，通过主界面上的"图书管理"→"浏览图书"，就可以管理图书书目，当弹出图书书目界面时，界面上会显示图书书目的所有信息，如图书编号、图书名、作者等书目的详细信息，其界面如图6-6所示。

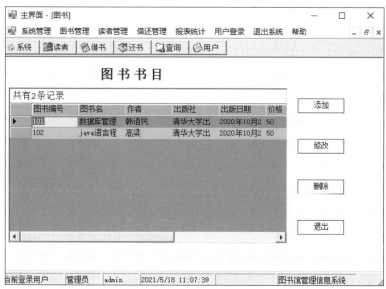

图6-6　图书书目管理界面

在该界面可以添加、删除、修改图书书目信息。单击"添加"按钮，会弹出"添加图书"界面，可以添加一条新的图书书目信息；当要删除过时或错误的信息时，选中要删除的信息，单击"删除"按钮，就会删除该条信息；当要修改信息时，单击"修改"按钮，就会弹出修改信息界面，可以修改被选中的信息；单击"退出"按钮，系统跳至主界面。如单击"添加"按钮，会弹出添加信息界面，在该界面就可以添加一条新的图书信息，效果如图6-7所示。

图6-7　"添加图书"界面

添加图书书目的主要代码如下。

```
private void btAdd_Click(object sender, System.EventArgs e)
{
```

```
if (textID.Text.Trim()==""||textName.Text.Trim()==
                ""||textNum.Text.Trim()==""||textWriter.Text.
                Trim()=="")
    MessageBox.Show("请填写完整信息","提示");
else
{
    oleConnection1.Open();
    string sql="select * from book where BID='"+textID.Text.Trim()+"'";
    SqlCommand cmd = new SqlCommand(sql,oleConnection1);
    if (null!=cmd.ExecuteScalar())
        MessageBox.Show("图书编号重复","提示");
    else
    {
        sql="insert into book values ('"+textID.Text.Trim()+"',
            '"+textName.Text.Trim()
            +"','"+textWriter.Text.Trim()+"',"+"'"+textPublish.Text.
            Trim()
            +"','"+date1.Text.Trim()+"','"+textPrice.Text.Trim()+"','"
            +textNum.Text.Trim()
            +"',"+ "'"+comboType.Text.Trim()+"','"+textRemark.Text.Trim()
            +"')";
        cmd.CommandText=sql;
        cmd.ExecuteNonQuery();
        MessageBox.Show("添加成功","提示");
        clear();
    }
    oleConnection1.Close();
}
```

（3）读者信息管理。该界面的管理权限也只有管理员才具有，管理员登录成功后进入管理员主界面，通过此界面，管理员可以管理读者的信息，如添加、修改、删除读者的信息。单击"读者管理"→"浏览读者"，就会弹出读者的信息，如图 6-8 所示。

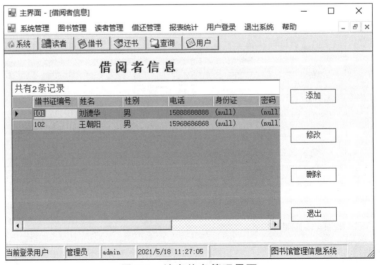

图 6-8　读者信息管理界面

在该界面可以添加、修改、删除读者的信息，如选中第二条信息，单击"修改"按钮，就会弹出修改借阅者信息的界面，在该界面除了借书证号不能修改外，可以任意地修改借阅者的信息。修改信息界面设计如图 6-9 所示。

图 6-9 修改借阅者信息界面

修改借阅者信息的主要代码如下。

```csharp
private void btAdd_Click(object sender, System.EventArgs e)
{
    if (textName.Text.Trim()==""||textPN.Text.Trim()==""
                      ||textCode.Text.Trim()=="")
        MessageBox.Show("请填写完整信息","提示");
    else
    {
        oleConnection1.Open();
        string sql1="select * from person where PID<>'"+textID.Text.ToString()
                    +"' and PN='"+textPN.Text.ToString()+"'";
        SqlCommand cmd = new SqlCommand(sql1,oleConnection1);
        if (null!=cmd.ExecuteScalar())
            MessageBox.Show("身份证号发生重复","提示");
        else
        {
            string sql2="update person set PName='"+textName.Text.Trim()+"',
                    PSex='"+comboSex.Text.Trim()+"','"+"PN='"+textPN.Text.
                    Trim()+"',
                    PPhone='"+textPhone.Text.Trim()+"',PCode='"+textCode.
                    Text.Trim()+"','"+
                    PRemark='"+textRemark.Text.Trim()+"',
                    PMoney='"+textMoney.Text.Trim()+"'
                    where PID='"+this.textID.Text.Trim()+"'";
            SqlCommand cmd2 = new SqlCommand(sql2,oleConnection1);
            cmd2.ExecuteNonQuery();
            MessageBox.Show("信息修改成功","提示");
            this.Close();
        }
        oleConnection1.Close();
    }
}
```

（4）借还管理功能。该模块主要由工作人员来管理，工作人员通过该模块来完成读者的借书和还书的工作。当读者第一次借书时，读者在图书馆注册自己的信息；当读者再次借书时，工作人员只需输入读者的借书证号，按 Enter 键，如果数据库中存在该读者的信息，在界面上就会显示出来，输入图书号，按 Enter 键，如果存在该书，图书的详细信息就会显示在界面上，单击"借书"按钮，读者就成功借阅了一本书，在界面上也会显示读者已借图书的情况，如图 6-10 所示。

图 6-10 借书管理界面

为操作方便，在输入借书证号或者图书编号时，用户只要按 Enter 键即可查询到当前证件及图书是否存在，这就要求在这两个输入框内的键盘事件当中完成如下代码。

借书证号查询验证代码如下。

```
DataSet ds;
private void textPID_KeyDown(object sender, System.Windows.Forms.KeyEventArgs e)
{
if (e.KeyCode == Keys.Enter)
    {
        oleConnection1.Open();
        string sql1 = "select PName as 姓名,PSex as 性别,PN as 身份证,PMoney as 罚款,
                    identityname as 身份 "+"from person where PID='"+textPID.
                    Text.Trim()+"'";
        string sql3 = "select BID from bookOut where PID = '"+textPID.Text.Trim()
            +"'";
        SqlDataAdapter adp = new SqlDataAdapter(sql1,oleConnection1);
        SqlDataAdapter adp3 = new SqlDataAdapter(sql3,oleConnection1);
        ds = new DataSet();
        ds.Clear();
        adp.Fill(ds,"person");
        adp3.Fill(ds,"bookid");
        dataGrid2.DataSource = ds.Tables["person"].DefaultView;
        dataGrid4.DataSource = ds.Tables["bookid"].DefaultView;
        if (ds.Tables[0].Rows.Count!=0)
        {
            textPName.Text = ds.Tables["person"].Rows[dataGrid2.CurrentCell.
```

```
                        RowNumber][0].ToString().Trim();
            textPSex.Text = ds.Tables["person"].Rows[dataGrid2.CurrentCell.
                        RowNumber][1].ToString().Trim();
            textPN.Text = ds.Tables["person"].Rows[dataGrid2.CurrentCell.
                        RowNumber][2].ToString().Trim();
            textMoney.Text = ds.Tables["person"].Rows[dataGrid2.CurrentCell.
                        RowNumber][3].ToString().Trim();
            textIden.Text = ds.Tables["person"].Rows[dataGrid2.CurrentCell.
                        RowNumber][4].ToString().Trim();
            dataGrid2.CaptionText = "共有"+ds.Tables["person"].Rows.Count+
                        "条记录";
        }
        else
            MessageBox.Show("没有该借书证号","提示");
        for (int x=0;x<ds.Tables["bookid"].Rows.Count;x++)
        {
            string sql2="select book.BID as 图书编号,BName as 图书名,BWriter as
                        作者,BPublish as 出版社,BDate as 出版日期,BPrice as 价格,"
                        + "type as 类型,ODate as 借书日期,(select longTime
                        from identityinfo
                        where identity=(select identity from person where PID='"
                        +textPID.Text.Trim()+"'))"+ " as 最长借书时间,dateAdd('m',
                        最长借书时间,ODate) as 应还日期 from book,bookOut where
                        book.BID=bookOut.BID and book.BID = '"+ds.Tables
                        ["bookid"].Rows[x][0]+"'"+" and PID= '"+textPID.Text.
                        Trim()+"'";
            SqlDataAdapter adp2 = new SqlDataAdapter(sql2,oleConnection1);
            adp2.Fill(ds,"bookout");
            dataGrid1.DataSource = ds.Tables["bookout"].DefaultView;
            dataGrid1.CaptionText = "已借图书"+ds.Tables["bookout"].Rows.Count
                +"本";
        }
        oleConnection1.Close();
    }
}
```

图书编号查询代码如下。

```
private void textBID_KeyDown(object sender, System.Windows.Forms.KeyEventArgs e)
{
    if (e.KeyCode == Keys.Enter)
    {
        oleConnection1.Open();
        string sql = "select BName as 图书名,BWriter as 作者,BPublish as 出版社,
                BDate as 出版日期,BPrice as 价格,"+ "type as 类型
                from book where BID='"+textBID.Text.Trim()+"'";
        SqlDataAdapter adp = new SqlDataAdapter(sql,oleConnection1);
        ds = new DataSet();
        ds.Clear();
        adp.Fill(ds,"book");
        dataGrid3.DataSource = ds.Tables["book"].DefaultView;
```

```
            if (ds.Tables[0].Rows.Count!=0)
            {
                textBName.Text = ds.Tables[0].Rows[dataGrid3.CurrentCell.
                    RowNumber][0].ToString().Trim();
                textWriter.Text = ds.Tables[0].Rows[dataGrid3.CurrentCell.
                        RowNumber][1].ToString().Trim();
                textPublish.Text = ds.Tables[0].Rows[dataGrid3.CurrentCell.
                        RowNumber][2].ToString().Trim();
                textBDate.Text = ds.Tables[0].Rows[dataGrid3.CurrentCell.
                        RowNumber][3].ToString().Trim();
                textPrice.Text = ds.Tables[0].Rows[dataGrid3.CurrentCell.
                        RowNumber][4].ToString().Trim();
                textType.Text = ds.Tables[0].Rows[dataGrid3.CurrentCell.
                        RowNumber][5].ToString().Trim();
                dataGrid3.CaptionText = "共有"+ds.Tables["book"].Rows.Count+"条记录";
            }
            else
            MessageBox.Show("没有该图书编号","提示");
            oleConnection1.Close();
        }
}
```

图书"借出"按钮事件代码如下。

```
private void btOut_Click(object sender, System.EventArgs e)
{
    if (textPID.Text.Trim() == " " || textBID.Text.Trim() == " ")
        MessageBox.Show("请输入完整信息","提示");
    else
    {
        oleConnection1.Open();
        string sql = "select * from bookOut where BID='" + textBID.Text.Trim()
            + "' and PID='" + textPID.Text.Trim() + "'";
        SqlCommand cmd = new SqlCommand(sql, oleConnection1);
        if (null != cmd.ExecuteScalar())
            MessageBox.Show("你已经借了一本该书","提示");
        else
        {
            sql = "insert into bookOut (BID,PID,ODate) values ('" + textBID.Text.
                Trim() + "','" + textPID.Text.Trim() + "','" + date1.Text.Trim()
                + "')";
            cmd.CommandText = sql;
            cmd.ExecuteNonQuery();
            MessageBox.Show("借出成功","提示");
        }
        oleConnection1.Close();
    }
}
```

当读者还书的时候，工作人员输入读者的图书证号和图书的图书号，按 Enter 键，读者所借的图书的信息以及读者借阅的时间、应还日期等信息就会显示在界面上，通过此界面可以判断读者借阅的图书是否超期，以及读者是否有罚款的记录等信息，单击"还书"按钮，读者还书过程就完成了。还书的界面如图 6-11 所示。

图 6-11 还书管理界面

在"图书编号"文本框的键盘事件当中添加如下代码,使用户按下 Enter 键就能够直接查询到所输入编号图书的详细信息。

```
DataSet ds;
private void textBID_KeyDown(object sender, System.Windows.Forms.KeyEventArgs e)
{
    if (e.KeyCode == Keys.Enter)
    {
        oleConnection1.Open();
        string sql = "select BName as 图书名,BWriter as 作者,BPublish as 出版社,
            BDate as 出版日期,BPrice as 价格,type as 类型," + "ODate as 借出日期,
                (select longTime from identityinfo where identityname = (select
                identityname from person where PID='"+textPID.Text.Trim()+"'))"
            + " as 最长借书时间,dateAdd('m',最长借书时间,ODate) as 应还日期,
                DateDiff('d',应还日期,Now) as 超出天数 from book,bookOut where "+"
                book.BID='"+textBID.Text.Trim()+"' and PID='"+textPID.Text.Trim
                ()+"'";
        SqlDataAdapter adp = new SqlDataAdapter(sql,oleConnection1);
        ds = new DataSet();
        ds.Clear();
        adp.Fill(ds,"book");
        dataGrid1.DataSource = ds.Tables["book"].DefaultView;
        if (ds.Tables[0].Rows.Count!=0)
        {
            textBName.Text = ds.Tables[0].Rows[dataGrid1.CurrentCell.
                RowNumber][0].
                    ToString().Trim();
            textWriter.Text = ds.Tables[0].Rows[dataGrid1.CurrentCell.
                RowNumber][1].
                    ToString().Trim();
```

```csharp
            textPublish.Text = ds.Tables[0].Rows[dataGrid1.CurrentCell.
                RowNumber][2].ToString().Trim();
            textBDate.Text = ds.Tables[0].Rows[dataGrid1.CurrentCell.
                RowNumber][3].ToString().Trim();
            textPrice.Text = ds.Tables[0].Rows[dataGrid1.CurrentCell.
                RowNumber][4].ToString().Trim();
            textType.Text = ds.Tables[0].Rows[dataGrid1.CurrentCell.RowNumber][5].
                ToString().Trim();
            textOutDate.Text=ds.Tables[0].Rows[dataGrid1.CurrentCell.
                RowNumber][6].ToString().Trim();
            textBigDay.Text= Convert.ToString(Convert.ToInt16(ds.Tables[0].
                Rows[dataGrid1.CurrentCell.RowNumber][7].ToString().Trim()) * 30);
            textInDate1.Text= ds.Tables[0].Rows[dataGrid1.CurrentCell.
                RowNumber][8].ToString().Trim();
            if (Convert.ToInt16(ds.Tables[0].Rows[dataGrid1.CurrentCell.
                RowNumber][9].ToString().Trim())>0)
            {
                textDay.Text = ds.Tables[0].Rows[dataGrid1.CurrentCell.
                    RowNumber][9].ToString().Trim();
                textMoney.Text = Convert.ToString(Convert.ToInt16(textDay.
                    Text) * 0.15);
            }
            else
            {
                textDay.Text="0";
                textMoney.Text="0";
            }
            textNow.Text = DateTime.Now.ToString();
            dataGrid1.CaptionText = "共有"+ds.Tables["book"].Rows.Count+"条记录";
        }
        else
        MessageBox.Show("该读者没有借该图书","提示");
        sql="update person set PMoney=PMoney+'"+textMoney.Text
                +"' where PID='"+textPID.Text.Trim()+"'";
        SqlCommand cmd = new SqlCommand(sql,oleConnection1);
        cmd.ExecuteNonQuery();
        oleConnection1.Close();
    }
}
```

单击"还书"按钮,实现还书管理,其主要代码如下。

```csharp
private void btIn_Click(object sender, System.EventArgs e)
{
    if (textBID.Text.Trim()==null)
        MessageBox.Show("请填写图书编号","提示");
    else
```

```
    {
        oleConnection1.Open();
        string sql = "delete * from bookOut where BID = '"+textBID.Text.Trim()
            +"'and PID='"+textPID.Text.Trim()+"'";
        SqlCommand cmd = new SqlCommand(sql,oleConnection1);
        cmd.ExecuteNonQuery();
        MessageBox.Show("还书成功","提示");
    }
}
```

(5) 图书查询界面。工作人员和读者都具有查询图书的权限,输入图书号、图书名或者作者中的任一条信息,单击"查询"按钮,图书信息就会显示到界面上。图书查询界面如图 6-12 所示。

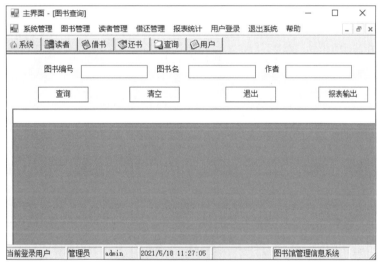

图 6-12　图书查询界面

主要代码如下。

```
private void btQuery_Click(object sender, System.EventArgs e)
{
    string sql1 = "(BNum-(select count(*) from bookOut where ";
    string sql = "select BID as 图书编号,BName as 图书名,BWriter as 作者,
        BPublish as 出版社,BDate as 出版日期,BPrice as 价格,"+"BNum as 数量,
        type as 类型,BRemark as 备注, ";
    if (textID.Text.Trim() != "")
    {
        sql1 = sql1+" BID= "+"'"+textID.Text.Trim()+"')) as 库存数量";
        sql = sql+sql1+"from book where BID= "+"'"+textID.Text.Trim()+"'";
    }
    else if (textName.Text.Trim() != "")
    {
        sql1 = sql1+" BID=(select BID from book where BName='"+textName.
            Text+"'))) as 库存数量";
        sql = sql+sql1+"from book where BName= "+"'"+textName.Text+"'";
    }
    else if (textWriter.Text.Trim() != "")
```

```
        {
            sql1 = sql1+" BID=(select BID from book where BWriter
                        ='"+textWriter.Text+"')))  as 库存数量";
            sql = sql+sql1+"from book where BWriter= "+"'"+textWriter.Text+"'";
        }
        else
        {
            MessageBox.Show("请输入查询条件","提示");    return;
        }
        oleConnection1.Open();
        OleDbDataAdapter adp = new OleDbDataAdapter(sql,oleConnection1);
        DataSet ds = new DataSet();
        ds.Clear();
        adp.Fill(ds,"book");
        dataGrid1.DataSource=ds.Tables[0].DefaultView;
        dataGrid1.CaptionText="共有"+ds.Tables[0].Rows.Count+"条查询记录";
        oleConnection1.Close();
}
```

（6）借阅查询界面。借阅查询主要实现读者对图书和自己所借图书的查询，只有读者本人才可以查看自己借阅图书的信息。当读者登录系统后，会进入读者管理的主界面，读者通过"报表统计"菜单中的"借阅报表"模块，可以查看自己的个人信息和自己借阅图书的信息，界面设计如图 6-13 所示。

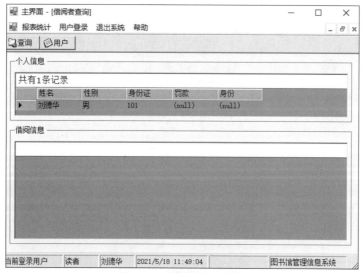

图 6-13　借阅查询界面

显示借阅者信息的主要代码如下。

```
DataSet ds;
private void PersonQuery_Load(object sender, System.EventArgs e)
{
    oleConnection1.Open();
    string sql1 = "select PName as 姓名,PSex as 性别,PN as 身份证,PMoney as 罚款,
        identityname as 身份 "+"from person where PID='"+this.Tag.ToString().
        Trim()+"'";
```

```
        string sql3 = "select BID from bookOut where PID = '"+this.Tag.ToString().
            Trim()+"'";
        SqlDataAdapter adp = new SqlDataAdapter(sql1,oleConnection1);
        SqlDataAdapter adp3 = new SqlDataAdapter(sql3,oleConnection1);
        ds = new DataSet();
        ds.Clear();
        adp.Fill(ds,"person");
        adp3.Fill(ds,"bookid");
        dataGrid2.DataSource = ds.Tables["person"].DefaultView;
        dataGrid2.CaptionText = "共有"+ds.Tables["person"].Rows.Count+"条记录";
        dataGrid3.DataSource = ds.Tables["bookid"].DefaultView;
        for (int x=0;x<ds.Tables["bookid"].Rows.Count;x++)
        {
            string sql2="select book.BID as 图书编号,BName as 图书名,BWriter as 作者,
                BPublish as 出版社,BDate as 出版日期,BPrice as 价格,"+"type as 类型,
                ODate as 借书日期,(select longTime from identityinfo where identity
                =(select identity from person where PID='"+this.Tag.ToString().
                    Trim()+"'))"+ "
                as 最长借书时间,dateAdd('m',最长借书时间,ODate) as 应还日期
                from book,bookOut where book.BID = bookOut.BID and
                book.BID = '"+ds.Tables["bookid"].Rows[x][0]+"'"+" and
                PID='"+this.Tag.ToString().Trim()+"'";
            SqlDataAdapter adp2 = new SqlDataAdapter(sql2,oleConnection1);
            adp2.Fill(ds,"bookout");
            dataGrid1.DataSource = ds.Tables["bookout"].DefaultView;
            dataGrid1.CaptionText = "已借图书"+ds.Tables["bookout"].Rows.Count+"本";
        }
        oleConnection1.Close();
}
```

6.4 程序打包

程序代码编写完成后，需要将程序交付给客户，但是一般情况下客户不懂计算机，因此他们不知道程序是如何部署的，这就要求开发人员将程序完成后进行程序打包，以便客户在拿到程序后直接安装就可以在计算机上运行，不需要或者只是进行简单的配置即可。本节结合本章所介绍的图书管理系统来详细介绍如何给一个程序打包和发布。

图书管理系统程序打包具体步骤如下。

（1）自 VS 2017 以后默认不再包含打包工程模板，所以如果想要实现程序打包，需要下载安装 Install 插件。有以下两种下载方式。

一种方式是通过以下网址下载：

https://marketplace.visualstudio.com/items?itemName=VisualStudioClient.MicrosoftVisualStudio2017InstallerProjects

打开网页后，单击 Download 按钮下载打包插件工具，如图 6-14 所示。

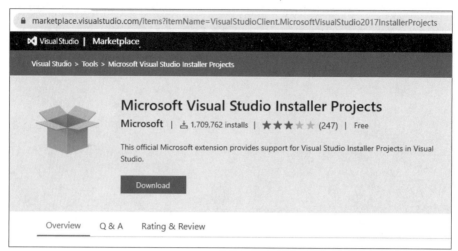

图 6-14 网页下载插件

另一种方式是,通过在 Visual Studio 2019 中选择"扩展"→"管理扩展"菜单项,打开"管理扩展"窗体,在其中找到 Microsoft Visual Studio Installer Projects 插件来下载,如图 6-15 所示。

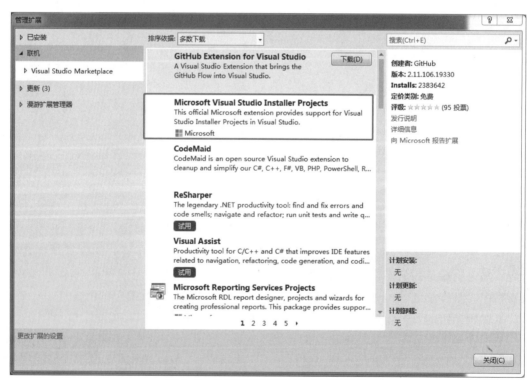

图 6-15 从"管理扩展"窗体上下载插件

(2) 安装成功后,重新打开 Visual Studio,选择"新建项目"→Setup Project 或者 Setup Wizard 都可以创建桌面类型的安装程序,如图 6-16 所示。

选择 Setup Project 后就会弹出"配置新项目"对话框,如图 6-17 所示。

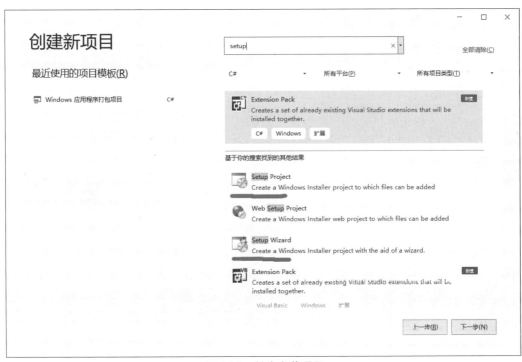

图 6-16 创建安装项目

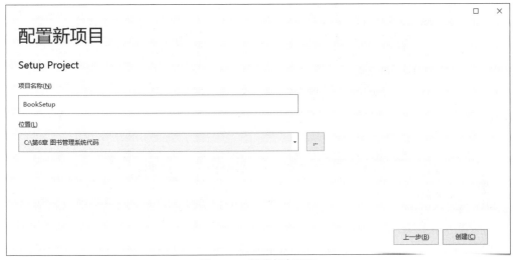

图 6-17 新建打包项目

单击"创建"按钮后进入部署页面，如图 6-18 所示。

（3）在 Application Folder 上右击→Add→"文件"，这里可以选择任何想要打包的程序文件，如图 6-19 所示。

（4）创建桌面或 ProgramMenu 菜单的快捷方式。

右击程序执行主文件，在弹出菜单中单击 Create Shortcut to LibraryMIS.exe 命令创建快捷方式，如图 6-20 所示。

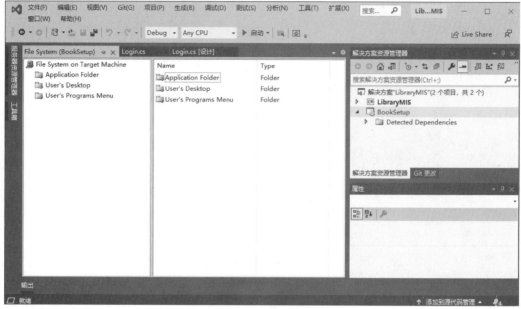

图 6-18 部署页面

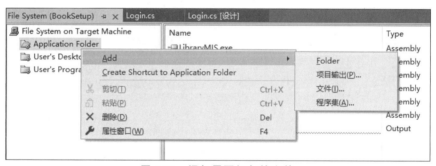

图 6-19 添加需要打包的文件

图 6-20 创建快捷方式

创建完成后可以更改快捷方式的名字,如图 6-21 所示。

用鼠标将此快捷方式分别拖至 User's Desktop 和 User's Programs Menu 文件夹中,如图 6-22 所示。

可以通过快捷方式的属性窗口修改快捷方式图标等信息,如图 6-23 所示。

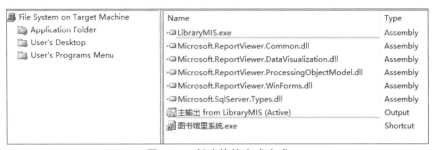

图 6-21 创建快捷方式完成

图 6-22 快捷方式设置

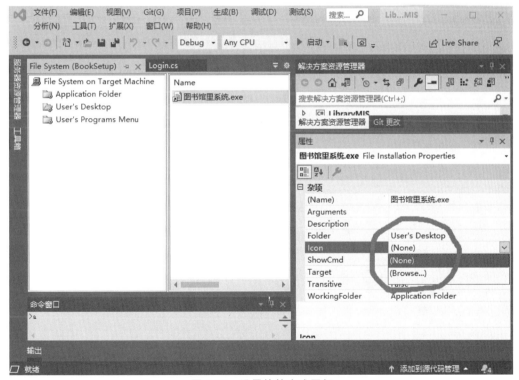

图 6-23 设置快捷方式图标

（5）设置打包项目的其他相关信息。

在解决方案资源管理器位置单击打包项目名称，即可以看到该项目的属性配置列表，如图 6-24 所示。

在这里可以配置安装程序的其他相关信息，例如，作者信息、选择安装程序默认主目录名称、是否有卸载旧代码等。

（6）完成以上步骤，就可以生成安装包了，右击项目"生成"命令，如图 6-25 所示。

（7）生成后，在 Debug 文件夹中能够找到对应的安装包，如图 6-26 所示。

图 6-24　项目打包属性配置列表

图 6-25　生成编译打包项目

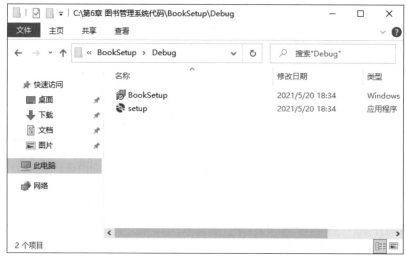

图 6-26　生成安装包

（8）双击安装包，即可执行程序安装。安装完成后，在"开始"菜单以及桌面上将会出现"图书管理系统"程序快捷方式，如图 6-27 所示。

图 6-27 安装后效果

小　　结

通过本章的学习,应基本掌握如何在 Visual Studio 2019 环境下进行管理信息系统开发的整个流程。通过一个简单的图书管理系统实例,讲解了基本的管理信息系统界面设计、代码书写、数据库设计等,并讲解如何将一个程序进行打包,生成安装包文件提交给客户的详细制作过程,至此完成了一个管理信息系统开发的全部过程。

习　　题

1. 结合自己日常生活完成一个简单的学籍信息数据库管理信息系统的开发。
2. 结合自己日常生活完成一个简单的小型商店商品信息数据库管理信息系统的开发。

第 7 章
超市商品进销存管理系统案例开发

本章将讲解利用 EF 开发简单的管理信息系统,围绕某超市进销存业务展开,系统分为商品管理、进货管理、销售管理、库存统计等模块。

通过本章的学习,读者应该重点掌握使用 EF 开发一般的信息管理系统。

7.1 系统需求

某超市为了节约人力成本,提高信息化管理水平,决定使用计算机对超市的进货、销售及库存进行一体化管理,开发一个商品进销存管理系统。

1. 主界面

(1) 主界面实现对每个功能模块的导航。

(2) 主界面默认显示商品管理模块内容。

2. 商品管理

包括商品基本信息的查询、新建、修改和删除等。详细描述如下。

(1) 界面加载时显示所有商品信息,按商品编号升序排列显示商品信息。

(2) 查询某个商品信息,可以实现商品名称的模糊查询;当没有输入商品名称时,查询出所有商品。

(3) 可以添加新的商品,添加后刷新商品列表;不允许添加已经存在的商品,若发生这种操作则提示用户。

(4) 当用户单击某商品时,则显示相应的商品信息。可对商品信息进行修改。

(5) 选中某个商品,可以实施删除操作。

3. 进货管理

商品进货管理功能完成进货信息登记等。详细描述如下。

(1) 当界面加载时,由于商品过多,默认情况下从列表中可以选择的商品为存货量最少的 10 件商品。

(2) 如果列表找不到相应商品,可以通过输入关键字在所有商品中筛选。

(3) 进货数量可以是正整数或正小数,不能为负数或非数字。

(4) 用户可以自行设置进货时间,默认为系统当前时间。

4. 销售管理

商品销售管理功能完成销售信息登记等。详细描述如下。

(1) 界面加载时,由于商品过多,默认情况下从列表中可以选择的商品为最近售出的 10 件商品。

(2) 如果选择商品时找不到相应商品,可以通过设置关键字在所有商品中筛选。
(3) 销售数量可以是正整数或正小数,不能为负数或非数字。
(4) 用户可以自行设置销售时间,默认为系统当前时间。

5. 库存统计

为了保证现有商品的数量、方便进货,统计出需要进货的商品。详细说明如下。
(1) 能够统计出存货量少于 N 件的商品,默认 $N=10$。
(2) 用户可以设置 N 值的大小。
(3) 把商品名称和剩余货量显示出来。

7.2 系 统 设 计

7.2.1 模块设计

该系统分为四个模块,分别是基本信息管理、进货管理、销售管理、库存统计。

7.2.2 数据库设计

1. 概念设计

数据库共有 3 个实体:商品信息(GoodsInfo)、进货(GoodsIn)和销售(GoodsOut)。其中,商品信息与进货、销售存在一对多的联系,如图 7-1 所示。

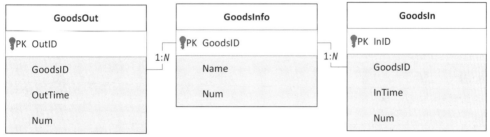

图 7-1 数据库模型

2. 逻辑设计

对应概念设计阶段的三个实体,系统需要创建三个数据表,分别是商品信息表、进货表、销售表。
(1) 商品信息表(GoodsInfo)。商品信息表表结构如表 7-1 所示,用来保存商品的基本信息。

表 7-1 商品信息表

列　　名	数 据 类 型	是否主键	是否允许空	说　　明
GoodsID	int	是	否	商品 ID
Name	nvarchar(255)	否	是	商品名称
Num	float	否	是	商品数量

（2）进货表（GoodsIn）。进货表表结构如表 7-2 所示，用来保存进货信息。

表 7-2 进货表

列 名	数 据 类 型	是否主键	是否允许空	说 明
InID	int	是	否	进货 ID
GoodsID	int	否	是	进货商品 ID
InTime	datetime	否	是	进货时间
Num	float	否	是	进货商品数量

（3）销售表（GoodsOut）。销售表表结构如表 7-3 所示，用来保存销售信息。

表 7-3 销售表

列 名	数 据 类 型	是否主键	是否允许空	说 明
OutID	int	是	否	销售 ID
GoodsID	int	否	是	销售商品 ID
OutTime	datetime	否	是	销售时间
Num	float	否	是	销售商品数量

7.3 系统实现

7.3.1 实体数据模型

1. 建立工程

（1）启动 Visual Studio 2019。

（2）在 Visual Studio 中，单击"创建新项目"。

（3）在"创建新项目"窗体中，选择 C♯、Windows 和"桌面"过滤条件，选择"Windows 窗体应用程序（.NET Framework）"模板，单击"下一步"按钮。

（4）在"配置新项目"窗体中，输入项目名称为"GoodsManage"。

（5）单击"创建"按钮。

2. 安装 EF

EF 的安装方法见 2.4.1 节。

3. 添加实体数据模型

在 Visual Studio 环境中，单击"项目"→"添加新项"按钮，弹出"添加新项"对话框。

在模板框中，选中"ADO.NET 实体数据模型"，在"名称"文本框中输入"GoodsManageModel"，单击"添加"按钮。后面的操作步骤可参考 2.4.2 节，注意在配置"实体数据模型向导"时，将"App.Config 中的连接设置另存为"GoodsManage。添加完成后，解决方案的视图如图 7-2 所示。

图 7-2 项目文件结构

实体数据模型类名为 GoodsManageModel，文件名为 GoodsManageModel.cs；数据库中每个表生成一个实体类，分别为 GoodsIn、GoodsOut 和 GoodsInfo。

7.3.2 主界面模块

1. 主界面设计

（1）自动生成的项目包含一个 Form1 窗体，该窗体无用，把该窗体删除。

（2）右击 GoodsManage 项目名称，在弹出的菜单中选中"添加"→"新建项"命令，弹出如图 7-3 所示"添加新项"对话框，选中类型"窗体（Windows 窗体）"，在"名称"文本框中输入窗体名称"GoodsManageMain"。

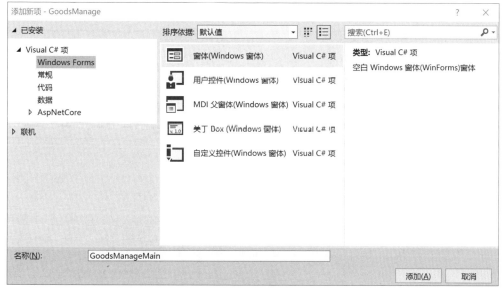

图 7-3　添加窗体

按照表 7-4 修改 GoodsManageMain 窗体的属性。

表 7-4　窗体属性

序号	属 性 名 称	属 性 值
1	MaximizeBox	False
2	MinimizeBox	False
3	Size	420，256
4	Text	超市商品进销存管理系统

（3）在工具栏中选中 MenuStrip（菜单）组件，拖放到 GoodsManageMain 窗体中，设计好的界面如图 7-4 所示。

GoodsManageMain 窗体中的有关控件对应的属性如表 7-5 所示。

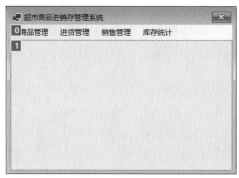

图 7-4 主界面

表 7-5 主窗体控件属性

Tab	控件类型	属性名	属性值
0	MenuStrip	Name	menuStrip1
1	Panel	Name	panel1
		Dock	Fill

单击 menuStrip1 控件的属性 Items,打开项集合编辑器(Items Collection Editor),如图 7-5 所示。

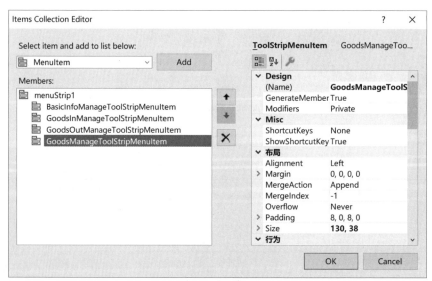

图 7-5 项集合编辑器窗体

给菜单添加四个 MenuItem 项,对应的属性值如表 7-6 所示。

表 7-6 菜单项属性

序 号	Name 属性值	Text 属性值
1	BasicInfoManageToolStripMenuItem	商品管理
2	GoodsInManageToolStripMenuItem	进货管理

续表

序号	Name 属性值	Text 属性值
3	GoodsOutManageToolStripMenuItem	销售管理
4	GoodsManageToolStripMenuItem	库存统计

(4) 修改 Programe.cs 文件代码如下。

```
[STAThread]
static void Main()
{
    Application.EnableVisualStyles();
    Application.SetCompatibleTextRenderingDefault(false);
    Application.Run(new GoodsManageMain());  //此处把 Form1 改为 GoodsManageMain
}
```

2．实现菜单

用户单击菜单中的按钮，触发相关的处理方法，显示有关的处理界面。下面以"商品管理"菜单项为例，描述实现方法。

双击"商品管理"菜单项，自动生成事件处理方法，打开代码编辑窗口。实现该方法，代码如下。

```
//"商品管理"菜单项单击事件的处理方法
private void BasicInfoManageToolStripMenuItem_Click(object sender, EventArgs e)
{
    //把主窗体的内容切换为商品管理
    changeWindow( new GoodsInfoManage());
}
```

changeWindow()方法用于当用户单击不同菜单项时，主窗体对显示的界面进行切换。

```
///<summary>
///切换主窗体中显示的界面
///</summary>
///<param name="uc">用户自定义的每种不同功能的界面,切换的目标界面</param>
private void changeWindow(UserControl uc)
{
    if (panel1.Controls.Count > 0)         //如果主界面面板中的控件不为空
    {
        //对于 panel1 来讲,里面只有一个控件,panel1.Controls[0]就是当前显示的界面
        //如果单击按钮要显示的界面和当前显示的界面类型不一致
        if (!(panel1.Controls[0].GetType()== uc.GetType()))
        {
            panel1.Controls.Clear();       //把面板中以前的界面控件给清除
        }
        else
        {
            return;    //如果当前显示的界面与单击按钮要显示的界面是一样的,就什么也不做
        }
    }
    uc.Dock = DockStyle.Fill;              //设置要添加的界面控件的显示样式为布满
```

```
        panel1.Controls.Add(uc);        //把目标界面控件添加到面板中
    }
```

其他菜单项的实现方法与上述相似,调用 changeWindow()方法,传入目标自定义控件作为参数即可。

3. 实现主窗体初始化

当主窗体加载时与单击"商品管理"菜单项一样,也显示商品管理的界面。主窗体的构造方法如下。

```
//主窗体类的构造方法
public GoodsManageMain()
{
    InitializeComponent();
    //初始化主窗体,显示内容为商品管理
    changeWindow(new GoodsInfoManage());
}
```

7.3.3 商品管理模块

该模块包括商品信息查询、新建、删除、更新商品的信息。

1. 界面设计

(1) 添加自定义控件。右击 GoodsManage 项目名称,在弹出的菜单中选择"添加"→"新建项"命令,弹出如图 7-6 所示"添加新项"对话框,选中类型"用户控件(Windows 窗体)",在"名称"文本框中输入窗体名称"GoodsInfoManage"。

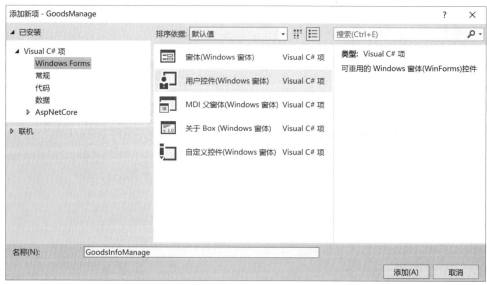

图 7-6 添加用户控件

(2) 设计界面。给用户控件添加两个文本框、四个按钮和一个数据显示控件等,并进行布局,如图 7-7 所示。

(3) 设置控件有关属性值。给控件设置有关的属性值,如表 7-7 所示。

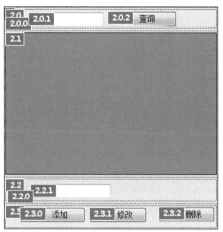

图 7-7 商品管理控件

表 7-7 商品管理控件属性

Tab 序号	控件类型	属性名称	属性值
2.0.1	TextBox	Name	tbxKey
2.0.2	Button	Name	btnGoodsQuery
		Text	查询
2.1	GataGridView	Name	dgvGoods
		AllowUserToAddRows	False
		Dock	Fill
		MultiSelect	False
		ReadOnly	True
		SelectionMode	FullRowSelect
2.2.1	TextBox	Name	tbxGoodsName
2.3.0	Button	Name	btnGoodsAdd
		Text	添加
2.3.1	Button	Name	btnGoodsMod
		Text	修改
2.3.2	Button	Name	btnGoodsDel
		Text	删除

2. 初始化实现

该控件对应的类名是 GoodsInfoManage,有一个字符串变量 filter,用来保存过滤关键字;有一个对象成员 GoodsManageModel gmm = new GoodsManageModel(),gmm 是数据库对象模型。通过 BindData() 方法绑定数据到数据显示控件。对应的代码如下:

```csharp
//定义一个数据库模型
GoodsManageModel gmm = new GoodsManageModel();
//过滤关键字
string filter = "";
public GoodsInfoManage()
{
    InitializeComponent();
    //初始化时绑定商品列表,传入空参数
    //当参数为空串时,显示所有商品
    BindData(filter);
}
```

BindData()方法实现绑定数据到数据显示控件。当传入参数值为空串时,表示加载所有商品数据;当传入的参数值非空时,表示对含有该字符串的商品进行过滤。该方法代码如下。

```csharp
//绑定商品列表
private void BindData(string key)
{
    //定义 Lambda 查询表达式
    var query = gmm.GoodsInfoes.
        //对数据按 GoodsID 升序排列
        OrderByDescending(g => g.GoodsID).
        //选取的记录组成新的表
        Select(n => new
        {
            //返回的 GoodsID 数据列名重命名为"商品编号"
            商品编号 = n.GoodsID,
            //返回的 Name 数据列名重命名为"商品名称"
            商品名称 = n.Name
        });
    var result = query;
    //如果有过滤条件,进行过滤数据集
    if (key != "")
    {
        //从返回结果中过滤出商品名称中包含 key 的商品列表
        result = query.Where(p => p.商品名称.Contains(key));
    }
    //把 Lambda 表达式的查询结果绑定到显示控件 dataGridView1 中
    dataGridView1.DataSource = result.ToList();
    //如果查询的结果不为空
    if (result.Count() > 0)
    {
        //商品名称文本框为商品列表中第一个商品的名称
        tbxGoodsName.Text = result.First().商品名称;
    }
    //重置过滤条件为空
    tbxKey.Text = "";
}
```

3. 实现商品查询功能

由于超市的商品很多,需要通过输入商品的名称进行查询。"查询"按钮功能实现代码如下。

```csharp
//"查询"按钮的单击事件的处理方法
private void btnGoodsQuery_Click(object sender, EventArgs e)
{
    //绑定数据列表
    BindData(tbxKey.Text);
}
```

该按钮的单击事件处理方法通过调用 BindData() 方法来实现,有关 BindData() 方法不再介绍。

4. 实现商品添加功能

当有新商品入库时,需要把商品的信息添加到系统中。"添加"商品按钮功能实现代码如下。

```csharp
//"添加"按钮的单击事件的处理方法
private void btnGoodsAdd_Click(object sender, EventArgs e)
{
    GoodsInfo goods = new GoodsInfo();              //定义一个商品实体对象
    goods.Name = tbxGoodsName.Text;                 //对该商品的名称赋值
    goods.Num = 0;                                  //新添加的商品数量为 0
    if (!goodsNameIsExit(tbxGoodsName.Text))        //检查该商品库中是否已经存在
    {
        gmm.GoodsInfoes.Add(goods);                 //把该入库商品的信息添加到数据库中
        gmm.SaveChanges();                          //提交对数据库的修改
        BindData(tbxKey.Text);                      //重新绑定数据控件
        tbxGoodsName.Text = "";                     //重置商品名称
    }
}
```

在商品入库的时候,对于系统中已经存在的商品,不需要添加该商品,只需要更新商品现存数量即可。检查系统中是否已经存在该商品的方法是 goodsNameIsExit(),该方法实现代码如下。

```csharp
//判断商品是否已经存在
private bool goodsNameIsExit(String goodsName)
{
    //定义 Lambda 查询表达式,以 goodsName 输入的内容作为查询关键字
    var query = gmm.GoodsInfoes.Where(g => g.Name == goodsName);
    if (query.Count() >= 1)                         //判断是否查询到该商品
    {
        MessageBox.Show("该商品名称已经存在!");
        return true;
    }
    else
        return false;
}
```

5. 实现修改功能

为了方便对商品信息的修改,当单击某一商品时把商品信息读取到对应的文本框中。实现读取商品信息到文本框中的方法是 dataGridView1_CellClick(),代码如下。

```csharp
//数据显示控件单击单元格时的处理方法
private void dataGridView1_CellClick(object sender, DataGridViewCellEventArgs e)
{
    if (e.RowIndex >= 0)                          //如果鼠标单击选中行的索引>0
    {
        //取出数据显示控件 dataGridView1 被选中行的索引
        DataGridViewRow row = dataGridView1.Rows[e.RowIndex];
        //取出选中行中对应商品名称的值,赋值给 tbxGoodsName 文本框中
        tbxGoodsName.Text = row.Cells[1].Value.ToString();
    }
}
```

单击"修改"按钮事件的处理方法的代码如下。

```csharp
//"修改"按钮的单击事件的处理方法
private void btnGoodsMod_Click(object sender, EventArgs e)
{
    //返回选中的当前行
    DataGridViewRow row = dataGridView1.SelectedRows[0];
    //用选中行的商品信息实例化一个商品对象
    GoodsInfo goods = findGoodsBySelectRow();
    //同时以文本框 tbxGoodsName.Text 修改数据显示控件中对应商品名称的值
    row.Cells[1].Value = tbxGoodsName.Text;
    //同时以文本框 tbxGoodsName.Text 修改商品对象名称的值
    goods.Name = tbxGoodsName.Text;
    //向数据库提交修改
    gmm.SaveChanges();
}
```

在该方法中使用了 findGoodsBySelectRow(),用来根据选中商品行返回一个商品对象,实现代码如下。

```csharp
//返回选中行对应的商品对象
private GoodsInfo findGoodsBySelectRow()
{
    //获取数据显示控件中被选中的行
    DataGridViewRow row = dataGridView1.SelectedRows[0];
    //取出选中商品对应的 ID
    int id = Int32.Parse(row.Cells[0].Value.ToString());
    //以 ID 作为关键字,构建 Lambda 表达式,实现查找该商品
    GoodsInfo good = gmm.GoodsInfoes.Where
        //商品 ID 等于 ID,所有找到记录的第一个被返回
        (g => g.GoodsID == id).First();
    //返回找到的商品
    return good;
}
```

6. 实现删除功能

当某个商品不再供货,需要从系统中把该商品删除。"删除"按钮功能的实现代码如下。

```csharp
//"删除"按钮的单击事件的处理方法
private void btnGoodsDel_Click(object sender, EventArgs e)
{
    //用选中行的商品信息实例化一个商品对象
```

```
    GoodsInfo good = findGoodsBySelectRow();
    gmm.CoodsInfoes.Remove(good);           //删除该对象
    gmm.SaveChanges();                      //提交对数据库的操作
    BindData(tbxKey.Text);                  //重新绑定数据
}
```

7.3.4 进货管理模块

该模块主要完成对已经存在的商品进行进货的管理。

图 7-8 进货管理控件

1. 界面设计

（1）添加自定义控件，名称为 GoodsInManage。

（2）设计界面，由两个文本框、一个下拉框、一个日期选择器和一个按钮组成，设计好的界面如图 7-8 所示。

（3）设置控件有关属性值。

给控件设置有关的属性值，如表 7-8 所示。

表 7-8 进货管理控件属性

Tab 序号	控 件 类 型	属 性 名 称	属 性 值
5.4	TextBox	Name	tbxFilterKey
5.5	CombBox	Name	cmbGoods
		DropDownStyle	DropDownList
5.6	TextBox	Name	tbxGoodsNum
5.7	DataTimePicker	Name	dtpGoodsIn
5.8	Button	Name	btnGoodsIn
		Text	进货

2. 初始化实现

该控件对应的类名是 GoodsInManage，有一个对象成员 GoodsManageModel gmm = new GoodsManageModel(); gmm 是数据库对象模型。该类实现初始界面的显示，其构造方法如下。

```
GoodsManageModel gmm = new GoodsManageModel();
//用户控件的构造方法
public GoodsInManage()
{
    //自动生成的控件初始化
    InitializeComponent();
    //构建 Lambda 查询表达式,查询出所有的商品.
    //在进行绑定的时候由于商品过多,可以选择库存最少的 10 件商品
    var query = gmm.GoodsInfoes.
        //按照商品存货量的升序排列
```

```
            OrderBy(g => g.Num).Select(g => g.Name);
        //把商品名称绑定到商品选择下拉框中
        cmbGoods.DataSource = query.Take(10).ToList();
}
```

3. 实现商品名称过滤功能

在进货时,有时系统中商品种类繁多,选择某一种商品很不方便。在实现进货时,系统提供了一个商品名称的过滤功能。用户输入商品的关键字,那么在商品选择的下拉框中就只显示包含该关键字的商品。对文本框的内容变化事件实现代码如下。

```
//过滤文本框控件文本发现变化事件处理方法
private void tbxFilterKey_TextChanged(object sender, EventArgs e)
{
    //构建以 tbxFilterKey.Text 为关键字的查询表达式
    var query = gmm.GoodsInfoes.
        //查询条件为商品名称包含传入的关键字
        Where(g => g.Name.Contains(tbxFilterKey.Text)).
        //以升序排列返回商品名称
        OrderBy(g => g.Name).Select(g => g.Name );
    //如果查询结果为空,设置 cmbGoods 控件没有任何项
    if (query.Count() == 0)
    {
        cmbGoods.Text = "";
    }
    else //绑定查询结果到 cmbGoods 控件
    {
        cmbGoods.DataSource = query.ToList();
    }
}
```

4. 实现进货量验证功能

在用户输入进货数量时,要对输入的值进行有效性的验证,必须是正整数或正小数,输入负数和非数字是无效的。验证的方法由数量文本框的失去焦点事件触发,代码如下。

```
//实现对数量文本框的输入有效性验证
private void tbxGoodsNum_Leave(object sender, EventArgs e)
{
    //返回验证结果,IsPositiveNumber()方法验证有效性
    bool isValidNum = IsPositiveNumber(tbxGoodsNum.Text);
    if (!isValidNum)
    {
        MessageBox.Show("不是数字或者为空,请重新输入!");
        //数量控件获取焦点
        tbxGoodsNum.Focus();
        //设置数量控件为空
        tbxGoodsNum.Text = "";
    }
}
```

方法 IsPositiveNumber()完成文本有效性的验证,并返回验证结果,该方法的实现代码如下。

```csharp
//验证数字的有效性
public bool IsPositiveNumber(string strNumber)
{
    //用来验证整数部分的表达式
    Regex objNotPositivePattern = new Regex("[^0-9.]");
    //用来验证小数部分的表达式
    Regex objPositivePattern = new Regex("^[.][0-9]+$|[0-9]*[.]*[0-9]+$");
    //用来验证包含整数和小数的表达式
    Regex objTwoDotPattern = new Regex("[0-9]*[.][0-9]*[.][0-9]*");
    //返回验证结果
    return objNotPositivePattern.IsMatch(strNumber) ||
        objPositivePattern.IsMatch(strNumber) ||
        objTwoDotPattern.IsMatch(strNumber);
}
```

该方法的实现使用了正则表达式,需要引用命名空间:System.Text.RegularExpressions。

5．实现商品进货功能

实现商品进货的功能,需要两个操作:一是修改商品的库存量,二是记录该次进货。"进货"按钮实现代码如下。

```csharp
//"进货"按钮单击的处理方法,实现进货处理
private void btnGoodsIn_Click(object sender, EventArgs e)
{
    //查询出选中的商品对象
    GoodsInfo good = gmm.GoodsInfoes.Where(g => g.Name == cmbGoods.Text).First();
    //把该商品的数量进行修改,现存量加上进货量
    good.Num = good.Num + Int32.Parse(tbxGoodsNum.Text);
    //实例化一个商品进货对象
    GoodsIn gi = new GoodsIn();
    //设置商品进货对象的商品ID等于商品对象的ID
    gi.GoodsID = good.GoodsID;
    //设置商品进货对象的进货数量等于tbxGoodsNum文本框的值
    gi.Num = Int32.Parse(tbxGoodsNum.Text);
    //设置商品进货时间
    gi.InTime = dtpGoodsIn.Value;
    //把商品进货对象插入到数据库
    gmm.GoodsIns.Add(gi);
    //提交对数据库的修改
    gmm.SaveChanges();
}
```

7.3.5 销售管理模块

该模块主要完成超市商品的销售管理。

1．界面设计

(1) 添加自定义控件,名称为 GoodsOutManage。

(2) 设计界面,由两个文本框、一个下拉框、一个日期选择器和一个按钮组成,设计好的界面如图 7-9 所示。

(3) 设置控件有关属性值,如表 7-9 所示。

图 7-9 销售管理控件

表 7-9 销售管理控件属性

Tab 序号	控件类型	属性名称	属性值
5.4	TextBox	Name	tbxFilterKey
5.5	CombBox	Name	cmbGoods
		DropDownStyle	DropDownList
5.6	TextBox	Name	tbxGoodsNum
5.7	DataTimePicker	Name	dtpGoodsOut
5.8	Button	Name	btnGoodsOut
		Text	销售

2. 初始化实现

该控件与控件 GoodsInManage 类似,对应的类名是 GoodsOutManage。该控件也有商品的过滤功能和销售数量验证功能,与类 GoodsInManage 的实现方法一样。在初始化界面加载时与 GoodsInManage 有一点小的区别,下拉框绑定是最近售出的 10 种商品名称。初始化方法如下。

```
//定义数据库模型
GoodsManageModel gmm = new GoodsManageModel();
//用户控件的构造方法
public GoodsOutManage()
{
    InitializeComponent();
    //定义 Lambda 表达式,返回商品销售记录
    var query = gmm.GoodsOuts.
        //对销售的记录按销售的时间降序排列
        OrderByDescending(g => g.OutTime).
        //取关联到的商品的名称
        Select(g => g.GoodsInfo.Name);
    //给下拉框绑定最近销售的 10 种商品,distinct 用来去除重复商品
    cmbGoods.DataSource = query.Distinct().Take(10).ToList();
}
```

3. 实现商品销售功能

实现商品销售的功能,需要两个操作:一是修改商品的剩余库存量,二是记录该次销售记录。"销售"按钮实现代码如下。

```csharp
//"销售"按钮的处理方法
private void btnGoodsOut_Click(object sender, EventArgs e)
{
    //返回一个商品对象,该项商品对象是用户从下拉框中选中的商品
    GoodsInfo good = gmm.GoodsInfoes.
        //查询条件为商品名称等于选中的商品名称
        Where(g => g.Name == cmbGoods.Text).
        //返回查询结果中的第一个对象
        First();
    //计算商品剩余数量,并赋值
    good.Num = good.Num - Int32.Parse(tbxGoodsNum.Text);
    //定义商品销售对象
    GoodsOut go = new GoodsOut();
    //售出的商品 ID 等于商品 ID
    go.GoodsID = good.GoodsID;
    //售出数量等于文本框内设置的数量
    go.Num = Int32.Parse(tbxGoodsNum.Text);
    //设置售出时间
    go.OutTime = dtpGoodsIn.Value;
    //向数据库对象中插入该条记录
    gmm.GoodsOuts.Add(go);
    //把对数据库的修改提交给服务器
    gmm.SaveChanges();
}
```

7.3.6 库存统计模块

该模块主要完成超市商品存货量的统计等,下面以统计存货量最小的商品为例说明。

1. 界面设计

(1) 添加自定义控件,名称为 GoodsStatic。

(2) 设计界面,由一个文本框和一个数据显示控件组成,界面设计如图 7-10 所示。

图 7-10 货存统计控件

(3) 设置控件有关属性值,如表 7-10 所示。

表 7-10 货存量统计控件属性

Tab 序号	控 件 类 型	属 性 名 称	属 性 值
2.0.1	TextBox	Name	tbNum
		Text	10
2.1	DataGridView	Name	dgvGoods

2. 初始化实现

该控件对应的类名是 GoodsStatic,有一个整型变量 num,用来存放存货量;有一个对象成员 GoodsManageModel gmm = new GoodsManageModel(),gmm 是数据库对象模型。通过 BindData()方法绑定数据到数据显示控件。对应的代码如下。

```csharp
//绑定数据到数据显示控件
private void bindData(int num)
{
    //重置数据显示控件的数据为空
    dgvGoods.DataSource = null;
    //定义查询存货量小于 num 的商品的 Lambda 表达式
    var query = gmm.GoodsInfoes.
        //查询条件为存货量小于 num
        Where(g => g.Num < num).
        //按照 num 的升序排列
        OrderBy(g=>g.Num).
        //把查询结果重组为对象
        Select(g => new
        {
            //查询的商品名称的列名为:商品名称
            商品名称 = g.Name,
            //查询的商品数量的列名为:商品数量
            商品数量 = g.Num
        });
    //把查询的结果绑定到数据显示控件中
    dgvGoods.DataSource = query.ToList();
}
```

3. 库存量筛选实现

当用户修改显示最少库存量的条件时,相应的商品能够在数据控件中显示出来。因此需要实现输入框的 TextChanged 事件,事件的处理方法如下。

```csharp
//文本输入框文本修改时的处理方法
private void tbNum_TextChanged(object sender, EventArgs e)
{
    int num = 0;
    try
    {
        //把用户输入的数字转换为数字类型
        num = Int32.Parse(tbNum.Text);
        //绑定数据到数据显示控件
        bindData(num);
    }
    catch
    {
        MessageBox.Show("数据格式有误,请重新输入!");
    }
}
```

7.4 技术经验总结

7.4.1 技术总结

本系统用到了以下技术及知识点。

(1) 使用 Visual Studio 的 EF 框架,自动生成数据库实体模型代码。
(2) 在进行界面设计时,使用了大量用户自定义控件,方便了实现。
(3) 本系统使用 LINQ to Enities 的方式完成对数据库操作。

7.4.2 经验总结

(1) 好的开发工具能大大提高系统的开发效率。
(2) 开发系统时,一定要从用户使用习惯出发来设计系统,提高用户使用的便利度。
(3) 养成对代码重构的习惯,提高代码的可重用性。

第 8 章 在线考试系统案例开发

本章以在线考试系统为例,讲解如何利用简单三层架构开发一个完整的管理信息系统。系统包括学生信息、班级信息、教师信息、课程信息、题库管理、组卷管理、在线考试等模块。

通过本章的学习,读者应重点掌握简单三层架构在管理信息系统开发中的应用。

8.1 项目概述

传统的纸质考试方式具有诸多缺点,如教师要花费较大时间和精力在出题、组卷和阅卷上,而且很难避免错判、漏判、计错分等错误的发生。随着计算机软件和互联网技术的迅速普及与飞速发展,在线考试系统应运而生,它不但可以在很大程度上减轻教师出题、组卷和阅卷上的工作量,还可以大幅度地降低人为错误,提升考试成绩的准确性、客观性和公正性。

8.2 系统需求

8.2.1 业务描述

传统考试方式的一般过程是教师出题,然后组成试卷再印刷试卷,接着安排考试时间、地点、监考教师,组织考生进行考试,最后人工阅卷、发布成绩。在这个过程中,教师选题、组卷、阅卷的工作量是巨大的,并且无论是在出卷还是阅卷环节都容易出错。

在线考试系统的考试过程是,首先教师向系统题库中录入大量试题,再按既定要求进行自动组卷;然后教师设定自己课程的考试时间;学生只有在规定的考试时间内才能进行考试,考试时间结束或者考生主动选择提交试卷则考试结束,不能继续答题。学生在考试期间,所有操作系统的热键将全部被屏蔽,防止出现作弊行为。

由于篇幅有限,本章介绍的在线考试系统只包含客观题型(单选题、多选题和判断题),系统可自动阅卷,大大提高了工作效率。

8.2.2 用户描述

本系统用户共分为三种角色:学生、教师、管理员。每一种用户的业务描述如下。

1. 学生

学生登录系统可完成以下操作。

(1) 考试:只有该学生在本时间段存在需要考试的课程时才能够进入该课程的考试界面进行考试。

(2) 查询成绩：学生只能查看自己的考试成绩，且必须是教师已经发布了该课程的考试成绩学生才可以看到。

2. 教师

教师主要负责授课课程及班级的设定、考试时间的设定、题库的维护、组卷以及学生成绩的发布审查。

3. 管理员

管理员主要负责对各类基础信息进行管理，包括学生信息、班级信息、教师信息、课程信息、章节信息。等此外，管理员也具有教师的全部功能。

8.2.3 功能分析

本系统包括两个子系统：教师子系统和学生子系统。教师子系统的用户是管理员及教师，学生子系统的用户是全体学生。

1. 教师功能

(1) 登录：登录验证成功才允许进入教师子系统。

(2) 修改个人设置：教师可以修改自己账户的登录密码。

(3) 授课信息管理：教师可设定自己本学期的授课课程及授课班级，一条授课信息代表教师的一个上课课头，教师可设定该课头的考试时间。

(4) 试题库管理：教师可以对系统试题库中的试题进行添加、删除、修改、查询等操作。

(5) 试卷管理：教师可以规定组卷份数、试卷所适用的课头，对组卷方式进行相应的设定，并且按照教师所设定的规则生成指定套数的试卷。

(6) 成绩管理：教师可以对成绩是否发布进行管理，并且可以根据不同条件对成绩进行查询。

(7) 注销：退出当前已经登录的用户，返回登录界面。

2. 管理员功能

(1) 管理员拥有教师的所有功能。

(2) 维护所有基础数据：管理员可以对班级、学生、教师、课程和章节进行添加、删除、修改、查询以及批量导入操作。

3. 学生功能

(1) 登录：登录验证成功才允许进入学生子系统。

(2) 考试：只有登录学生所属班级在当前服务器时间存在考试科目，该学生才能进入考试界面进行考试。在进入考试界面后，应做一些必要的限制，如禁止用户使用任务管理器、系统组合键等，以防学生利用这些功能切换出考试界面进行其他操作。

(3) 提交试卷：如果考试时间结束，系统将自动提交试卷，结束考试。考生也可手动提前提交试卷，结束考试。考试结束时考试界面自动关闭，同时解除客户端对当前计算机的限制。

(4) 查看考试成绩：学生提交试卷后，系统会自动阅卷，但是成绩必须经教师确认并发布后学生才可以查看到，且只能看到自己的考试成绩。

(5) 注销：退出当前已经登录的用户，返回登录界面。

8.3 系统分析设计

8.3.1 模块设计

根据 8.2 节的需求分析，对系统进行总体结构设计，如图 8-1 所示。

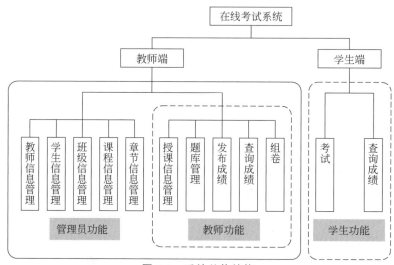

图 8-1 系统总体结构

8.3.2 数据库设计

根据系统需求分析，设计满足要求的数据库逻辑模型，如图 8-2 所示。

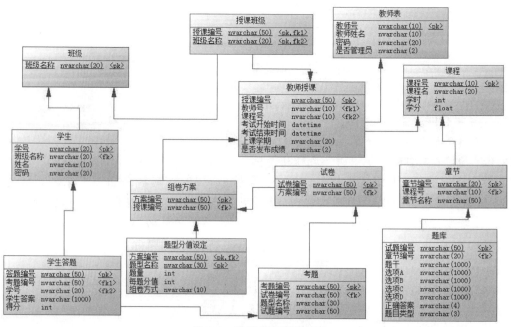

图 8-2 数据库逻辑模型

(1) 章节信息表(Chapter)如表 8-1 所示。

表 8-1 章节信息表

列　　名	数据类型	长度	允许空	是否为主键	说　　明
chapterId	nvarchar	20	否	是	章节编号
courseId	nvarchar	10	否	否	课程号
chapterName	nvarchar	50	否	否	章节名称

(2) 班级信息表(Classes)如表 8-2 所示。

表 8-2 班级信息表

列　　名	数据类型	长度	允许空	是否为主键	说　　明
className	nvarchar	20	否	是	班级名称

(3) 课程信息表(Course)如表 8-3 所示。

表 8-3 课程信息表

列　　名	数据类型	长度	允许空	是否为主键	说　　明
courseId	nvarchar	10	否	是	课程号
courseName	nvarchar	20	否	否	课程名
courseHour	int		是	否	学时
courseCredit	float		是	否	学分

(4) 组卷方案表(CreatePaperScheme)如表 8-4 所示。

表 8-4 组卷方案表

列　　名	数据类型	长度	允许空	是否为主键	说　　明
schemeId	nvarchar	50	否	是	方案编号
teachId	nvarchar	50	否	否	授课编号

(5) 考题信息表(Questions)如表 8-5 所示。

表 8-5 考题信息表

列　　名	数据类型	长度	允许空	是否为主键	说　　明
testQuestionID	nvarchar	50	否	是	考题编号
paperID	nvarchar	50	否	否	试卷编号
typeName	nvarchar	30	否	否	题型名称
questionId	nvarchar	50	否	否	试题编号

(6) 题型分值设定信息表(QuestionTypeScore)如表 8-6 所示。

表 8-6 题型分值设定信息表

列　　名	数 据 类 型	长度	允许空	是否为主键	说　　明
schemeId	nvarchar	50	否	是	方案编号
typeName	nvarchar	30	否	是	题型名称
questionNum	int		否	否	题量
questionScore	int		否	否	每题分值
createType	nvarchar	10	否	否	组卷方式

(7) 学生信息表(Student)如表 8-7 所示。

表 8-7 学生信息表

列　　名	数 据 类 型	长度	允许空	是否为主键	说　　明
studentId	nvarchar	20	否	是	学号
className	nvarchar	20	否	否	班级名称
studentName	nvarchar	10	是	否	姓名
studentPwd	nvarchar	20	是	否	密码

(8) 学生答题信息表(StudentAnswer)如表 8-8 所示。

表 8-8 学生答题信息表

列　　名	数 据 类 型	长度	允许空	是否为主键	说　　明
answerId	nvarchar	50	否	是	答题编号
testQuestionID	nvarchar	50	否	否	考题编号
studentId	nvarchar	20	否	否	学号
answer	nvarchar	1000	是	否	学生答案
score	int		是	否	得分

(9) 授课班级信息表(TeachClass)如表 8-9 所示。

表 8-9 授课班级信息表

列　　名	数 据 类 型	长度	允许空	是否为主键	说　　明
teachId	nvarchar	50	否	是	授课编号
className	nvarchar	20	否	是	班级名称

(10) 教师授课信息表(TeachCourse)如表 8-10 所示。

表 8-10 教师授课信息表

列 名	数据类型	长度	允许空	是否为主键	说 明
teachId	nvarchar	50	否	是	授课编号
teacherId	nvarchar	10	否	否	教师号
courseId	nvarchar	10	否	否	课程号
beginTime	datetime		是	否	考试开始时间
endTime	datetime		是	否	考试结束时间
teachTerm	nvarchar	20	否	否	上课学期
isPublic	nvarchar	2	否	否	是否发布成绩

(11) 教师信息表(Teacher)如表 8-11 所示。

表 8-11 教师信息表

列 名	数据类型	长度	允许空	是否为主键	说 明
teacherId	nvarchar	10	否	是	教师号
teacherName	nvarchar	10	是	否	教师姓名
teacherPwd	nvarchar	20	是	否	密码
isAdmin	nvarchar	2	否	否	是否管理员

(12) 试卷信息表(TestPaper)如表 8-12 所示。

表 8-12 试卷信息表

列 名	数据类型	长度	允许空	是否为主键	说 明
paperID	nvarchar	50	否	是	试卷编号
schemeId	nvarchar	50	否	否	方案编号

(13) 题库信息表(TestQuestion)如表 8-13 所示。

表 8-13 题库信息表

列 名	数据类型	长度	允许空	是否为主键	说 明
questionID	nvarchar	50	否	是	试题编号
chapterId	nvarchar	20	否	否	章节编号
questionTitle	nvarchar	1000	否	否	题干
answerA	nvarchar	1000	是	否	选项 A
answerB	nvarchar	1000	是	否	选项 B
answerC	nvarchar	1000	是	否	选项 C

续表

列　名	数据类型	长度	允许空	是否为主键	说　明
answerD	nvarchar	1000	是	否	选项 D
currectAnswer	nvarchar	4	否	否	正确答案
questionType	nvarchar	3	否	否	题目类型

8.4　技　术　准　备

该项目涉及一些本书前面没有提到的技术，如在实现学生信息批量导入时，需要用到 Excel 电子表格的相关操作技术；在实现组卷时，需随机从数据库抽取试题，可借助 SQL Server 数据库的相关函数来实现；在线考试过程中，应杜绝考生切出考试界面，需借助系统 API 来实现；同样是在线考试过程中，还应杜绝考生使用任务管理器强制结束程序，需借助注册表来完成限制；此外，在线考试时，考生的答题界面中的控件需根据组卷时设定的试题数，自动产生相应的操作控件，需实现控件的动态生成。本节将针对上述问题，给出相应的技术解决方案。

8.4.1　Excel 组件使用

Excel 是微软公司 Office 办公自动化套件中的一个软件，它主要是用来处理电子表格的。Excel 以其功能强大、界面友好等特点受到了广大用户的欢迎。利用程序操作 Excel 不仅使得程序设计简单，而且满足了用户的数据交换和数据复用要求，更加实用。那么用 Visual C♯ 如何调用 Excel、如何读写 Excel 呢？

要在项目中调用 Excel，向其中写入数据，首先需要引用 Excel 的 COM 组件。在 Visual Studio 的解决方案资源管理器中右击要调用 Excel 的项目中的"引用"节点，在弹出菜单中选择"添加引用"命令，弹出如图 8-3 所示的"引用管理器"对话框。在"引用管理器"对话框中选择 COM 选项卡，在列表中勾选 Microsoft Excel 11.0 Object Library（随着计算

图 8-3　"引用管理器"对话框

机中安装的 Office 版本不同,组件名称也不相同。Microsoft Excel 11.0 Object Library 是 Office 2003 所带的 COM 组件名称)组件,单击"确定"按钮完成引用的添加。

添加 COM 组件之后还要在源代码中引入相应的命名空间,代码如下。

```
using Microsoft.Office.Interop;
using Excel = Microsoft.Office.Interop.Excel;
```

引用之后就可以进行写入操作。

```
Excel.Application app = new Excel.Application();        //创建 Excel 程序实例对象
app.Application.Workbooks.Add(true);                    //添加工作簿
Excel.Workbook book = (Excel.Workbook)app.ActiveWorkbook;
                                                        //获得当前活动的工作簿
Excel.Worksheet sheet = (Excel.Worksheet)book.ActiveSheet;
                                                        //获得当前活动的工作表
```

完成这些准备操作后,就可以利用赋值语句来为指定单元格赋值,例如:

```
sheet.Cells[1, 1] ="ABC";        //指定当前工作表中第　行第　列的值为 ABC
```

还可以通过对 Visible 属性的设置来控制 Excel 程序窗口是否显示。

```
app.Visible = true;
```

如果要结束操作,用以下代码进行"善后"工作。

```
//保存文件
book.SaveCopyAs("c:\\source.xls");
//关闭文件
book.Close(false);
//退出 Excel
app.Quit();
```

从 Excel 数据表中读取数据,需要通过 OleDb 进行连接,引用如下命名空间。

```
using System.Data.OleDb;
using System.Data;
```

接下来的操作类似于数据库操作,可以将一个 Excel 工作簿理解为一个数据库,其中的一个工作表(sheet)就相当于数据库的一个数据表,代码如下。

```
string oleconstr = @"Provider=Microsoft.Jet.OLEDB.4.0;Extended Properties=
Excel 12.0; data source=Excel 文件路径";          //定义连接字符串
OleDbConnection oleConn = new OleDbConnection(oleconstr);  //创建连接对象
oleConn.Open();                                            //打开连接
```

建立数据库连接后即可通过 SQL 语句进行查询,并读取数据,最后关闭数据库连接,代码如下。

```
string sqlexcel = "SELECT * FROM [sheet1$]";    //从工作表 sheet1 中查询所有数据
OleDbCommand olecmd = new OleDbCommand();
olecmd.Connection = oleConn;
olecmd.CommandText = sqlexcel;
using (OleDbDataReader odr = olecmd.ExecuteReader())
```

```
{
    while (odr.Read())
    {
        //从当前表的当前行中读取第一、二、三、四列的内容,并删除前后空格
        string para1 = Convert.ToString(odr[0]).Trim(); ;
        string para2 = Convert.ToString(odr[1]).Trim();
        string para3 = Convert.ToString(odr[2]).Trim();
        string para4 = Convert.ToString(odr[3]).Trim();
    }
    odr.Close();
    oleConn.Close();
}
```

8.4.2 数据库的随机排序方法

Transact-SQL 中有一个 newid() 函数,该函数可以创建一个 uniqueidentifier 类型的唯一值。可以在使用 select 语句查询数据时,加入 order by newid() 子句,这样在扫描每条记录的时候都生成一个值,而生成的值是随机的,没有大小写顺序,然后再按这个值排序,排序的结果即为随机结果。使用 newid() 函数进行试题的随机抽取,要比写 C♯ 程序算法更简洁且随机性更高。

以下语句是从学生表中随机抽取 10 个学号的 SQL 语句。

```
Select top 10 studentId from students order by newid()
```

8.4.3 API 的使用

API(Application Programming Interface,应用编程接口)其实就是操作系统留给应用程序的一套调用接口,应用程序通过调用操作系统的 API 函数可以完成一些系统级的操作,如截获 Windows 消息、进程控制、内存操作等。

本系统所需要的 API 都包含在以下 3 个 DLL 库中:Kernel、User、GDI,本节以调用 User 库中的 MessageBox() 函数为例,介绍在 C♯ 中如何声明及使用 API 函数。User 库在 32 位的 Windows 操作系统中名叫 USER32.DLL,它允许管理全部的用户接口,如窗口、菜单、对话框、图标等。

要使用 API 函数,需要以外部函数的方式声明该 API 函数,并且用 DllImport 属性指明该函数所在的库。函数正确声明后,即可像调用普通的 C♯ 函数一样调用该 API 函数。

要使用 DllImport 属性需引入如下命名空间。

```
using System.Runtime.InteropServices;
```

接下来声明 API 函数 MessageBox(),并调用它,以实现在控制台程序中,弹出 Windows 消息框的效果,代码如下。

```
using System;
using System.Runtime.InteropServices;
class Program
{
```

```
//以下两行代码是在声明 API 函数,API 函数的用法、结构可查阅相应的 API 文档
[DllImport("User32.dll")]
public static extern int MessageBox(int h, string m, string c, int type);
static int Main()
{
    //调用 API 函数 MessageBox(),参数一代表是否隐藏,参数二为消息框内容
    //参数三为标题栏名称,参数四标识消息框按钮类型
    MessageBox(0, "Hello Win32 API", "标题栏", 4);
    Console.ReadLine();
    return 0;
}
```

8.4.4 注册表的使用

注册表是 Windows 操作系统中的一个核心数据库,其中存放着各种参数,直接控制着 Windows 的启动、硬件驱动程序的装载以及一些 Windows 应用程序的运行,从而在整个系统中起着核心作用。

Windows 操作系统的注册表包含很多有关计算机运行的配置,打开注册表可以看到注册表是按类似于目录的树状结构组织的,其中,第二级目录包含 5 个预定义主键,分别是 HKEY_CLASSES_ROOT、HKEY_CURRENT_USER、HKEY_LOCAL_MACHINE、HKEY_USERS 和 HKEY_CURRENT_CONFIG。每个主键内包含非常多的子键,子键中还有若干值项,一个值项则由名称、数据类型以及分配的值组成。读者可自行查阅注册表操作手册以深入了解注册表的操作。本系统利用注册表实现了屏蔽系统热键功能。

下面简单介绍如何实现对注册表的读、写操作。

(1) 读取注册表指定值项的值。

示例代码如下。

```
private string GetRegistData(string name)
{
    string registData;
    RegistryKey hkml = Registry.LocalMachine;
                                //指明要访问的主键是 HKEY_LOCAL_MACHINE
    //打开 HKEY_LOCAL_MACHINE 下的子键
    RegistryKey software = hkml.OpenSubKey("@"Software\Microsoft\Windows\
            CurrentVersion\Policies\System",true);
    RegistryKey aimdir = software.OpenSubKey("XXX",true);
    registData = aimdir.GetValue(name).ToString();
                                //获得指定名称的值项的值
    return registData;
}
```

以上代码的作用是读取注册表中 HKEY_LocalMachine \ Software \ Microsoft \ Windows\CurrentVersion\Policies\System 子键下的 XXX 子键中名称为 name 的值项的值。

(2) 向注册表中写数据。

示例代码如下。

```csharp
private void WTRegedit(string name, string tovalue)
{
    RegistryKey hklm = Registry.LocalMachine;
    RegistryKey software = hklm.OpenSubKey("@"Software\Microsoft\Windows\
                           CurrentVersion\Policies\System",true);
    RegistryKey aimdir = software.CreateSubKey("XXX");    //创建子键
    aimdir.SetValue(name,tovalue);                         //向子键中写入值项的名称和值
}
```

以上是在注册表中 HKEY _ LocalMachine \ Software \ Microsoft \ Windows \ CurrentVersion\Policies\System 子键下新建 XXX 子键并在此子键下创建名称为 name、值为 tovalue 的值项。

8.4.5 控件的代码生成法

本系统的学生考试界面，涉及控件的代码生成技术，即要根据本次考试抽取到的数据库中的试题数据，用代码动态自动生成相应的控件，并完成试题在界面中的显示及相应的事件处理。

以代码生成 Button 控件及其 Click 事件为例介绍控件的代码生成方法。

示例代码如下。

```csharp
private void FrmTest_Load(object sender, EventArgs e)   //窗体的 Load 事件
{
    Button btn = new Button();                           //实例化一个按钮对象
    btn.Text = "代码产生的按钮";                          //设置按钮的 Text 属性
    btn.Left = 50;                                       //设置按钮的左上角横坐标
    btn.Top = 50;                                        //设置按钮的左上角纵坐标
    btn.AutoSize = true;                                 //设置按钮自动控制大小
    btn.Click+=new EventHandler(btn_Click);              //为按钮添加 Click 事件处理函数
    plContainer.Controls.Add(btn);                       //将按钮添加到面板控件 plContainer 中
}
public void btn_Click(object sender, EventArgs e)        //按钮的 Click 事件处理函数
{
    MessageBox.Show("这是代码生成的按钮事件");
}
```

8.5 实体类库实现

Model 即实体类库，该类库利用面向对象的思想，将数据表封装成类。本系统共涉及 13 个数据表的操作：Chapter、Classes、Course、CreatePaperScheme、Questions、QuestionTypeScore、Student、StudentAnswer、TeachClass、TeachCourse、Teacher、TestPaper、TestQuestion，因此需在 Model 类库中添加 13 个类，每个类的命名与对应的数据表相同，如图 8-4 所示。每个类中包含若干属性的定义，每个属性与数据表中的字段相对应，需要注意各个属性应定义为 public 公有属性。

由于篇幅所限，本章后续内容仅以学生信息管理模块、题库管理模块、组卷模块、学生端主界面以及学生考试模块的实现为例进行详细介绍。所列各实体类、数据访问层类、业务逻

辑层类也仅与上述模块相关,更多内容可参照本书网络资源中的完整项目代码。

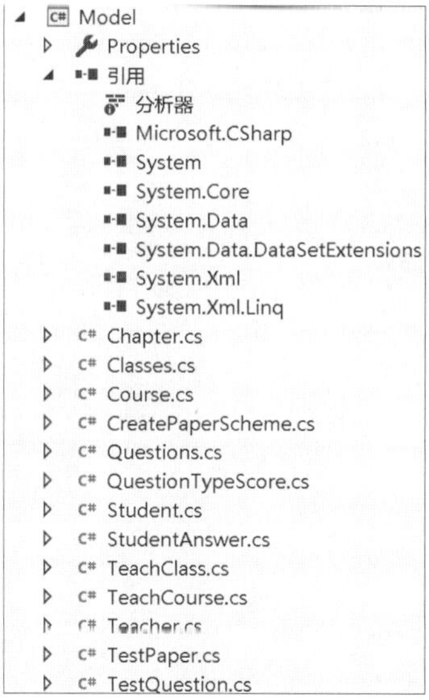

图 8-4　Model 类库结构

8.5.1　Student 类

该类是学生信息表 Student 的实体类。学生信息管理模块的实现需要调用此类。实现代码如下。

```csharp
public class Student
{
    private string studentId;
    private string studentPwd;
    private string className;
    private string studentName;
    ///<summary>
    ///获取或设置学生的学号
    ///</summary>
    public string StudentId
    {
        get
        { return studentId; }
        set
        { studentId = value; }
    }
    ///<summary>
    ///获取或设置学生的密码
    ///</summary>
    public string StudentPwd
    {
        get
        { return studentPwd; }
        set
        { studentPwd = value; }
    }
```

```csharp
    }
    ///<summary>
    ///获取或设置学生的班级名称
    ///</summary>
    public string ClassName
    {
        get
        { return className; }
        set
        { className = value; }
    }
    ///<summary>
    ///获取或设置学生的姓名
    ///</summary>
    public string StudentName
    {
        get
        { return studentName; }
        set
        { studentName = value; }
    }
}
```

8.5.2 TestQuestion 类

该类是题库表 TestQuestion 的实体类。题库管理、组卷管理等多个模块的实现需要调用此类。实现代码如下。

```csharp
public class TestQuestion
{
    private string questionId;
    private string chapterId;
    private string questionTitle;
    private string answerA;
    private string answerB;
    private string answerC;
    private string answerD;
    private string currectAnswer;
    private string questionType;
    ///<summary>
    ///获取或设置题目试题编号
    ///</summary>
    public string QuestionId
    {
        get
        { return questionId; }
        set
        { questionId = value; }
    }
    ///<summary>
    ///获取或设置题目章节编号
    ///</summary>
```

```csharp
public string ChapterId
{
    get
    { return chapterId; }
    set
    { chapterId = value; }
}
///<summary>
///获取或设置题目题干
///</summary>
public string QuestionTitle
{
    get
    { return questionTitle; }
    set
    { questionTitle = value; }
}
///<summary>
///获取或设置题目选项 A 的内容
///</summary>
public string AnswerA
{
    get
    { return answerA; }
    set
    { answerA = value; }
}
///<summary>
///获取或设置题目选项 B 的内容
///</summary>
public string AnswerB
{
    get
    { return answerB; }
    set
    { answerB = value; }
}
///<summary>
///获取或设置题目选项 C 的内容
///</summary>
public string AnswerC
{
    get
    { return answerC; }
    set
    { answerC = value; }
}
///<summary>
///获取或设置题目选项 D 的内容
///</summary>
public string AnswerD
{
    get
```

```csharp
        { return answerD; }
        set
        { answerD = value; }
    }
    ///<summary>
    ///获取或设置题目正确答案
    ///</summary>
    public string CurrectAnswer
    {
        get
        { return currectAnswer; }
        set
        { currectAnswer = value; }
    }
    ///<summary>
    ///获取或设置题目的类型
    ///</summary>
    public string QuestionType
    {
        get
        { return questionType; }
        set
        { questionType = value; }
    }
}
```

8.5.3 CreatePaperScheme 类

该类是组卷方案表 CreatePaperScheme 的实体类。组卷管理模块的实现需要调用此类。实现代码如下。

```csharp
public class CreatePaperScheme
{
    private string schemeId;
    private string teachId;
    ///<summary>
    ///获取或设置试卷方案的方案编号
    ///</summary>
    public string SchemeId
    {
        get
        { return schemeId; }
        set
        { schemeId = value; }
    }
    ///<summary>
    ///获取或设置试卷方案的授课编号
    ///</summary>
    public string TeachId
    {
        get
        { return teachId; }
```

```
            set
            { teachId = value; }
        }
    }
```

8.5.4 TestPaper 类

该类是试卷表 TestPaper 的实体类。组卷管理模块的实现需要调用此类。实现代码如下。

```
public class TestPaper
{
    private string paperId;
    private string schemeId;
    ///<summary>
    ///获取或设置试卷的试卷编号
    ///</summary>
    public string PaperId
    {
        get
        { return paperId; }
        set
        { paperId = value; }
    }
    ///<summary>
    ///获取或设置试卷的方案编号
    ///</summary>
    public string SchemeId
    {
        get
        { return schemeId; }
        set
        { schemeId = value; }
    }
}
```

8.5.5 QuestionTypeScore 类

该类是题型分值设定表 QuestionTypeScore 的实体类。组卷管理模块的实现需要调用此类。实现代码如下。

```
public class QuestionTypeScore
{
    private string schemeId;
    private string typeName;
    private int questionNum;
    private int questionScore;
    private string createType;
    ///<summary>
    ///获取或设置题型分值设定的方案编号
    ///</summary>
    public string SchemeId
```

```csharp
{
    get
    { return schemeId; }
    set
    { schemeId = value; }
}
///<summary>
///获取或设置题型分值设定的题型名称
///</summary>
public string TypeName
{
    get
    { return typeName; }
    set
    { typeName = value; }
}
///<summary>
///获取或设置题型分值设定的题量
///</summary>
public int QuestionNum
{
    get
    { return questionNum; }
    set
    { questionNum = value; }
}
///<summary>
///获取或设置题型分值设定的每题分值
///</summary>
public int QuestionScore
{
    get
    { return questionScore; }
    set
    { questionScore = value; }
}
///<summary>
///获取或设置题型分值设定的组卷方式
///</summary>
public string CreateType
{
    get
    { return createType; }
    set
    { createType = value; }
}
}
```

8.5.6 Questions 类

该类是考题表 Questions 的实体类。组卷管理模块的实现需要调用此类。实现代码如下。

```csharp
public class Questions
{
    private string testQuestionId;
    private string paperId;
    private string typeName;
    private string questionId;
    ///<summary>
    ///获取或设置考题的考题编号
    ///</summary>
    public string TestQuestionId
    {
        get
        { return testQuestionId; }
        set
        { testQuestionId = value; }
    }
    ///<summary>
    ///获取或设置考题的试卷编号
    ///</summary>
    public string PaperId
    {
        get
        { return paperId; }
        set
        { paperId = value; }
    }
    ///<summary>
    ///获取或设置考题的题型名称
    ///</summary>
    public string TypeName
    {
        get
        { return typeName; }
        set
        { typeName = value; }
    }
    ///<summary>
    ///获取或设置考题的试题编号
    ///</summary>
    public string QuestionId
    {
        get
        { return questionId; }
        set
        { questionId = value; }
    }
}
```

8.5.7　StudentAnswer 类

该类是学生答题信息表 StudentAnswer 的实体类。学生考试模块的实现需要调用此类。实现代码如下。

```csharp
public class StudentAnswer
{
    private string answerId;
    private string testQuestionId;
    private string studentId;
    private string answer;
    private int score;
    ///<summary>
    ///获取或设置学生答卷的答题编号
    ///</summary>
    public string AnswerId
    {
        get
        { return answerId; }
        set
        { answerId = value; }
    }
    ///<summary>
    ///获取或设置学生答卷的考题编号
    ///</summary>
    public string TestQuestionId
    {
        get
        { return testQuestionId; }
        set
        { testQuestionId = value; }
    }
    ///<summary>
    ///获取或设置学生答卷的学号
    ///</summary>
    public string StudentId
    {
        get
        { return studentId; }
        set
        { studentId = value; }
    }
    ///<summary>
    ///获取或设置学生答卷的学生答案
    ///</summary>
    public string Answer
    {
        get
        { return answer; }
        set
        { answer = value; }
    }
    ///<summary>
    ///获取或设置学生答卷的得分
    ///</summary>
    public int Score
    {
        get
```

```
            { return score; }
            set
            { score = value; }
        }
    }
}
```

8.6 数据访问层实现

数据访问层的主要任务是与数据库交互,实现对数据库各表的添加、删除、修改、查询等功能。本系统数据访问层包含的类如图 8-5 所示。

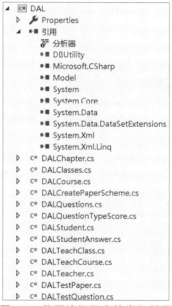

图 8-5 数据访问层中的类和引用

8.6.1 DALStudent 类

DALStudent 类是学生信息表 Student 的数据访问层类。学生管理、学生登录等多个模块的业务逻辑层需要调用此类。实现代码如下:

```
public class DALStudent
{
    //添加一条学生信息
    public bool Insert(Model.Student stu)
    {
        List<SqlParameter> parms = new List<SqlParameter>();
        parms.Add(new SqlParameter("@studentId", stu.StudentId));
        parms.Add(new SqlParameter("@className", stu.ClassName));
        parms.Add(new SqlParameter("@studentName", stu.StudentName));
        parms.Add(new SqlParameter("@studentPwd", stu.StudentPwd));
        return DBUtility.DbHelperSQL.ExecuteSql("insert into Student values
```

```
                (@studentId, eierScnType@className, @studentName, @studentPwd)",
parms);
    }
    //修改学生信息
    public bool Update(Model.Student stu, string currStudentId)
    {
        List<SqlParameter> parms = new List<SqlParameter>();
        parms.Add(new SqlParameter("@studentId", currStudentId));
        parms.Add(new SqlParameter("@studentName", stu.StudentName));
        parms.Add(new SqlParameter("@className", stu.ClassName));
        parms.Add(new SqlParameter("@studentPwd", stu.StudentPwd));
        return DBUtility.DbHelperSQL.ExecuteSql("update Student set
            studentName=@studentName,
            className=@className,studentPwd=@studentPwd where studentId=
            @studentId", parms);
    }
    //删除一条学生信息
    public bool Delete(string currStudentId)
    {
        List<SqlParameter> parms = new List<SqlParameter>();
        parms.Add(new SqlParameter("@studentId", currStudentId));
        return DBUtility.DbHelperSQL.ExecuteSql("delete from Student where
            studentId=@studentId", parms);
    }
    //查询学生信息
    public DataTable Select(string strwhere)
    {
        string sql = "select * from Student";
        if (strwhere != "")
        {
            sql += " where " + strwhere;
        }
        return DBUtility.DbHelperSQL.Query(sql);
    }
    //按条件查询
    public DataTable Select(string str, string type)
    {
        if ("学生姓名" == type)
        { return Select("studentName like'" + str + "%'"); }
        else if ("班级名称" == type)
        { return Select("className like '" + str + "%'"); }
        else
        { return Select("studentId='" + str + "'"); }
    }
}
```

8.6.2 DALTestQuestion 类

DALTestQuestion 类是题库表 TestQuestion 的数据访问层类。题库管理、组卷管理等多个模块的业务逻辑层需要调用此类。实现代码如下。

```
public class DALTestQuestion
```

```csharp
{
    //添加一条题目信息
    public bool Insert(Model.TestQuestion cq)
    {
        List<SqlParameter> parms = new List<SqlParameter>();
        parms.Add(new SqlParameter("@questionId", cq.QuestionId));
        parms.Add(new SqlParameter("@chapterId", cq.ChapterId));
        parms.Add(new SqlParameter("@questionTitle", cq.QuestionTitle));
        parms.Add(new SqlParameter("@answerA", cq.AnswerA));
        parms.Add(new SqlParameter("@answerB", cq.AnswerB));
        parms.Add(new SqlParameter("@answerC", cq.AnswerC));
        parms.Add(new SqlParameter("@answerD", cq.AnswerD));
        parms.Add(new SqlParameter("@currectAnswer", cq.CurrectAnswer));
        parms.Add(new SqlParameter("@questionType", cq.QuestionType));
        return DBUtility.DbHelperSQL.ExecuteSql("insert into
            TestQuestion values
            (@questionId,@chapterId,@questionTitle,@answerA,@answerB,
                @answerC,
            @answerD,@currectAnswer,@questionType)", parms);
    }
    //修改题目信息
    public bool Update(Model.TestQuestion cq, string currQuestionId)
    {
        List<SqlParameter> parms = new List<SqlParameter>();
        parms.Add(new SqlParameter("@questionId", currQuestionId));
        parms.Add(new SqlParameter("@chapterId", cq.ChapterId));
        parms.Add(new SqlParameter("@questionTitle", cq.QuestionTitle));
        parms.Add(new SqlParameter("@answerA", cq.AnswerA));
        parms.Add(new SqlParameter("@answerB", cq.AnswerB));
        parms.Add(new SqlParameter("@answerC", cq.AnswerC));
        parms.Add(new SqlParameter("@answerD", cq.AnswerD));
        parms.Add(new SqlParameter("@currectAnswer", cq.CurrectAnswer));
        parms.Add(new SqlParameter("@questionType", cq.QuestionType));
        return DBUtility.DbHelperSQL.ExecuteSql("update TestQuestion set
            chapterId=@chapterId,
            questionTitle=@questionTitle,answerA=@answerA,answerB=@answerB,
            answerC=@answerC,answerD=@answerD,currectAnswer=@currectAnswer,
            questionType=@questionType where questionId=@questionId", parms);
    }
    //删除一条题目信息
    public bool Delete(string currQuestionId)
    {
        List<SqlParameter> parms = new List<SqlParameter>();
        parms.Add(new SqlParameter("@questionId", currQuestionId));
        return DBUtility.DbHelperSQL.ExecuteSql("delete from TestQuestion where
            questionId=@questionId", parms);
    }
    //查询题目信息
    public DataTable Select(string QuestionTitle, string CourseId, string
        ChapterId, string typeName)
    {
        string sql = "select * from TestQuestion left join Chapter on
```

```csharp
            TestQuestion.chapterId=Chapter.chapterId left join Course
                on Chapter.courseId=Course.courseId where Course.courseId='" +
                CourseId + "' and TestQuestion.questionType='" + typeName + "'";
            if ("" != QuestionTitle && "" != ChapterId)
            {
                sql += " and Chapter.chapterId ='" + ChapterId + "' and
                    TestQuestion.questionTitle
                    like '%" + QuestionTitle + "%'";
            }
            else if ("" == QuestionTitle && "" != ChapterId)
            {
                sql += " and Chapter.chapterId ='" + ChapterId + "'";
            }
            else if ("" != QuestionTitle && "" == ChapterId)
            {
                sql += " and TestQuestion.questionTitle like'%" + QuestionTitle
                    + "%'";
            }
            return DBUtility.DbHelperSQL.Query(sql);
        }
        //完全随机生成试题
        public DataTable AllRandomQuestion(int QuestionNum, string QuestionType,
            string CourseId)
        {
            string sql = "Select top " + QuestionNum + " * from testQuestion
                left join chapter on testQuestion.chapterId=chapter.chapterId
                left join course on course.courseId=chapter.courseId where
                testQuestion.questionType='" + QuestionType + "' and
                course.courseId='" + CourseId + "' order by newid()";
            return DBUtility.DbHelperSQL.Query(sql);
        }
        //按章节随机生成试卷
        public DataTable ChapterRandomQuestion(int QuestionNum, string QuestionType,
            string CourseId, string ChapterId)
        {
            string sql = "Select top " + QuestionNum + " * from testQuestion
                left join chapter on testQuestion.chapterId=chapter.chapterId
                left join course on course.courseId=chapter.courseId where
                testQuestion.questionType='" + QuestionType + "' and course.
                courseId='" + CourseId + "' and chapter.chapterId='" + ChapterId + "
                ' order by newid()";
            return DBUtility.DbHelperSQL.Query(sql);
        }
    }
```

8.6.3 DALCreatePaperScheme 类

DALCreatePaperScheme 类是组卷方案表 CreatePaperScheme 的数据访问层类。组卷管理模块的业务逻辑层需要调用此类。实现代码如下。

```csharp
public class DALCreatePaperScheme
```

```csharp
{
    //添加一条试卷方案信息
    public bool Insert(Model.CreatePaperScheme cps)
    {
        List<SqlParameter> parms = new List<SqlParameter>();
        parms.Add(new SqlParameter("@schemeId", cps.SchemeId));
        parms.Add(new SqlParameter("@teachId", cps.TeachId));
        return DBUtility.DbHelperSQL.ExecuteSql("insert into createPaperScheme 
            values(@schemeId,@teachId)", parms);
    }
}
```

8.6.4 DALTestPaper 类

DALTestPaper 类是试卷表 TestPaper 的数据访问层类。组卷管理模块的业务逻辑层需要调用此类。实现代码如下。

```csharp
public class DALTestPaper
{
    ///<summary>
    ///添加一条试卷信息
    ///</summary>
    ///<param name="tp">试卷类的对象</param>
    ///<returns></returns>
    public bool Insert(Model.TestPaper tp)
    {
        List<SqlParameter> parms = new List<SqlParameter>();
        parms.Add(new SqlParameter("@paperId", tp.PaperId));
        parms.Add(new SqlParameter("@schemeId", tp.SchemeId));
        return DBUtility.DbHelperSQL.ExecuteSql("insert into TestPaper values
            (@paperId,@schemeId)", parms);
    }
    ///<summary>
    ///查询试卷信息
    ///</summary>
    ///<param name="teachId">授课编号</param>
    ///<returns>返回 DataTable 类型的数据</returns>
    public DataTable Select(string teachId)
    {
        string sql = "select * from TestPaper left join CreatePaperScheme
            on CreatePaperScheme.SchemeId=testpaper.SchemeId where
            CreatePaperScheme.teachId='" + teachId + "'";
        return DBUtility.DbHelperSQL.Query(sql);
    }
}
```

8.6.5 DALQuestionTypeScore 类

DALQuestionTypeScore 类是题型分值设定表 QuestionTypeScore 的数据访问层类。组卷管理模块的业务逻辑层需要调用此类。实现代码如下。

```csharp
public class DALQuestionTypeScore
{
    ///<summary>
    ///添加一条题型分值设定信息
    ///</summary>
    ///<param name="qts">题型分值设定类的对象</param>
    ///<returns></returns>
    public bool Insert(Model.QuestionTypeScore qts)
    {
        List<SqlParameter> parms = new List<SqlParameter>();
        parms.Add(new SqlParameter("@schemeId", qts.SchemeId));
        parms.Add(new SqlParameter("@typeName", qts.TypeName));
        parms.Add(new SqlParameter("@questionNum", qts.QuestionNum));
        parms.Add(new SqlParameter("@questionScore", qts.QuestionScore));
        parms.Add(new SqlParameter("@createType", qts.CreateType));
        return DBUtility.DbHelperSQL.ExecuteSql("insert into QuestionTypeScore
            values(@schemeId,@typeName,@questionNum,@questionScore,
            @createType)", parms);
    }
}
```

8.6.6　DALQuestions 类

DALQuestions 类是考题表 Questions 的数据访问层类。组卷管理模块的业务逻辑层需要调用此类。实现代码如下。

```csharp
public class DALQuestions
{
    ///<summary>
    ///添加一条考题信息
    ///</summary>
    ///<param name="q">考题类的对象</param>
    ///<returns></returns>
    public bool Insert(Model.Questions q)
    {
        List<SqlParameter> parms = new List<SqlParameter>();
        parms.Add(new SqlParameter("@testQuestionId", q.TestQuestionId));
        parms.Add(new SqlParameter("@paperId", q.PaperId));
        parms.Add(new SqlParameter("@typeName", q.TypeName));
        parms.Add(new SqlParameter("@questionId", q.QuestionId));
        return DBUtility.DbHelperSQL.ExecuteSql("insert into questions values
            (@testQuestionId,@paperId,@typeName,@questionId)", parms);
    }
    ///<summary>
    ///查询考题信息
    ///</summary>
    ///<param name="teachId">授课编号</param>
    ///<param name="paperId">试卷编号</param>
    ///<returns>返回 DataTable 类型的数据</returns>
    public DataTable Select(string teachId, string paperId)
    {
        string sql = "select * from questions left join testpaper on
```

```
            testpaper.paperId=questions.paperId left join CreatePaperScheme on
            CreatePaperScheme.SchemeId=testpaper.SchemeId where
            CreatePaperScheme.teachId='" + teachId + "' and testpaper.paperId=
               '" + paperId + "'";
        return DBUtility.DbHelperSQL.Query(sql);
    }
}
```

8.6.7　DALStudentAnswer 类

DALStudentAnswer 类是学生答题表 StudentAnswer 的数据访问层类。学生考试模块的业务逻辑层需要调用此类。实现代码如下。

```
///<summary>
///学生答题 DAL 类
///<summary>
public class DALStudentAnswer
{
    ///<summary>
    ///添加学生答卷信息
    ///<summary>
    ///<param name="sa">Model.StudentAnswer 类</param>
    ///<returns>返回 false 代表添加失败,返回 true 代表添加成功</returns>
    public bool Insert(Model.StudentAnswer sa)
    {
        //parms 表示 SqlParameter 类集合的对象,用于存储参数并传递
        List<SqlParameter> parms = new List<SqlParameter>();
        parms.Add(new SqlParameter("@answerId", sa.AnswerId));      //答题编号
        parms.Add(new SqlParameter("@testQuestionId", sa.TestQuestionId));
                                                                    //试题编号
        parms.Add(new SqlParameter("@studentId", sa.StudentId));    //学号
        parms.Add(new SqlParameter("@answer", sa.Answer));          //答案
        parms.Add(new SqlParameter("@score", sa.Score));            //分数
        return DBUtility.DbHelperSQL.ExecuteSql("insert into StudentAnswer values
           (@answerId,@testQuestionId,@studentId,@answer,@score)", parms);
    }
    ///<summary>
    ///修改学生答卷信息
    ///<summary>
    ///<param name="sa">Model.StudentAnswer 类</param>
    ///<param name="currAnswerId">所选择的答题编号</param>
    ///<returns>返回 false 代表修改失败,返回 true 代表修改成功</returns>
    public bool Update(Model.StudentAnswer sa, string currAnswerId)
    {
        List<SqlParameter> parms = new List<SqlParameter>();
        parms.Add(new SqlParameter("@answerId", currAnswerId));
        parms.Add(new SqlParameter("@answer", sa.Answer));
        parms.Add(new SqlParameter("@score", sa.Score));
        return DBUtility.DbHelperSQL.ExecuteSql("update StudentAnswer set
            answer=@answer,
            score=@score where answerId=@answerId", parms);
```

```csharp
    }
    ///<summary>
    ///查询学生答卷信息
    ///</summary>
    ///<param name="strwhere">sql 语句 select 语句的 where 子句,可为空</param>
    ///<returns>返回 null 为查询失败,返回非 null 为查询成功,且结果存于返回的对象中
</returns>
    public DataTable Select(string strwhere)
    {
        string sql = "select * from studentAnswer";
        if (strwhere != "")
        {
            sql += " " + strwhere;              //sql 为 SQL 查询语句
        }
        return DBUtility.DbHelperSQL.Query(sql);
    }
    ///<summary>
    ///读取已存试卷信息
    ///</summary>
    ///<param name="teachId">授课编号</param>
    ///<param name="studentId">学号</param>
    ///<returns>返回 null 为查询失败,返回非 null 为查询成功,且结果存于返回的对象中
</returns>
    public DataTable Select(string teachId, string studentId)
    {
        return Select("where studentId='" + studentId + "' and answerId like '"
            + teachId + "%' ");
    }
    ///<summary>
    ///查询学生成绩
    ///</summary>
    ///<param name="studentId">学号</param>
    ///<returns>返回 null 为查询失败,返回非 null 为查询成功,且结果存于返回的对象中
        </returns>
    public DataTable ScoreSelect(string studentId)
    {
        string sql = "select course.courseName,course.courseHour,course.
            courseCredit,
            StudentAnswer.score from teachCourse,course,CreatePaperScheme,
            TestPaper,
            StudentAnswer,questions where course.courseId=teachCourse.
            courseId and
            teachCourse.teachId=CreatePaperScheme.teachId and
            CreatePaperScheme.schemeId=TestPaper.schemeId and
            TestPaper.paperId=questions.paperId and questions.testQuestionId=
            StudentAnswer.testQuestionId and teachCourse.isPublic='是' and
            studentId='" + studentId + "'";
        return DBUtility.DbHelperSQL.Query(sql);
    }
    ///<summary>
    ///读取所选试卷
    ///</summary>
    ///<param name="questionType">题型</param>
```

```csharp
///<param name="studentId">学号</param>
///<param name="teachId">授课编号</param>
///<returns>返回null为查询失败,返回非null为查询成功,且结果存于返回的对象中</returns>
    public DataTable LoadTestPaper (string questionType, string studentId, string teachId)
    {
        string where = "";
        if (questionType != "")
        {
            where = " and testQuestion.questiontype='" + questionType + "'";
        }
        string sql = "select * from CreatePaperScheme,QuestionTypeScore,
            testPaper,testquestion,
            questions,studentAnswer where QuestionTypeScore.schemeId=
            CreatePaperScheme.schemeId
            and CreatePaperScheme.schemeId=testPaper.schemeId and testPaper.paperId=
            questions.paperId and questions.questionId=testquestion.questionId and
            questions.testquestionId=studentAnswer.testquestionId and
            questionTypeScore.TypeName=questions.typeName  and studentAnswer.
            studentId='" + studentId + "' and studentAnswer.answerId like '" +
            teachId + "%'"+where;
        return DBUtility.DbHelperSQL.Query(sql);
    }
    //查询学生成绩
    public DataTable ScoreSelect(string TeachTerm, string CourseId, string TeacherId)
    {
        string sql = "select student.studentId,student.studentName,teacher.teacherName,
            Classes.className,course.courseName,studentAnswer.score from
            course,teacher,
            teachCourse,teachClass,classes,student,CreatePaperScheme,TestPaper,
            StudentAnswer,questions where teachCourse.teacherId=teacher.teacherId and
            teachCourse.teachId=teachClass.teachId and teachClass.className=
            classes.className and
            classes.className=student.className and student.studentId=
            studentAnswer.studentId and
            teachCourse.teachId=CreatePaperScheme.teachId and
            CreatePaperScheme.schemeId=
            TestPaper.schemeId and TestPaper.paperId=questions.paperId and
            questions.testQuestionId=
            StudentAnswer.testQuestionId and teachCourse.teachTerm='" +
            TeachTerm + "' and
            course.courseId='" + CourseId + "' and teacher.teacherId='" +
            TeacherId + "'";
        return DBUtility.DbHelperSQL.Query(sql);
    }
}
```

8.7 业务逻辑层实现

业务逻辑层的主要任务是负责处理系统的业务逻辑,当业务逻辑层需要访问数据库时,要通过调用数据访问层来实现。本系统业务逻辑层包含的类如图 8-6 所示。

图 8-6 业务逻辑层中的类和引用

8.7.1 BLLStudent 类

BLLStudent 类是学生信息管理模块的业务逻辑层类。实现代码如下。

```csharp
public class BLLStudent
{
    //添加
    public bool StudentInsert(Model.Student stu)
    {
        DAL.DALStudent dStu = new DAL.DALStudent();
        return dStu.Insert(stu);
    }
    //修改
    public bool StudentUpdate(Model.Student stu, string StudentId)
    {
        DAL.DALStudent dStu = new DAL.DALStudent();
        return dStu.Update(stu, StudentId);
    }
    //删除
    public bool StudentDelete(string StudentId)
    {
        DAL.DALStudent dStu = new DAL.DALStudent();
        return dStu.Delete(StudentId);
```

```csharp
        }
        //查询全部
        public DataTable StudentSelectAll()
        {
            DAL.DALStudent dStu = new DAL.DALStudent();
            return dStu.Select("");
        }
        //按条件查询
        public DataTable StudentSelectCondition(string str, string type)
        {
            DAL.DALStudent dStu = new DAL.DALStudent();
            return dStu.Select(str, type);
        }
        //学生登录
        public int StudentLogin(string Uid, string Pwd)
        {
            DAL.DALStudent dStu = new DAL.DALStudent();
            DataTable dt = dStu.Select(Uid, "学号");
            if (dt.Rows.Count != 0)
            {
                if (dt.Rows[0]["studentPwd"].ToString() == Pwd)
                {
                    return 1;
                }
                else
                {
                    return 0;
                }
            }
            else
            {
                return 0;
            }
        }
}
```

8.7.2 BLLTestQuestion 类

BLLTestQuestion 类是题库管理模块的业务逻辑层类。实现代码如下。

```csharp
///<summary>
///BLLTestQuestion 的摘要说明
///</summary>
public class BLLTestQuestion
{
    ///<summary>
    ///添加题目信息
    ///</summary>
    public bool testQuestionInsert(Model.TestQuestion tq)
    {
        DAL.DALTestQuestion dTq = new DAL.DALTestQuestion();
        return dTq.Insert(tq);
    }
```

```csharp
///<summary>
///修改题目信息
///</summary>
public bool testQuestionUpdate(Model.TestQuestion tq, string QuestionId)
{
    DAL.DALTestQuestion dTq = new DAL.DALTestQuestion();
    return dTq.Update(tq, QuestionId);
}
///<summary>
///删除题目信息
///</summary>
public bool testQuestionDelete(string QuestionId)
{
    DAL.DALTestQuestion dTq = new DAL.DALTestQuestion();
    return dTq.Delete(QuestionId);
}
///<summary>
///查询
///</summary>
public DataTable testQuestionSelect(string QuestionTitle, string CourseId,
                    string ChapterId, string typeName)
{
    DAL.DALTestQuestion dTq = new DAL.DALTestQuestion();
    return dTq.Select(QuestionTitle, CourseId, ChapterId, typeName);
}
///<summary>
///完全随机
///</summary>
public DataTable AllRandomQuestion(int QuestionNum, string QuestionType,
    string CourseId)
{
    DAL.DALTestQuestion dTq = new DAL.DALTestQuestion();
    return dTq.AllRandomQuestion(QuestionNum, QuestionType, CourseId);
}
///<summary>
///按章节随机
///</summary>
public DataTable ChapterRandomQuestion(int QuestionNum, string
                    QuestionType, string CourseId, string ChapterId)
{
    DAL.DALTestQuestion dTq = new DAL.DALTestQuestion();
    return dTq.ChapterRandomQuestion(QuestionNum, QuestionType, CourseId,
        ChapterId);
}
}
```

8.7.3 BLLCreatePaperScheme 类

BLLCreatePaperScheme 类是组卷方案数据表的业务逻辑层封装,组卷模块的业务逻辑层类需要调用该类。实现代码如下。

```
///<summary>
///BLLCreatePaperScheme 的摘要说明
///</summary>
public class BLLCreatePaperScheme
{
    ///<summary>
    ///添加组卷方案
    ///</summary>
    public bool Insert(Model.CreatePaperScheme cps)
    {
        DAL.DALCreatePaperScheme dCps = new DAL.DALCreatePaperScheme();
        return dCps.Insert(cps);
    }
}
```

8.7.4 BLLTestPaper 类

BLLTestPaper 类是试卷数据表的业务逻辑层封装，组卷模块的业务逻辑层类需要调用该类。实现代码如下。

```
///<summary>
///BLLTestPaper 的摘要说明
///</summary>
public class BLLTestPaper
{
    ///<summary>
    ///添加试卷
    ///</summary>
    public bool Insert(Model.TestPaper tp)
    {
        DAL.DALTestPaper dTp = new DAL.DALTestPaper();
        return dTp.Insert(tp);
    }
}
```

8.7.5 BLLQuestionTypeScore 类

BLLQuestionTypeScore 类是题型分值设定数据表的业务逻辑层封装，组卷模块的业务逻辑层类需要调用该类。实现代码如下。

```
///<summary>
///BLLQuestionTypeScore 的摘要说明
///</summary>
public class BLLQuestionTypeScore
{
    ///<summary>
    ///添加
    ///</summary>
    public bool Insert(Model.QuestionTypeScore qts)
    {
        DAL.DALQuestionTypeScore dQts = new DAL.DALQuestionTypeScore();
```

```
            return dQts.Insert(qts);
        }
    }
```

8.7.6　BLLQuestions 类

BLLQuestions 类是试题数据表的业务逻辑层封装,同时加入了大量的组卷业务逻辑,是组卷模块的核心业务逻辑层类。实现代码如下。

```
public class BLLQuestions
{
    public bool Insert(Model.Questions q)
    {
        DAL.DALQuestions dQ = new DAL.DALQuestions();
        return dQ.Insert(q);
    }
    //随机组卷
    public bool CreatePaperChapterRandom(List<Model.QuestionTypeScore> qts,
        List<string> chapterId_Num, Model.CreatePaperScheme cps, string
        CourseId, int paperCount)
    {
        for (int i = 0; i < paperCount; i++)
        {
            BLLQuestionTypeScore bQts = new BLLQuestionTypeScore();
            BLLCreatePaperScheme bCps = new BLLCreatePaperScheme();
            BLLTestPaper bTp = new BLLTestPaper();
            BLLQuestions bQ = new BLLQuestions();
            BLLTestQuestion bTq = new BLLTestQuestion();
            DataTable dt = new DataTable();
            Model.TestPaper tp = new Model.TestPaper();
            Model.Questions q = new Model.Questions();
            bCps.Insert(cps);
            tp.PaperId = DateTime.Now.ToString();
            tp.SchemeId = cps.SchemeId;
            bTp.Insert(tp);
            for (int j = 0; j < qts.Count; j++)
            {
                bQts.Insert(qts[j]);
                if ("按章节随机" == qts[j].CreateType)
                {
                    for (int m = 0; m < chapterId_Num.Count; m++)
                    {
                        if (qts[j].TypeName == chapterId_Num[m].Split('|')[0])
                        {
                            dt = bTq.ChapterRandomQuestion(
                                int.Parse(chapterId_Num[m].Split('|')[2].
                                ToString())), chapterId_Num[m].Split('|')[0],
                                CourseId,
                                chapterId_Num[m].Split('|')[1]);
                                            //题型|章节号|数量
                            for (int k = 0; k < dt.Rows.Count; k++)
                            {
```

```
                    q.TestQuestionId =
                        DateTime.Now.ToString("yyyyMMddHHmmssfff");
                    q.PaperId = tp.PaperId;
                    q.TypeName = qts[j].TypeName;
                    q.QuestionId = dt.Rows[k]["questionId"].ToString();
                    bQ.Insert(q);
                    System.Threading.Thread.Sleep(9);
                }
            }
        }
        else
        {
            dt = bTq.AllRandomQuestion(qts[j].QuestionNum, qts[j].
                TypeName, CourseId);
            for (int k = 0; k < dt.Rows.Count; k++)
            {
                q.TestQuestionId = DateTime.Now.ToString
                    ("yyyyMMddHHmmssfff");
                q.PaperId = tp.PaperId;
                q.TypeName = qts[j].TypeName;
                q.QuestionId = dt.Rows[k]["questionId"].ToString();
                bQ.Insert(q);
                System.Threading.Thread.Sleep(9);
            }
        }
    }
    System.Threading.Thread.Sleep(200);
}
return true;
}
///<summary>
///获取随机出的试卷下的试题
///</summary>
///<param name="teachId">授课编号</param>
public DataTable QuestionsSelect(string teachId)
{
    DAL.DALTestPaper bTp = new DAL.DALTestPaper();
    DataTable dt = bTp.Select(teachId);
    DAL.DALQuestions bQ = new DAL.DALQuestions();
    return bQ.Select(teachId, dt.Rows[new Random().Next(0, dt.Rows.Count)]
        ["paperId"].ToString());
}
}
```

8.7.7 BLLStudentAnswer 类

BLLStudentAnswer 类是学生答题数据表的业务逻辑层封装，同时加入了大量学生考试相关的业务逻辑，该类是学生考试模块的核心业务逻辑层类。实现代码如下。

```
public class BLLStudentAnswer
{
```

```csharp
///<summary>
///查询是否第一次进入本次考试
///</summary>
///<param name="teachId">授课编号</param>
///<param name="studentId">学号</param>
public DataTable isSavePaper(string teachId, string studentId)
{
    DAL.DALStudentAnswer dSa = new DAL.DALStudentAnswer();
    return dSa.Select(teachId, studentId);
}
///<summary>
///第一次进入本次考试,存储考试试卷
///</summary>
///<param name="sa">学生答题类</param>
public bool SaveTestPaper(Model.StudentAnswer sa)
{
    DAL.DALStudentAnswer dSa = new DAL.DALStudentAnswer();
    return dSa.Insert(sa);
}
///<summary>
///读取学生试题
///</summary>
///<param name="questionType">试题类型</param>
///<param name="studentId">学号</param>
///<param name="teachId">授课编号</param>
public DataTable LoadTestPaper(string questionType, string studentId,
    string teachId)
{
    DAL.DALStudentAnswer dSa = new DAL.DALStudentAnswer();
    return dSa.LoadTestPaper(questionType, studentId, teachId);
}
///<summary>
///查询成绩
///</summary>
///<param name="studentId">学号</param>
public DataTable ScoreSelect(string studentId)
{
    DAL.DALStudentAnswer dSa = new DAL.DALStudentAnswer();
    DataTable dt = new DataTable();
    DataTable dtOrigin = dSa.ScoreSelect(studentId);
    dt.TableName = dtOrigin.TableName;
    //设置新的数据表的表头
    for (int i = 0; i < dtOrigin.Columns.Count; i++)
    {
        dt.Columns.Add(dtOrigin.Columns[i].Caption);
    }
    //筛选整合数据
    for (int i = 0; i < dtOrigin.Rows.Count; i++)
    {
        bool isExist = false;
        for (int j = 0; j < dt.Rows.Count; j++)
        {
            if (dtOrigin.Rows[i]["courseName"].ToString() ==
```

```csharp
                        dt.Rows[j]["courseName"].ToString())
                {
                    dt.Rows[j]["score"] = int.Parse(dt.Rows[j]["score"].
                        ToString()) + int.Parse(dtOrigin.Rows[i]["score"].
                        ToString());
                    isExist = true;
                    break;
                }
            }
            if (!isExist)
            {
                if ("0" != dtOrigin.Rows[i]["score"].ToString())
                {
                    DataRow dr = dt.NewRow();
                    for (int ii = 0; ii < dtOrigin.Columns.Count; ii++)
                    {
                        dr[ii] = dtOrigin.Rows[i][ii];
                    }
                    dt.Rows.Add(dr);
                }
            }
        }
        return dt;
    }
    ///<summary>
    ///提交答案
    ///</summary>
    ///<param name="sa">学生答题类</param>
    ///<param name="AnswerId">答题编号</param>
    public bool SubmitPaper(Model.StudentAnswer sa, string AnswerId)
    {
        DAL.DALStudentAnswer dSa = new DAL.DALStudentAnswer();
        return dSa.Update(sa, AnswerId);
    }
    //查询成绩
    public DataTable ScoreSelect(string TeachTerm, string CourseId, string
        TeacherId)
    {
        DAL.DALStudentAnswer dSa = new DAL.DALStudentAnswer();
        return dSa.ScoreSelect(TeachTerm, CourseId, TeacherId);
    }
}
```

8.8 表示层实现

表示层 UI 负责界面的显示及用户交互,教师端该层共有章节编辑(FrmChapterEdit)、章节管理(FrmChapterManage)、班级信息管理(FrmClassManage)、课程编辑(FrmCourseEdit)、课程管理(FrmCourseManage)、组卷(FrmCreatePaper)、登录(FrmLogin)、成绩查询(FrmMarkManage)、成绩发布管理(FrmMarkPublishManage)、题库编辑(FrmQuestionEdit)、题库管理(FrmQuestionManage)、学生信息编辑(FrmStudentEdit)、学生信息管理(FrmStudentManage)、教

师信息编辑（FrmTeacherEdit）、教师信息管理（FrmTeacherManage）、教师密码修改（FrmTeacherPwdChange）、授课信息编辑（FrmTeachMessageEdit）、授课信息管理（FrmTeachMessageManage）以及主窗体（FrmMain）共 19 个 Windows 窗体，分别负责实现不同的功能。学生端该层共有登录（FrmLogin）、主窗体（FrmMain）、成绩查询（FrmScore）、考试（FrmTest）4 个窗体。

注意： 在 UI 中需要添加对 BLL 和 Model 的引用。UI 中的类和引用如图 8-7 和图 8-8 所示。

图 8-7　教师端 UI 层中的类和引用

图 8-8　学生端 UI 层中的类和引用

8.8.1　学生信息管理模块——"学生信息管理"窗体

学生信息管理模块主要实现对学生信息的维护，"学生信息管理"窗体（FrmStudentManage）与 8.8.2 节介绍的"学生信息编辑"窗体（FrmStudentEdit）共同完成对学生信息的添加、修改、删除、查询以及批量导入功能。"学生信息管理"窗体如图 8-9 所示。

"学生信息管理"窗体的属性设置如表 8-14 所示。

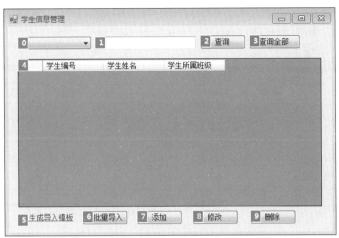

图 8-9 "学生信息管理"窗体

表 8-14 "学生信息管理"窗体属性设置

属 性 名	属 性 值	作 用
Name	FrmStudentManage	窗体名称
Text	学生信息管理	设置窗体的标题文本

"学生信息管理"窗体中的控件,按 Tab 顺序,描述如表 8-15 和表 8-16 所示。

表 8-15 "学生信息管理"窗体中的控件

Tab 序号	控件类型	属 性 名	属 性 值
0	ComboBox	Name	CmbCondition
		DropDownStyle	DropDownList
1	TextBox	Name	txtKeyword
2	Button	Name	btnSearch
		Text	查询
3	Button	Name	btnAll
		Text	查询全部
4	DataGridView	Name	dgvStudent
		AllowUserToAddRows	False
		AllowUserToDeleteRows	False
		ColumnHeadersHeightSizeMode	AutoSize
		MultiSelect	False
		ReadOnly	True
5	LinkLabel	Name	llImportModel
		Text	生成导入模板

续表

Tab 序号	控件类型	属性名	属性值
6	Button	Name	btnImport
		Text	批量导入
7	Button	Name	btnAdd
		Text	添加
8	Button	Name	btnModify
		Text	修改
9	Button	Name	btnDelete
		Text	删除

表 8-16　dgvStudent 中各列的属性设置

列头文本	属性名	属性值
学生编号	DataPropertyName	studentid
学生姓名	DataPropertyName	studentname
学生密码	DataPropertyName	studentpwd
	Visible	False
学生所属班级	DataPropertyName	classname

首先，在该窗体的类文件 FrmStudentManage.cs 中声明两个成员变量。

```
OpenFileDialog ofd;                //打开文件对话框,用于在批量导入时定位导入文件的路径
bool isPressedAllLast = true;      //判断最后单击的是否是"查询全部"
```

加载窗体时，DataGridView 控件 dgvStudent 中会显示 Student 数据表中所有的学生信息。窗体的 Load 事件代码如下。

```
private void FrmStudentManage_Load(object sender, EventArgs e)
{
    updateDataGridViewDataSource();
}
```

updateDataGridViewDataSource 函数代码如下。

```
public void updateDataGridViewDataSource()
{
    if (isPressedAllLast)
    {
        btnAll_Click(null, null);
                        //调用 btnAll_Click 函数,在 dgvStudent 中显示所有学生数据
    }
    else
    {
```

```
        //调用 btnSearch_Click 函数,在 dgvStudent 中显示满足上一次查询条件的查询
          结果
        btnSearch_Click(null, null);
    }
}
```

在 ComboBox 控件 CmbCondition 中选择要查询的字段,并在 TextBox 控件 txtKeyword 中输入要查询的内容后,单击"查询"按钮实现学生信息的查询并将查询结果显示在 dgvStudent 中。单击"查询全部"按钮可再次在 dgvStudent 中查看到全部的学生所有信息。

"查询"按钮的事件处理代码如下。

```
private void btnSearch_Click(object sender, EventArgs e)
{
    if ("" == txtKeyword.Text) { MessageBox.Show("请输入查询关键字!"); return; }
    BLL.BLLStudent ssc = new BLL.BLLStudent();
    dgvStudent.DataSource = ssc.StudentSelectCondition(txtKeyword.Text,
cmbCondition.Text);
    isPressedAllLast = false;
}
```

"查询全部"按钮的事件处理代码如下。

```
private void btnAll_Click(object sender, EventArgs e)
{
    BLL.BLLStudent ssc = new BLL.BLLStudent();
    dgvStudent.DataSource = ssc.StudentSelectAll();
    isPressedAllLast = true;
}
```

单击"批量导入"按钮可以将 Excel 中的学生数据导入到数据库中。但系统对 Excel 的表格样式是有要求的,单击"生成导入模板"超链接按钮可以生成 Excel 数据模板。"生成导入模板"超链接按钮的事件处理代码如下。

```
private void llImportModel_LinkClicked(object sender,
LinkLabelLinkClickedEventArgs e)
{
    List<string> t = new List<string>();
    t.Add("学生编号");
    t.Add("学生名");
    t.Add("学生密码");
    t.Add("所属班级名");
    ExcelHelper.generateModel(t);
}
```

ExcelHelper 类中的 generateModel 函数是生成 Excel 模板的核心代码,如下。

```
public static void generateModel(List<string> headerList)
                                                //headerList 内存储所有列的列头文本
{
    Excel.Application app = new Excel.Application();   //创建 Excel 程序实例对象
    app.Application.Workbooks.Add(true);               //添加工作集
```

```csharp
    Excel.Workbook book = (Excel.Workbook)app.ActiveWorkbook;        //激活工作集
    Excel.Worksheet sheet = (Excel.Worksheet)book.ActiveSheet;
                                                //为当前工作集添加一个工作表
    for (int i = 0; i < headerList.Count; i++)
    {
        sheet.Cells[1, i + 1] = headerList[i];
    }
    app.Visible = true;
}
```

导入操作就是逐行将 Excel 中的数据取出并插入到数据库的过程,"批量导入"按钮的事件处理代码如下。

```csharp
private void btnImport_Click(object sender, EventArgs e)
{
    ofd = new OpenFileDialog();
    ofd.Filter = "*.xls|*.xls";                //过滤文件格式,只接受 Excel 文件
    DialogResult dr = ofd.ShowDialog();        //弹出打开文件对话框
    if (dr == DialogResult.OK)
    {
        DialogResult d = MessageBox.Show("确定要导入 " + ofd.FileName +
            " 中的内容到学生表中么?", "警告!", MessageBoxButtons.OKCancel);
        if (DialogResult.OK == d)
        {
            //开始导入
            ExcelHelper.importFromExcelFile(ofd.FileName, "student");
        }
    }
    updateDataGridViewDataSource();
}
```

ExcelHelper 类中的 importFromExcelFile 函数是导入数据的核心代码,该函数不仅在导入学生信息时需要,在批量导入教师信息时也会调用。具体代码如下。

```csharp
public static void importFromExcelFile(string path, string importType)
//path 代表 Excel 文件路径, importType 标示当前导入的是教师信息、学生信息还是课程信息
{
    //连接 Excel 文件的连接字符串
    string oleconstr = @"Provider=Microsoft.Jet.OLEDB.4.0;Extended Properties=
        Excel 8.0;
    data source=" + path;
    OleDbConnection oleConn = new OleDbConnection(oleconstr);
    //选取 sheet1 中的全部数据(学生信息、教师信息或课程信息)
    string sqlexcel = "SELECT * FROM [sheet1$]";
    OleDbCommand olecmd = new OleDbCommand();
    oleConn.Open();
    olecmd.Connection = oleConn;
    olecmd.CommandText = sqlexcel;
    //执行上述 SELECT 语句,并返回 DataReader 对象
    using (OleDbDataReader odr = olecmd.ExecuteReader())
    {
        while (odr.Read())                            //遍历查询到的所有数据
        {
```

```csharp
            //取出当前遍历到的数据的各字段的值
            string para1 = Convert.ToString(odr[0]).Trim(); ;
            string para2 = Convert.ToString(odr[1]).Trim();
            string para3 = Convert.ToString(odr[2]).Trim();
            string para4 = Convert.ToString(odr[3]).Trim();
            //将当前遍历到的数据按 importType 的值进行封装并将该数据插入到相应的数据表中
            //如果 importType 的值是 teacher,则代表要导入的数据是教师信息
            //如果 importType 的值是 student,则代表要导入的数据是学生信息
            //如果 importType 的值是 course,则代表要导入的数据是课程信息
            if ("teacher" == importType)
            {
                Model.Teacher t = new Model.Teacher();
                t.TeacherId = para1;
                t.TeacherName = para2;
                t.TeacherPwd = para3;
                t.IsAdmin = para4;
                BLL.BLLTeacher ssc = new BLL.BLLTeacher();
                if (ssc.TeacherInsert(t)) { }
            }
            else if ("student" == importType)
            {
                Model.Student t = new Model.Student();
                t.StudentId = para1;
                t.StudentName = para2;
                t.StudentPwd = para3;
                t.ClassName = para4;
                BLL.BLLStudent ssc = new BLL.BLLStudent();
                if (ssc.StudentInsert(t)) { }
            }
            else if ("course" == importType)
            {
                Model.Course t = new Model.Course();
                t.CourseId = para1;
                t.CourseName = para2;
                t.CourseHour = int.Parse(para3);
                t.CourseCredit = int.Parse(para4);
                BLL.BLLCourse ssc = new BLL.BLLCourse();
                if (ssc.CourseInsert(t)) { }
            }
        }
        odr.Close();
        oleConn.Close();
        MessageBox.Show("导入完成!");
    }
}
```

单击"添加"按钮可以打开学生信息编辑界面(FrmStudentEdit),此时打开的学生信息编辑界面可以实现学生信息的添加。"添加"按钮的处理代码如下。

```csharp
private void btnAdd_Click(object sender, EventArgs e)
{
    FrmStudentEdit frm = new FrmStudentEdit();
    //设定学生信息编辑界面的 MdiParent 与当前学生信息管理界面的 MdiParent
```

```
        //是同一个窗体对象,即主窗体 FrmMain
        frm.MdiParent = this.MdiParent;
        //将当前 FrmStudentManage 类的实例对象传递给学生信息编辑界面 FrmStudentEdit
        //以便在 FrmStudentEdit 类中调用 FrmStudentMange 类的 updateDataGridViewDataSource
          方法
        //达到刷新 dgvStudent 的目的
        frm.studentManage = this;
        frm.Show();
    }
```

在 dgvStudent 中,选中一条学生记录,单击"修改"按钮可以打开学生信息编辑界面(FrmStudentEdit),但此时所打开的学生信息编辑界面可以实现学生信息的修改,且在打开学生信息编辑界面的同时会将当前选中的学生记录封装成 Model.Student 实体类对象并传递给学生信息编辑界面,以便在学生信息编辑界面可以查看到要修改学生信息的当前数据状况。"修改"按钮的处理代码如下。

```
private void btnModify_Click(object sender, EventArgs e)
{
    if (null == dgvStudent.CurrentRow)
    {
        MessageBox.Show("请先选择一行数据!");
        return;
    }
    FrmStudentEdit frm = new FrmStudentEdit();
    frm.MdiParent = this.MdiParent;
    Model.Student t = new Model.Student();
    //取出当前 dgvStudent 中选中的学生学号
    t.StudentId = dgvStudent.CurrentRow.Cells["studentid"].Value.ToString();
    //取出当前 dgvStudent 中选中的学生姓名
    t.StudentName = dgvStudent.CurrentRow.Cells["studentname"].Value.ToString();
    //取出当前 dgvStudent 中选中的学生密码
    t.StudentPwd = dgvStudent.CurrentRow.Cells["studentpwd"].Value.ToString();
    //取出当前 dgvStudent 中选中的学生班级
    t.ClassName = dgvStudent.CurrentRow.Cells["classname"].Value.ToString();
    //将当前学生对象传递给学生信息编辑界面的 student 成员变量
    frm.student = t;
    frm.studentManage = this;
    frm.Show();
}
```

在 dgvStudent 中,选中一条学生记录,单击"删除"按钮,会弹出确认对话框,询问用户是否确定删除该学生,如果选择"是"则执行删除,并刷新 dgvStudent 控件,如果选择"否"则中止删除操作。"删除"按钮事件处理代码如下。

```
private void btnDelete_Click(object sender, EventArgs e)
{
    if (DialogResult.Cancel == MessageBox.Show("确定要删除此条信息?", "警告!",
        MessageBoxButtons.OKCancel))
    {
        return;
    }
```

```
        BLL.BLLStudent ssc = new BLL.BLLStudent();
        if (ssc.StudentDelete(dgvStudent.CurrentRow.Cells["studentid"].Value.
            ToString()))
        {
            MessageBox.Show("删除成功!");
        }
        else
        {
            MessageBox.Show("删除失败!");
        }
        updateDataGridViewDataSource();
    }
```

8.8.2 学生信息管理模块——"学生信息编辑"窗体

学生信息编辑窗体负责实现学生信息的添加及修改,其界面如图 8-10 所示。窗体属性设计如表 8-17 所示,窗体的控件如表 8-18 所示。

图 8-10 "学生信息编辑"窗体

表 8-17 "学生信息编辑"窗体属性设置

属 性 名	属 性 值	作 用
Name	FrmStudentEdit	窗体名称
Text	学生信息编辑	设置窗体的标题文本

表 8-18 "学生信息编辑"窗体中的控件

Tab 序号	控件类型	属 性 名	属 性 值
1	TextBox	Name	txtId
3	TextBox	Name	txtName
5	ComboBox	Name	cmbClassName
		DropDownStyle	DropDownList
6	CheckBox	Name	ckbResetPwd
		Text	是否重置密码

续表

Tab 序号	控件类型	属性名	属性值
7	Button	Name	btnDone
		Text	

首先,在该窗体的类文件 FrmStudentEdit.cs 中声明两个成员变量。

```
public Model.Student student;
//接收 FrmStudentManage 对象,以便调用其 updateDataGridViewDataSource 函数刷
//新 dgvStudent
public FrmStudentManage studentManage;
```

加载窗体时,需要做一些初始化操作:首先,需要将班级表中的班级信息绑定到 cmbClassName 控件中;其次,要根据当前窗体的操作目的是添加还是修改进行相应的信息设置。

窗体的 Load 事件代码如下。

```
private void FrmStudentEdit_Load(object sender, EventArgs e)
{
    BLL.BLLClasses ssc = new BLL.BLLClasses();
    cmbClassName.DataSource = ssc.ClassesSelcet("");    //设置 cmbClassName 的数据源
    cmbClassName.DisplayMember = "classname";
                                        //设置 cmbClassName 中要显示哪个字段的数据
    if (null == student)                //添加
    {
        btnDone.Text = "添加";
        this.Text = "学生添加";
        ckbResetPwd.Visible = false;
    }
    else                                //修改
    {
        btnDone.Text = "修改";
        this.Text = "学生修改";
        txtId.Enabled = false;
        //以下三行代码是将学生的原始信息显示在各控件内
        txtId.Text = student.StudentId;
        txtName.Text = student.StudentName;
        cmbClassName.Text = student.ClassName;
    }
}
```

输入各类信息后,单击 btnDone 按钮可实现学生信息的添加或修改,事件处理代码如下。

```
private void btnDone_Click(object sender, EventArgs e)
{
    if ("" == txtId.Text || "" == txtName.Text || -1 ==
        cmbClassName.SelectedIndex)
    {
        //Localizable 是自定义的类,CHECK_INPUT_STRING 是其中定义的一个常量,
        //具体可查阅网络资源中的源代码
```

```csharp
            MessageBox.Show(Localizable.CHECK_INPUT_STRING); return;
        }
        BLL.BLLStudent ssc = new BLL.BLLStudent();
        if (null == student)   //添加
        {
            Model.Student t = new Model.Student();   //构造学生实体类对象,对数据进行封装
            t.StudentId = txtId.Text;
            t.StudentName = txtName.Text;
            t.StudentPwd = "123";                    //学生初始密码为 123
            t.ClassName = cmbClassName.Text;
            if (ssc.StudentInsert(t))                //执行添加操作
            {
                MessageBox.Show("添加成功!");
            }
            else
            {
                MessageBox.Show("添加失败!");
            }
            this.Close();
        }
        else                                         //修改
        {
            student.StudentId = txtId.Text;
            student.StudentName = txtName.Text;
            if (ckbResetPwd.Checked)                 //如果修改时勾选了"重置密码"选项,则
                                                     //将密码重置为"123"
            {
                student.StudentPwd = "123";
            }
            student.ClassName = cmbClassName.Text;
            if (ssc.StudentUpdate(student, student.StudentId))   //执行修改操作
            {
                MessageBox.Show("修改成功!");
            }
            else
            {
                MessageBox.Show("修改失败!");
            }
            this.Close();
        }
        this.studentManage.updateDataGridViewDataSource();
    }
```

8.8.3 题库管理模块——"题库管理"窗体

题库管理模块主要实现对题库中试题的维护,"题库管理"窗体(FrmQuestionManage)与 8.8.4 节介绍的"题库编辑"窗体(FrmQuestionEdit)共同完成对题库中试题的添加、修改、删除、查询功能。"题库管理"窗体如图 8-11 所示,窗体属性设置如表 8-19 所示,窗体的控件如表 8-20 和表 8-21 所示。

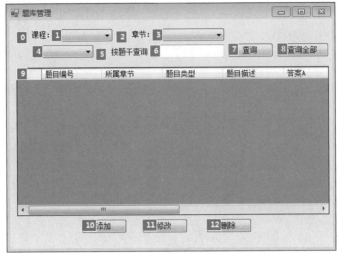

图 8-11 "题库管理"窗体

表 8-19 "题库管理"窗体属性设置

属 性 名	属 性 值	作 用
Name	FrmQuestionManage	窗体名称
Text	题库管理	设置窗体的标题文本

表 8-20 "题库管理"窗体中的控件

Tab 序号	控件类型	属 性 名	属 性 值
1	ComboBox	Name	cmbCourse
		DropDownStyle	DropDownList
3	ComboBox	Name	cmbChapter
		DropDownStyle	DropDownList
4	ComboBox	Name	cmbCondition
		DropDownStyle	DropDownList
6	TextBox	Name	txtKeyword
7	Button	Name	btnSearch
		Text	查询
8	Button	Name	btnAll
		Text	查询全部
9	DataGridView	Name	dgvQuestion
		AllowUserToAddRows	False
		AllowUserToDeleteRows	False
		ColumnHeadersHeightSizeMode	AutoSize

续表

Tab 序号	控件类型	属性名	属性值
9	DataGridView	MultiSelect	False
		ReadOnly	True
10	Button	Name	btnAdd
		Text	添加
11	Button	Name	btnModify
		Text	修改
12	Button	Name	btnDelete
		Text	删除

表 8-21 dgvQuestion 中各列的属性设置

列头文本	属性名	属性值
题目编号	Name	questionid
	DataPropertyName	
所属章节	Name	chapterid
	DataPropertyName	
题目类型	Name	questiontype
	DataPropertyName	
题目描述	Name	questiontitle
	DataPropertyName	
答案 A	Name	answera
	DataPropertyName	
答案 B	Name	answerb
	DataPropertyName	
答案 C	Name	answerc
	DataPropertyName	
答案 D	Name	answerd
	DataPropertyName	
正确答案	Name	currectanswer
	DataPropertyName	

首先，在该窗体的类文件 FrmQuestionManage.cs 中声明一个成员变量。

```
bool isPressedAllLast = true;       //判断最后单击的是否是"查询全部"
```

加载窗体时，首先向 cmbCourse 控件中绑定课程表中的当前登录教师讲授的所有课程，因为只有该课程的授课教师才有权限维护该课程的题库，接着刷新 dgvQuestion，令其显示当前默认选中课程、选中题型的所有试题。窗体的 Load 事件处理代码如下。

```csharp
private void FrmQuestionManage_Load(object sender, EventArgs e)
{
    BLL.BLLTeachCourse ssc = new BLL.BLLTeachCourse();
    dgvQuestion.AutoGenerateColumns = false;    //禁止 dgvQuestion 自动生成列
    cmbCondition.SelectedIndex = 0;
    //Teacher_CourseSelect 函数的作用是取出当前登录教师讲授的所有课程
    cmbCourse.DataSource = ssc.Teacher_CourseSelect(LoginHelper.teacherID);
    //设定 cmbCourse 显示 coursename(课程名)字段的数据
    cmbCourse.DisplayMember = "coursename";
    //设定 cmbCourse 各选项实际的值是 courseid(课程号)字段的数据
    cmbCourse.ValueMember = "courseid";
    cmbCourse.SelectedIndex = 0;
    //以下两行代码设定 cmbChapter 控件的部分绑定信息
    cmbChapter.DisplayMember = "chaptername";
    cmbChapter.ValueMember = "chapterid";
    updateDataGridViewDataSource();
}
```

当在 cmbCourse 控件中选择一个课程时，会触发该控件的 SelectedValueChanged 事件，在该事件处理函数中，需要把当前选中课程的所有章节绑定到 cmbChapter 控件中。代码如下。

```csharp
private void cmbCourse_SelectedValueChanged(object sender, EventArgs e)
{
    BLL.BLLChapter ssc = new BLL.BLLChapter();
    DataTable dt = ssc.ChapterSelectCondition(cmbCourse.SelectedValue.
        ToString(), "课程号");
    //ChapterSelectCondition 函数的作用是查询当前选中课程所有的章节信息
    DataRow dr = dt.NewRow();                //产生一个新的行对象，该行的列样式与 dt 相同
    //以下两行代码是在为新行的各列赋值，目的是在课程列表中加入"全部章节"字符串
    //这样在将 dt 作为数据源绑定给 cmbChapter 控件时，在该控件中可以具有"全部章节"的选项
    //以方便查询
    dr["chaptername"] = "全部章节";
    dr["chapterid"] = "-1";
    dt.Rows.InsertAt(dr, 0);                 //将行对象 dr 添加到表 dt 中
    cmbChapter.DataSource = dt;
}
```

当在 cmbCondtion 控件中选择不同的题型时，会导致 dgvQuestion 控件中的列发生变化，例如，选择查询选择题与判断题相比，dgvQuestion 中的会多出"答案 A""答案 B""答案 C""答案 D"等列。需要编写 cmbCondition 控件的 SelectedIndexChanged 事件处理函数如下。

```csharp
private void cmbCondition_SelectedIndexChanged(object sender, EventArgs e)
{
    if (0 == cmbCondition.SelectedIndex)    //选择题
        //控制"答案 A""答案 B"等列可见
        //answera、answerb 等是 dgvQuestion 控件中的各列的名称，参见表 8-21
        answera.Visible = answerb.Visible = answerc.Visible = answerd.Visible = true;
```

```
            else
                answera.Visible =answerb.Visible =answerc.Visible =answerd.Visible =
                    false;
            dgvQuestion.DataSource = null;
}
```

当选择完课程、章节、题型并输入要查询的内容后,单击"查询"按钮可实现题库的查询并将查询结果显示在 dgvQuestion 中。单击"查询全部"按钮可在 dgvQuestion 中查看到当前选中课程指定章节(cmbChapter 中选中的章节,如果选中的是"全部章节"则查询全部章节)、指定题型(cmbCondition 中选中的题型)的所有题库信息。

"查询"按钮的事件处理代码如下。

```
private void btnSearch_Click(object sender, EventArgs e)
{
    BLL.BLLTestQuestion ssc = new BLL.BLLTestQuestion();
    //testQuestionSelect 函数的功能是从题库中查询满足指定条件的试题
    DataTable dt = ssc.testQuestionSelect(txtKeyword.Text,cmbCourse.
        SelectedValue.ToString(),
        cmbChapter.SelectedValue.ToString(),cmbCondition.Text);
    dgvQuestion.DataSource = dt;
}
```

"查询全部"按钮的事件处理代码如下。

```
private void btnAll_Click(object sender, EventArgs e)
{
    BLL.BLLTestQuestion ssc = new BLL.BLLTestQuestion();
    if ("-1" == cmbChapter.SelectedValue.ToString())
        //如果当前选中的章节是"全部章节",则查询当前选中课程,选中题型的所有试题
        dgvQuestion.DataSource = ssc.testQuestionSelect("", cmbCourse.
            SelectedValue.ToString(), "",
            cmbCondition.Text);
    else
        //否则查询当前选中课程的指定章节、指定题型的所有试题
        dgvQuestion.DataSource = ssc.testQuestionSelect("", cmbCourse.
            SelectedValue.ToString(),
            cmbChapter.SelectedValue.ToString(), cmbCondition.Text);
}
```

单击"添加"按钮可以打开题库编辑界面(FrmQuestionEdit),此时打开的题库编辑界面可以实现题库中试题的添加。"添加"按钮的处理代码如下。

```
private void btnAdd_Click(object sender, EventArgs e)
{
    FrmQuestionEdit frm = new FrmQuestionEdit();
    frm.MdiParent = this.MdiParent;
    frm.questionManage = this;
    frm.Show();
}
```

在 dgvQuestion 中,选中一条试题记录,单击"修改"按钮可以打开题库编辑界面(FrmQuestionEdit),但此时所打开的题库编辑界面可以实现题库中试题信息的修改,且在

打开题库编辑界面的同时会将当前选中的试题记录封装成 Model.TestQuestion 实体类对象并传递给题库编辑界面，以便在题库编辑界面可以查看到要修改试题信息的当前数据状况。"修改"按钮的处理代码如下。

```csharp
private void btnModify_Click(object sender, EventArgs e)
{
    if (null == dgvQuestion.CurrentRow)
    {
        MessageBox.Show("请先选择一行数据!");
        return;
    }
    FrmQuestionEdit frm = new FrmQuestionEdit();
    frm.MdiParent = this.MdiParent;
    Model.TestQuestion t = new Model.TestQuestion();
    t.ChapterId = dgvQuestion.CurrentRow.Cells["chapterid"].Value.ToString();
    t.QuestionId = dgvQuestion.CurrentRow.Cells["QuestionId"].Value.ToString();
    t.QuestionTitle = dgvQuestion.CurrentRow.Cells["QuestionTitle"].Value.
        ToString();
    t.QuestionType = dgvQuestion.CurrentRow.Cells["QuestionType"].Value.
        ToString();
    t.AnswerA = dgvQuestion.CurrentRow.Cells["AnswerA"].Value.ToString();
    t.AnswerB = dgvQuestion.CurrentRow.Cells["AnswerB"].Value.ToString();
    t.AnswerC = dgvQuestion.CurrentRow.Cells["AnswerC"].Value.ToString();
    t.AnswerD = dgvQuestion.CurrentRow.Cells["AnswerD"].Value.ToString();
    t.CurrectAnswer = dgvQuestion.CurrentRow.Cells["CurrectAnswer"].Value.
        ToString();
    frm.testQuestion = t;
    frm.questionManage = this;
    frm.Show();
}
```

在 dgvQuestion 中，选中一条试题记录，单击"删除"按钮，会弹出确认对话框，询问用户是否确定删除该试题，如果选择"是"则执行删除，并刷新 dgvQuestion 控件，如果选择"否"则中止删除操作。"删除"按钮事件处理代码如下。

```csharp
private void btnDelete_Click(object sender, EventArgs e)
{
    if (DialogResult.Cancel == MessageBox.Show("确定要删除此条信息?", "警告!",
        MessageBoxButtons.OKCancel))
        return;
    BLL.BLLTestQuestion ssc = new BLL.BLLTestQuestion();
    //执行删除操作
    if (ssc.testQuestionDelete(dgvQuestion.CurrentRow.Cells["questionid"].
        Value.ToString()))
        MessageBox.Show("删除成功!");
    else
        MessageBox.Show("删除失败!");
    updateDataGridViewDataSource();
}
```

updateDataGridViewDataSource 函数代码如下。

```
public void updateDataGridViewDataSource()
{
    if (isPressedAllLast)
        btnAll_Click(null, null);
    else
        btnSearch_Click(null, null);
}
```

8.8.4 题库管理模块——"题库编辑"窗体

题库编辑窗体负责实现对题库的试题信息的添加及修改,其界面如图 8-12 所示,窗体属性设置如表 8-22 所示,窗体的控件设置如表 8-23 所示。

图 8-12 "题库编辑"窗体

表 8-22 "题库编辑"窗体属性设置

属 性 名	属 性 值	作 用
Name	FrmQuestionEdit	窗体名称
Text	题库编辑	设置窗体的标题文本

表 8-23 "题库编辑"窗体中的控件

Tab 序号	控 件 类 型	属 性 名	属 性 值	说 明
1	ComboBox	Name	cmbCourseName	
		DropDownStyle	DropDownList	
3	ComboBox	Name	cmbChapterName	
		DropDownStyle	DropDownList	

续表

Tab 序号	控件类型	属性名	属性值	说明
5	ComboBox	Name	cmbType	
		DropDownStyle	DropDownList	
7	TextBox	Name	txtName	
8	GroupBox	Name	gbSelect	
		Text	请选择正确的答案	
8.0	CheckBox	Name	cbA	gbSelect 的子控件
		RightToLeft	Yes	
		Text	答案 A	
8.1	TextBox	Name	txtA	gbSelect 的子控件
8.2	CheckBox	Name	cbB	gbSelect 的子控件
		RightToLeft	Yes	
		Text	答案 B	
8.3	TextBox	Name	txtB	gbSelect 的子控件
8.4	CheckBox	Name	cbC	gbSelect 的子控件
		RightToLeft	Yes	
		Text	答案 C	
8.5	TextBox	Name	txtC	gbSelect 的子控件
8.6	CheckBox	Name	cbD	gbSelect 的子控件
		RightToLeft	Yes	
		Text	答案 D	
8.7	TextBox	Name	txtD	gbSelect 的子控件
9	RadioButton	Name	rbYes	
		CheckAlign	MiddleRight	
		Text	对	
10	RadioButton	Name	rbNo	
		CheckAlign	MiddleRight	
		Text	错	
11	Button	Name	btnDone	

首先，在该窗体的类文件 FrmQuestionEdit.cs 中声明两个成员变量。

```
public Model.TestQuestion testQuestion;
public FrmQuestionManage questionManage;
```

加载窗体时,需要做一些初始化操作:首先,需要将当前教师承担的课程信息绑定到 cmbCourseName 控件中;其次,要根据当前窗体的操作目的是添加还是修改进行相应的信息设置。

窗体的 Load 事件代码如下。

```
private void FrmQuestionEdit_Load(object sender, EventArgs e)
{
    cmbChapterName.DisplayMember = "chaptername";
    cmbChapterName.ValueMember = "chapterid";
    BLL.BLLTeachCourse ssc = new BLL.BLLTeachCourse();
    cmbCourseName.DataSource = ssc.Teacher_CourseSelect(LoginHelper.
        teacherID);
    cmbCourseName.DisplayMember = "coursename";
    cmbCourseName.ValueMember = "courseid";
    if (null == testQuestion)                      //添加
    {
        btnDone.Text = "添加";
        this.Text = "试题添加";
        cmbType.SelectedIndex = 0;
    }
    else                                           //修改
    {
        btnDone.Text = "修改";
        this.Text = "试题修改";
        //以下代码是将要修改试题的原始信息显示在各控件内
        txtName.Text = testQuestion.QuestionTitle;
        if ("选择题" == testQuestion.QuestionType)
            cmbType.SelectedIndex = 0;
        else
            cmbType.SelectedIndex = 1;
        BLL.BLLChapter sscCpt = new BLL.BLLChapter();
        //ChapterSelectCondition 函数的作用是查询当前章节号所属的课程信息
        //该行代码的作用是获取当前试题的章节号所属课程的课程号
        //并令 cmbCourseName 默认选中是该课程
        cmbCourseName.SelectedValue = (sscCpt.ChapterSelectCondition
            (testQuestion.ChapterId, "章节号")).Rows[0]["courseid"];
        cmbChapterName.SelectedValue = testQuestion.ChapterId;
        //以下四行代码的目的是勾选选择题正确答案所对应的 CheckBox
        if (testQuestion.CurrectAnswer.Contains("A")) {cbA.Checked = true;}
        if (testQuestion.CurrectAnswer.Contains("B")) { cbB.Checked = true; }
        if (testQuestion.CurrectAnswer.Contains("C")) { cbC.Checked = true; }
        if (testQuestion.CurrectAnswer.Contains("D")) { cbD.Checked = true; }
        //以下四行代码的目的是将该试题目前的所有选项内容显示在对应的文本框中
        txtA.Text = testQuestion.AnswerA;
        txtB.Text = testQuestion.AnswerB;
        txtC.Text = testQuestion.AnswerC;
        txtD.Text = testQuestion.AnswerD;
        //以下两行代码的目的是勾选判断题正确答案所对应的 RadioButton
```

```
            if ("0" == testQuestion.CurrectAnswer) { rbNo.Checked = true; }
            else { rbYes.Checked = true; }
        }
}
```

在 cmbType 控件中选择不同的题型时,题库编辑窗体中显示的控件会有所变化:选择判断题时,应显示 rbYes 和 rbNo 控件;而选择选择题时应显示 GroupBox 控件 gbSelect 中的所有控件。需要处理 cmbType 控件的 SelectedIndexChanged 事件代码如下。

```
private void cmbType_SelectedIndexChanged(object sender, EventArgs e)
{
    if (0 == cmbType.SelectedIndex)
    {
        //选择题
        gbSelect.Visible = true;
        gbSelect.BringToFront();
        rbYes.Checked = true;
    }
    else
    {
        //判断题
        gbSelect.Visible = false;
        cbA.Checked = false;
        cbB.Checked = false;
        cbC.Checked = false;
        cbD.Checked = false;
    }
}
```

当在 cmbCourse 控件中选择一个课程时,会触发该控件的 SelectedValueChanged 事件,在该事件处理函数中,需要把当前选中课程的所有章节绑定到 cmbChapterName 控件中,代码如下。

```
private void cmbCourseName_SelectedValueChanged(object sender, EventArgs e)
{
    updateChapterbyCourse();
    clearMulSelInputs();
}
```

updateChapterbyCourse 函数的作用就是根据当前选中的课程重新向 cmbChapterName 控件中绑定章节,代码如下。

```
void updateChapterbyCourse()
{
    BLL.BLLChapter ssc = new BLL.BLLChapter();
    cmbChapterName.DataSource = ssc.ChapterSelectCondition
                    (cmbCourseName.SelectedValue.ToString(), "课程号");
}
```

clearMulSelInputs 函数的作用是清空 gbSelect 控件中所有子控件的内容,代码如下。

```
void clearMulSelInputs()
```

```
{
    txtA.Text =txtB.Text =txtC.Text =txtD.Text = "";
    cbA.Checked =cbB.Checked =cbC.Checked = cbD.Checked = false;
}
```

输入各类信息后,单击 btnDone 按钮可实现试题信息的添加或修改,事件处理代码如下。

```
private void btnDone_Click(object sender, EventArgs e)
{
    if (-1 == cmbChapterName.SelectedIndex|| -1 == cmbCourseName.SelectedIndex||
        -1 == cmbType.SelectedIndex|| "" == txtName.Text)
    {
        MessageBox.Show(Localizable.CHECK_INPUT_STRING);
        return;
    }
    if (0 == cmbType.SelectedIndex)
    {
        if ("" == txtA.Text || "" == txtB.Text || "" == txtC.Text || "" == txtD.Text)
        {
            MessageBox.Show(Localizable.CHECK_INPUT_ABCD_STRING);
            return;
        }
    }
    BLL.BLLTestQuestion ssc = new BLL.BLLTestQuestion();
    if (null == testQuestion)                //添加
    {
        Model.TestQuestion t = new Model.TestQuestion();
        t.QuestionId=DateTime.Now.ToString("yyyyMMddHHmmss ");
        t.QuestionTitle = txtName.Text;
        t.QuestionType = cmbType.Text;
        t.ChapterId = cmbChapterName.SelectedValue.ToString();
        t.AnswerA = txtA.Text;
        t.AnswerB = txtB.Text;
        t.AnswerC = txtC.Text;
        t.AnswerD = txtD.Text;
        t.CurrectAnswer = "";
        if (0 == cmbType.SelectedIndex)
        {
            //选择题
            if (cbA.Checked) { t.CurrectAnswer += "A"; }
            if (cbB.Checked) { t.CurrectAnswer += "B"; }
            if (cbC.Checked) { t.CurrectAnswer += "C"; }
            if (cbD.Checked) { t.CurrectAnswer += "D"; }
        }
        else
        {
            //判断题
            if (rbYes.Checked) { t.CurrectAnswer = "1"; }
            else { t.CurrectAnswer = "0"; }
```

```
            }
            if ("" == t.CurrectAnswer)
            {
                MessageBox.Show("请选上正确答案之后再进行添加操作!");
                return;
            }
            if (ssc.testQuestionInsert(t))              //执行添加操作
                MessageBox.Show("添加成功!");
            else
                MessageBox.Show("添加失败!");
            this.Close();
        }
        else                                            //修改
        {
            testQuestion.QuestionTitle = txtName.Text;
            testQuestion.QuestionType = cmbType.Text;
            testQuestion.ChapterId = cmbChapterName.SelectedValue.ToString();
            testQuestion.AnswerA = txtA.Text;
            testQuestion.AnswerB = txtB.Text;
            testQuestion.AnswerC = txtC.Text;
            testQuestion.AnswerD = txtD.Text;
            testQuestion.CurrectAnswer = "";
            if (0 == cmbType.SelectedIndex)
            {
                //选择题
                if (cbA.Checked) { testQuestion.CurrectAnswer += "A"; }
                if (cbB.Checked) { testQuestion.CurrectAnswer += "B"; }
                if (cbC.Checked) { testQuestion.CurrectAnswer += "C"; }
                if (cbD.Checked) { testQuestion.CurrectAnswer += "D"; }
            }
            else
            {
                //判断题
                if (rbYes.Checked) { testQuestion.CurrectAnswer = "1"; }
                else { testQuestion.CurrectAnswer = "0"; }
            }
            if (ssc.testQuestionUpdate(testQuestion, testQuestion.QuestionId))
                //执行修改操作
                MessageBox.Show("修改成功!");
            else
                MessageBox.Show("修改失败!");
            this.Close();
        }
    }
    this.questionManage.updateDataGridViewDataSource();
}
```

8.8.5 组卷模块

组卷管理模块的主要功能是实现学生考试用卷的组卷功能,该模块是教师端子系统中最复杂的一个模块，也是最核心的模块。其窗体设计如图 8-13 所示，窗体的属性设置如表 8-24 所示，窗体中的控件设置如表 8-25～表 8-27 所示。

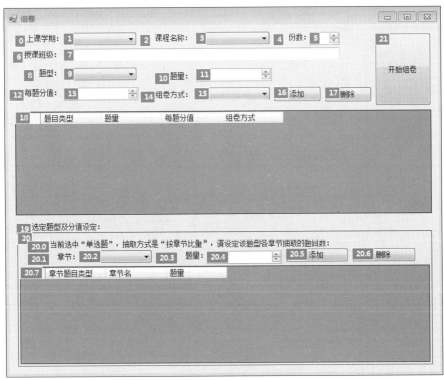

图 8-13 "组卷"窗体

表 8-24 "组卷"窗体属性设置

属 性 名	属 性 值	作 用
Name	FrmCreatePaper	窗体名称
Text	组卷	设置窗体的标题文本

表 8-25 "组卷"窗体中的控件

Tab 序号	控 件 类 型	属 性 名	属 性 值	说 明
1	ComboBox	Name	cmbTakeTerm	
		DropDownStyle	DropDownList	
3	ComboBox	Name	cmbCourse	
		DropDownStyle	DropDownList	
5	NumericUpDown	Name	nudPaper	
7	TextBox	Name	txtTeachClass	
9	ComboBox	Name	cmbQuestionType	
		DropDownStyle	DropDownList	

续表

Tab序号	控件类型	属性名	属性值	说明
11	NumericUpDown	Name	nudQuestionCount	
13	NumericUpDown	Name	nudQuestionValue	
15	ComboBox	Name	cmbCreateMethod	
		DropDownStyle	DropDownList	
16	Button	Name	btnAddScheme	
		Text	添加	
17	Button	Name	btnDeleteScheme	
		Text	删除	
18	DataGridView	Name	dgvPaperScheme	
		AllowUserToAddRows	False	
		AllowUserToDeleteRows	False	
		ColumnHeadersHeightSizeMode	AutoSize	
		MultiSelect	False	
		ReadOnly	True	
20	Panel	Name	panelChapter	
20.2	ComboBox	Name	cmbChapter	panelChapter 的子控件
		DropDownStyle	DropDownList	
20.4	NumericUpDown	Name	nudChapterCount	panelChapter 的子控件
20.5	Button	Name	btnAddChapter	panelChapter 的子控件
		Text	添加	
20.6	Button	Name	btnDeleteChapter	panelChapter 的子控件
		Text	删除	
20.7	DataGridView	Name	dgvChapterScheme	panelChapter 的子控件
		AllowUserToAddRows	False	
		AllowUserToDeleteRows	False	
		ColumnHeadersHeightSizeMode	AutoSize	
		MultiSelect	False	
		ReadOnly	True	
21	Button	Name	btnCreatePaper	
		Text	开始组卷	

表 8-26　dgvPaperScheme 中各列的属性设置

列头文本	属性名	属性值
题目类型	DataPropertyName	questionType
题量	DataPropertyName	questionCount
每题分值	DataPropertyName	questionValue
组卷方式	DataPropertyName	method

表 8-27　dgvChapterScheme 中各列的属性设置

列头文本	属性名	属性值
章节题目类型	DataPropertyName	chapterQuestionType
章节编号	DataPropertyName	chapterId
	Visible	False
章节名	DataPropertyName	chapterName
题量	DataPropertyName	chapterQuestionCount

首先,在该窗体的类文件 FrmCreatePaper.cs 中声明三个成员变量。

```
DataTable dtTerm;
Model.TeachCourse teachCourse = new Model.TeachCourse();
DataTable dtTeachCourse;                    //用于存储当前教师某一学期的授课信息
```

接下来,进行窗体加载,需要做一些初始化操作。

(1) 对 DataGridView 控件 dgvPaperScheme 中的列的 Name 属性进行设置,方便后续操作。

(2) 对 DataGridView 控件 dgvChapterScheme 中的列的 Name 属性进行设置,方便后续操作。

(3) 从数据库中提取当前登录教师的授课信息,并将数据暂存至共用数据表 dtTerm 中。

(4) 遍历 dtTerm 中的授课信息,将其中的授课学期提取出来,并显示在 cmbTakeTerm 中,由于可能有多门课程在同一学期,即 dtTerm 中同一个学期会出现多次,所以要进行重复项过滤。过滤完成后,选择第一项,保证该下拉列表选项不为空。

(5) 设置 cmbChapter 的绑定显示字段与值字段,方便后续操作。

(6) 从数据库中获取当前登录教师所有教授的课程列表(不重复),并绑定至 cmbCourse。选择第一项,保证默认不为空。

窗体的 Load 事件代码如下。

```
private void FrmCreatePaper_Load(object sender, EventArgs e)
{
    for (int i = 0; i < dgvPaperScheme.Columns.Count; i++)
    //为 dgvPaperScheme 中各列的 Name 属性赋值为该列的绑定字段名
        dgvPaperScheme.Columns[i].Name = dgvPaperScheme.Columns[i].
           DataPropertyName;
```

```csharp
            for (int i = 0; i < dgvChapterScheme.Columns.Count; i++)
                //为 dgvChapterScheme 中各列的 Name 属性赋值为该列的绑定字段名
                dgvChapterScheme.Columns[i].Name = dgvChapterScheme.Columns[i].
                    DataPropertyName;
            //授课信息的业务逻辑层类,可参考本书网络资源的源代码
            BLL.BLLTeachInformation ssc = new BLL.BLLTeachInformation();
            //TeachInformationSelectCondition 函数的作用是取出指定教师号的教师的详细授课信息,
            //包括上课学期
            dtTerm = ssc.TeachInformationSelectCondition(LoginHelper.teacherID,"教师号");
            for (int i = 0; i < dtTerm.Rows.Count; i++)
            //遍历 dtTerm,将其中的上课学期添加到 cmbTakeTerm 选项集合中
            {
                bool isExist = false;
                for (int j = 0; j < cmbTakeTerm.Items.Count; j++)
                //循环遍历 cmbTakeTerm 的选项集合,
                //查看当前遍历到的上课学期是否已经存在于 cmbTakeTerm 的选项集合中
                {
                    if (dtTerm.Rows[i]["teachterm"].ToString() == cmbTakeTerm.Items[j].
                        ToString())
                    {
                        isExist = true;
                    }
                }
                //如果当前遍历到的上课学期不在 cmbTakeTerm 的选项集合中,
                //则把该上课学期添加进 cmbTakeTerm
                if (!isExist)
                    cmbTakeTerm.Items.Add(dtTerm.Rows[i]["teachterm"]);
            }
            cmbTakeTerm.SelectedIndex = 0;
            cmbChapter.DisplayMember = "chaptername";
            cmbChapter.ValueMember = "chapterid";
            updateCmbCourse();
            cmbQuestionType.SelectedIndex = 0;
            cmbCreateMethod.SelectedIndex = 0;
            checkChapterPanelEnable();
            checkSchemeButtonEnable();
        }
```

updateCmbCourse 函数的作用是根据当前选中的上课学期,为 cmbCourse 控件绑定当前登录教师在该学期讲授的所有课程,代码如下。

```csharp
void updateCmbCourse()
{
    BLL.BLLTeachInformation sscLT = new BLL.BLLTeachInformation();
    //TeachInformationSelectConditionWithTeacherId 的作用是查询指定教师,
    //满足指定条件的详细授课信息
    dtTeachCourse= sscLT.TeachInformationSelectConditionWithTeacherId
        (LoginHelper.teacherID,cmbTakeTerm.Text, "上课学期");
    cmbCourse.DataSource =dtTeachCourse;
    cmbCourse.DisplayMember = "coursename";
    cmbCourse.ValueMember = "courseid";
}
```

checkChapterPanelEnable 函数的作用是控制 panelChapter 的可用性,如果用户在

dgvPaperScheme 中选中了一条题型的设置信息,并且该题型的组卷方式是"按章节随机"则 panelChapter 可用,即允许用户操作按章节随机组卷的情况下各章试题的抽取比例。代码如下。

```
private void checkChapterPanelEnable()
{
    if (null == dgvPaperScheme.CurrentRow) { panelChapter.Enabled = false;
        return; }
        panelChapter.Enabled = ("按章节随机"==
            dgvPaperScheme.CurrentRow.Cells["method"].Value.ToString());
}
```

checkSchemeButtonEnable 函数的作用是控制 btnDeleteScheme 和 btnAddScheme 按钮的可用性,代码如下。

```
private void checkSchemeButtonEnable()
{
    btnDeleteScheme.Enabled = (0 != dgvPaperScheme.RowCount);
    btnAddScheme.Enabled = (0 != cmbQuestionType.Items.Count);
    if (0 != cmbQuestionType.Items.Count) { cmbQuestionType.SelectedIndex = 0; }
}
```

当在 cmbTakeTerm 控件中选择一个学期时,会触发该控件的 SelectedIndexChanged 事件,在该事件处理函数中,需要把当前教师在当前选中学期中承担的所有课程绑定到 cmbCourse 控件中。代码如下。

```
private void cmbTakeTerm_SelectedIndexChanged(object sender, EventArgs e)
{
    updateCmbCourse();
}
```

当在 cmbCourse 控件中选择一个课程时,会触发该控件的 SelectedIndexChanged 事件,在该事件处理函数中,需要把当前选中课程的章节信息绑定到 cmbChapter 控件中,同时要刷新 txtTeachClass 控件,显示当前课程的授课班级。代码如下。

```
private void cmbCourse_SelectedIndexChanged(object sender, EventArgs e)
{
    if (dgvChapterScheme.Rows.Count != 0)
    {
        if (DialogResult.OK == MessageBox.Show
            ("变换课程将清空下方已经选好的章节配置,还要继续么?", "警告!",
            MessageBoxButtons.OKCancel))
            dgvChapterScheme.Rows.Clear();
        else
            return;
    }
    updateCmbChapter();
    updateTxtTeachClass();
}
```

updateCmbChapter 函数的作用是查询当前选中课程的所有章节,并绑定到 cmbChapter 控件中,代码如下。

```csharp
void updateCmbChapter()
{
    BLL.BLLChapter ssc = new BLL.BLLChapter();
    //ChapterSelectCondition 的作用是查询满足指定条件的章节信息
    cmbChapter.DataSource = ssc.ChapterSelectCondition(cmbCourse.
        SelectedValue.ToString(),
        "课程号");
}
```

updateTxtTeachClass 函数的作用是查询当前选中课程的授课班级并将结果显示在 txtTeachClass 控件中。代码如下。

```csharp
void updateTxtTeachClass()
{
    txtTeachClass.Text = "";
    if (null == cmbCourse.SelectedValue) { return; }
    //取出当前所选课程的授课班级
    txtTeachClass.Text = dtTeachCourse.Rows[cmbCourse.SelectedIndex]
        ["classname"].ToString();
    if ("" == txtTeachClass.Text)
    {
        btnCreatePaper.Text = "没有上课班级,不能组卷!";
        btnCreatePaper.Enabled = false;
    }
    else
    {
        btnCreatePaper.Text = "组卷";
        btnCreatePaper.Enabled = true;
    }
}
```

选择好学期、课程、确认授课班级,输入组卷份数后,即可为试卷进行详细配置。选择题型、输入这种题型的题量、每题分值并选择组卷方式后,单击"添加"按钮(btnAddScheme),可将当前选中题型的配置信息添入 dgvPaperScheme 中。该"添加"按钮的事件处理代码如下。

```csharp
private void btnAddScheme_Click(object sender, EventArgs e)
{
    if (!checkSchemeCanAdd())
    { MessageBox.Show(Localizable.CHECK_COUNT_VALUE_STRING); return; }
    BLL.BLLTestQuestion ssc = new BLL.BLLTestQuestion();
    if (ssc.testQuestionSelect("", cmbCourse.SelectedValue.ToString(), "",
        cmbQuestionType.Text).
        Rows.Count < nudQuestionCount.Value)
    //testQuestionSelect 函数,验证题库中该题型是否有足够的题量,
    //可查阅本书网络资源中的源代码
    { MessageBox.Show("题库中当前类型没有足够的题目!"); return; }
    DataGridViewRow dgvr = new DataGridViewRow();
                                    //产生一个 DataGridView 控件的行对象
    //为该行对象创建单元格,单元格样式与 dgvPaperScheme 中的列相同
    dgvr.CreateCells(dgvPaperScheme);
```

```csharp
            //以下四行代码是为新产生的行对象的各单元格赋值
            dgvr.Cells[0].Value = cmbQuestionType.Text;
            dgvr.Cells[1].Value = int.Parse(nudQuestionCount.Text);
            dgvr.Cells[2].Value = int.Parse(nudQuestionValue.Text);
            dgvr.Cells[3].Value = cmbCreateMethod.Text;
            dgvPaperScheme.Rows.Add(dgvr);
                            //将新产生的行对象添加到dgvPaperScheme控件中进行显示。
            //将已设置的题型从cmbQuestionType中删除，避免用户重复设置
            cmbQuestionType.Items.Remove(cmbQuestionType.Text);
            checkSchemeButtonEnable();
            checkChapterPanelEnable();
        }
```

checkSchemeCanAdd 函数的作用是对题型配置信息进行一次基本验证，即题量不能为 0，每题分值不能为 0。代码如下。

```csharp
        private bool checkSchemeCanAdd()
        {
            return (0 != nudQuestionCount.Value && 0 != nudQuestionValue.Value);
        }
```

如果要修改已设置题型的配置信息，需要在 dgvPaperScheme 中删除该配置信息之后再添加。在 dgvPaperScheme 中选中要删除的配置信息，单击"删除"按钮（btnDeleteScheme），完成配置信息的删除。代码如下。

```csharp
        private void btnDeleteScheme_Click(object sender, EventArgs e)
        {
            //将当前题型加回cmbQuestionType
            cmbQuestionType.Items.Add(dgvPaperScheme.CurrentRow.Cells
                ["questionType"].Value.ToString());
            deleteChapterSetForType(dgvPaperScheme.CurrentRow.Cells["questionType"].
                Value.ToString());
            dgvPaperScheme.Rows.Remove(dgvPaperScheme.CurrentRow);
            checkSchemeButtonEnable();
            checkChapterPanelEnable();
        }
```

如果用户已配置了每种题型是"按章节随机"的组卷方式，且已经在 dgvChapterScheme 中配置了详细的各章节试题的抽取策略，那么在删除该题型的配置信息时，应同时删除 dgvChapterScheme 中与该题型相关的抽取策略。deleteChapterSetForType 函数的作用就是删除 dgvChapterScheme 中的抽取策略。代码如下。

```csharp
        private void deleteChapterSetForType(string type)
        {
            List<DataGridViewRow> dgvrs = new List<DataGridViewRow>();
                                            //用于存储所有的待删行
            for (int i = 0; i < dgvChapterScheme.RowCount; i++)
                                            //找到所有的待删行,加入到dgvrs集合中
            {
                if (type == dgvChapterScheme.Rows[i].Cells["chapterQuestionType"].
                    Value.ToString())
                {
```

```
            dgvrs.Add(dgvChapterScheme.Rows[i]);
        }
    }
    for (int i = 0; i < dgvrs.Count; i++)     //删除所有的待删行
    {
        dgvChapterScheme.Rows.Remove(dgvrs[i]);
    }
}
```

如果用户配置了某题型是"按章节随机"的组卷方式,还需要针对这种组卷方式进行更详细的配置,即配置各章节试题的抽取策略。在 dgvPaperScheme 中选中一条组卷方式是"按章节随机"的配置信息,panelChapter 中的所有子控件呈可用状态。代码如下。

```
private void dgvPaperScheme_SelectionChanged(object sender, EventArgs e)
{
    if (null == dgvPaperScheme.CurrentRow) { return; }
    checkChapterPanelEnable();
    lblNotifyWord.Text = "当前选中"" +dgvPaperScheme.CurrentRow.Cells[
        "questionType"].Value.
        ToString() + "",抽取方式是"" + dgvPaperScheme.CurrentRow.Cells[
        "method"].Value.
        ToString() + "",请设定该题型各章节抽取的题目数:";
}
```

选择好章节、该题型在本章抽取的题量后,单击"添加"按钮(btnAddChapter),可将当前选中章节的抽取策略添入 dgvChapterScheme 中。该"添加"按钮的事件处理代码如下。

```
private void btnAddChapter_Click(object sender, EventArgs e)
{
    if (!checkCanAddNewChapterForCurrentRow())
    {
        MessageBox.Show(Localizable.INSERT_CHAPTER_COUNT_OVERFLOW); return;
    }
    DataGridViewRow dgvr = new DataGridViewRow();
    dgvr.CreateCells(dgvChapterScheme);
    dgvr.Cells[0].Value = dgvPaperScheme.CurrentRow.Cells["questionType"].
        Value.ToString();
    dgvr.Cells[1].Value = cmbChapter.SelectedValue.ToString();    //章节编号
    dgvr.Cells[2].Value = cmbChapter.Text;                         //章节名
    dgvr.Cells[3].Value = int.Parse(nudChapterCount.Text);         //章节题目数量
    dgvChapterScheme.Rows.Add(dgvr);
}
```

checkCanAddNewChapterForCurrentRow 函数的作用是检验是否还能够向 dgvChapterScheme 中添加抽取策略信息,如果当前已经设置的抽取策略中,各章节的题量之和加上本次要添加的抽取策略中的题量总和已经大于当前选中题型需要抽取的题量,则不允许继续添加该抽取策略;此外,如果 dgvChapterScheme 中已经存在了选中题型下该章节的抽取策略,则不允许继续添加该抽取策略。具体代码如下。

```
private bool checkCanAddNewChapterForCurrentRow()
{
```

```
    //获取当前选中题型
    string type = dgvPaperScheme.CurrentRow.Cells["questionType"].Value.
        ToString();
    for (int i = 0; i < dgvChapterScheme.RowCount; i++)
    {
        //判断dgvChapterScheme中是否已存在了题型是当前选中题型
        //并且章节与即将添加的抽取策略章节相同的记录
        if (type == dgvChapterScheme.Rows[i].Cells["chapterquestiontype"].
            Value.ToString()
            &&cmbChapter.SelectedValue.ToString()==dgvChapterScheme.Rows[i].
            Cells["chapterid"].Value.ToString())
        { return false; }
    }
    //计算当前抽取策略+即将添加的抽取策略题量总和,并与当前选中题型需要的最大题量相比较
    return (getChapterCountByType(type) + (int)nudChapterCount.Value <=
        int.Parse(dgvPaperScheme.CurrentRow.Cells["questionCount"].Value.
ToString()));
}
```

getChapterCountByType函数的作用是计算dgvChapterScheme中指定题型的抽取策略包含的总题量。代码如下。

```
private int getChapterCountByType(string type)
{
    int t = 0;
    for (int i = 0; i < dgvChapterScheme.RowCount; i++)
    {
        if (type == dgvChapterScheme.Rows[i].Cells["chapterQuestionType"].
            Value.ToString())
        {
            t += int.Parse(dgvChapterScheme.Rows[i].Cells
                ["chapterQuestionCount"].Value.ToString());
        }
    }
    return t;
}
```

如果要修改已设置章节的抽取策略,需要在dgvChapterScheme中删除该抽取策略之后再添加。在dgvChapterScheme中选中要删除的抽取策略,单击"删除"按钮(btnDeleteChapter),完成抽取策略的删除。代码如下。

```
private void btnDeleteChapter_Click(object sender, EventArgs e)
{
    dgvChapterScheme.Rows.Remove(dgvChapterScheme.CurrentRow);
}
```

各项配置完成后,即可单击"组卷"按钮执行组卷操作。代码如下。

```
private void btnCreatePaper_Click(object sender, EventArgs e)
{
    //检查所需数据是否合法,不合法就报错,并停止组卷
    if (-1 == cmbTakeTerm.SelectedIndex|| -1 == cmbCourse.SelectedIndex||
        nudPaper.Value <= 0
```

```csharp
            || dgvPaperScheme.RowCount <= 0)
        {
            MessageBox.Show(Localizable.CHECK_INPUT_STRING); return;
        }
        //按题目类型设定信息进行遍历检查信息合法性,主要遍历按章节随机的部分
        for (int i =0; i<dgvPaperScheme.RowCount;i++)
        {
            //是否是按章节随机
            if ("按章节随机" == dgvPaperScheme.Rows[i].Cells["method"].Value.
                ToString())
            {
                //题目类型组卷信息是否大于 0
                if (dgvChapterScheme.RowCount <= 0)
                {
                    MessageBox.Show(Localizable.CHECK_INPUT_STRING); return;
                }
                else
                {
                    //按章节随机的题目,设定章节题目总数是否符合题目类型规则
                    if (getChapterCountByType(dgvPaperScheme.Rows[i].Cells
                        ["questionType"].Value.ToString())< int.Parse
                        (dgvPaperScheme.Rows[i].
                        Cells["questionCount"].Value.ToString()))
                    {
                        MessageBox.Show("章节设定总数小于当前类型,请检查!");
                        return;
                    }
                }
            }
        }
        Model.CreatePaperScheme cps = new Model.CreatePaperScheme();
        //存储所有的题型、题量、分值信息
        List<Model.QuestionTypeScore> qtsList = new List<Model.QuestionTypeScore>();
        if (0 == dgvPaperScheme.Rows.Count)
        {
            MessageBox.Show("没有添加任何规则,无法组卷!");
            return;
        }
        cps.SchemeId = DateTime.Now.ToString();              //生成组卷方案 ID
                //获取授课 ID 号
        cps.TeachId = dtTeachCourse.Rows[cmbCourse.SelectedIndex]["teachid"].
            ToString();
        List<string> chapterList = new List<string>();      //存储所有的章节抽取策略
        //按题型设定信息进行遍历,构造题型、题量、分值信息集合
        for (int i = 0;i < dgvPaperScheme.Rows.Count;i++)
        {
            Model.QuestionTypeScore qts = new Model.QuestionTypeScore();
            //获取组卷方式:完全随机、按章节随机
            qts.CreateType = dgvPaperScheme.Rows[i].Cells["method"].Value.
                ToString();
            qts.QuestionNum = int.Parse(dgvPaperScheme.Rows[i].Cells
                ["questionCount"].Value.ToString());        //获取题量
```

```
        qts.QuestionScore = int.Parse(dgvPaperScheme.Rows[i].Cells
            ["questionValue"].Value.ToString());        //获取每题分值
        qts.SchemeId = cps.SchemeId;
        qts.TypeName = dgvPaperScheme.Rows[i].Cells["questionType"].Value.
            ToString();                                 //题型
        qtsList.Add(qts);
    }
    //按题目章节设定信息进行遍历,构造章节抽取策略集合
    for (int i = 0; i < dgvChapterScheme.Rows.Count; i++)
    {
        string str = "";
        for (int j = 0; j < dgvChapterScheme.Rows[i].Cells.Count; j++)
        {
            if (2 == j) { continue; }//跳过章节名称列
            //将信息组合成"题型|章节|题量"的格式
            str += dgvChapterScheme.Rows[i].Cells[j].Value.ToString() + "|";
        }
        str = str.Substring(0,str.Length-1);            //删除 str 最后边的"|"
        chapterList.Add(str);
    }
    //尝试与数据逻辑层交互,并组卷,显示反馈信息
    BLL.BLLQuestions ssc = new BLL.BLLQuestions();
    if (ssc.CreatePaperChapterRandom(qtsList, chapterList, cps, cmbCourse.
        SelectedValue.ToString(),
        int.Parse(nudPaper.Value.ToString())))//关于 CreatePaperChapterRandom
                                              //请查阅 8.7.6 节
    {
        MessageBox.Show("组卷成功!");
    }
    else
    {
        MessageBox.Show("组卷失败!");
    }
}
```

8.8.6 学生端主界面

学生登录成功后会进入学生端主界面(FrmMain),如图 8-14 所示。

该界面是学生端各功能模块的入口点。学生可选择"操作"→"参加考试"命令查看自己是否有正在进行的考试。如果有正在进行的考试,可在"参加考试"菜单项内选择一个考试菜单项,进入考试;如果当前时间没有正在进行的考试,则"参加考试"菜单项中无考试选项。选择"操作"→"成绩查询"命令,可以查阅已经发布成绩的课程的自己的成绩。选择"操作"→"注销"命令,系统注销当前用户,退回到登录界面。选择"操作"→"退出"命令,即可退出学生端子系统。

该窗体的属性设置如表 8-28 所示。

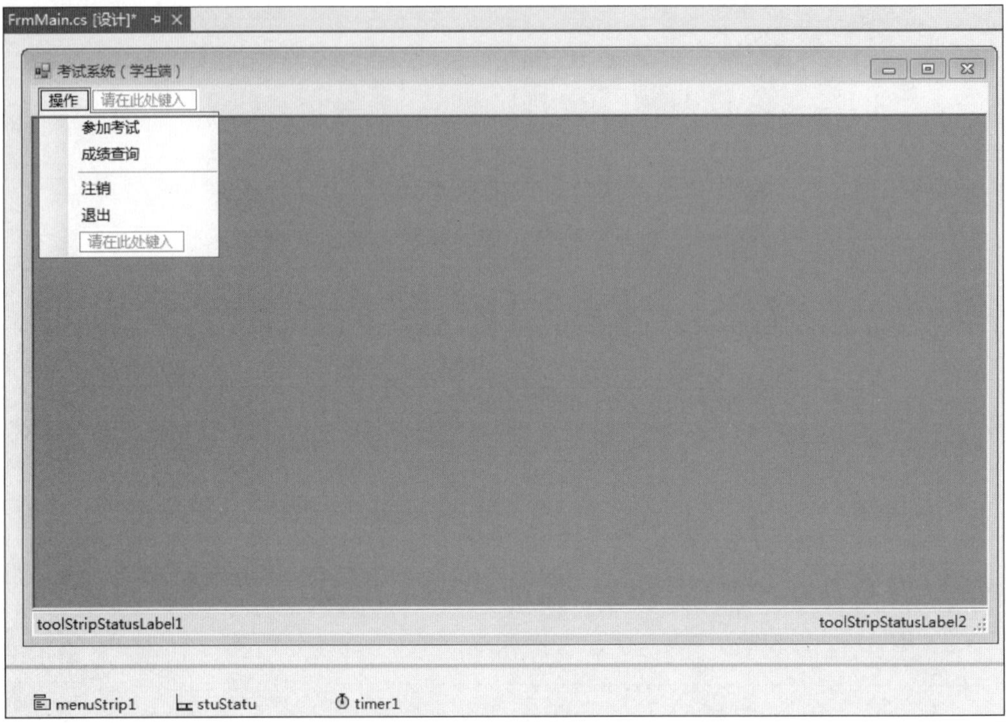

图 8-14　学生端主界面

表 8-28　学生端主界面属性设置

属 性 名	属 性 值	作　　用
Name	FrmMain	窗体名称
Text	在线考试系统（学生端）	设置窗体的标题文本
WindowState	Maximized	设置窗体的初始状态为最大化
IsMdiContainer	True	设置该窗体为 MDI 父窗体

首先，在该窗体的类文件 FrmMain.cs 中声明一个成员变量。

```
public string studentId = "";              //用于接收从登录窗体传过来的学生学号
```

编写 FrmMain 类的构造函数，用于在登录窗体实例化本窗体对象时，调用该构造函数并传递学号，代码如下。

```
public FrmMain(string StudentId)
{
    studentId = StudentId;
    InitializeComponent();
}
```

主界面窗体加载时，首先访问数据库，查询当前时间段该考生可以考试的科目，并将考试科目添加在"操作"→"参加考试"（tsmiAttendTest）菜单项中，并且为该考生随机选择一份可考科目的试卷，考生可以选择考试科目进行考试。窗体的 Load 事件代码如下。

```csharp
private void FrmMain_Load(object sender, EventArgs e)
{
    //启动定时器timer1,触发其Tick事件,
    //事件的核心功能是更新主窗体状态栏显示的当前时间,请查阅网络资源中的源代码
    timer1.Start();
    toolStripStatusLabel1.Text = "学号:" + studentId;
                                            //在状态栏中显示当前登录学生学号
    BLL.BLLCourse bC = new BLL.BLLCourse();
    //TestCourseSelect 函数的作用是获得当前登录学生当前时间能考试的科目,
    //请查阅网络资源中的源代码
    DataTable dt = bC.TestCourseSelect(studentId);
    if (dt.Rows.Count != 0)
    {
        //遍历所有的能考试的科目,向"参加考试"菜单项增加可选项,并随机抽取试卷
        for (int i = 0; i < dt.Rows.Count; i++)
        {
            string teachId = dt.Rows[i]["teachid"].ToString();
            int count= new BLL.BLLStudentAnswer().isSavePaper("|"+teachId+"|",
                studentId).Rows.Count;
            //isSavePaper 函数的作用是从 studentAnswer 表中获取当前登录学生指定授课
            //课程的答题情况,如果 count=0 则说明该学生第一次登录,还没有抽取试卷
            if (!tsmiAttendTest.DropDownItems.ContainsKey(dt.Rows[i][
                "courseName"].ToString()))
            {
                //如果学生还没有抽取试卷
                if (count == 0)
                {
                    Model.StudentAnswer sa = new Model.StudentAnswer();
                    //构造该课程的考试菜单项
                    ToolStripMenuItem tsmi = new ToolStripMenuItem();
                    //设置菜单项上的文本为课程名称
                    tsmi.Text = dt.Rows[i]["courseName"].ToString();
                    tsmi.Tag = teachId;          //保存该课程的授课 ID
                    //将该菜单项添加到"参加考试"菜单中
                    tsmiAttendTest.DropDownItems.Add(tsmi);
                    //为"参加考试"菜单添加 DropDownItemClicked 事件处理函数
                    tsmiAttendTest.DropDownItemClicked += new
                        ToolStripItemClickedEventHandler
                                (tsmiAttendTest_DropDownItemClicked);
                    //QuestionSelect 函数的作用是随机抽取一份试卷,
                    //返回结果中含有本试卷所有的试题
                    DataTable dtPaper = new BLL.BLLQuestions().QuestionsSelect
                                (dt.Rows[i]["teachId"].ToString());
                    for (int j = 0; j < dtPaper.Rows.Count; j++)
                    //遍历所有的试题,保存到 studentAnswer 中,作为该生的试卷内容
                    {
                        //AnswerId字段的内容格式是"|授课ID|年月日时分秒毫秒",
                        //在保证该字段唯一性的同时,带入授课 ID 信息,方便后面的操作
                        sa.AnswerId = "|"+teachId+"|" +
                            DateTime.Now.ToString("yyyyMMddHHmmssfff");
                        //试题在题库中的唯一编号
                        sa.TestQuestionId = dtPaper.Rows[j]["testQuestionId"].
                            ToString();
```

```
                    sa.StudentId = studentId;              //学号
                    sa.Answer = "";                        //答案
                    sa.Score = 0;                          //得分
                    new BLL.BLLStudentAnswer().SaveTestPaper(sa);
                                                           //为该生保存试卷
                }
            }
        }
    }
}
```

"参加考试"菜单项的 DropDownItemClicked 事件处理函数如下。

```
private void tsmiAttendTest_DropDownItemClicked(object sender,
ToolStripItemClickedEventArgs e)
{
    //调用有参构造函数,将当前考试菜单项的课程名、学号及授课 ID 传递过去
    FrmTest frm = new FrmTest(e.ClickedItem.Text, studentId,
        e.ClickedItem.Tag .ToString());
    frm.Show();
    //进入考试界面后删除主界面中该考试菜单项,默认为已经参加了考试,
    //但如果学生进入考试界面后未回答任何问题,在二次登录时,依然可以看到本考试菜单项,
    //允许参加考试。
    tsmiAttendTest.DropDownItems.Remove(e.ClickedItem);
}
```

8.8.7　学生考试模块

单击"参加考试"菜单中的某个考试菜单项,即可进入考试模块,如图 8-15 所示,窗体的属性设置如表 8-29 所示,窗体中的控件设置如表 8-30 所示。

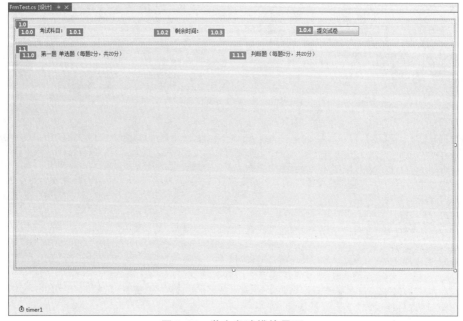

图 8-15　学生考试模块界面

表 8-29 学生考试界面属性设置

属 性 名	属 性 值	作 用
Name	FrmTest	窗体名称
WindowState	Maximized	设置窗体的初始状态为最大化
FormBorderStyle	None	清除界面标题栏

表 8-30 学生考试界面中的控件

Tab 序号	控 件 类 型	属 性 名	属 性 值
1	TableLayoutPanel	Name	tlpTest
1.0.1	Label	Name	lbCourse
1.0.3	Label	Name	lbTimeRemainder
1.0.4	Button	Name	btnFinish
		Text	提交试卷
1.1	Panel	Name	plTest
1.1.0	Label	Name	lbTitle_1
1.1.1	Label	Name	lbTitle_2

考试模块运行效果如图 8-16 所示。

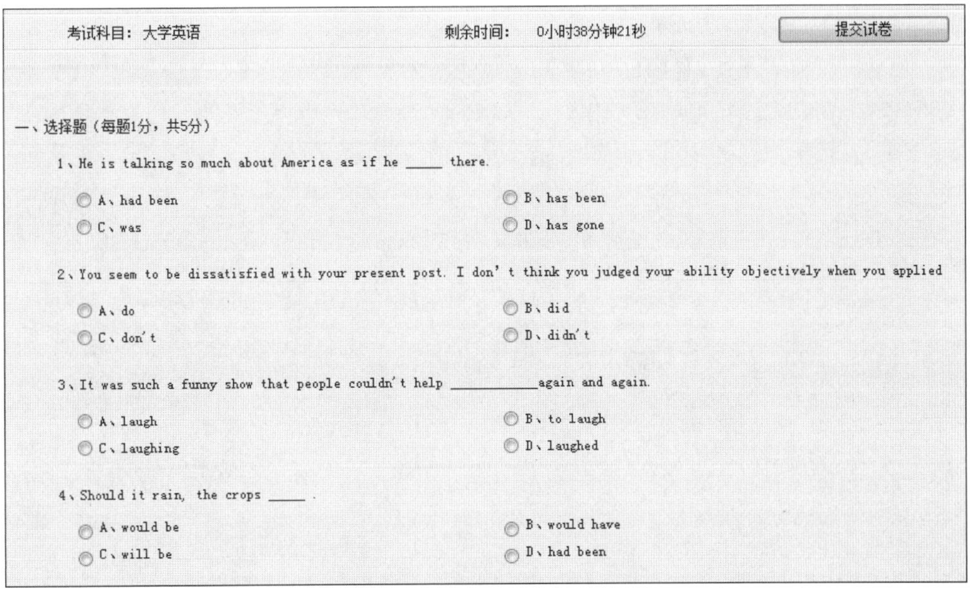

图 8-16 考试模块运行效果

首先，在该窗体的类文件 FrmTest.cs 中声明六个成员变量，并加入一个有参构造函数，代码如下。

```
Hook hook = new Hook();
public static string courseName = "", studentId = "", teachId="";
Dictionary<string, string> rbAnswer = new Dictionary<string, string>();
                                           //存储题目及其对应的学生答案
DateTime endTime;                          //存储考试结束时间
//在 FrmMain 中用该构造函数实例化对象,并将参数传递过来
public FrmTest(string CourseName, string StudentId, string TeachId)
{
    courseName = CourseName;
    studentId = StudentId;
    teachId = TeachId;
    InitializeComponent();
}
```

Hook 类用于屏蔽热键及任务管理器。学生一旦进入本界面,系统会自动屏蔽 Alt+F4、Alt+Tab、Windows+D、任务管理器等热键,以防止学生在考试过程中作弊。Hook 类调用 API 函数,利用 Hook(钩子)技术实现热键屏蔽。Hook 类代码如下。

```
public class Hook : IDisposable
{
    public delegate int HookProc(int nCode, int wParam, IntPtr lParam);
    static int hHook = 0;
    public const int WH_KEYBOARD_LL = 13;
    HookProc KeyBoardHookProcedure;
    [StructLayout(LayoutKind.Sequential)]
    public class KeyBoardHookStruct
    {
        public int vkCode;
        public int scanCode;
        public int flags;
        public int time;
        public int dwExtraInfo;
    }
    [DllImport("user32.dll")]
    public static extern int SetWindowsHookEx(int idHook, HookProc lpfn, IntPtr
        hInstance, int threadId);
    [DllImport("user32.dll", CharSet = CharSet.Auto, CallingConvention =
        CallingConvention.StdCall)]
    public static extern bool UnhookWindowsHookEx(int idHook);
    [DllImport("user32.dll")]
    public static extern int CallNextHookEx(int idHook, int nCode, int wParam,
        IntPtr lParam);
    [DllImport("kernel32.dll")]
    public static extern IntPtr GetModuleHandle(string name);
    public void Start()                     //安装键盘钩子
    {
        if (hHook == 0)
        {
            KeyBoardHookProcedure = new HookProc(KeyBoardHookProc);
            hHook = SetWindowsHookEx(WH_KEYBOARD_LL, KeyBoardHookProcedure,
                GetModuleHandle(Process.GetCurrentProcess().MainModule.
                ModuleName), 0);
```

```csharp
        //如果设置钩子失败
        if (hHook == 0)
            Close();
        else
        {
            RegistryKey key = Registry.CurrentUser.OpenSubKey
                (@"Software\Microsoft\Windows\CurrentVersion\Policies\
                System", true);
            if (key == null)              //如果该项不存在的话,则创建该项
                key = Registry.CurrentUser.CreateSubKey
                    (@"Software\Microsoft\Windows\CurrentVersion\Policies\
                    System");
            //禁用任务管理器
            key.SetValue("DisableTaskMgr", 1, RegistryValueKind.DWord);
            key.Close();
        }
    }
}
public void Close()                       //去掉钩子
{
    bool retKeyboard = true;
    if (hHook != 0)
    {
        retKeyboard = UnhookWindowsHookEx(hHook);
        hHook = 0;
    }
    RegistryKey key = Registry.CurrentUser.OpenSubKey
        (@"Software\Microsoft\Windows\CurrentVersion\Policies\System",
            true);
    if (key != null)
    {
        key.DeleteValue("DisableTaskMgr", false);
        key.Close();
    }
}
public static int KeyBoardHookProc(int nCode, int wParam, IntPtr lParam)
{
    if (nCode >= 0)
    {
        KeyBoardHookStruct kbh = (KeyBoardHookStruct)
            Marshal.PtrToStructure
            (lParam, typeof(KeyBoardHookStruct));
        if (kbh.vkCode == 91)             //截获左 Win(开始菜单键)
            return 1;
        if (kbh.vkCode == 92)             //截获右 Win
            return 1;
        if (kbh.vkCode == (int)Keys.Escape &&
            (int)Control.ModifierKeys == (int)Keys.Control)   //截获 Ctrl+Esc
            return 1;
        if (kbh.vkCode == (int)Keys.F4 && (int)Control.ModifierKeys == (int)
            Keys.Alt)
        //截获 Alt+F4
            return 1;
```

```csharp
            if (kbh.vkCode == (int)Keys.Tab && (int)Control.ModifierKeys ==
                (int)Keys.Alt)
            //截获 Alt+Tab
                return 1;
            if (kbh.vkCode == (int)Keys.Escape && (int)Control.ModifierKeys
                == (int)Keys.Control + (int)Keys.Shift) //截获 Ctrl+Shift+Esc
                return 1;
            if (kbh.vkCode == (int)Keys.Space && (int)Control.ModifierKeys ==
                (int)Keys.Alt)
            //截获 Alt+空格
                return 1;
            if (kbh.vkCode == 241)                        //截获 F1
                return 1;
            if (kbh.vkCode == (int)Keys.Control && kbh.vkCode == (int)Keys.
                Alt &&
                kbh.vkCode == (int)Keys.Delete)
                return 1;
            if ((int)Control.ModifierKeys == (int)Keys.Control + (int)Keys.Alt
                + (int)Keys.Delete)
            //截获 Ctrl+Alt+Delete
                return 1;
            if ((int)Control.ModifierKeys == (int)Keys.Control + (int)Keys.
                Shift)
            //截获 Ctrl+Shift
                return 2;
            if ((int)Control.ModifierKeys == (int)Keys.Control + (int)Keys.Alt)
            //截获 Ctrl+Alt
                return 1;
            if (kbh.vkCode == (int)Keys.Escape)           //截获 Esc
                return 1;
            if (kbh.vkCode == (int)Keys.Decimal)          //截获 。
                return 1;
            if ((int)Control.ModifierKeys == (int)Keys.Control + (int)Keys.
                Alt &&
                kbh.vkCode == (int)Keys.Decimal)          //截获任务管理器
                return 1;
        }
        return CallNextHookEx(hHook, nCode, wParam, lParam);
    }
    public void Dispose()
    {
        Close();
    }
}
```

考试界面加载时,首先调用 Hook 类的 Start 方法安装钩子,屏蔽热键操作;然后启动定时器控件 timer1,开始考试时间的倒计时;接下来,将该学生随机抽取到的试卷中所有的试题按题型分类进行遍历,并生成合适的控件将试题信息放置在各控件内,并将控件添加到窗体中的 Panel 控件 plTest 的合适位置上。代码如下。

```csharp
private void FrmTest_Load(object sender, EventArgs e)
{
```

```csharp
hook.Start();                                          //安装钩子,屏蔽热键操作
this.Text = courseName;
lbCourse.Text = courseName;
DataTable dt = new BLL.BLLCourse().TestCourseSelect(studentId);
//查询登录学生当前能够考试的所有科目
if (dt.Rows.Count != 0)
{
    for (int a = 0; a < dt.Rows.Count; a++)            //遍历到当前考试课程的相关信息
    {
        if (teachId == dt.Rows[a]["teachId"].ToString())
        {
            endTime = DateTime.Parse(dt.Rows[a]["endTime"].ToString());
        }
    }
    timer1.Start();                                    //开启计时器,进行考试时间的倒计时显示
}
int i = 0;
//获取该生试卷中的所有选择题
DataTable dtXz = new BLL.BLLStudentAnswer().LoadTestPaper
    ("选择题", studentId, "|"+teachId+"|");
if (dtXz.Rows.Count != 0)//如果试卷中存在选择题
{
    //以下四行代码,设定选择题的题头信息、坐标及可见性
    lbTitle_1.Text = "一、选择题(每题" + dtXz.Rows[0]["questionScore"].
        ToString() + "分,共"+ (int.Parse(dtXz.Rows[0]["questionNum"].ToString()) *
        int.Parse(dtXz.Rows[0]["questionScore"].ToString())).ToString()
        + "分)";
    lbTitle_1.Left = 10;
    lbTitle_1.Top = 5;
    lbTitle_1.Visible = true;
    for (i = 0; i < dtXz.Rows.Count; i++)
    //遍历所有的选择题,生成相应控件承载试题信息,并加以显示
    {
        Panel p = new Panel();
        p.Tag = dtXz.Rows[i]["answerId"].ToString();
        p.Left = 35;
        p.Top = 30 + i * 90;
        p.Width = 750;
        p.Height = 75;
        plTest.Controls.Add(p);
        Label lbTitle = new Label();
        lbTitle.Location = new Point(10, 5);
        lbTitle.Size = new Size(1000, lbTitle.Size.Height);
        if (dtXz.Rows[i]["CurrectAnswer"].ToString().Length > 1)
                                                       //如果是多选题
        {
            lbTitle.Text = (i + 1).ToString() + "、(多选题)" +
                dtXz.Rows[i]["questionTitle"].ToString();
            p.Controls.Add(lbTitle);
            CheckBox cbAnswerA = new CheckBox();
                                                       //多选题选项用 checkBox 承载
            cbAnswerA.Location = new Point(28, 29);
```

```csharp
            cbAnswerA.Text = "A、" + dtXz.Rows[i]["answerA"].ToString();
                                                        //存储选项内容
            cbAnswerA.Tag = dtXz.Rows[i]["answerId"];
                                                        //存储 answerId
            p.Controls.Add(cbAnswerA);                  //将 checkBox 加入 panel 中
            cbAnswerA.CheckedChanged += new EventHandler(cbAnswer_
                CheckedChanged);
            //为 checkBox 添加 CheckedChanged 事件处理函数
            CheckBox cbAnswerB = new CheckBox();
            cbAnswerB.Location = new Point(380, 29);
            cbAnswerB.Text = "B、" + dtXz.Rows[i]["answerB"].ToString();
            cbAnswerB.Tag = dtXz.Rows[i]["answerId"];
            p.Controls.Add(cbAnswerB);
            cbAnswerB.CheckedChanged += new EventHandler(cbAnswer_
                CheckedChanged);
            CheckBox cbAnswerC = new CheckBox();
            cbAnswerC.Location = new Point(28, 51);
            cbAnswerC.Text = "C、" + dtXz.Rows[i]["answerC"].ToString();
            cbAnswerC.Tag = dtXz.Rows[i]["answerId"];
            p.Controls.Add(cbAnswerC);
            cbAnswerC.CheckedChanged += new EventHandler(cbAnswer_
                CheckedChanged);
            CheckBox cbAnswerD = new CheckBox();
            cbAnswerD.Location = new Point(380, 51);
            cbAnswerD.Text = "D、" + dtXz.Rows[i]["answerD"].ToString();
            cbAnswerD.Tag = dtXz.Rows[i]["answerId"];
            p.Controls.Add(cbAnswerD);
            cbAnswerD.CheckedChanged += new EventHandler(cbAnswer_
                CheckedChanged);
        }
        else
        {
            lbTitle.Text = (i + 1).ToString() + "、" + dtXz.Rows[i]
                ["questionTitle"].ToString();
            p.Controls.Add(lbTitle);
            RadioButton rbAnswerA = new RadioButton();
                                                //单选题用 RadioButton 承载选项
            rbAnswerA.Location = new Point(28, 29);
            rbAnswerA.Text = "A、" + dtXz.Rows[i]["answerA"].ToString();
            rbAnswerA.Tag = dtXz.Rows[i]["answerId"];
            p.Controls.Add(rbAnswerA);
            rbAnswerA.CheckedChanged += new EventHandler(rbAnswer_
                CheckedChanged);
            RadioButton rbAnswerB = new RadioButton();
            rbAnswerB.Location = new Point(380, 29);
            rbAnswerB.Text = "B、" + dtXz.Rows[i]["answerB"].ToString();
            rbAnswerB.Tag = dtXz.Rows[i]["answerId"];
            p.Controls.Add(rbAnswerB);
            rbAnswerB.CheckedChanged += new EventHandler(rbAnswer_
                CheckedChanged);
            RadioButton rbAnswerC = new RadioButton();
            rbAnswerC.Location = new Point(28, 51);
            rbAnswerC.Text = "C、" + dtXz.Rows[i]["answerC"].ToString();
```

```csharp
                    rbAnswerC.Tag = dtXz.Rows[i]["answerId"];
                    p.Controls.Add(rbAnswerC);
                    rbAnswerC.CheckedChanged += new EventHandler(rbAnswer_
                        CheckedChanged);
                    RadioButton rbAnswerD = new RadioButton();
                    rbAnswerD.Location = new Point(380, 51);
                    rbAnswerD.Text = "D、" + dtXz.Rows[i]["answerD"].ToString();
                    rbAnswerD.Tag = dtXz.Rows[i]["answerId"];
                        p.Controls.Add(rbAnswerD);
                        rbAnswerD.CheckedChanged += new
                            EventHandler(rbAnswer_CheckedChanged);
                }
            }
        }
        //获取该生试卷中所有判断题
        DataTable dtPd = new BLL.BLLStudentAnswer().LoadTestPaper("判断题",
            studentId,"|"+teachId+"|");
        if (dtPd.Rows.Count != 0)                    //如果试卷中存在判断题
        {
            lbTitle_2.Text = "二、判断题(每题" + dtPd.Rows[0]["questionScore"].
                ToString() + "分,共" +
                (int.Parse(dtPd.Rows[0]["questionNum"].ToString()) *
                int.Parse(dtPd.Rows[0]["questionScore"].ToString())).ToString()
                + "分)";
            lbTitle_2.Left = 10;
            lbTitle_2.Top = i * 90 + 30;
            lbTitle_2.Visible = true;
            for (int j = 0; j < dtPd.Rows.Count; j++)
            {
                Panel p = new Panel();
                p.Left = 35;
                p.Top = i * 90 + 60 + j * 65;
                p.Width = 750;
                p.Height = 55;
                plTest.Controls.Add(p);
                Label lbTitle = new Label();
                lbTitle.Location = new Point(10, 5);
                lbTitle.Text = (j + 1).ToString() + "、" + dtPd.Rows[j]
                    ["questionTitle"].ToString();
                p.Controls.Add(lbTitle);
                RadioButton rbAnswerT = new RadioButton();
                rbAnswerT.Location = new Point(28, 29);
                rbAnswerT.Text = "对";
                rbAnswerT.Tag = dtPd.Rows[j]["answerId"];
                p.Controls.Add(rbAnswerT);
                rbAnswerT.CheckedChanged += new EventHandler(rbAnswer_
                    CheckedChanged);
                RadioButton rbAnswerF = new RadioButton();
                rbAnswerF.Location = new Point(380, 29);
                rbAnswerF.Text = "错";
                rbAnswerF.Tag = dtPd.Rows[j]["answerId"];
                p.Controls.Add(rbAnswerF);
```

```
            rbAnswerF.CheckedChanged += new EventHandler(rbAnswer_
                CheckedChanged);
        }
    }
}
```

定时器 timer1 的 Tick 事件主要用来进行考试时间的倒计时,并且在考试结束时自动提交试卷,代码如下。

```
private void timer1_Tick(object sender, EventArgs e)
{
    DateTime dt1 = new DateTime(DateTime.Now.Ticks);
    DateTime dt2 = new DateTime(endTime.Ticks);
    TimeSpan ts = dt2 - dt1;                 //计算当前时间距离考试结束时间的时间差
    lbTimeRemainder.Text = ts.Hours.ToString() + "小时" + ts.Minutes.ToString()
        + "分钟" +ts.Seconds.ToString() + "秒";
    if (lbTimeRemainder.Text == "0 小时 0 分钟 0 秒")
                                        //如果考试时间到,则提交试卷,结束考试
    {
        timer1.Stop();                  //停止计时
        MessageBox.Show("考试时间到");
        submitPaper();                  //提交试卷
        this.Close();
    }
}
```

submitPaper 函数的作用是提交试卷。将学生的答案与正确答案进行匹配,并根据组卷时的分值设定信息计算得分,最终将学生答案与得分更新到 studentAnswer 数据表,完成试卷提交。代码如下。

```
void submitPaper()
{
    try
    {
        DataTable dt = new BLL.BLLStudentAnswer().LoadTestPaper("", studentId,
            "|"+teachId+"|");
        for (int i = 0; i < dt.Rows.Count; i++)       //遍历该生试卷中所有题
        {
            Model.StudentAnswer sa = new Model.StudentAnswer();
            sa.Score = 0;
            if (rbAnswer.ContainsKey(dt.Rows[i]["answerId"].ToString()))
            //如果 rbAnswer 中包含该试题的 answerId,说明学生答了该题,
            //则获取学生对该试题的答案
            {
                if ("对" == rbAnswer[dt.Rows[i]["answerId"].ToString()])
                { sa.Answer = "1"; }
                else if ("错" == rbAnswer[dt.Rows[i]["answerId"].ToString()])
                { sa.Answer = "0"; }
                else { sa.Answer = rbAnswer[dt.Rows[i]["answerId"].ToString()]; }
            }
            if (dt.Rows[i]["CurrectAnswer"].ToString() ==sa.Answer)
            //判断学生答案是否正确,如果正确,则设定分值
            {
```

```
                sa.Score = int.Parse(dt.Rows[i]["questionScore"].ToString());
            }
            //向数据库提交结果
            new BLL.BLLStudentAnswer().SubmitPaper(sa, dt.Rows[i]["AnswerId"].
                ToString());
        }
        MessageBox.Show("提交成功!");
        this.Close();
    }
    catch { MessageBox.Show("提交失败!"); }
}
```

学生在考试界面中,每选择一个单选题或判断题的选项(RadioButton)时,会触发该控件的 CheckedChanged 事件,该事件负责将学生选择的单选题、判断题答案添加到字典对象 rbAnswer 中,代码如下。

```
public void rbAnswer_CheckedChanged(object sender, EventArgs e)
{
    RadioButton rb = (RadioButton)sender;
    if (rb.Checked)
    {
        if (rbAnswer.ContainsKey(rb.Tag.ToString()))
        {
            rbAnswer.Remove(rb.Tag.ToString());
        }
        rbAnswer.Add(rb.Tag.ToString(), rb.Text.Substring(0, 1));
    }
}
```

学生在考试界面中,每选择一个多选题的选项(CheckBox)时,会触发该控件的 CheckedChanged 事件,该事件处理程序负责将学生选择的多选题答案添加到字典对象 rbAnswer 中,代码如下。

```
public void cbAnswer_CheckedChanged(object sender, EventArgs e)
{
    CheckBox cb = (CheckBox)sender;
    Panel p = (Panel)(cb.Parent);
    string str="";
    for (int i = 0; i < p.Controls.Count; i++)
    {
        if (p.Controls[i] is CheckBox)
        {
            CheckBox cbTemp=(CheckBox)(p.Controls[i]);
            if(cbTemp.Checked)
                str +=cbTemp.Text.Substring(0, 1);
        }
    }
    if (rbAnswer.ContainsKey(cb.Tag.ToString()))
    {
        rbAnswer.Remove(cb.Tag.ToString());
    }
```

```
        rbAnswer.Add(cb.Tag.ToString(), str);
    }
```

答题完毕,单击"提交试卷"按钮,完成试卷提交,并退出考试界面,回到学生端主界面,代码如下。

```
private void btnFinish_Click(object sender, EventArgs e)
{
    DialogResult dr = MessageBox.Show("提交后无法继续答卷,您确定提交试卷?",
                "提示框", MessageBoxButtons.YesNo);
    if (dr == DialogResult.Yes)
    {
        submitPaper();
    }
}
```

8.9 技术经验总结

8.9.1 技术总结

本系统用到了以下技术及知识点。

(1) 本系统使用了简单三层架构,使用三层架构可以使程序结构更清晰、可维护性更强。

(2) 本系统使用了 API 函数和操作注册表,合理利用 API 函数及注册表可以做到很多系统级的操作,达到一些常规操作无法实现的效果,如禁用系统热键、屏蔽任务管理器等。

(3) 本系统操作了 Excel 文件,实现了从 Excel 文件读取数据的功能。事实上,操作 Excel 文件与操作 Access 数据库极其类似,只是数据库连接字符串不同。

(4) 在实现从数据库随机读取试题时,在 SQL 语句中使用了 newid() 函数,该函数可以进行随机排序动作,并选取符合条件的前 N 条数据,有效提高了随机抽取效率和随机性。

(5) 本系统学生考试模块使用了控件的代码生成技术,可以使界面的生成更灵活,适应性更强。

8.9.2 经验总结

在进行软件项目开发时,不应急于进入编码阶段,尤其是对于业务逻辑复杂、功能较多的应用系统。应遵循软件工程思想,将更多的时间花在需求调研及系统设计上,要经过反复论证。尤其是对于三层架构的项目,如果需求和设计阶段做得不够严谨,在开发阶段势必会因为需求理解的失误或者设计缺陷导致级联修改。

本系统充分体现了三层架构的优越性。本系统分为两个子系统:教师端子系统、学生端子系统。教师端子系统与学生端子系统都访问相同的数据库,甚至部分业务逻辑相同。系统分层后,Model、DAL、BLL 均可为两个子系统所使用,大大提高了代码复用度。在今后面临需求变更,如数据库类型更换等问题时,只需更改同一个数据访问层即可。

另外要说明的是,为方便读者阅读源代码及系统调试,特将教师端子系统和学生端子系统分为两个项目,并各自拥有一套 Model、DAL 和 BLL 类库源代码,但两端这三个类库的代码是相同的。

第 9 章 高校实践课题管理系统案例开发

本章描述的是高校实践课题管理系统。该系统首先对高校实践课题管理中的学生、专业、班级、年级等基本信息进行维护;其次,系统对实践课题管理过程中的教师题目维护、课题申报、课题选报等一系列业务操作进行管理,保证各阶段数据的一致性和连续性;对教师及课题负责人工作中需要的学生名单、课题选报情况等进行统计分析。本章介绍了项目的开发过程,描述了项目的需求获取、分析设计、测试以及最后的交付运行等环节的实现。

9.1 项 目 描 述

软件学院在校各年级学生每个学期都要参与实践课题作为一门必修的课程。目前各实践环节中教师指导学生是采用双向选择的方式,即指导教师发布题目之后,由学生选择其感兴趣的任一教师的题目。教师也可以在已选报自己题目的学生中选择合适的学生。

这种双向选择的方式效果很好,深受教师和学生的欢迎。但是整个实践课题管理工作需要经历:教师添加题目→教师申报课题→学生选报课题→教师确认学生→课题负责人汇总结果等步骤,且各步骤之间衔接非常紧密,每个步骤又都有各自的操作规则。以往的实践课题工作主要以文件方式(Excel 文件)管理,这种方式容易发生数据重复、遗漏及统计数据出错等问题,因此,必须有一套管理系统作为工具来支持整个实践课题管理工作的正常进行。

软件学院实践课题管理系统主要分为三种用户:教师、学生和管理员。以下对这三种用户所需要的功能分别进行描述。

1. 教师用户

(1) 教师用户需要在每学期课题申报工作开始后通过系统申报实践课题。

(2) 在学生选报过课题后,教师可以从已选报的学生组中确定自己要指导的学生,也可以驳回某个组或者某个学生的选报。

(3) 教师可以查询并打印学生点名册。

(4) 修改密码及查看个人信息。

2. 学生用户

(1) 学生用户可登录系统查看本专业方向已公布的实践课题情况,并进行课题选报。

(2) 学生可以查看自己的选报状况,即教师是否同意指导自己做课题。

(3) 修改密码及查看个人信息。

3. 管理员

(1) 负责设置系统基本参数,包括专业管理、年级及班级管理等。

(2) 负责学生基本信息维护,查看学生信息及信息导入。

(3) 课题负责人可对课题申报、选报等情况进行统计和导出。

(4) 修改密码。

通过该系统,最终实现对所需的基础数据的维护管理,如学生信息、专业信息、班级信息、年级信息等进行维护。对实践课题生命周期中的各环节工作进行管理,以保证课题负责人、教师及学生能按步骤正常完成各自的任务。在实践课题各阶段,能为教师及课题负责人提供完善的查询、统计功能。

9.2 系统需求分析

实践课题管理的业务流程阶段性很强,每个阶段产生的数据都要求准确无误,并且各阶段之间的数据连续性及相关性要求很高,后一阶段的工作必须依据前一阶段的数据并满足当前阶段的业务规则限制。

由于开发人员本身即为实践课题管理系统的用户——教师及管理员,对系统的需求非常熟悉,因此系统需求分析阶段及设计阶段基本上是同步进行的。并且由于系统的核心业务模块之间数据联系很紧密,每个模块的功能都受相关模块的牵制,因此系统的功能需求获取不可能一步到位,经常是设计另一功能模块时才发现原有的需求中存在的问题及不足。另外,在系统设计、开发及测试的过程中,还会增加及修改一些需求,主要是模块之间的数据联系。每次需求变动,均需完整地记录下来,并同步修改设计、编码及测试计划。

以下将给出系统最终的需求描述、用例规约及用例图。中间修改及完善的过程略去。

9.2.1 总体需求

系统采用 B/S 架构设计,主要功能包括课题操作、查询统计、个人信息及基础信息管理。系统功能模块图如图 9-1 所示。

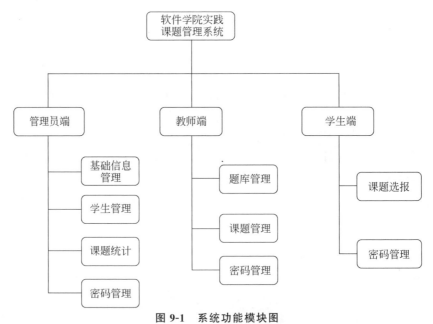

图 9-1 系统功能模块图

系统总体业务活动图如图 9-2 所示。

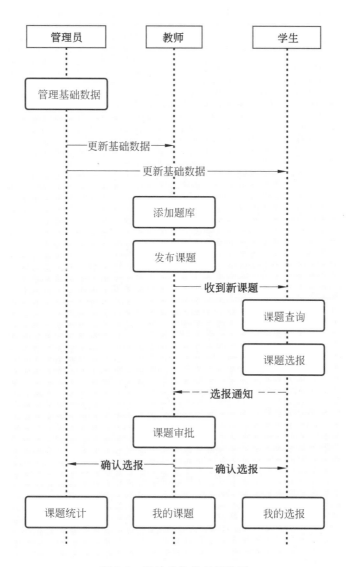

图 9-2　系统总体业务活动图

9.2.2　需求描述

1. 课题管理

课题管理是实践课题系统的主要业务模块，教师和学生都需要参与，以下按业务流程逐个描述课题操作模块的各项功能。课题管理的用例图如图 9-3 所示。

课题管理是本系统的核心业务模块，教师和学生用户均需参与到课题管理的生命周期中。

（1）题库管理。教师个人题库只供教师个人查看，在未申报之前课题管理员和学生都无法查看。教师可维护自己的题库，包括添加、修改及删除题目操作。个人题库包括题目名

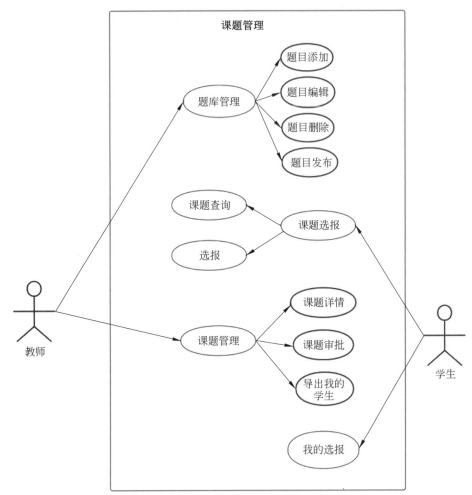

图 9-3　课题管理用例图

称、题目描述及题目备注等数据项。

① 个人题目添加。教师可以随时向个人课题库中添加新题目，用以在实践课题工作开始时进行申报。

② 个人题目修改。教师可以修改个人题库中的题目信息。

③ 个人题目删除。教师可以删除个人题库中的题目。

④ 个人题目信息查看。教师可以只读方式查看题目的详细信息。操作方式是在题目维护页面的题库列表中单击要查看的题目的详情，系统将显示题目详细信息页面。

⑤ 题目发布。教师在发布题目时需从个人题库中选择一个题目，然后输入适合专业、要求使用的语言，题目允许的组数及每组允许的人数等信息。如教师想指定特定学生做某个题目，可以为该题目设定密码。学生选报时需输入这个密码才允许选报。用例规约如表 9-1 所示。

表 9-1　课题发布用例规约

用例编号	UC-05
用例名称	题目发布

用例描述	教师对外发布题目
参与者	教师
前置条件	1. 参与者成功登录系统 2. 教师个人题库中已存在题目信息
后置条件	成功发布题目
涉众利益	1. 参与者希望登录后能从个人题库中选择合适的题目进行申报 2. 参与者希望能为指定题目设置密码
基本路径	1. 参与者请求题库管理 2. 系统显示题库信息页面 3. 系统在题库信息页面的题目列表中显示数据库中现有的属于该教师的题目信息 4. 参与者选择要发布的题目信息 5. 系统显示题目申报详情页面 6. 系统提示当前用户可指导的学生人数上限,及可申报课题的容纳人数 7. 参与者填写发布题目所需补充信息 8. 参与者请求发布题目 9. 系统计算参与者本次所发布题目容纳人数是否超过可申报课题的容纳人数 10. 系统返回是否发布成功 11. 系统返回题库信息页面
字段列表	年级、选报专业、要求语言、允许组数、每组人数、课题密码(可选项)
业务规则	"课题密码"是供教师用户设置的,如教师想让指定的学生做某个课题,可设置课题密码

(2) 课题选报。学生用户的课题选报功能是课题操作过程中业务最复杂的一个环节,每位学生仅能选报本专业、本年级的课题。

① 课题查询。学生可以根据自己的所在年级、专业查看符合条件的所有课题信息。操作方式是在课题选报页面的题目列表中单击要查看课题的详情,系统将显示课题详细信息页面。

② 学生在选报实践课题时的操作步骤为:学生首先对想选报的课题创建组,同时设置组密码,其他学生在选报时需输入"组密码"才能加入该组。每组所能容纳的学生人数由教师申报课题时指定。用例规约如表 9-2 所示。

表 9-2 课题选报(组长)用例规约

用例编号	UC-06
用例名称	课题选报
用例描述	学生选报课题
参与者	学生
前置条件	1. 参与者成功登录系统 2. 当前系统时间处于课题选报时间段内
后置条件	学生成功选报课题
涉众利益	1. 参与者希望能通过系统查看待选报课题信息 2. 参与者希望能选报课题

续表

基本路径	1. 参与者请求课题选报 2. 系统显示课题选报页面 3. 参与者输入教师姓名、语言，请求查询 4. 系统显示已发布的实践课题列表、该课题是否已经报满、是否能新建组或加入组等信息 5. 如课题未报满且能新建组，则参与者可请求新建组（如该课题是教师加密课题，则参与者新建选报组时系统要求输入课题密码） 6. 参与者设置并确认该组的密码后请求提交选报 7. 如参与者希望加入组且有未报满组，则参与者请求加入组 8. 如该组创建人设置了组密码，则参与者需输入组密码并提交选报 9. 系统提示是否选报成功
字段列表	指导教师、课题名称、语言、组数、每组人数、是否已满

（3）课题管理。实践课题是允许教师和学生双向选择的，当学生选报课题完成后，教师可对选报自己课题的学生进行确认或驳回。教师可按课题名称查询到所有选报该课题的学生，这些学生是以组为单位列出的，教师整组地确认学生。

① 确认选报组。教师用户在学生选报过课题之后可以确认选报自己的学生，确认选报时是按课题和分组来操作的，确认用例规约如表 9-3 所示。

表 9-3 确认选报组用例规约

用例编号	UC-09
用例名称	确认选报组
用例描述	教师用户确认选报自己课题的选报组
参与者	教师
前置条件	1. 参与者成功登录系统 2. 已有学生选报该教师的课题
后置条件	参与者完成选报组的确认
涉众利益	整组确定组员
基本路径	1. 参与者请求确认选报组 2. 系统显示确认选报组页面 3. 参与者选择年级、课题类别及课题名称，并请求查询 4. 系统显示查询出来的学生的选报组列表 5. 参与者选中待确认的组 6. 参与者请求确认选报组 7. 系统提示是否成功确认 8. 系统显示选报组列表，已确认的组将不再出现在列表中

② 课题详情。教师对自己发布的课题查看详细的选报情况，包括课题已经报了几组、每组学生的名单等信息。在教师确认完选报组后，可以随时查看当前已确认的学生名单。

③ 导出我的学生。学生名单主要是方便教师在指导课题时记录学生的考勤及其他平时成绩，名单可以按学号排序，也可以按课题分组排序。

（4）我的选报。学生可以查看自己选报课题的情况，包括已经成功选报和选报失败的。学生选报过课题之后，可以查看自己的选报状况，选报状况有以下三种。

① 未确认：即教师尚未确认是否指导该学生做课题。这时学生可以选择退出选报组，另行选报其他题目，如不退出原有选报组，则不能再选报其他课题。

② 已确认：即教师已确认指导该学生做课题。已确认过的学生不能再修改自己的选报情况，如有特殊情况，则需课题负责人处理。

③ 已驳回：即教师驳回了学生的选报，这时学生可以重新选报其他课题。

学生选报过课题后，可以查看选报状况，即教师是否确认指导自己做课题。用例规约如表 9-4 所示。选报状况是撤销选报的包含用例。

表 9-4 "我的选报"用例规约

用例编号	UC-11
用例名称	我的选报
用例描述	学生查看自己选报课题是否成功
参与者	学生
前置条件	参与者成功登录系统
后置条件	参与者能查看自己选报课题的状况
涉众利益	参与者希望能查看自己所选报课题的状况
基本路径	1. 参与者请求查看选报状况 2. 系统显示选报状况界面 3. 系统在选报状况界面显示参与者已选报过的所有课题信息列表 4. 系统显示该学生选报课题的选报状况
业务规则	选报状况有三种：未确认、已确认和已驳回

2. 查询统计

管理员为了能够准确、直观地了解课题的选报情况，需要对课题的选报进行统计。查询统计的用例图如图 9-4 所示。

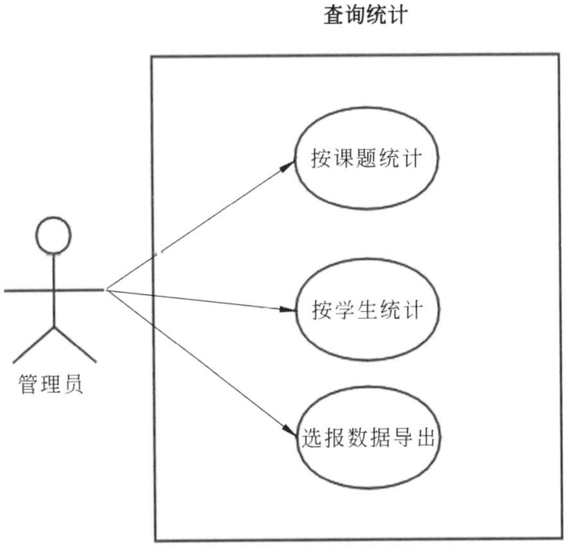

查询统计

图 9-4 查询统计用例图

（1）按课题统计。在教师课题申报工作进行到一定程度之后，课题负责人希望能统计所有指导教师所报题目能容纳的各专业方向学生数，并与各专业方向的实际学生人数进行对比，算出两者之间的差额，以便确定下一步的管理策略。

① 如差额较小，则可以安排个别老师增加题目，并适当加大其所带学生人数的上限。

② 如差额较大，则可以将没报上课题的学生交给合作实训公司指导。

由于教师在申报课题时，同一个课题可以由多个专业的学生共同选报，所以统计出来的各专业课题数及可容纳学生的人数和一定会超过真正的题目总数和学生总数。

当教师申报课题工作进行到一定程度时，管理员需要对已申报的课题进行统计，主要目的是想了解教师所申报的课题在各专业方向上的分布情况，再对比各专业实际的学生数，从而得出以下结论。

① 教师申报的题目容纳学生总数是否大于学生总数。

② 教师申报题目在各专业方向的容纳人数是否大于该专业方向的学生。

根据以上统计结果，课题负责人要确定应对的措施。用例规约如表9-5所示。

表 9-5 按课题统计用例规约

用例编号	UC-12
用例名称	按课题统计
用例描述	课题负责人对教师申报的课题进行统计
参与者	课题负责人
前置条件	参与者成功登录系统
后置条件	参与者可对教师已申报的所有实践课题题目总数及能容纳的学生人数按组合条件进行统计
涉众利益	参与者希望能按专业方向统计教师所申报课题容纳的学生人数，并与该专业方向的实际学生人数进行对比
基本路径	1. 用户成功登录系统 2. 用户请求按课题统计 3. 系统显示课题统计页面

（2）按学生统计。课题负责人可在学生结束选报后对学生选报的整体情况进行统计。在统计的时候可以选择年级、课题类别、专业、班级等条件，也可以按选报状态进行统计，课题负责人对统计结果的相应处理方式有以下几种情况。

① 统计出的未选报学生的总数，结合课题统计的结果进行分析，如果教师申报的课题还有余量，则需要辅导员通知学生抓紧时间选报；如果教师申报的课题已报满，则需要根据未选报学生的人数安排实训公司指导学生做课题。

② 对于已选报未被确认学生，课题负责人需要通知相关教师尽快确认学生。

③ 对于已确认学生，课题负责人可以统计出其总数以掌握当前学生总体的选报情况。

（3）选报数据导出。为了及时掌握学生选报课题的情况，为下一步的工作做好准备，在学生选报课题工作进行到一定程度后，课题负责人可能对学生的选报情况进行导出。用例规约如表9-6所示。

表 9-6　选报数据导出用例规约

用例编号	UC-12
用例名称	选报数据导出
用例描述	课题负责人希望能导出学生选报课题的情况
参与者	课题负责人
前置条件	参与者正常登录系统
后置条件	参与者导出学生的选报数据
涉众利益	1. 参与者希望能对实践课题的学生选报情况进行统计 2. 参与者希望能导出及打印学生选报情况详单
基本路径	参与者可将记录导出至 Excel
字段列表	学号、姓名、专业、班级、课题名称、指导教师

3. 个人信息

本模块包括学生及教师注册、基本信息查看、修改密码及登录，用例图如图 9-5 所示。

个人信息

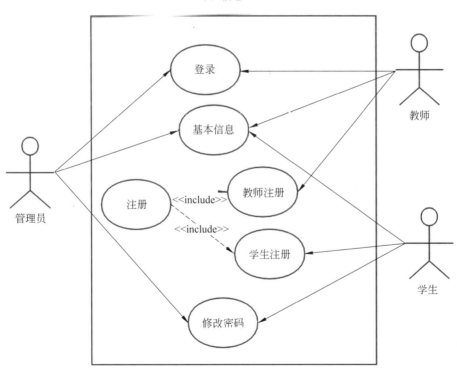

图 9-5　个人信息用例图

4. 基础信息设置

基础信息设置包括系统运行各种支撑数据的管理，包括专业、年级和班级信息设置，用例图如图 9-6 所示。

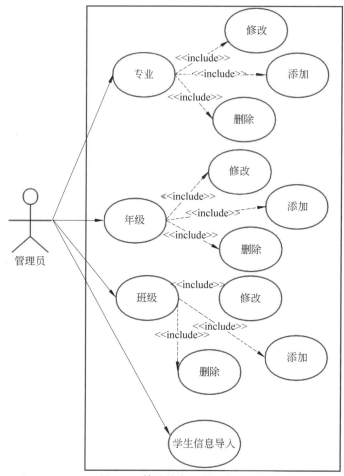

图 9-6 基础信息设置用例图

9.3 系统设计

9.3.1 总体设计

1. 技术架构设计

由于系统的使用者为众多的教师和学生,因此该项目使用 B/S 的技术方案。在考虑到项目实施时相关开发者的技术储备及技术先进性,拟使用 ASP.NET MVC 技术架构。

2. 前端框架设计

考虑到前端 UI 对于后端开发者有一定的难度和需要很大的工作量,前端页面拟基于 AdminLTE 模板来实现。AdminLTE 是一个完全响应管理模板,基于 Bootstrap 3 和 jQuery 3.3.1 的框架,适合多种屏幕分辨率,从小型移动设备到大型台式计算机。它内置了多个页面,包括仪表盘、邮箱、日历、锁屏、登录及注册、404 错误、500 错误等页面。对于后台站点的模板渲染,有很大的作用。

3. 数据持久层设计

本项目采用 Database First 方式，使用 Entity Framework 进行持久层设计，由数据库生成数据模型类。

9.3.2 业务流程建模

顺序图可以描述在设计中对象如何控制它的方法和行为，展示了活动或者行为发生的顺序。本节对主要用例建立了顺序图，建立顺序图是为了进一步描述用例。

1. 管理员查看学生名单顺序图

学生名单顺序图描述的是学生名单用例。参与者在 Index.cshtml 请求学生名单，视图将请求提交到控制类 StudentsController，控制类通过 EF 框架请求数据对象列表，将结果封装成 IPagedList 格式返回给视图 Index.cshtml，参与者可以看到学生名单。管理员查看学生名单顺序图如图 9-7 所示。

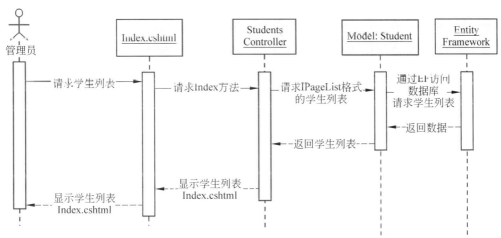

图 9-7 管理员查看学生名单顺序图

2. 管理员导入学生数据顺序图

管理员导入学生数据顺序图描述的是导入学生数据用例。管理员在 Import.cshtml 选择导入学生数据的 Excel 文件，视图将请求提交到控制类 StudentsController。控制类先通过 NPOI 库的 XSSFWorkbook 类将 Excel 文件的内容处理成 Student 对象列表，控制类再通过 EF 框架请求将学生数据保存到数据库中，最后将处理的结果返回给参与者。管理员导入学生数据顺序图如图 9-8 所示。

3. 教师创建题目顺序图

教师创建题目顺序图描述的是题目添加用例。教师在题目添加页面 Create.cshtml 输入题目名称、描述、备注等信息后，通过视图将请求发送到控制类 SubjectsController。控制类通过 Create 方法来处理业务逻辑，通过 EF 框架请求将题目数据对象保存到数据库中，若保存成功则返回给教师题目列表页面 Index.cshtml。教师创建题目顺序图如图 9-9 所示。

4. 教师发布题目顺序图

教师发布题目顺序图是描述题目发布用例。教师在题目发布页面 Create.cshtml 请求题目发布，在题目发布页面中选择所选题目针对哪种专业的学生，以及所选题目开设多少课

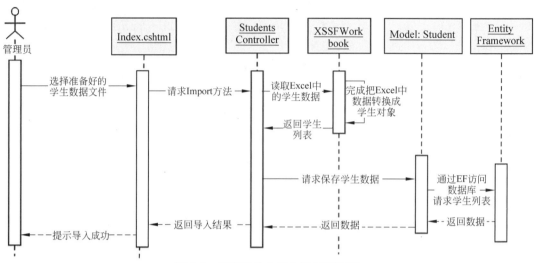

图 9-8 管理员导入学生数据顺序图

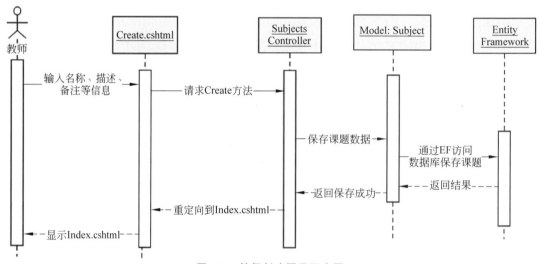

图 9-9 教师创建题目顺序图

题组、选报密码等信息。提交后交给控制类 TopicsController 的 Create 方法进行处理。在处理时先进行传递的数据的格式化，如语言、年级、专业要拼接成字符串。最后，把 Topic 对象交给 EF 框架保存到数据库中。保存成功后，控制类最终把发布的课题列表页面返回给教师。教师发布题目顺序图如图 9-10 所示。

5. 教师课题审批顺序图

教师课题审批顺序图描述的是教师确认选报组用例。教师在课题选报处理页面 Index.cshtml 对选报组进行同意操作，将请求发送给 GroupsController 控制类，控制类通过 AgreeApply 方法完成相应业务处理。控制类先修改 Group 对象的状态为同意，然后调用 EF 框架进行数据的保存，最后将选择成功返回给参与者。教师课题审批顺序图如图 9-11 所示。

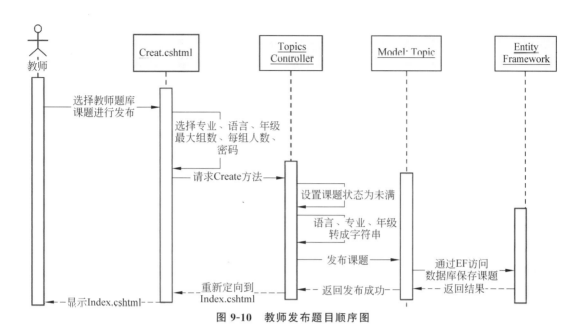

图 9-10 教师发布题目顺序图

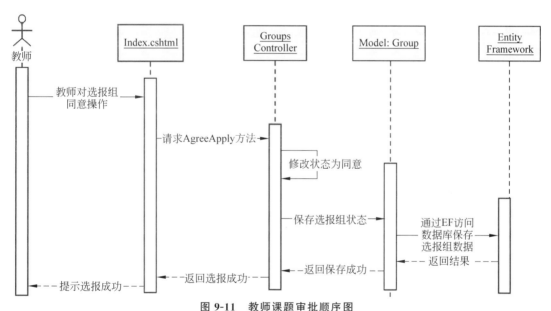

图 9-11 教师课题审批顺序图

6. 学生课题查询顺序图

学生课题查询顺序图描述的是学生查看课题列表用例。学生打开课题列表页面 Index.cshtml，请求发送给控制类 TopicsController，控制类通过 IndexStudent 方法处理业务逻辑。首先检查该生是否已经选报，如果已经选报进行提示；再通过 EF 框架访问数据库返回适合该生年级的课题列表；接下来控制类对课题列表进行筛选，筛选出适合本专业、语言和未满的课题列表。最后将课题列表返回给视图 Index.cshtml，视图呈现给学生。学生课题查询顺序图如图 9-12 所示。

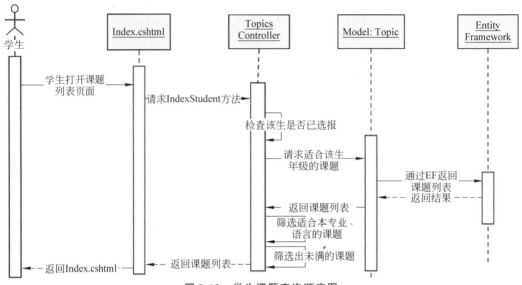

图 9-12 学生课题查询顺序图

7. 学生（组长）选报顺序图

学生（组长）选报顺序图描述的是课题选报用例。参与者以组长身份访问课题选报页面 ApplyForLeader.cshtml，输入本课题对应的密码（可能为空），然后进行选报。选报请求发送到 GroupsController 控制类，控制类调用 ApplyForLeader 方法进行业务逻辑处理。首先检查密码的正确性，如果不正确进行提示。然后在 Group 表中添加一个新的选报组，该 group 的状态为选报中。接下来为 GroupStu 对象添加新的成员，并保存到数据库中。最后，如果操作都成功了，返回"我的选报"页面 MyApply.cshtml 给参与者。学生（组长）选报顺序图如图 9-13 所示。

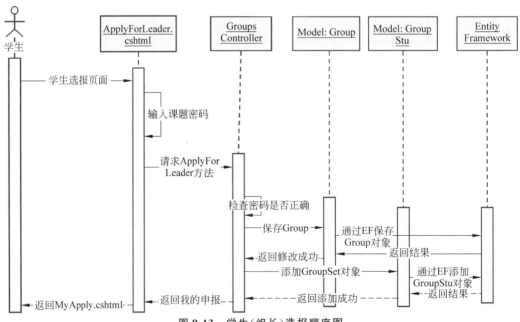

图 9-13 学生（组长）选报顺序图

8．学生（组员）选报顺序图

学生（组员）选报顺序图描述的是课题选报用例。参与者访问课题选报页面 ApplyForMember.cshtml，参与者选择加入的选报组，输入本组对应的密码，然后进行选报。选报请求发送到 GroupsController 控制类，控制类调用 ApplyForMember 方法进行业务逻辑处理。首先检查密码的正确性，如果不正确进行提示。然后修改 Group 对象，若 Group 组已满修，改 IsFull 为"是"，并保存到数据库中。接下来为 GroupStu 对象添加新的成员，并保存到数据库中。最后，如果操作都成功了，返回"我的选报"页面 MyApply.cshtml 给参与者。学生（组员）选报顺序图如图 9-14 所示。

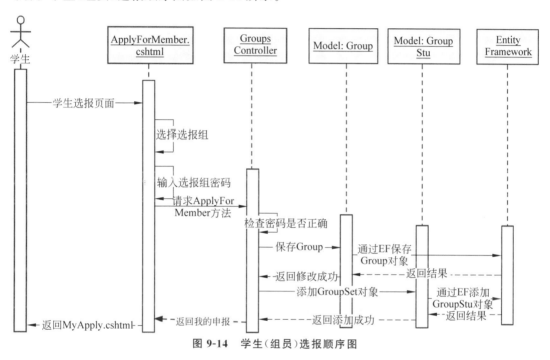

图 9-14　学生（组员）选报顺序图

9.4　数据库设计与实现

9.4.1　数据库设计

1．概念模型

为了便于展示，概念模型只标出了属性中的主键，其他属性没有标出，系统的概念模型如图 9-15 所示。

2．逻辑模型

转换后的关系模式如下。

专业(<u>编号</u>,专业名称,类型)

语言(<u>编号</u>,语言名称)

年级(<u>编号</u>,年级名称)

用户(<u>编号</u>,真实姓名,密码,角色)

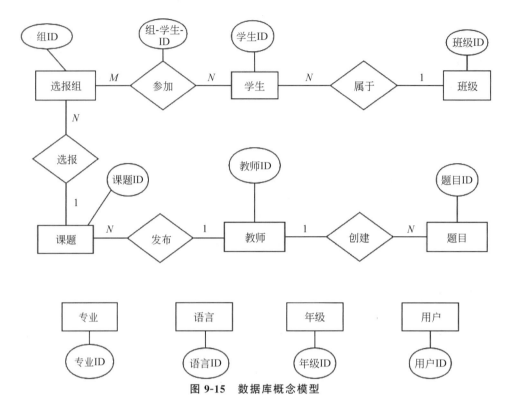

图 9-15 数据库概念模型

班级(<u>编号</u>,班级名称,年级,专业编号)

学生(<u>编号</u>,学生用户名,学生姓名,班级编号)

选报组(<u>编号</u>,组密码,组长,是否报满,是否确认,课题编号)

组员表(<u>编号</u>,学生 ID,组 ID)

课题(<u>编号</u>,名称,描述,年级,语言,专业,最大组数,每组最多人数,是否审核通过,审核建议,是否已满,备注,密码,教师编号)

教师(<u>编号</u>,名称,真实姓名,职称,邮箱,电话,状态,备注)

题目(<u>编号</u>,题目名称,题目描述,题目备注,教师编号)

9.4.2 数据库实现

本项目采用 SQL Server 2019 实现,数据库名称为 exercise,具体实现如下。

(1) 专业表(MajorSet)。专业表的表结构如表 9-7 所示。

表 9-7 MajorSet 表的表结构

字 段 名	数据类型	长 度	主 键	含 义
Id	int		是	专业编号
name	nvarchar	Max	否	专业名称
type	nvarchar	Max	否	专业类型

(2) 语言表(LanguageSet)。语言表的表结构如表 9-8 所示。

表 9-8 语言表的表结构

字 段 名	数据类型	长 度	主 键	含 义
Id	int		是	语言编号
name	nvarchar	Max	否	语言名称

（3）年级表（GradeSet）。年级表的表结构如表 9-9 所示。

表 9-9 年级表的表结构

字 段 名	数据类型	长 度	主 键	含 义
Id	int		是	年级编号
name	nvarchar	Max	否	年级名称

（4）用户表（UserSet）。为了验证用户合法身份，用户表只记录用户的用户名和密码，用户角色用来识别用户身份，控制用户可以访问哪些页面。用户表的表结构如表 9-10 所示。

表 9-10 用户表的表结构

字 段 名	数据类型	长 度	主 键	含 义
Id	int		是	账户编号
name	nvarchar	Max	否	账户名称
pwd	nvarchar	Max	否	账户密码
role	nvarchar	Max	否	账户角色

（5）班级表（ClassSet）。班级与专业相关，学生通过与班级的关系确定专业，班级表的表结构如表 9-11 所示。

表 9-11 班级表的表结构

字 段 名	数据类型	长 度	主 键	含 义
Id	int		是	班级编号
name	nvarchar	Max	否	班级名称
grade	nvarchar	Max	否	班级年级
Major_Id	int		否	外键：专业 Id

（6）学生表（StudentSet）。学生表的表结构如表 9-12 所示。

表 9-12 学生表的表结构

字 段 名	数据类型	长 度	主 键	含 义
Id	int		是	学生编号
name	nvarchar	Max	否	学生账户

续表

字 段 名	数据类型	长 度	主 键	含 义
userName	nvarchar	Max	否	真实姓名
Class_Id	int		否	外键：班级 Id

(7) 选报组表（GroupSet）。选报课题的时候需要分组，每组的成员合作完成一个题目。教师申报题目的时候需指定某个课题允许多少个组选报。每个分组都需要记录其所属的课题的编号，作为外键，参照已申报课题表。出于业务流程的考虑，对于课题选报分组需要增加"是否报满"字段用来记录该分组是否已报满，还需增加"是否确认"字段用来记录指导教师是否已确认选报组的成员。选报组表的表结构如表 9-13 所示。

表 9-13 选报组表的表结构

字 段 名	数据类型	长 度	主 键	含 义
Id	int		是	组编号
password	nvarchar	Max	否	组密码
leader	nvarchar	Max	否	组长名称
isFull	nvarchar	Max	否	是否为满
isConfirm	nvarchar	Max	否	是否已确认
Topic_Id	int		否	外键：课题 Id

(8) 组员表（GroupStuSet）。学生与组之间是多对多的关系，需要衍生出一个新的关系。组员表的表结构如表 9-14 所示。

表 9-14 组员表的表结构

字 段 名	数据类型	长 度	主 键	含 义
Id	int		是	编号
Student_Id	nvarchar	Max	否	外键：学生 Id
Group_Id	nvarchar	Max	否	外键：选报组 Id

(9) 课题表（TopicSet）。教师的个人题库中的题目经申报之后就成为课题，这时即使教师修改了个人题库中的题目内容或者删除了该题目，也不会影响到已申报课题的内容。另外，基于系统需求中描述的题目申报及课题选择的业务流程，需要增加是否报满字段；课题密码字段是选填字段。课题表的表结构如表 9-15 所示。

表 9-15 课题表的表结构

字 段 名	数据类型	长 度	主 键	含 义
Id	int		是	课题编号
name	nvarchar	Max	否	课题名称

续表

字 段 名	数据类型	长 度	主 键	含 义
[desc]	nvarchar	Max	否	课题描述
grade	nvarchar	Max	否	课题所属年级
languages	nvarchar	Max	否	课题适合语言
majors	nvarchar	Max	否	课题适合专业
groupsMax	smallint		否	最多选报组
stusMax	smallint		否	每组最多人数
hasApproved	nvarchar	Max	否	是否审核通过
suggest	nvarchar	Max	否	审核建议
ifFull	nvarchar	Max	否	选报组是否满
memo	nvarchar	Max	否	备注
password	nvarchar	Max	否	课题密码
TeacherInfo_Id	int		否	外键，教师 Id

（10）教师表（TeacherInfoSet）。教师基本信息包括教师的姓名、学历等。教师表的表结构如表 9-16 所示。

表 9-16 教师表的表结构

字 段 名	数据类型	长 度	主 键	含 义
Id	int		是	编号
name	nvarchar	Max	否	教师账户
userName	nvarchar	Max	否	真实姓名
title	nvarchar	Max	否	职称
tel	nvarchar	Max	否	电话
email	nvarchar	Max	否	邮箱
state	nvarchar	Max	否	状态
memo	nvarchar	Max	否	备注

（11）题目表（Subject）。每个教师都可以维护自己的题库信息，题库中的题目只属于教师，在申报之前其他用户都无法访问。题目表的表结构如表 9-17 所示。

表 9-17 题目表的表结构

字 段 名	数据类型	长 度	主 键	含 义
Id	int		是	题目编号
name	nvarchar	Max	否	名称

续表

字 段 名	数据类型	长 度	主 键	含 义
des	nvarchar	Max	否	描述
memo	nvarchar	Max	否	备注
TeacherInfo_Id	int		否	外键：教师 Id

9.5 系统实现

9.5.1 项目总体实现

1. 创建 ASP.NET MVC 项目

创建 ASP.NET MVC 项目，创建方法参考 4.2 节。

2. 在项目中使用 AdminLTE 模板

本项目使用的 AdminLTE 版本是 2.4.18，下载的网站为 https://github.com/ColorlibHQ/AdminLTE。打开 index.html 的显示效果如图 9-16 所示。

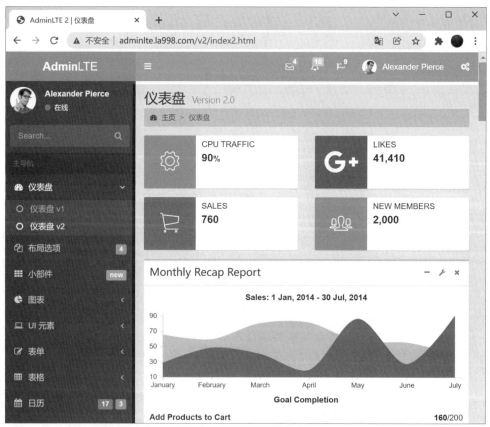

图 9-16 AdminLTE 模板效果

可以看到该项目提供了很多友好的组件及页面可供参考使用，下载后解压包含的主要目录和文件如图 9-17 所示。

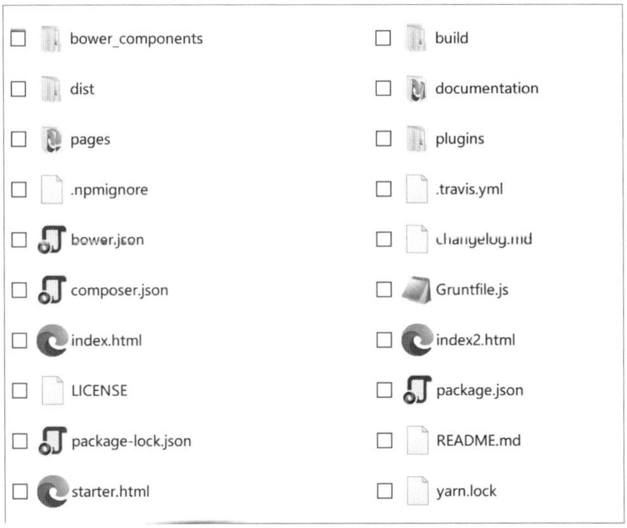

图 9-17　AdminLTE 模板文件

- bower_components：存放了这个框架依赖的其他框架，如 bootstrap、jquery、字体样式、图标样式等。
- build：编译前的源文件目录。
- dist：编译后的静态资源目录。
- pages：目录下是一些示例页面。
- plugins：目录存放依赖的插件。
- starter.html：是 AdminLTE 建议用来作为起点的参考示例。
- index.html：是 AdminLTE 中比较完善的展示品，用于参考、借鉴。

把 AdminLTE 模板整合到 ASP.NET 项目中的方法如下。

（1）把 AdminLTE 目录下 dist 内的 JavaScript 所有文件复制到 ASP.NET MVC 项目下的 Scripts 目录中。

（2）把 AdminLTE 目录下 dist 内的 css 所有文件复制到 ASP.NET MVC 项目下的 Contents 目录中。

（3）把 AdminLTE 目录下 dist 内的 img 复制到 ASP.NET MVC 项目根目录中。

（4）把 AdminLTE 目录下 bower_components、plugins 复制到 ASP.NET MVC 项目根目录中。

（5）把 AdminLTE 目录下 index.html 文件复制到 ASP.NET MVC 项目下 Views 目录的 Home 目录中。

注：如果创建的 ASP.NET MVC 项目内已经包含对 jQuery 和 Bootstrap 库的引用，先删除掉相关文件，使用 AdminLTE 项目引用的 jQuery 和 Bootstrap 库。

3．配置项目路由信息及加载前端依赖文件

（1）配置项目的路由信息，修改 RouteConfig.cs 文件，内容如下。

```
public static void RegisterRoutes(RouteCollection routes)
```

```
{
    routes.IgnoreRoute("{resource}.axd/{*pathInfo}");
    routes.MapRoute(
        name: "Default",
        url: "{controller}/{action}/{id}",
        defaults: new { controller = "Home", action = "Login",
            id = UrlParameter.Optional }
    );
}
```

配置了页面 URL 请求的格式及拦截处理规则，并设置默认页面为 Views 下的 Home 下的 Login.cshtml。

（2）修改 BundleConfig.cs 文件，使项目在启动时自动引用依赖的 JavaScript 库及样式表文件。修改内容如下。

```
public static void RegisterBundles(BundleCollection bundles)
{
    //jQuery js
    bundles.Add(new ScriptBundle("~/bundles/jquery").Include(
            "~/Scripts/jquery-{version}.js"));
    //jQuery validate
    bundles.Add(new ScriptBundle("~/bundles/jqueryval").Include(
            "~/Scripts/jquery.validate*"));
    //bootstrap js
    bundles.Add(new ScriptBundle("~/bundles/bootstrap").Include(
            "~/Scripts/bootstrap.js"));
    //adminlte.js
    bundles.Add(new ScriptBundle("~/bundles/adminlte").Include(
            "~/Scripts/adminlte.js"));
    //adminlte.css
    bundles.Add(new StyleBundle("~/Content/css").Include(
            "~/Content/bootstrap.css",
            "~/Content/AdminLTE.css"));
    //使用要用于开发和学习的 Modernizr 的开发版本
    bundles.Add(new ScriptBundle("~/bundles/modernizr").Include(
            "~/Scripts/modernizr-*"));
}
```

9.5.2 实体及数据访问层实现

使用 EF 设计工具由数据库生成数据模型类最主要的文件是 edmx 文件，下面介绍由现成数据库生成该文件的方法。

1. 生成过程

（1）在"解决方案资源管理器"中右击该项目的名称→"添加"→"新建项"。

（2）在"添加新项"对话框的"数据"栏目中，选择"ADO.NET 实体数据模型"，如图 9-18 所示。

输入该文件的名称"DataModel"，然后单击"添加"按钮。

（3）此时将显示"实体数据模型向导"的第一页，如图 9-19 所示。

在"选择模型内容"对话框中选择"来自数据库的 EF 设计器"，然后单击"下一步"按钮。

图 9-18　添加实体数据模型

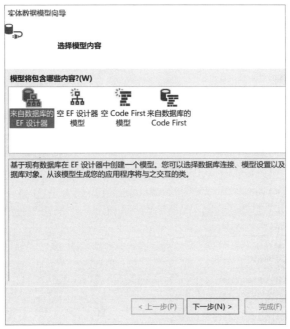

图 9-19　选择模型内容

（4）弹出"实体数据模型向导"对话框，如图 9-20 所示。

如果没有建立好的连接，需要单击"新建连接"按钮。可以将配置好的连接保存到 Web.config 文件中，最后单击"下一步"按钮继续。

（5）此时弹出"选择您的数据库对象和设置"对话框，如图 9-21 所示。选择数据库中创建的表与视图，选中"在模型中包括外键列"和"将所选存储过程和函数导入到实体模型中"复选框。单击"完成"按钮创建 DataModel.edmx 文件。

图 9-20　选择数据库连接

图 9-21　选择数据库对象

2. 文件说明

本项目数据模型最终生成的文件结构如图 9-22 所示。

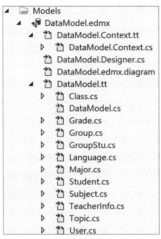

图 9-22　数据模型文件结构

（1）edmx 文件的本质就是一个 XML 文件，它用于定义概念模型、存储模型和这些模型之间的映射，结构如图 9-23 所示。

```
  1   <?xml version="1.0" encoding="utf-8"?>
  2   <edmx:Edmx Version="3.0" xmlns:edmx="http://schemas.microsoft.com/ado/2009/11/edmx">
  3     <!-- EF Runtime content -->
  4     <edmx:Runtime>
  5       <!-- SSDL content -->
  6       <edmx:StorageModels>...</edmx:StorageModels>
244       <!-- CSDL content -->
245       <edmx:ConceptualModels>...</edmx:ConceptualModels>
457       <!-- C-S mapping content -->
458       <edmx:Mappings>...</edmx:Mappings>
633     </edmx:Runtime>
634     <!-- EF Designer content (DO NOT EDIT MANUALLY BELOW HERE) -->
635     <edmx:Designer xmlns="http://schemas.">...</edmx:Designer>
653   </edmx:Edmx>
654
```

图 9-23　edmx 文件内容结构

从代码中可以看到，edmx 大致由 SSDL、CSDL、C-S 三部分组成，分别对应着对于数据库、实体、数据库表与实体之间的映射这三方面的解析，SSDL 中有对数据库表、字段等的规定，CSDL 中有对实体名、实体属性等的规定，C-S 中有对数据库表与实体之间的映射。edmx 文件就是用来解析存储模型、概念模型以及这两者之间的映射，其对应的图形化展示如图 9-24 所示。

（2）DataModel.tt 就是 T4 模板，下面对应的实体类是 T4 模板根据 edmx 配置文件生成的。这些实体类使数据库对象与实体类对象匹配。如果想要执行数据库的操作，可以直接通过对创建出的实体类对象操作就可以同步到数据库中。

（3）本项目数据库对象对应的名称为 DataModelContainer，实体名称与数据库表名称一致，不再复述。

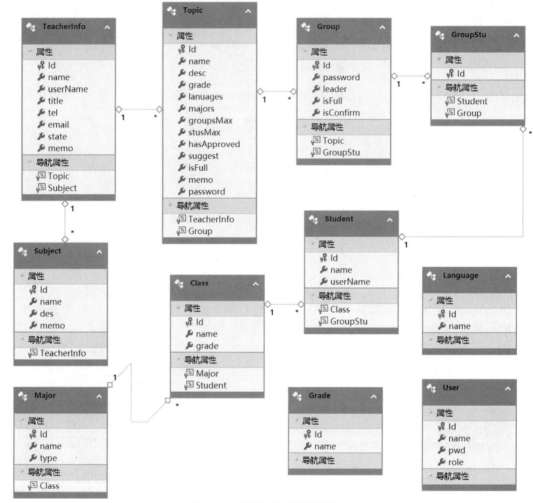

图 9-24　数据实体模型及其关系

9.5.3　管理员模块实现

ASP.NET MVC 项目在实现某一功能时，视图可采用 cshtml 文件来展示，业务逻辑使用 C#代码来完成。完成每一个功能的大致流程分为如下 3 步。

（1）生成对应的基础页面及控制器模板。

（2）使用合适 AdminLTE 的示例页来修改基础页面。

（3）修改或添加控制器对应的方法。

1. 登录

本系统的用户身份分为三种，分别是管理员、教师和学生。管理员主要权限是基础信息维护和查询统计等，教师的主要权限是对课题的申报和对学生选报的确认等，学生的主要权限是对课题的选报。

实现系统登录涉及的数据主要来源于数据库的 UserSet 表，对应的实体为 User。

(1) 生成 Login.cshtml 页面及 UserController 控制器。

① 在项目的 Controllers 文件夹上单击右键,选择"添加"后再选择"控制器"命令。

② 弹出"添加已搭建基架的新项"窗口,选择"控制器"栏目内的"包含视图的 MVC 5 控制器(使用 Entity Framework)",单击"添加"按钮。

③ 弹出"添加控制器"对话框,模型类选择 User,勾选"生成视图"复选框,其他设置如图 9-25 所示。

图 9-25　添加控制器

④ 单击"添加"按钮,可在 Controllers 文件夹生成 UsersController 文件,在 Views 文件夹下生成 Users 文件夹,内包括五个视图文件,分别为 Create.cshtml、Edit.cshtml、Delete.cshtml、Index.cshtml 及 Details.cshtml。这几个文件后续会用到。

⑤ 复制 AdminLTE 项目中的 Login.html 到 Views 目录下的 Home 目录中,并修改文件名为 Login.cshtml。

(2) 修改 Login.cshtml 文件。

修改后的 Login.cshtml 内容如下。

```
@model ExerciseManagement.Models.User
@{
    Layout = null;
}
<!DOCTYPE html>
<html>
<head>
    <meta charset="utf-8">
    <meta http-equiv="X-UA-Compatible" content="IE=edge">
    <meta http-equiv="Content-Type" content="text/html; charset=utf-8" />
    <title>高校实践课题管理系统</title>
    <!-- Tell the browser to be responsive to screen width -->
    <meta content="width=device-width, initial-scale=1, maximum-scale=1,
        user-scalable=no" name="viewport">
    @Styles.Render("~/bower_components/font-awesome/css/font-awesome.min.css")
    @Styles.Render("~/bower_components/Ionicons/css/ionicons.min.css")
```

```
        @Styles.Render("~/plugins/iCheck/square/blue.css")
        @Styles.Render("~/Content/css")
</head>
<body class="hold-transition login-page">
    <div class="login-box">
        <div class="login-logo">
            <b>高校实践课题管理系统</b>
        </div>
        <!-- /.login-logo -->
        <div class="login-box-body">
            <p class="login-box-msg">欢迎登录使用</p>
            @using (Html.BeginForm("Login", "Users", FormMethod.Post))
            {
                @Html.AntiForgeryToken()
                <div class="form-group has-feedback">
                    @Html.EditorFor(model => model.name, new
                    {
                        htmlAttributes = new
                        {
                            @class = "form-control",
                            placeholder = "用户名"
                        }
                    })
                    <span class="glyphicon glyphicon-envelope form-control-
                        feedback"></span>
                </div>
                <div class="form-group has-feedback">
                    @Html.PasswordFor(model => model.pwd, new
                    {
                        @class = "form-control",
                        placeholder = "密码"
                    })
                    <span class="glyphicon glyphicon-lock form-control-
                        feedback"></span>
                </div>
                <div class="row">
                    <div class="col-xs-8">
                        <div class="checkbox icheck">
                            <label>
                                <input type="checkbox"> 记住我
                            </label>
                        </div>
                    </div>
                    <!-- /.col -->
                    <div class="col-xs-4">
                        <button type="submit" class="btn btn-primary btn-block
                            btn-flat">
                            确定
                        </button>
                    </div>
                    <!-- /.col -->
                </div>
                @*</form>*@
```

```
            }
            @Html.ActionLink("注册新用户", "Create", "Users", null, new { @class =
                "text-center" })
        </div>
        <!-- /.login-box-body -->
    </div>
    <!-- /.login-box -->
    @Scripts.Render("~/bundles/jquery")
    @Scripts.Render("~/bundles/bootstrap")
    @Scripts.Render("~/bundles/adminlte")
    @Scripts.Render("~/plugins/iCheck/icheck.min.js")
    <script>
        $(function () {
            $('input').iCheck({
                checkboxClass: 'icheckbox_square-blue',
                radioClass: 'iradio_square-blue',
                increaseArea: '20%' /* optional */
            });
        });
    </script>
</body>
</html>
```

说明：

① 视图中的模型对象 model 为 User 类型，当单击"确定"按钮提交数据时，会传递给控制器。

② "@using（Html.BeginForm("Login"，"Users"，FormMethod.Post））"表明该页面以 post 方式提交到 UsersConstroller 的 Login 方法。

（3）修改 UsersController 文件。

修改后 UsersController 文件的 Login 方法如下。

```
[HttpPost]
[ValidateAntiForgeryToken]
public ActionResult Login(FormCollection form)
{
    string name = form["name"];
    string pwd = form["pwd"];
    User user = null;
    IQueryable< User > users= db.UserSet.Where(u => u.name == name && u.pwd == pwd);
    if (users.Count() ==1)
    {
        user = users.First();
        Session["user"] = user;

        return RedirectToAction("IndexAdmin", "Home", new { name=name,role=
            user.role});
    }
    else
    {
        return RedirectToAction("Login", "Home",new {msg= "用户名或密码错误!" });
    }
}
```

其中，db 为数据库对象。

2. 主界面

本项目三个不同角色的用户共用一个主界面文件，只是在显示效果上有所不同。首先复制 AdminLTE 项目中的 index.html 到 Views 目录下的 Home 目录内，并修改文件名称为 indexAdmin.cshtml。

（1）使用布局页_LayoutPage.cshtml。

_LayoutPage.cshtml 布局页提供了对页面的整体设置以及库文件的引用，该文件内容如下。

```html
<!DOCTYPE html>
<html>
<head>
    <meta charset="utf-8">
    <meta http-equiv="X-UA-Compatible" content="IE=edge">
    <meta http-equiv="Content-Type" content="text/html; charset=utf-8" />
    <title>高校实践课题管理系统</title>
    <!-- Tell the browser to be responsive to screen width -->
    <meta content="width=device-width, initial-scale=1, maximum-scale=1,
        user-scalable=no" name="viewport">
    @Styles.Render("~/bower_components/font-awesome/css/font-awesome.min.
        css")
    @Styles.Render("~/bower_components/Ionicons/css/ionicons.min.css")
    @Styles.Render("~/Content/css")
    @Styles.Render("~/Content/skins/_all-skins.min.css")
    @Styles.Render("~/bower_components/morris.js/morris.css")
    @Styles.Render("~/bower_components/jvectormap/jquery-jvectormap.css")
    @Styles.Render("~/bower_components/bootstrap-datepicker/dist/css/
        bootstrap-datepicker.min.css")
    @Styles.Render("~/bower_components/bootstrap-daterangepicker/
        daterangepicker.css")
    @Styles.Render("~/plugins/bootstrap-wysihtml5/bootstrap3-wysihtml5.min.
        css")
    @Styles.Render("~/Content/PagedList.css")
    @Styles.Render("~/bower_components/datatables.net-bs/css/dataTables.
        bootstrap.min.css")
    @Styles.Render("~/bower_components/bootstrap-fileinput/css/fileinput.
        min.css")
</head>
<body class="hold-transition skin-blue sidebar-mini">
    @RenderBody()
    @Scripts.Render("~/bundles/jquery")
    @Scripts.Render("~/bundles/bootstrap")
    @Scripts.Render("~/bundles/adminlte")
    @Scripts.Render("~/bower_components/jquery-ui/jquery-ui.min.js")
    <script>$.widget.bridge('uibutton', $.ui.button);</script>
    @Scripts.Render("~/bower_components/raphael/raphael.min.js")
    @Scripts.Render("~/bower_components/morris.js/morris.min.js")
    @Scripts.Render("~/bower_components/jquery-sparkline/dist/jquery.
        sparkline.min.js")
    @Scripts.Render("~/plugins/jvectormap/jquery-jvectormap-1.2.2.min.js")
    @Scripts.Render("~/plugins/jvectormap/jquery-jvectormap-world-mill-en.js")
```

```
    @Scripts.Render("~/bower_components/jquery-knob/dist/jquery.knob.min.js")
    @Scripts.Render("~/bower_components/moment/min/moment.min.js")
    @Scripts.Render("~/bower_components/bootstrap-daterangepicker/
        daterangepicker.js")
    @Scripts.Render("~/bower_components/bootstrap-datepicker/dist/js/
        bootstrap-datepicker.min.js")
    @Scripts.Render("~/plugins/bootstrap-wysihtml5/bootstrap3-wysihtml5.all.
        min.js")
    @Scripts.Render("~/bower_components/jquery-slimscroll/jquery.slimscroll.
        min.js")
    @Scripts.Render("~/bower_components/fastclick/lib/fastclick.js")
    @Scripts.Render("~/Scripts/pages/dashboard.js")
    @Scripts.Render("~/Scripts/demo.js")
    @Scripts.Render("~/bower_components/datatables.net/js/jquery.dataTables.
        min.js")
    @Scripts.Render("~/bower_components/datatables.net-bs/js/dataTables.
        bootstrap.min.js")
    @Scripts.Render("~/bower_components/chart.js/Chart.js")
    @Scripts.Render("~/bower_components/bootstrap-fileinput/js/fileinput.
        min.js")
    @Scripts.Render("~/bower_components/bootstrap-fileinput/js/locales/zh.
        js")
    @RenderSection("scripts", required: false)
</body>
</html>
```

（2）修改视图页 indexAdmin.cshtml。

修改后的文件内容如下。

```
@{
    Layout = "~/Views/Shared/_LayoutPage.cshtml";
    ViewBag.Title = "高校实践课题管理系统";
}
<div class="wrapper">
    <header class="main-header">
        <a href="#" class="logo">
            <span class="logo-mini">课题</span>
            <span class="logo-lg">高校课题申报管理系统</span>
        </a>
        <nav class="navbar navbar-static-top">
            <a href="#" class="sidebar-toggle" data-toggle="push-menu" role=
                "button">
                <span class="sr-only">Toggle navigation</span>
            </a>
            <div class="navbar-custom-menu">
                <ul class="nav navbar-nav">
                    <li class="dropdown user user-menu">
                        <a class="btn btn-primary-outline"
                            href="@Url.Action("Logout", "Users")"> 退出</a>
                    </li>
                </ul>
            </div>
        </nav>
```

```html
</header>
<aside class="main-sidebar">
    <section class="sidebar">
        <div class="user-panel">
            <div class="pull-left image">
                <img src="~/img/user2-160x160.jpg" class="img-circle"
                    alt="User Image">
            </div>
            <div class="pull-left info">
                <p>@Request["name"]</p>
                <a href="#"><i class="fa fa-circle text-success"></i> 在线
                </a>
            </div>
        </div>
        <ul class="sidebar-menu" data-widget="tree">
            @if (Request["role"] == "管理员")
            {
                <li class=" treeview">
                    <a href="#">
                        <i class="fa fa-dashboard"></i> <span>基础信息</span>
                        <span class="pull-right-container">
                            <i class="fa fa-angle-left pull-right"></i>
                        </span>
                    </a>
                    <ul class="treeview-menu">
                        <li><a target="content" href="@Url.Action("Index",
                            "Majors",
                            new RouteValueDictionary { { "name",
                            Model.name } })">
                            <i class="fa fa-circle-o"></i> 专业</a></li>
                        <li><a target="content" href="@Url.Action("Index",
                            "Grades",
                            new RouteValueDictionary { { "name",
                            Model.name } })">
                            <i class="fa fa-circle-o"></i> 年级</a></li>
                        <li><a target="content" href="@Url.Action("Index",
                            "Classes",
                            new RouteValueDictionary { { "name",
                            Model.name } })">
                            <i class="fa fa-circle-o"></i> 班级</a></li>
                    </ul>
                </li>
                <li class=" treeview">
                    <a href="#">
                        <i class="fa fa-dashboard"></i> <span>学生管理</
                            span>
                        <span class="pull-right-container">
                            <i class="fa fa-angle-left pull-right"></i>
                        </span>
                    </a>
                    <ul class="treeview-menu">
                        <li><a target="content" href="@Url.Action("Index",
                            "Students")">
```

```html
                        <i class="fa fa-circle-o"></i> 学生列表</a>
                    </li>
                    <li><a target="content" href="@Url.Action("Import",
                        "Students")">
                        <i class="fa fa-circle-o"></i> 学生导入</a>
                    </li>
                </ul>
            </li>
            <li>
                <a target="content" href="@Url.Action
                    ("StaticsByStudent", "Statics")">
                    <i class="fa fa-pie-chart"></i> 课题统计</a>
            </li>
}
@if (Request["role"] == "教师")
{
    <li class=" treeview">
        <a href="#">
            <i class="fa fa-dashboard"></i> <span>题库管理</span>
            <span class="pull-right-container">
                <i class="fa fa-angle-left pull-right"></i>
            </span>
        </a>
        <ul class="treeview-menu">
            <li><a target="content" href="@Url.Action("Create",
                "Subjects",
                new RouteValueDictionary { { "name",
                    Model.name } })">
                <i class="fa fa-circle-o"></i> 创建题目</a>
            </li>
            <li><a target="content" href="@Url.Action("Index",
                "Subjects",
                new RouteValueDictionary { { "name",
                    Model.name } })">
                <i class="fa fa-circle-o"></i> 我的题库</a>
            </li>
        </ul>
    </li>
    <li class=" treeview">
        <a href="#">
            <i class="fa fa-dashboard"></i> <span>课题管理
                </span>
            <span class="pull-right-container">
                <i class="fa fa-angle-left pull-right"></i>
            </span>
        </a>
        <ul class="treeview-menu">
            <li><a target="content" href="@Url.Action("Index",
                "Topics",
                new RouteValueDictionary { { "name",
                Model.name } })">
                <i class="fa fa-circle-o"></i> 我的课题</a>
            </li>
```

```html
                <li><a target="content" href="@Url.Action
                    ("Confirm", "Groups",
                        new RouteValueDictionary { { "name",
                        Model.name } })">
                            <i class="fa fa-circle-o"></i> 课题审批</a>
                        </li>
                </ul>
            </li>
        }
        @if (Request["role"] == "学生")
        {
            <li class=" treeview">
                <a href="#">
                    <i class="fa fa-dashboard"></i> <span>课题选报</span>
                    <span class="pull-right-container">
                        <i class="fa fa-angle-left pull-right"></i>
                    </span>
                </a>
                <ul class="treeview-menu">
                    <li><a target="content" href="@Url.Action
                        ("IndexStudent", "Topics",
                            new RouteValueDictionary { { "name",
                            Model.name } })">
                                <i class="fa fa-circle-o"></i> 课题查询</a>
                            </li>
                    <li><a target="content" href="@Url.Action
                        ("MyApply", "Groups",
                            new RouteValueDictionary { { "name",
                            Model.name } })">
                                <i class="fa fa-circle-o"></i> 我的选报</a>
                            </li>
                </ul>
            </li>
        }
        <li>
            <a target="content" href="@Url.Action("Password", "Users")">
                <i class="fa fa-pie-chart"></i> 修改密码</a>
        </li>
    </ul>
</section>
</aside>
<div class="content-wrapper" >
    <iframe scrolling="yes" frameborder="0"
            src="@Url.Action(ViewBag.action, ViewBag.controller)"
            style="width: 100%; min-height:700px; overflow: visible;"
            id="content" name="content"></iframe>
</div>
</div>
```

说明：

① "<a target="content" href=""><i class="fa fa-pie-chart"></i> 修改密码</a>"其中，target="content"表明新的页面将在名称为 content 的 iframe 中打开。

② "@if (Request["role"] == "管理员")"三种不同角色共用一个视图文件,通过访问该页面时传递过来的 role 角色来区分不同角色,从而达到不同角色显示不同内容。

③ "<a class="btn btn-primary-outline" href="@Url.Action("Logout","Users")">退出</a>"退出登录是通过调用 UsersController 控制器的 Logout 方法实现的。

(3) 修改 UsersController 控制器。

```
public ActionResult Logout()
{
    Session["user"] = null;
    return RedirectToAction("Login", "Home");
}
```

3. 专业管理

专业管理属于基础数据的管理,除此之外,还包括班级管理、年级管理等,由于它们的实现过程都是类似的,这里仅以专业管理为代表讲述基础数据的管理。

添加控制器及视图,方法参考"登录"创建的过程,选择模型为 Major,控制器名称为 MajorController。

(1) 专业列表。

专业列表的视图内容如下。

```
@model PagedList.IPagedList<ExerciseManagement.Models.Major>
@{
    Layout = "~/Views/Shared/_LayoutPage.cshtml";
}
@using PagedList.Mvc;
@using PagedList;
<div class="box">
    <div class="box-header">
        <div class="row">
            <div class="col-xs-2">
                <h3 class="box-title">专业信息</h3>
            </div>
            <div class="col-xs-10">
                @Html.ActionLink("创建", "Create")
            </div>
        </div>
    </div>
    <div class="box-body">
        <table id="example1" class="table table-bordered table-striped">
            <thead>
                <tr>
                    <th>
                        名称
                    </th>
                    <th>
                        类型
                    </th>
                    <th>操作</th>
                </tr>
```

```
            </thead>
            <tbody>
                @foreach (var item in Model)
                {
                    <tr>
                        <td>@Html.DisplayFor(modelItem => item.name)</td>
                        <td>@Html.DisplayFor(modelItem => item.type)</td>
                        <td>
                            @Html.ActionLink("编辑", "Edit", new { id = item.Id }) |
                            @Html.ActionLink("删除", "Delete", new { id = item.Id })
                        </td>
                    </tr>
                }
            </tbody>
            <tfoot>
                <tr>
                    <th>
                        名称
                    </th>
                    <th>
                        类型
                    </th>
                    <th>操作</th>
                </tr>
            </tfoot>
        </table>
        @Html.PagedListPager(Model, page => Url.Action("Index", new { page }))
    </div>
</div>
```

说明：

① 在分页显示多条记录时，使用了 PagedList 分页插件，官方网址为 https://github.com/troygoode/PagedList，使用方法请读者自行查阅。

② 单击"创建""编辑"链接可打开新的页面，单击"删除"链接可对相应的专业信息进行删除操作。

控制器的 Index 方法代码如下。

```
public ActionResult Index(int ? page)
{
    var majors = db.MajorSet.OrderBy(g => g.name);
    foreach(var v in majors)
    {
        string s = v.name;
    }
    var pageNumber = page ?? 1;
    ///每页显示项目数量
    var pageSize = 10;
    ///进行分页生成 model
    IPagedList<Major> model = majors.ToPagedList(pageNumber, pageSize);
    return View(model);
}
```

控制器的 Delete 方法代码如下。

```
public ActionResult Delete(int? id)
{
    try
    {
        Major major = db.MajorSet.Find(id);
        db.MajorSet.Remove(major);
        db.SaveChanges();
        return RedirectToAction("Index");
    }
    catch (Exception ex)
    {
        var info = string.Format("<script>alert('" + ex.Message + "');" +
            "location.href='{0}'</script>", Url.Action("Index"));
        return Content(info, "text/html");
    }
}
```

如果删除失败,进行提示。

(2) 专业创建。

专业创建视图的内容如下。

```
@model ExerciseManagement.Models.Major
@{
    Layout = "~/Views/Shared/_LayoutPage.cshtml"; ;
}
<div class="box box-primary">
    <div class="box-header with-border">
        <h3 class="box-title">专业</h3>
    </div>
    @using (Html.BeginForm())
    {
        @Html.AntiForgeryToken()
        <div class="box-body">
            <div class="form-group">
                @Html.EditorFor(model => model.name, new { htmlAttributes =
                    new { @class = "form-control", placeholder = "请输入名称" } })
            </div>
            <div class="form-group has-feedback">
                <div class="radio,row">
                    <label class="col-xs-1">
                        @Html.RadioButtonFor(model => model.type, "本科",
                            new { @checked = true, @id = "type1", @name = "type" })<label>
                        本科</label>
                    </label>
                    <label class="col-xs-1">
                        @Html.RadioButtonFor(model => model.type, "专科",
                            new { @id = "type2", @name = "type" })<label>专科</label>
                    </label>
                </div>
            </div>
        </div>
```

```html
            <div class="box-footer">
                <button type="submit" class="btn btn-primary">创建</button>
                @Html.ActionLink("返回", "Index", null, new { @class =
                    "btn btn-default" })
            </div>
        }
</div>
```

创建时对应的控制器方法如下。

```csharp
[HttpPost]
[ValidateAntiForgeryToken]
public ActionResult Create([Bind(Include = "Id,name,type")] Major major)
{
    if (ModelState.IsValid)
    {
        db.MajorSet.Add(major);
        db.SaveChanges();
        return RedirectToAction("Index");
    }
    return View(major);
}
```

(3) 专业编辑。

当需要修改专业名称及相关信息时，可以对专业信息进行编辑。专业编辑的视图内容如下。

```html
@model ExerciseManagement.Models.Major
@{
    Layout = "~/Views/Shared/_LayoutPage.cshtml"; ;
}
<div class="box box-primary">
    <div class="box-header with-border">
        <h3 class="box-title">专业</h3>
    </div>
    @using (Html.BeginForm())
    {
        @Html.AntiForgeryToken()
        @Html.HiddenFor(model => model.Id)
        <div class="box-body">
            <div class="form-group">
                @Html.EditorFor(model => model.name, new { htmlAttributes =
                    new { @class = "form-control", placeholder = "请输入名称" } })
            </div>
            <div class="form-group has-feedback">
                <div class="radio,row">
                    <label class="col-xs-1">
                        @Html.RadioButtonFor(model => model.type, "本科",
                            new { @checked = true, @id = "type1", @name = "type" })
                        <label>本科</label>
                    </label>
                    <label class="col-xs-1">
                        @Html.RadioButtonFor(model => model.type, "专科",
```

```
                    new { @id = "type2", @name = "type" })<label>专科
                    </label>
                </label>
            </div>
        </div>
    </div>
    <div class="box-footer">
        <button type="submit" class="btn btn-primary">确定</button>
        @Html.ActionLink("返回", "Index", null, new { @class =
            "btn btn-default" })
    </div>
}
</div>
```

修改专业信息的控制器方法代码如下。

```
public ActionResult Edit(int? id)
{
    if (id == null)
    {
        return new HttpStatusCodeResult(HttpStatusCode.BadRequest);
    }
    Major major = db.MajorSet.Find(id);
    if (major == null)
    {
        return HttpNotFound();
    }
    return View(major);
}
[HttpPost]
[ValidateAntiForgeryToken]
public ActionResult Edit([Bind(Include = "Id,name,type")] Major major)
{
    if (ModelState.IsValid)
    {
        db.Entry(major).State = EntityState.Modified;
        db.SaveChanges();
        return RedirectToAction("Index");
    }
    return View(major);
}
```

其中,第一个 Edit 为进行编辑前调用的方法,第二个为编辑后提交调用的方法。

4. 学生列表

学生列表是参加本次实践课题的所有学生,其来源于导入或者学生注册。添加控制器及视图方法参考"登录"创建的过程,选择模型为 Student,控制器名称为 StudentsController。修改 Views 目录下 Students 内的 Index.cshtml 学生列表的视图文件内容如下。

```
@model PagedList.IPagedList<ExerciseManagement.Models.Student>
@using PagedList.Mvc;
@{
    ViewBag.Title = "Index";
```

```
        Layout = "~/Views/Shared/_LayoutPage.cshtml";
}
<div class="box">
    @using (Html.BeginForm("ImportFile", "Students", FormMethod.Post,
        new { enctype = "multipart/form-data" }))
    {
        <div class="box-header">
            <div class="row">
                <div class="col-xs-2">
                    <h3 class="box-title">学生列表</h3>
                </div>
            </div>
        </div>
        <div class="box-body">
            <table id="example1" class="table table-bordered table-striped">
                <thead>
                    <tr>
                        <th>账户</th>
                        <th>姓名</th>
                        <th>班级</th>
                    </tr>
                </thead>
                <tbody>
                    @foreach (var item in Model)
                    {
                        <tr>
                            <td>@Html.DisplayFor(modelItem => item.name)</td>
                            <td>@Html.DisplayFor(modelItem => item.userName)</td>
                            <td>@Html.DisplayFor(modelItem => item.Class.name)
                            </td>
                        </tr>
                    }
                </tbody>
                <tfoot>
                    <tr>
                        <th>账户</th>
                        <th>姓名</th>
                        <th>班级</th>
                    </tr>
                </tfoot>
            </table>
            @Html.PagedListPager(Model, page => Url.Action("Index", new
                { page }))
        </div>
    }
</div>
```

对应的分页显示学生的控制器代码如下。

```
public ActionResult Index(int ? page)
{
    var pageNumber = page ?? 1;
    ///每页显示项目数量
```

```
        var pageSize = 10;
        ///进行分页生成 model
        IPagedList<Student> model = db.StudentSet.OrderBy(s=>
              s.Class.Id).ToPagedList(pageNumber, pageSize);
        return View(model);
    }
```

5. 学生导入

由于学生人数比较多,因此采用导入 Excel 的方式添加学生。导入学生的视图文件内容如下。

```
@model PagedList.IPagedList<ExerciseManagement.Models.Student>
@using PagedList.Mvc;
@{
    ViewBag.Title = "Index";
    Layout = null;
}
<!DOCTYPE html>
<html>
<head>
    <meta charset="utf-8">
    <meta http-equiv="X-UA-Compatible" content="IE=edge">
    <meta http-equiv="Content-Type" content="text/html; charset=utf-8" />
    <title>高校实践课题管理系统</title>
    <meta content="width=device-width, initial-scale=1, maximum-scale=1,
        user-scalable=no" name="viewport">
    @Styles.Render("~/Content/css")
    @Styles.Render("~/Content/skins/_all-skins.min.css")
    @Scripts.Render("~/bundles/jquery")
    @Scripts.Render("~/bundles/bootstrap")
    @Scripts.Render("~/bundles/adminlte")
    @Styles.Render("~/Content/PagedList.css")
    @Styles.Render("~/bower_components/font-awesome/css/font-awesome.min.
        css")
    @Styles.Render("~/bower_components/Ionicons/css/ionicons.min.css")
    @Styles.Render("~/bower_components/bootstrap-fileinput/css/fileinput.
        min.css")
    @Scripts.Render("~/Scripts/demo.js")
    @Scripts.Render("~/bower_components/bootstrap-fileinput/js/fileinput.
        min.js")
    @Scripts.Render("~/bower_components/bootstrap-fileinput/js/locales/zh.js")
</head>
<body class="hold-transition skin-blue sidebar-mini">
    <div class="box">

            <div class="box-header">
                <div class="row">
                    <div class="col-xs-2">
                        <h3 class="box-title">学生导入</h3>
                    </div>
                    <div class="col-xs-10">
                        @Html.ActionLink("下载模板", "DowntTemplate")
                    </div>
```

```html
                </div>
            </div>
            <div class="box-body">
                <div class="row">
                    <div class="col-xs-10">
                        <input id="input-id" type="file" />
                    </div>
                </div>
            </div>
        </div>
        <script>
            initFileInput( "/Students/ImportData");
            function initFileInput( uploadUrl) {
                var control = $("#input-id")
                control.fileinput({
                    language: 'zh',                                  //设置语言
                    uploadUrl: uploadUrl,                            //上传的地址
                    enctype: 'multipart/form-data',
                    allowedFileExtensions: ['xls', 'xlsx'],          //接收的文件后缀
                    showUpload: true,                                //是否显示"上传"按钮
                    showCaption: true,                               //是否显示标题
                    browseClass: "btn btn-primary",                  //按钮样式
                    showPreview: true,
                    previewFileIconSettings: {
                        'xlsx': '<i class="fa fa-file-excel-o text-success"></i>'
                    },
                    previewFileIcon: "<i class='glyphicon glyphicon-file'></i>",
                }).on('fileuploaded', function (event, data, previewId, index) {
                    alert(data.jqXHR.responseJSON);
                });
            }
        </script>
</body>
</html>
```

说明：该部分使用了 bootstrap-fileinput 文件上传组件，该插件的网址为 https://plugins.krajee.com/file-input，使用方法请读者自行查阅。

上传文件前需要先下载模板文件，下载模板文件对应的控制器的代码如下。

```csharp
public ActionResult DowntTemplate()
{
    //模板文件的路径
    string filePath = Server.MapPath("~/Document/students.xlsx");
    if (System.IO.File.Exists(filePath))
    {
        string strfileName = Path.GetFileName(filePath);            //获取文件名称
        return File(new FileStream(filePath, FileMode.Open),
            "application/octet-stream", strfileName);
    }
    else
    {
        return Content("模板文件找不到!请检查文件是否存在!");          //提示用户
```

```
    }
}
```

上传文件到后台，相应的控制器处理方法代码如下。

```
[HttpPost]
public JsonResult ImportData()
{
    string result = "";
    var file = HttpContext.Request.Files["file_data"];
    //声明二进制数组存放文件
    byte[] fileBytes = new byte[file.ContentLength];
    //将传入的文件转换为二进制的数组存入
    file.InputStream.Read(fileBytes, 0, file.ContentLength);
    //将二进制数组转换为内存流
    MemoryStream excelFileStream = new MemoryStream(fileBytes);
    //将内存流转换为工作簿
    IWorkbook workbook = new XSSFWorkbook(excelFileStream);
    if (workbook.NumberOfSheets > 0)
    {
        DataTable dbExcel = new DataTable();
        ISheet sheet = workbook.GetSheetAt(0);                    //获取第一个工作表
        int rowCount = sheet.LastRowNum + 1;                      //获取表格行数
        if (rowCount > 1)
        {
            IRow rowHeader = sheet.GetRow(0);
            int cellCount = rowHeader.LastCellNum;                //获取表格列数
            for (int i = rowHeader.FirstCellNum; i < cellCount; i++)
            {
                DataColumn dtColumn = new DataColumn(rowHeader.
                    GetCell(i).StringCellValue);
                dbExcel.Columns.Add(dtColumn);
            }
            for (int i = (sheet.FirstRowNum) + 1; i < rowCount; i++)
            {
                IRow row = sheet.GetRow(i);                       //获取行的数据
                DataRow dtRow = dbExcel.NewRow();                 //创建行
                if (row != null)
                {
                    for (int j = row.FirstCellNum; j < cellCount; j++)
                    {
                        if (row.GetCell(j) != null)
                        {
                            dtRow[j] = row.GetCell(j).ToString();
                        }
                    }
                }
                dbExcel.Rows.Add(dtRow);                          //执行添加
            }
            foreach (DataRow row in dbExcel.Rows)
            {
                string className= row["班级"].ToString();
                Class c = db.ClassSet.Where(c2 => c2.name == className).
```

```
                    FirstOrDefault();
                string sno = row["学号"].ToString();
                bool isNotExist = db.StudentSet.Where(s => s.name ==
                    sno).Count()==0;
                if (c != null && isNotExist)
                {
                    User user = new User();
                    user.name = row["学号"].ToString();
                    user.pwd = row["密码"].ToString();
                    user.role = "学生";
                    db.UserSet.Add(user);
                    Student stu = new Student();
                    stu.name= row["学号"].ToString();
                    stu.userName= row["姓名"].ToString();
                    stu.Class = c;
                    db.StudentSet.Add(stu);
                }
            }
            db.SaveChanges();
            result = "导入成功!";
        }
        else
        {
            result = "数据为空,无须导入!";
        }
    }
    else
    {
        result = "数据为空,无须导入!";
    }
    JsonResult jr = new JsonResult();
    jr.Data = result;
    jr.JsonRequestBehavior = JsonRequestBehavior.AllowGet;
    return jr;
}
```

在导入 Excel 格式的学生数据时,使用了 NPOI 组件。NPOI 是开源的 POI 项目的.NET 版,在处理 Excel 文件上,NPOI 可以同时兼容 xls 和 xlsx。NPOI 的网址为 https://github.com/nissl-lab/npoi,具体使用方法请读者自行查阅。

6. 课题统计

在进行课题统计时采用了按学生、按课题两种方式的统计,课题统计的视图文件内容如下。

```
@{
    Layout = null;
}
<!DOCTYPE html>
<html>
<head>
    <meta charset="utf-8">
    <meta http-equiv="X-UA-Compatible" content="IE=edge">
    <meta http-equiv="Content-Type" content="text/html; charset=utf-8" />
```

```html
        <title>高校实践课题管理系统</title>
        <meta content="width=device-width, initial-scale=1,
            maximum-scale=1, user-scalable=no" name="viewport">
    @Styles.Render("~/bower_components/font-awesome/css/font-awesome.min.css")
    @Styles.Render("~/bower_components/Ionicons/css/ionicons.min.css")
    @Styles.Render("~/Content/css")
    @Styles.Render("~/Content/skins/_all-skins.min.css")
</head>
<body class="hold-transition skin-blue sidebar-mini">
    <div class="box">
        <div class="box-header">
            <div class="row">
                <div class="col-xs-4">
                    <h3 class="box-title">课题统计</h3>
                </div>
                <div class="col-xs-4">
                    @Html.ActionLink("导出数据", "ExportData", "Statics")
                </div>
                <div class="col-xs-4">
                </div>
            </div>
        </div>
        <div class="box-body">
            <div class="row">
                <div class="col-sm-4">
                    <div class="text-center">按学生统计</div>
                    <canvas id="pieChart1" ></canvas>
                </div>
                <div class="col-sm-4">
                    <div class="text-center">按课题统计</div>
                    <canvas id="pieChart2"></canvas>
                </div>
            </div>
        </div>
    </div>
    @Scripts.Render("~/bundles/jquery")
    @Scripts.Render("~/bundles/bootstrap")
    @Scripts.Render("~/bundles/adminlte")
    @Scripts.Render("~/bower_components/fastclick/lib/fastclick.js")
    @Scripts.Render("~/Scripts/demo.js")
    @Scripts.Render("~/bower_components/chart.js/Chart.js")
    <script>
        var pieChartCanvas1 = $('#pieChart1').get(0).getContext('2d')
        var pieChart1 = new Chart(pieChartCanvas1)
        var pieChartCanvas2 = $('#pieChart2').get(0).getContext('2d')
        var pieChart2 = new Chart(pieChartCanvas2)
        var pieChartCanvas3 = $('#pieChart3').get(0).getContext('2d')
        var pieChart3 = new Chart(pieChartCanvas3)
        var pieOptions = {
            segmentShowStroke: true,
            segmentStrokeColor: '#fff',
            segmentStrokeWidth: 2,
            percentageInnerCutout: 0,
```

```
            animationSteps: 100,
            animationEasing: 'easeOutBounce',
            animateRotate: true,
            animateScale: false,
            responsive: true,
            maintainAspectRatio: true,
            legendTemplate: '<ul class="<%-name.toLowerCase()%>-legend">
              <% for (var i=0; i<segments.length; i++)
              {%><li><span style="background-color:<%=segments[i].
                fillColor%>"></span>
              <%if(segments[i].label){%><%=segments[i].label%><%}%></li>
                <%}%></ul>'
        }
        $.get('@Url.Action("StaticsDataByStudent", "Statics")',
            function (data) {
                var PieData =[];
                $.each(data, function (index, sd) {
                    var o = { value: sd.num,label:sd.name};
                    PieData.push(o);
                });
                pieChart1.Pie(PieData, pieOptions)
            });
        $.get('@Url.Action("StaticsDataByTopic", "Statics")',
            function (data) {
                var PieData =[];
                $.each(data, function (index, sd) {
                    var o = { value: sd.num,label:sd.name};
                    PieData.push(o);
                });
                pieChart2.Pie(PieData, pieOptions)
            });
</script>
</body>
</html>
```

在进行图形化显示时，为了绘图方便使用了 Chart.js 组件，Chart.js 的网址为 https://www.chartjs.org/，使用方法请自行查阅。

如果想把学生的课题选报情况进行导出，可以单击"导出"按钮，对应的控制器代码如下。

```
public ActionResult ExportData()
{
    //课题名称,学生名称,所在班级
    User user = (User)Session["user"];
    if (user == null)
    {
        return RedirectToAction("Login", "Home");
    }
    List<Student> stus = new List<Student>();
    List<string> subName = new List<string>();
    List<string> teaName = new List<string>();
    List<Group> list = db.GroupSet.Where(gs=>gs.isConfirm == "同意").ToList();
```

```csharp
        foreach (Group g in list)
        {
            //该组有哪些学生
            List<GroupStu> gs = db.GroupStuSet.Where(gss => gss.Group.Id ==
                g.Id).ToList();
            foreach (GroupStu a in gs)
            {
                stus.Add(a.Student);
                subName.Add(g.Topic.name);
                teaName.Add(g.Topic.TeacherInfo.userName);
            }
        }
        XSSFWorkbook excelBook = new XSSFWorkbook();                    //创建工作簿 Excel
        ISheet sheet1 = excelBook.CreateSheet("学生选报情况");
                                                                        //为工作簿创建工作表并命名
        //编写工作表 (1)表头 (2)数据:listStudent
        NPOI.SS.UserModel.IRow row1 = sheet1.CreateRow(0);              //创建第一行
        row1.CreateCell(0).SetCellValue("学生姓名");
        row1.CreateCell(1).SetCellValue("所在班级");
        row1.CreateCell(2).SetCellValue("课题名称");
        row1.CreateCell(3).SetCellValue("指导老师");
        for (int i = 0; i < stus.Count(); i++)
        {
            IRow rowTemp = sheet1.CreateRow(i + 1);
            rowTemp.CreateCell(0).SetCellValue(stus[i].userName);
            rowTemp.CreateCell(1).SetCellValue(stus[i].Class.name);
            rowTemp.CreateCell(2).SetCellValue(subName[i]);
            rowTemp.CreateCell(3).SetCellValue(teaName[i]);
        }
        var fileName = "学生选报情况" + ".xlsx";                         //文件名
        //将 Excel 表格转换为流,输出
        NpoiMemoryStream bookStream = new NpoiMemoryStream();          //创建文件流
        bookStream.AllowClose = false;
        excelBook.Write(bookStream);
        bookStream.Flush();
        bookStream.Seek(0, SeekOrigin.Begin);
        bookStream.AllowClose = true;
        return File(bookStream, "application/vnd.ms-excel", fileName);
                                                                        //最后以文件形式返回
}
```

为了便于展示信息,定义了 StudentsData 类,内容如下。

```csharp
class StudentsData
{
    public string  name;
    public int num;
}
```

按学生统计对应的控制器代码如下。

```csharp
public JsonResult StaticsDataByStudent()
{
    IList<StudentsData> listSD = new List<StudentsData>();
```

```csharp
    StudentsData sd1 = new StudentsData();
    sd1.name = "已申报";
    sd1.num = db.GroupStuSet.Where(gs =>
    gs.Group.isConfirm == "同意").Count();
    listSD.Add(sd1);
    StudentsData sd2 = new StudentsData();
    sd2.name = "申报中";
    sd2.num = db.GroupStuSet.Where(gs =>
    gs.Group.isConfirm == "申请中").Count();;
    listSD.Add(sd2);
    StudentsData sd3 = new StudentsData();
    sd3.name = "未申报";
    sd3.num = db.StudentSet.Count()-(sd1.num+sd2.num);
    listSD.Add(sd3);
    return Json(listSD, JsonRequestBehavior.AllowGet);
}
```

按课题统计对应的控制器代码如下。

```csharp
public JsonResult StaticsDataByTopic()
{
    int total = db.TopicSet.Count();              //总数
    //已报满
    int full = db.TopicSet.Where(gs => gs.isFull == "是")
            .Count();
    //未报满
    int half = db.TopicSet.Where(gs => gs.isFull == "否"
    && gs.Group.Count > 0).Count();
    //没有人报
    int blank = db.TopicSet.Where(gs => gs.isFull == "否"
    && gs.Group.Count == 0).Count();
    List<object> list = new List<object>();
    list.Add(new { name = "已报满", num = full });
    list.Add(new { name = "未报满", num = half });
    list.Add(new { name = "未报", num = blank });
    return Json(list, JsonRequestBehavior.AllowGet);
}
```

7. 修改密码

修改密码的视图文件内容如下。

```
@model ExerciseManagement.Models.UserVm
@{
    ViewBag.Title = "Password";
    Layout = "~/Views/Shared/_LayoutPage.cshtml";
}
<div class="box">
    <div class="box-header">
        <div class="row">
            <div class="col-xs-2">
                <h3 class="box-title">修改密码</h3>
            </div>
            <div class="col-xs-10">
                @{
```

```
                    string role = ((ExerciseManagement.Models.User)Session
                        ["user"]).role;
                }
                @if (role == "教师")
                {
                    @Html.ActionLink("账户详情", "Details", "TeacherInfoes");
                }
                @if (role == "学生")
                {
                    @Html.ActionLink("账户详情", "Details", "Students");
                }
            </div>
        </div>
    </div>
    @using (Html.BeginForm("PasswordUpdate", "Users", FormMethod.Post))
    {
        @Html.AntiForgeryToken()
        <div class="box-body">
            <div class="form-group has-feedback">
                @Html.EditorFor(model => model.name, new { htmlAttributes = new
        { @class = "form-control", @readonly = "readonly" } })
                    <span class="glyphicon glyphicon-user form-control-feedback">
                    </span>
            </div>
            <div class="form-group has-feedback">
                @Html.PasswordFor(model => model.pwdOld, new { @class = "form-
                    control",
                placeholder = "原密码" })
                    <span class="glyphicon glyphicon-lock form-control-feedback">
                    </span>
            </div>
            <div class="form-group has-feedback">
                @Html.PasswordFor(model => model.pwdNew, new { @class = "form-
                    control",
                placeholder = "新密码" })
                    <span class="glyphicon glyphicon-lock form-control-feedback">
                    </span>
            </div>
            <div class="form-group has-feedback">
                @Html.PasswordFor(model => model.pwdNew2, new { @class = "form-
                    control",
                placeholder = "重复新密码" })
                    <span class="glyphicon glyphicon-lock form-control-feedback">
                    </span>
            </div>
        </div>
        <div class="box-footer">
            <button type="submit" class="btn btn-primary">确定</button>
        </div>
    }
</div>
```

说明：

① 管理员、教师和学生共用该页面进行密码的修改，通过判断登录者的角色来确定身份。

② 由于该页面的数据需要原密码、新密码和重复密码，与模型中的实体属性不一致，因此需要定义一个虚拟实体 UserVm，内容如下。

```csharp
public class UserVm
{
    public string name { set; get; }
    public string pwdOld { set; get; }
    public string pwdNew { set; get; }
    public string pwdNew2 { set; get; }
}
```

修改密码控制器代码如下。

```csharp
public ActionResult Password()
{
    UserVm vm = new UserVm();
    User user = ((User)Session["user"]);
    if (user == null)
    {
        return RedirectToAction("Login", "Home");
    }
    else
    {
        vm.name = user.name;
        return View(vm);
    }
}
[HttpPost]
[ValidateAntiForgeryToken]
public ActionResult PasswordUpdate(UserVm vm)
{
    User user = db.UserSet.Where(u => u.name == vm.name).FirstOrDefault();
    if (user.pwd == vm.pwdOld && vm.pwdNew==vm.pwdNew2)
    {
        user.pwd = vm.pwdNew;
        db.SaveChanges();
        var info = string.Format("<script>alert('更新成功!');" +
            "location.href='{0}'</script>", Url.Action("Password", "Users"));
        return Content(info, "text/html");
    }
    else
    {
        var info = string.Format("<script>alert('输入信息有误,请重试!');" +
            "location.href='{0}'</script>", Url.Action("Password", "Users"));
        return Content(info, "text/html");
    }
}
```

第一个方法为进入修改密码页面调用的方法，第二个为确定修改密码调用的方法。

9.5.4 教师模块实现

1. 注册教师

注册教师分为两步完成,第一步注册账号,第二步完善教师信息。

(1) 注册账号。

修改后的 Users 目录下 Create.cshtml 注册页面内容如下。

```
@model ExerciseManagement.Models.User
@{
    Layout = null;
}
<!DOCTYPE html>
<html>
<head>
    <meta charset="utf-8">
    <meta http-equiv="X-UA-Compatible" content="IE=edge">
    <meta http-equiv="Content-Type" content="text/html; charset=utf-8" />
    <title>注册新用户</title>
    <meta content="width=device-width, initial-scale=1, maximum-scale=1,
        user-scalable=no" name="viewport">
    @Styles.Render("~/bower_components/font-awesome/css/font-awesome.min.
        css")
    @Styles.Render("~/bower_components/Ionicons/css/ionicons.min.css")
    @Styles.Render("~/plugins/iCheck/square/blue.css")
    @Styles.Render("~/Content/css")
</head>
<body class="hold-transition register-page">
    <div class="register-box">
        <div class="register-box-body">
            <p class="login-box-msg">注册新用户</p>
            @using (Html.BeginForm("Create", "Users", FormMethod.Post))
            {
                @Html.AntiForgeryToken()
                <div class="form-group has-feedback">
                    @Html.EditorFor(model => model.name, new { htmlAttributes =
                    new { @class = "form-control", placeholder = "用户名" } })
                    <span class="glyphicon glyphicon-user form-control-
                        feedback"></span>
                </div>
                <div class="form-group has-feedback">
                    @Html.PasswordFor(model => model.pwd, new { @class = "form-
                        control",
                    placeholder = "密码" })
                    <span class="glyphicon glyphicon-lock form-control-
                        feedback"></span>
                </div>
                <div class="form-group has-feedback">
                    @Html.PasswordFor(model => model.pwd, new { @class = "form-
                        control",
                    placeholder = "确认密码" })
                    <span class="glyphicon glyphicon-log-in form-control-
                        feedback"></span>
```

```
                    </div>
                    <div class="form-group has-feedback">
                        @Html.DropDownListFor(model => model.role, ViewBag.Roles as
                            IEnumerable<SelectListItem>, new { @class = "form-control" })
                        <span class="glyphicon glyphicon-wrench form-control-
                            feedback"></span>
                    </div>
                    <div class="row">
                        <div class="col-xs-8">
                            <div class="checkbox icheck">
                                <label>
                                    <input type="checkbox"> 我同意相关协议!
                                </label>
                            </div>
                        </div>
                        <div class="col-xs-4">
                            <button type="submit" class="btn btn-primary btn-block
                                btn-flat">
                                注册</button>
                        </div>
                    </div>
                    @Html.ActionLink("我已经有账号", "Login", "Home", null,
                        new { @class = "text-center" })
                }
            </div>
        </div>
        @Scripts.Render("~/bundles/jquery")
        @Scripts.Render("~/bundles/bootstrap")
        @Scripts.Render("~/bundles/adminlte")
        @Scripts.Render("~/plugins/iCheck/icheck.min.js")
        <script>
            $(function () {
                $('input').iCheck({
                    checkboxClass: 'icheckbox_square-blue',
                    radioClass: 'iradio_square-blue',
                    increaseArea: '20%' /* optional */
                });
            });
        </script>
    </body>
</html>
```

在注册时,需要选择注册的角色类型,下拉框绑定的数据为 ViewBag.Roles。进入注册页面的控制器代码如下。

```
public ActionResult Create()
{
    var hold = new SelectListItem { Text = "--请选择--", Value = "0", Disabled =
        true, Selected = true };
    var roleList = new List<SelectListItem>();
    roleList.Add(hold);
    var o1 = new SelectListItem();
    o1.Text = "教师";o1.Value = "教师"; o1.Selected = false;
```

```csharp
        roleList.Add(o1);
        var o2 = new SelectListItem();
        o2.Text = "学生"; o2.Value = "学生"; o2.Selected = false;
        roleList.Add(o2);
        ViewBag.Roles = roleList;
        return View();
}
```

注册提交执行的控制器代码如下。

```csharp
[HttpPost]
[ValidateAntiForgeryToken]
public ActionResult Create([Bind(Include = "Id,name,pwd,role")] User user)
{
    if (ModelState.IsValid)
    {
        db.UserSet.Add(user);
        db.SaveChanges();
        if (user.role== "教师")  //
        {
            TeacherInfo teacherInfo = new TeacherInfo();
            teacherInfo.name = user.name;
            return RedirectToAction("Create", "TeacherInfoes", teacherInfo);
        }
        else if (user.role == "学生")  //
        {
            Student student = new Student();
            student.name = user.name;
            return RedirectToAction("Create", "Students", student);
        }
    }
    return View(user);
}
```

（2）完善教师信息。

教师添加涉及的模型为 TeacherInfo，添加控制器及视图方法参考"登录"创建的过程，选择模型为 TeacherInfo，控制器名称为 TeacherInfoesController。其中生成的 Create.cshtml 可视为注册页面，参考 AdminLTE 下的 Register.html 进行修改。修改教师的 Create.cshtml 内容如下。

```html
@model ExerciseManagement.Models.TeacherInfo
@{
    Layout = null;
}
<!DOCTYPE html>
<html>
<head>
    <meta charset="utf-8">
    <meta http-equiv="X-UA-Compatible" content="IE=edge">
    <meta http-equiv="Content-Type" content="text/html; charset=utf-8" />
    <title>注册新用户</title>
    <meta content="width=device-width, initial-scale=1, maximum-scale=1,
```

```
            user-scalable=no" name="viewport">
    @Styles.Render("~/bower_components/font-awesome/css/font-awesome.min.
        css")
    @Styles.Render("~/bower_components/Ionicons/css/ionicons.min.css")
    @Styles.Render("~/plugins/iCheck/square/blue.css")
    @Styles.Render("~/Content/css")
</head>
<body class="hold-transition register-page">
    <div class="register-box">
        <div class="register-box-body">
            <p class="login-box-msg">补全教师信息</p>
            @using (Html.BeginForm("Create", "TeacherInfoes", FormMethod.Post))
            {
                @Html.AntiForgeryToken()
                <div class="form-group has-feedback">
                    @Html.EditorFor(model => model.name, new { htmlAttributes =
                    new { @class = "form-control", @readonly = "readonly" } })
                    <span class="glyphicon glyphicon-user form-control-
                        feedback"></span>
                </div>
                <div class="form-group has-feedback">
                    @Html.EditorFor(model => model.userName, new { htmlAttributes =
                    new { @class = "form-control", placeholder = "真实姓名" } })
                    <span class="glyphicon glyphicon-user form-control-
                        feedback"></span>
                </div>
                <div class="form-group has-feedback">
                    @Html.EditorFor(model => model.title, new { htmlAttributes =
                    new { @class = "form-control", placeholder = "职称" } })
                    <span class="glyphicon glyphicon-subtitles form-control-
                        feedback"></span>
                </div>
                <div class="form-group has-feedback">
                    @Html.EditorFor(model => model.email, new {
                        htmlAttributes =
                    new { @class = "form-control", placeholder = "邮箱" } })
                    <span class="glyphicon glyphicon-folder-close form-control-
                        feedback"></span>
                </div>
                <div class="form-group has-feedback">
                    @Html.EditorFor(model => model.tel, new { htmlAttributes =
                    new { @class = "form-control", placeholder = "电话" } })
                    <span class="glyphicon glyphicon-phone form-control-
                        feedback"></span>
                </div>
                <div class="form-group has-feedback">
                    @Html.EditorFor(model => model.memo, new { htmlAttributes =
                    new { @class = "form-control", placeholder = "备注" } })
                    <span class="glyphicon glyphicon-comment form-control-
                        feedback"></span>
                </div>
                <div class="row">
```

```
                    <!-- /.col -->
                    <div class="col-xs-12">
                        <button type="submit" class="btn btn-primary btn-block
                            btn-flat">
                            确定</button>
                    </div>
                </div>
            }
        </div>
    </div>
    @Scripts.Render("~/bundles/jquery")
    @Scripts.Render("~/bundles/bootstrap")
    @Scripts.Render("~/bundles/adminlte")
    @Scripts.Render("~/plugins/iCheck/icheck.min.js")
    <script>
        $(function () {
            $('input').iCheck({
                checkboxClass: 'icheckbox_square-blue',
                radioClass: 'iradio_square-blue',
                increaseArea: '20%' /* optional */
            });
        });
    </script>
</body>
</html>
```

添加教师信息的控制器代码如下。

```
[HttpPost]
[ValidateAntiForgeryToken]
public ActionResult Create([Bind(Include = "Id,name,userName,title," +
    "tel,email,state,memo")] TeacherInfo teacherInfo)
{
    if (ModelState.IsValid)
    {
        teacherInfo.state = "启用";
        db.TeacherInfoSet.Add(teacherInfo);
        db.SaveChanges();
        //弹出消息,跳转
        var info = string.Format("<script>alert('添加成功,请登录!');" +
            "location.href='{0}'</script>", Url.Action("Login","Home"));
        return Content(info, "text/html");
    }
    return View(teacherInfo);
}
```

2. 创建题目

创建题目涉及的模型为 Subject,首先添加控制器及视图,方法参考"登录"创建的过程,选择模型为 Subjects,控制器名称为 SubjectsController。

修改 Create.cshtml 内容如下。

```
@model ExerciseManagement.Models.Subject
@{
```

```
        ViewBag.Title = "Create";
        Layout = "~/Views/Shared/_LayoutPage.cshtml";
    }
    <div class="box box-primary">
        <div class="box-header with-border">
            <h3 class="box-title">创建题目</h3>
        </div>
        @using (Html.BeginForm())
        {
            @Html.AntiForgeryToken()
            <div class="box-body">
                <div class="form-group">
                    @Html.EditorFor(model => model.name, new { htmlAttributes =
                      new { @class = "form-control", placeholder = "请输入题目名称" } })
                </div>
                <div class="form-group has-feedback">
                    @Html.TextAreaFor(model => model.des,  new { rows = "20",
                        @class = "form-control", placeholder = "请输入题目描述" })
                </div>
                <div class="form-group has-feedback">
                    @Html.TextAreaFor(model => model.memo, new { @class = "form-
                        control",
                        placeholder = "请输入题目备注"   })
                </div>
            </div>
            <div class="box-footer">
                <button type="submit" class="btn btn-primary">创建</button>
                @Html.ActionLink("返回", "Index", null, new { @class =
                    "btn btn-default" })
            </div>
        }
    </div>
```

创建题目对应的控制器代码如下。

```
[HttpPost]
[ValidateAntiForgeryToken]
public ActionResult Create([Bind(Include = "Id,name,des,memo")]
Subject subject)
{
    User user = (User)Session["user"];
    if (user == null)
    {
        return RedirectToAction("Login", "Home");
    }
    if (ModelState.IsValid)
    {

        var ti = db.TeacherInfoSet.Where(t => t.name == user.name).
            FirstOrDefault();
        subject.TeacherInfo = ti;
        db.SubjectSet.Add(subject);
        db.SaveChanges();
```

```
            return RedirectToAction("Index");
        }
        return View(subject);
}
```

3. 我的题库

教师所有创建的题目都可以在"我的题库"中找到,通过"我的题库"可以完成对题库的管理及发布。

(1) 题目列表。

题目列表视图文件为 Index.cshtml,修改内容如下。

```
@model PagedList.IPagedList<ExerciseManagement.Models.Subject>
@using PagedList.Mvc;
@{
    Layout = "~/Views/Shared/_LayoutPage.cshtml"; ;
}
<div class="box">
    <div class="box-header">
        <div class="row">
            <div class="col-xs-2">
                <h3 class="box_title">题库信息</h3>
            </div>
            <div class="col-xs-10">
                @Html.ActionLink("创建", "Create")
            </div>
        </div>
    </div>
    <div class="box-body">
        <table id="example1" class="table table-bordered table-striped">
            <thead>
                <tr>
                    <th>名称</th>
                    <th>描述</th>
                    <th>备注</th>
                    <th>操作</th>
                </tr>
            </thead>
            <tbody>
                @foreach (var item in Model)
                {
                <tr>
                    <td>@Html.DisplayFor(modelItem => item.name)</td>
                    @{
                        string parameterValue = item.des.Substring(0,
                            item.des.Length > 30 ? 30 : item.des.Length)+"...";
                    }
                    <td>@Html.DisplayFor(modelItem => parameterValue)</td>
                    <td>@Html.DisplayFor(modelItem => item.memo)</td>
                    <td>
                        @Html.ActionLink("详情", "Details", new { id = item.Id }) |
                        @Html.ActionLink("编辑", "Edit", new { id = item.Id }) |
                        @Html.ActionLink("发布", "Create","Topics", item,null) |
```

```
                    @Html.ActionLink("删除", "Delete", new { id = item.Id })
                </td>
            </tr>
            }
        </tbody>
        <tfoot>
            <tr>
                <th>名称</th>
                <th>描述</th>
                <th>备注</th>
                <th>操作</th>
            </tr>
        </tfoot>
    </table>
    @Html.PagedListPager(Model, page => Url.Action("Index", new { page }))
</div>
</div>
```

题目列表控制器的代码如下。

```
public ActionResult Index(int ? page)              //教师用
{
    User user = (User)Session["user"];
    if (user == null)
    {
        return RedirectToAction("Login", "Home");
    }
    TeacherInfo teacher = db.TeacherInfoSet.Where(
        t => t.name == user.name).FirstOrDefault();
    var subjects = db.SubjectSet.Where(
        s=>s.TeacherInfo.Id==teacher.Id).OrderByDescending(s => s.Id);
    var pageNumber = page ?? 1;
    ///每页显示项目数量
    var pageSize = 10;
    ///进行分页生成 model
    IPagedList<Subject> model = subjects.
            ToPagedList(pageNumber, pageSize);
    return View(model);
}
```

由于使用了分页显示,所以使用了 IPagedList 组件。

当单击"删除"链接时的控制器代码如下。

```
public ActionResult Delete(int? id)
{
    try
    {
        Subject subject = db.SubjectSet.Find(id);
        db.SubjectSet.Remove(subject);
        db.SaveChanges();
        return RedirectToAction("Index");
    }
    catch (Exception ex)
```

```csharp
        {
            var info = string.Format("<script>alert('" +
                ex.Message + "');location.href='{0}'</script>",
                Url.Action("Index"));
            return Content(info, "text/html");
        }
    }
}
```

（2）题目详情。

题目详情的视图文件内容如下。

```cshtml
@model ExerciseManagement.Models.Subject
@{
    ViewBag.Title = "Details";
    Layout = "~/Views/Shared/_LayoutPage.cshtml";
}
<div class="box">
    <div class="box-header with-border">
        <h3 class="box-title">课目详情</h3>
    </div>
    <div class="box-body">
        <div class="form-group">
            <label class="col-sm-2 control-label">名称</label>
            @Html.DisplayFor(model => model.name, new { @class = "form-
                control" })
        </div>
            <div class="row form-group">
                <label class="col-sm-2 control-label">
                    描述
                </label>
                <div class="col-sm-10 ">
                    @Html.DisplayFor(model => model.des, new { @class = "form-
                        control" })
                </div>
            </div>
        <div class="form-group">
            <label class="col-sm-2 control-label">备注</label>
            @Html.DisplayFor(model => model.memo, new { @class = "form-
                control" })
        </div>
    </div>
    <div class="box-footer">
        @Html.ActionLink("返回", "Index", null, new { @class = "btn btn-
            primary" })
        @Html.ActionLink("编辑", "Edit", new {
    id = Model.Id },new { @class = "btn btn-default" })
    </div>
</div>
```

对应的控制器代码如下。

```csharp
public ActionResult Details(int? id)
{
```

```
        if (id == null)
        {
            return new HttpStatusCodeResult(HttpStatusCode.BadRequest);
        }
        Subject subject = db.SubjectSet.Find(id);
        if (subject == null)
        {
            return HttpNotFound();
        }
        return View(subject);
    }
```

(3) 题目编辑。

题目编辑的视图文件内容如下。

```
@model ExerciseManagement.Models.Subject
@{
    ViewBag.Title = "Edit";
    Layout = "~/Views/Shared/_LayoutPage.cshtml";
}
<div class="box box-primary">
    <div class="box-header with-border">
        <h3 class="box-title">编辑题目</h3>
    </div>
    @using (Html.BeginForm())
    {
        @Html.AntiForgeryToken()
        @Html.HiddenFor(model => model.Id)
        <div class="box-body">
            <div class="form-group">
                @Html.EditorFor(model => model.name, new { htmlAttributes = new
    { @class = "form-control", placeholder = "请输入题目名称" } })
            </div>
            <div class="form-group has-feedback">
                @Html.TextAreaFor(model => model.des, new { rows = "20",
      @class = "form-control", placeholder = "请输入题目描述" })
            </div>
            <div class="form-group has-feedback">
                @Html.TextAreaFor(model => model.memo, new {
      @class = "form-control", placeholder = "请输入题目备注" })
            </div>
        </div>
        <div class="box-footer">
            <button type="submit" class="btn btn-primary">确定</button>
            @Html.ActionLink("返回", "Index", null, new { @class = "btn btn-default" })
        </div>
    }
</div>
```

编辑页面进入时的控制器代码如下。

```
public ActionResult Edit(int? id)
```

```
{
    if (id == null)
    {
        return new HttpStatusCodeResult(HttpStatusCode.BadRequest);
    }
    Subject subject = db.SubjectSet.Find(id);
    if (subject == null)
    {
        return HttpNotFound();
    }
    return View(subject);
}
```

编辑页面修改后提交的控制器代码如下。

```
[HttpPost]
[ValidateAntiForgeryToken]
public ActionResult Edit([Bind(Include = "Id,name,des,memo")] Subject subject)
{
    if (ModelState.IsValid)
    {
        db.Entry(subject).State = EntityState.Modified;
        db.SaveChanges();
        return RedirectToAction("Index");
    }
    return View(subject);
}
```

(4) 题目发布。

题目发布的视图文件内容如下。

```
@using MvcCheckBoxList.Model
@model ExerciseManagement.Models.TopicVm
@{
    ViewBag.Title = "Create";
    Layout = "~/Views/Shared/_LayoutPage.cshtml";
}
<div class="box box-primary">
    <div class="box-header with-border">
        <h3 class="box-title">发布课题</h3>
    </div>
    @using (Html.BeginForm())
    {
        @Html.AntiForgeryToken()
        <div class="box-body">
            <div class="form-group">
                @Html.LabelFor(model => model.topic.name, "题目名称")
                @Html.EditorFor(model => model.topic.name, new {
                    htmlAttributes =
                    new { @class = "form-control", @readonly = "readonly" } })
            </div>
            <div class="form-group">
                @Html.LabelFor(model => model.topic.desc, "题目描述")
```

```
            @Html.TextAreaFor(model => model.topic.desc, new { rows = "10",
          @class = "form-control", @readonly = "readonly" })
        </div>
        <div class="form-group">
            @Html.LabelFor(model => model.topic.memo, "题目备注")
            @Html.TextAreaFor(model => model.topic.memo, new {
          @class = "form-control", @readonly = "readonly" })
        </div>
        <div class="form-group">
            @Html.LabelFor(model => model.topic.groupsMax, "最大组数")
            @Html.EditorFor(model => model.topic.groupsMax, new {
                htmlAttributes =
          new { @class = "form-control", @type = "number", @Value = "1" } })
        </div>
        <div class="form-group">
            @Html.LabelFor(model => model.topic.stusMax, "每组最多人数")
            @Html.EditorFor(model => model.topic.stusMax, new {
                htmlAttributes =
          new { @class = "form-control", @type = "number", @Value = "3" } })
        </div>
        <div class="form-group">
            @Html.LabelFor(model => model.topic.password, "课题密码")
            @Html.EditorFor(model => model.topic.password, new {
                htmlAttributes =
          new { @class = "form-control", placeholder = "请输入课题密码,可为空" } })
        </div>
        <div class="form-group has-feedback">
            @Html.LabelFor(model => model.topic.grade, "课题适用于年级")
            @Html.DropDownListFor(model => model.topic.grade, ViewBag.
                Grades as
          IEnumerable<SelectListItem>, new { @class = "form-control" })
        </div>
        <div class="form-group has-feedback">
            @Html.LabelFor(model => model.selectedLanguagesIds, "选择语言");
            <ul style="list-style: none;">
                @foreach (var a in Model.allLanguages)
                {
                    <li class="checkbox">
                        @if (Model.selectedLanguagesIds.Contains(a.Id))
                        {
                            <label>
                                <input type="checkbox" name=
                                    "selectedLanguagesIds"
                                       value="@a.Id" id="@a.Id" checked=
                                           "checked" />
                                @a.name
                            </label>
                        }
                        else
                        {
                            <label>
                                <input type="checkbox" name=
                                    "selectedLanguagesIds"
```

```
                                    value="@a.Id" id="@a.Id" />
                                @a.name
                            </label>
                        }
                    </li>
                }
            </ul>
        </div>
        <div class="form-group has-feedback">
            @Html.LabelFor(model => model.selectedMajarsIds, "选择专业");
            <ul style="list-style:none;">
                @foreach (var a in Model.allMajars)
                {
                    <li class="checkbox">
                        @if (Model.selectedMajarsIds.Contains(a.Id))
                        {
                            <label>
                                <input type="checkbox" name=
                                    "selectedMajarsIds"
                                        value="@a.Id" id="@a.Id" checked=
                                            "checked" />
                                @a.name
                            </label>
                        }
                        else
                        {
                            <label>
                                <input type="checkbox" name=
                                    "selectedMajarsIds"
                                        value="@a.Id" id="@a.Id" />
                                @a.name
                            </label>
                        }
                    </li>
                }
            </ul>
        </div>
    </div>
    <div class="box-footer">
        <button type="submit" class="btn btn-primary">提交</button>
        @Html.ActionLink("返回", "Index", "Subjects", null,
          new { @class = "btn btn-default" })
    </div>
    }
</div>
```

由于视图文件涉及的数据较多，实体模型 Topic 无法满足需要，定义 TopicVm 虚拟实体模型。TopicVm 类的定义如下。

```
public class TopicVm
{
    public Topic topic { get; set; }
    public List<Language> allLanguages { get; set; }
```

```
    public List<Language> topicLanguages { get; set; }
    public int[] selectedLanguagesIds { get; set; }
    public string languageNames { get; set; }
    public List<Major> allMajars { get; set; }
    public List<Major> topicMajars { get; set; }
    public int[] selectedMajarsIds { get; set; }
    public string majorNames { get; set; }
    public string isFull { get; set; }
    public int applyGroupsCount { get; set; }
    public int conformGroupsCount { get; set; }
}
```

在进入发布页面时,相应的控制器代码需要准备模型数据,代码如下。

```
public ActionResult Create(Subject  subject)
{
    //准备年级数据
    var holdGrade = new SelectListItem { Text = "--请选择年级--",
        Value = "0", Disabled = true, Selected = true };
    var grades = new List<SelectListItem>();
    grades.Add(holdGrade);
    var gs = db.GradeSet.ToList();
    foreach (Grade c in gs)
    {
        SelectListItem item = new SelectListItem();
        item.Text = c.name;
        item.Value = c.name;
        item.Selected = false;
        grades.Add(item);
    }
    ViewBag.Grades = grades;
    TopicVm vm = new TopicVm();
    vm.topic = new Topic();
    vm.topic.name = subject.name;
    vm.topic.desc = subject.des;
    vm.topic.memo = subject.memo;
    //准备语言数据
    vm.allLanguages = db.LanguageSet.ToList();
    vm.selectedLanguagesIds = new int[] { };
    vm.topicLanguages = new List<Language>();
    //准备专业数据
    vm.allMajars = db.MajorSet.ToList();
    vm.selectedMajarsIds = new int[] { };
    vm.topicMajars = new List<Major>();
    return View(vm);
}
```

发布题目的控制器代码如下。

```
[HttpPost]
[ValidateAntiForgeryToken]
public ActionResult Create( TopicVm vm)
{
    User user = (User)Session["user"];
```

```
        if(user==null)
        {
            return RedirectToAction("Login", "Home");
        }
        if (ModelState.IsValid)
        {
            Topic topic = vm.topic;
            string ls = "";
            string ms = "";
            List<Language> llist = db.LanguageSet.ToList();
            foreach(var l in llist)
            {
                if (vm.selectedLanguagesIds.Contains(l.Id))
                {
                    ls += l.Id.ToString() + "|";
                }
            }
            topic.lanuages = ls;
            List<Major> mlist = db.MajorSet.ToList();
            foreach(var m in mlist)
            {
                if (vm.selectedMajarsIds.Contains(m.Id))
                {
                    ms += m.Id.ToString()+"|";
                }
            }
            TeacherInfo teacher = db.TeacherInfoSet.Where(
                t => t.name == user.name).FirstOrDefault();
            topic.TeacherInfo = teacher;
            topic.majors = ms;
            topic.suggest = "";
            if (topic.password == null)
            {
                topic.password = "";
            }
            topic.hasApproved = "是";
            topic.isFull = "否";
            db.TopicSet.Add(topic);
            db.SaveChanges();
            return RedirectToAction("Index","Subjects",null);
        }
        return View(vm);
}
```

视图传递过来的是 TopicVm 对象,存入数据库时必须重新封装成 Topic 对象进行存储。

4. 我的课题

"我的课题"列表视图文件内容如下。

```
@model PagedList.IPagedList<ExerciseManagement.Models.Topic>
@using PagedList.Mvc;
@{
```

```html
    ViewBag.Title = "Index";
    Layout = "~/Views/Shared/_LayoutPage.cshtml";
}
<div class="box">
    <div class="box-header">
        <div class="row">
            <div class="col-xs-2">
                <h3 class="box-title">我的课题</h3>
            </div>
        </div>
    </div>
    <div class="box-body">
        <table id="example1" class="table table-bordered table-striped">
            <thead>
                <tr>
                    <th>课题名称</th>
                    <th>设置年级</th>
                    <th>是否已满</th>
                    <th>操作</th>
                </tr>
            </thead>
            <tbody>
                @foreach (var item in Model)
                {
                <tr>
                    <td>@Html.DisplayFor(modelItem => item.name)</td>
                    <td>@Html.DisplayFor(modelItem => item.grade)</td>
                    <td>@Html.DisplayFor(modelItem => item.isFull)</td>
                    <td>
                        @Html.ActionLink("课题详情", "DetailsTeacher",
                        new { id = item.Id })
                    </td>
                </tr>
                }
            </tbody>
            <tfoot>
                <tr>
                    <th>课题名称</th>
                    <th>设置年级</th>
                    <th>是否已满</th>
                    <th>操作</th>
                </tr>
            </tfoot>
        </table>
        @Html.PagedListPager(Model, page => Url.Action("Index",
        new { page }))
    </div>
</div>
```

对应的控制器代码如下。

```
public ActionResult Index(int? page)
{
```

```
User user = (User)Session["user"];
if (user == null)
{
    return RedirectToAction("Login", "Home");
}
TeacherInfo tea = db.TeacherInfoSet.Where(t => t.name == user.name).
    FirstOrDefault();
List<Topic> list = db.TopicSet.Where(t => t.TeacherInfo.Id == tea.Id).
    ToList();
var pageNumber = page ?? 1;
///每页显示项目数量
var pageSize = 10;
///进行分页生成model
IPagedList<Topic> model = list.ToPagedList(pageNumber, pageSize);
return View(model);
}
```

5. 课题审批

当一组学生申请某个课题后,需要指导老师进行审批,审批的视图文件内容如下。

```
@model PagedList.IPagedList<ExerciseManagement.Models.GroupVm>
@using PagedList.Mvc;
@{
    ViewBag.Title = "Confirm";
    Layout = "~/Views/Shared/_LayoutPage.cshtml";
}
<div class="box">
    <div class="box-header">
        <div class="row">
            <div class="col-xs-2">
                <h3 class="box-title">申报处理</h3>
            </div>
            <div class="col-xs-10">
                @Html.ActionLink("导出我的学生", "ExportStudents", "Groups")
            </div>
        </div>
    </div>
    <div class="box-body">
        <table id="example1" class="table table-bordered table-striped">
            <thead>
                <tr>
                    <th>课题名称</th>
                    <th>组长</th>
                    <th>组员</th>
                    <th>成员已满</th>
                    <th>状态</th>
                    <th>操作</th>
                </tr>
            </thead>
            <tbody>
                @foreach (var item in Model)
                {
                    <tr>
```

```html
                        <td>@Html.DisplayFor(modelItem => item.TopicName)</td>
                        <td>@Html.DisplayFor(modelItem => item.Leader)</td>
                        <td>@Html.DisplayFor(modelItem => item.Members)</td>
                        <td>@Html.DisplayFor(modelItem => item.IsFull)</td>
                        <td>@Html.DisplayFor(modelItem => item.IsConfirm)</td>
                        <td>
                            @if (item.IsConfirm == "申请中" && item.IsFull == "是")
                            {
                                @Html.ActionLink("同意", "AgreeApply", new { id = item.GroupId })
                                @Html.Label("|")
                                @Html.ActionLink("驳回", "DisAgreeApply", new { id = item.GroupId })
                            }
                        </td>
                    </tr>
                }
            </tbody>
            <tfoot>
                <tr>
                    <th>课题名称</th>
                    <th>组长</th>
                    <th>组员</th>
                    <th>成员已满</th>
                    <th>状态</th>
                    <th>操作</th>
                </tr>
            </tfoot>
        </table>
        @Html.PagedListPager(Model, page => Url.Action("Confirm", new { page }))
    </div>
</div>
```

所在的实体模型为 GroupVm，GroupVm 类定义如下。

```csharp
public class GroupVm
{
    public int GroupId { get; set; }
    public int TopicId { get; set; }
    public string Teacher { set; get; }
    public string TopicName { get; set; }
    public string Leader { set; get; }
    public string Members { set; get; }
    public string IsFull { set; get; }
    public string IsConfirm { set; get; }
}
```

课题列表页面对应的控制器代码如下。

```csharp
public ActionResult Confirm(int ? page)
{
    List<GroupVm> listGV = new List<GroupVm>();
    User user = (User)Session["user"];
    if (user == null)
```

```
{
    return RedirectToAction("Login", "Home");
}
TeacherInfo teacher = db.TeacherInfoSet.Where(t => t.name == user.name)
    .FirstOrDefault();
List<Group> listGroup = db.GroupSet.Where(g => g.Topic.TeacherInfo.Id ==
teacher.Id).OrderByDescending(g=>g.Id).ToList();
foreach(Group gg in listGroup)
{
    GroupVm gv = new GroupVm();
    gv.TopicName = gg.Topic.name;
    gv.Leader = gg.leader;
    gv.GroupId = gg.Id;
    gv.IsConfirm = gg.isConfirm;
    gv.IsFull = gg.isFull;
    List<GroupStu> listGS = db.GroupStuSet.Where(
        gs => gs.Group.Id == gg.Id).ToList();
    foreach(GroupStu gs in listGS)
    {
        if (gs.Student.userName != gg.leader)
        {
            gv.Members += gs.Student.userName + ";";
        }
    }
    listGV.Add(gv);
}
var pageNumber = page ?? 1;
///每页显示项目数量
var pageSize = 10;
///进行分页生成model
IPagedList<GroupVm> model = listGV.ToPagedList(pageNumber, pageSize);
return View(model);
}
```

课题审批对应的同意处理代码如下。

```
public ActionResult AgreeApply(int ? id)
{
    Group group = db.GroupSet.Find(id);
    group.isConfirm = "同意";
    db.SaveChanges();
    var info = string.Format("<script>alert('通过成功！');" +
        "location.href='{0}'</script>", Url.Action("Confirm", "Groups"));
    return Content(info, "text/html");
}
```

课题审批对应的驳回处理代码如下。

```
public ActionResult DisAgreeApply(int? id)
{
    Group group = db.GroupSet.Find(id);
    group.isConfirm = "驳回";
    group.Topic.isFull = "否";
    db.SaveChanges();
```

```
    var info = string.Format("<script>alert('驳回成功！');" +
        "location.href='{0}'</script>", Url.Action("Confirm", "Groups"));
    return Content(info, "text/html");
}
```

如果把选报的所有学生下载，单击"导出我的学生"，相应处理代码如下。

```
public ActionResult ExportStudents()
{
    //课题名称,学生名称,所在班级
    User user = (User)Session["user"];
    if (user == null)
    {
        return RedirectToAction("Login", "Home");
    }
    List<Student> stus = new List<Student>();
    List<string> subName = new List<string>();
    List<string> teaName = new List<string>();
    TeacherInfo teacher = db.TeacherInfoSet.Where(t => t.name == user.name).
        FirstOrDefault();
    //选报该老师有哪些组
    List<Group> list = db.GroupSet.Where(gs => gs.Topic.TeacherInfo.Id
      == teacher.Id && gs.isConfirm=="同意").ToList();
    foreach(Group g in list)
    {
        //该组有哪些学生
        List<GroupStu> gs = db.GroupStuSet.Where(gss => gss.Group.Id == g.Id).
            ToList();
        foreach(GroupStu a in gs)
        {
            stus.Add(a.Student);
            subName.Add(g.Topic.name);
            teaName.Add(g.Topic.TeacherInfo.userName);
        }
    }
    XSSFWorkbook excelBook = new XSSFWorkbook();              //创建工作簿 Excel
    ISheet sheet1 = excelBook.CreateSheet("学生选报情况");
                                                //为工作簿创建工作表并命名
    //编写工作表 (1)表头 (2)数据:listStudent
    NPOI.SS.UserModel.IRow row1 = sheet1.CreateRow(0);        //创建第一行
    row1.CreateCell(0).SetCellValue("学生姓名");
    row1.CreateCell(1).SetCellValue("所在班级");
    row1.CreateCell(2).SetCellValue("课题名称");
    row1.CreateCell(3).SetCellValue("指导老师");
    for (int i = 0; i < stus.Count(); i++)
    {
        IRow rowTemp = sheet1.CreateRow(i + 1);
        rowTemp.CreateCell(0).SetCellValue(stus[i].userName);
        rowTemp.CreateCell(1).SetCellValue(stus[i].Class.name);
        rowTemp.CreateCell(2).SetCellValue(subName[i]);
        rowTemp.CreateCell(3).SetCellValue(teaName[i]);
    }
    var fileName = "学生选报情况" + ".xlsx";                    //文件名
```

```
//将 Excel 表格转换为流,输出
NpoiMemoryStream bookStream = new NpoiMemoryStream();        //创建文件流
bookStream.AllowClose = false;
excelBook.Write(bookStream);
bookStream.Flush();
bookStream.Seek(0, SeekOrigin.Begin);
bookStream.AllowClose = true;
//最后以文件形式返回
return File(bookStream, "application/vnd.ms-excel", fileName);
}
```

6. 账户详情

账户详情比较简单,视图文件内容如下。

```
@model ExerciseManagement.Models.TeacherInfo
@{
    ViewBag.Title = "Details";
    Layout = "~/Views/Shared/_LayoutPage.cshtml";
}
<div class="box">
    <div class="box-header with-border">
        <h3 class="box-title">教师详情</h3>
    </div>
    <div class=" box-body">
        <div class="form-group">
            <label class="col-sm-2  control-label">账户</label>
            @Html.DisplayFor(model => model.name, new { @class = "form-
                control" })
        </div>
        <div class="form-group">
            <label class="col-sm-2 control-label">姓名</label>
            @Html.DisplayFor(model => model.userName, new { @class = "form-
                control" })
        </div>
        <div class="form-group">
            <label class="col-sm-2  control-label">职称</label>
            @Html.DisplayFor(model => model.title, new { @class = "form-
                control" })
        </div>
        <div class="form-group">
            <label class="col-sm-2  control-label">电话</label>
            @Html.DisplayFor(model => model.tel, new { @class = "form-
                control" })
        </div>
        <div class="form-group">
            <label class="col-sm-2  control-label">邮箱</label>
            @Html.DisplayFor(model => model.email, new { @class = "form-
                control" })
        </div>
        <div class="form-group">
            <label class="col-sm-2 control-label">备注</label>
            @Html.DisplayFor(model => model.memo, new { @class = "form-
                control" })
```

```
        </div>
    </div>
</div>
```

控制器代码如下。

```csharp
public ActionResult Details()
{
    User user = ((User)(Session["user"]));
    if (user == null)
    {
        return RedirectToAction("Login", "Homne");
    }
    string name = user.name;
    TeacherInfo teacherInfo = db.TeacherInfoSet.Where(
        t => t.name == name).FirstOrDefault();
    if (teacherInfo == null)
    {
        return HttpNotFound();
    }
    return View(teacherInfo);
}
```

9.5.5 学生模块实现

1. 课题查询

学生在选报课题时先进行课题的查询,查询出符合学生本人专业的、可以选报的课题。课题查询的视图文件内容如下。

```
@model PagedList.IPagedList<ExerciseManagement.Models.TopicVm>
@using PagedList.Mvc;
@{
    ViewBag.Title = "Index";
    Layout = "~/Views/Shared/_LayoutPage.cshtml";
}
<div class="box">
    <div class="box-header">
        <div class="row">
            <div class="col-xs-2">
                <h3 class="box-title">课题列表</h3>
            </div>
        </div>
    </div>
    <div class="box-body">
        <table id="example1" class="table table-bordered table-striped">
            <thead>
                <tr>
                    <th>课题名称</th>
                    <th>指导老师</th>
                    <th>适合专业</th>
                    <th>适合语言</th>
                    <th>组数已满</th>
```

```html
            <th>人数已满</th>
            <th>操作</th>
        </tr>
    </thead>
    <tbody>
        @foreach (var item in Model)
        {
            <tr>
                <td>@Html.DisplayFor(modelItem => item.topic.name)</td>
                <td>@Html.DisplayFor(modelItem => item.topic.TeacherInfo.
                    userName)</td>
                <td>@Html.DisplayFor(modelItem => item.majorNames)</td>
                <td>@Html.DisplayFor(modelItem => item.languageNames)</td>
                <td>@Html.DisplayFor(modelItem => item.topic.isFull)</td>
                <td>@Html.DisplayFor(modelItem => item.isFull)</td>
                <td>
                    @Html.ActionLink("详情", "DetailsStudent", new { id =
                        item.topic.Id })
                    @if (!ViewBag.isApply)
                    {
                        @Html.Label("|")
                        @Html.ActionLink("组员选报", "ApplyForMember", new {
                        id = item.topic.Id })
                        if (item.topic.isFull == "否")
                        {
                            @Html.Label("|")
                            @Html.ActionLink("组长选报", "ApplyForLeader",
                                new {
                                    id = item.topic.Id })
                        }
                    }
                </td>
            </tr>
        }
    </tbody>
    <tfoot>
        <tr>
            <th>课题名称</th>
            <th>指导老师</th>
            <th>适合专业</th>
            <th>适合语言</th>
            <th>组数已满</th>
            <th>人数已满</th>
            <th>操作</th>
        </tr>
    </tfoot>
</table>
@Html.PagedListPager(Model, page => Url.Action("Index", new { page }))
</div>
</div>
```

对应学生查询到的课题列表控制器代码如下。

```csharp
public ActionResult IndexStudent(int? page)
{
    User user = (User)Session["user"];
    if (user == null)
    {
        return RedirectToAction("Login", "Home");
    }
    Student student = db.StudentSet.Where(s => s.name ==
        user.name).FirstOrDefault();
    //检测该生是否已经申报
    bool isApply = db.GroupStuSet.Where(gs => gs.Student.Id == student.Id
        &&gs.Group.isConfirm!="驳回").Count()>0;
    ViewBag.isApply = isApply;
    List<Topic> listTopic = db.TopicSet.Where(t=> t.grade==student.Class.
        grade).ToList();
    List<TopicVm> listTV = new List<TopicVm>();
    foreach(var topic in listTopic)
    {
        if ( topic.majors.Split('|').Contains(student.Class.Major.Id.ToString()))
        {
            TopicVm vm = new TopicVm();
            vm.topic = topic;
            if (topic.isFull == "否")                //都没满
            {
                vm.majorNames = MajorIdsToNames(topic.majors);
                vm.languageNames = LanIdsToNames(topic.lanuages);
                vm.isFull = "否";
                listTV.Add(vm);
            }
            else                                     //组已满,人未满
            {
                int count = db.GroupSet.Where(g => g.Topic.Id == topic.Id &&
                g.isFull == "是" &&g.isConfirm!="驳回").Count();
                if (topic.groupsMax > count)
                {
                    vm.majorNames = MajorIdsToNames(topic.majors);
                    vm.languageNames = LanIdsToNames(topic.lanuages);
                    vm.isFull = "否";
                    listTV.Add(vm);
                }
            }
        }
    }
    var pageNumber = page ?? 1;
    ///每页显示项目数量
    var pageSize = 10;
    ///进行分页生成 model
    IPagedList<TopicVm> model = listTV.ToPagedList(pageNumber, pageSize);
    return View(model);
}
```

对于该生可以查看课题详情,如果没有选报,可以以组长身份建立一组进行选报,对应的视图文件内容如下。

```
@model ExerciseManagement.Models.Group
@{
    ViewBag.Title = "Apply";
    Layout = "~/Views/Shared/_LayoutPage.cshtml";
}
<div class="box box-primary">
    <div class="box-header with-border">
        <h3 class="box-title">申报课题</h3>
    </div>
    @using (Html.BeginForm("ApplyForLeader", "Groups", FormMethod.Post))
    {
        @Html.AntiForgeryToken()
        <div class="box-body">
    @Html.HiddenFor(model => model.Topic.Id)
    <div class="form-group">
        @Html.LabelFor(model => model.Topic.name, "课题名称")
        @Html.EditorFor(model => model.Topic.name, new { htmlAttributes = new {
      @class = "form-control", @readonly = "readonly" } })
    </div>
    <div class="form-group">
        @Html.LabelFor(model => model.isFull, "课题密码")
        @Html.EditorFor(model => model.isFull, new { htmlAttributes = new {
      @class = "form-control", placeholder = "请输入本课题密码,可为空" } })
    </div>
    <div class="form-group has-feedback">
        @Html.LabelFor(model => model.password, "本组密码")
        @Html.EditorFor(model => model.password, new { htmlAttributes = new {
      @class = "form-control", placeholder = "请设置本小组密码,可为空" } })
    </div>
</div>
        <div class="box-footer">
            <button type="submit" class="btn btn-primary">提交</button>
            @Html.ActionLink("返回", "IndexStudent", "Topics", null, new {
              @class = "btn btn-default" })
        </div>
    }
</div>
```

对应的控制器代码如下。

```
public ActionResult ApplyForLeader(int ? id)
{
    Topic topic = db.TopicSet.Find(id);
    Group group = new Group();
    group.Topic = topic;
    return View(group);
}
```

当需要提交时对应的控制器代码如下。

```
[HttpPost]
[ValidateAntiForgeryToken]
public ActionResult ApplyForLeader( Group group)
{
```

```csharp
if (ModelState.IsValid)
{
    User user = ((User)Session["user"]);
    if (user == null)
    {
        return RedirectToAction("Login","Home");
    }
    string name = user.name;
    string passwd = group.isFull;                      //isFull 为借用
    //添加 Group 表
    Topic t = db.TopicSet.Find(group.Topic.Id);
    if (passwd == t.password    )                      //密码正确
    {
        group.Topic = t;
        int stusMax = t.stusMax;
        if (stusMax == 1)
        {
            group.isFull = "是";
        }
        else
        {
            group.isFull = "否";
        }
        group.isConfirm = "申请中";

        Student leader = db.StudentSet.Where(ss => ss.name == name).
            FirstOrDefault();
        group.leader = leader.userName;
        //groupstu
        db.GroupSet.Add(group);
        db.SaveChanges();
        //添加 GroupStu 表
        GroupStu gs = new GroupStu();
        gs.Group = group;
        gs.Student = leader;
        db.GroupStuSet.Add(gs);
        db.SaveChanges();
        //修改 Topic 表
        int groupCount = db.GroupSet.Where(g => g.Topic.Id
        == group.Topic.Id &&g.isConfirm!="驳回").Count();
        if (groupCount >= group.Topic.groupsMax)
        {
            group.Topic.isFull = "是";
            db.SaveChanges();
        }
        return RedirectToAction("MyApply");             //回到我的申报
    }
    else                                                //密码错误
    {
        var info = string.Format("<script>alert('密码错误!');" +
            "location.href='{0}'</script>", Url.Action("IndexStudent",
                "Topics"));
        return Content(info, "text/html");
```

```
            }
        }
        return View(group);
    }
```

该生如果以组员的身份进行选报,对应的视图文件内容如下。

```
@model ExerciseManagement.Models.Group
@{
    ViewBag.Title = "Apply";
    Layout = "~/Views/Shared/_LayoutPage.cshtml";
}
<div class="box box-primary">
    <div class="box-header with-border">
        <h3 class="box-title">申报课题</h3>
    </div>
    @using (Html.BeginForm("ApplyForMember", "Groups", FormMethod.Post))
    {
        @Html.AntiForgeryToken()
    <div class="box-body">
    @Html.HiddenFor(model => model.Topic.Id)
    <div class="form-group">
        @Html.LabelFor(model => model.Topic.name, "课题名称")
        @Html.EditorFor(model => model.Topic.name, new { htmlAttributes =
      new { @class = "form-control", @readonly = "readonly" } })
    </div>
    <div class="form-group has-feedback">
        @Html.Label("选择申报组")
        @Html.DropDownListFor(model => model.leader, ViewBag.Leaders as
      IEnumerable<SelectListItem>, new { @class = "form-control" })
    </div>
    <div class="form-group has-feedback">
        @Html.Label("输入本组密码")
        @Html.EditorFor(model => model.isFull, new { htmlAttributes = new {
        @class = "form-control", placeholder = "请设置本小组密码,可为空" } })
    </div>
</div>
        <div class="box-footer">
            <button type="submit" class="btn btn-primary">提交</button>
            @Html.ActionLink("返回", "IndexStudent", "Topics",
          null, new { @class = "btn btn-default" })
        </div>
    }
</div>
```

进行选报页面的控制器代码如下。

```
public ActionResult ApplyForMember(int? id)
{
    Topic topic = db.TopicSet.Find(id);
    Group group = new Group();
    group.Topic = topic;
    var holdLeader = new SelectListItem { Text = "--请选择组长--",
        Value = "0", Disabled = true, Selected = true };
```

```csharp
        var leads = new List<SelectListItem>();
        leads.Add(holdLeader);
        var gs = db.GroupSet.Where(g=>g.Topic.Id==id &&
        g.isConfirm=="申请中").ToList();
        foreach (Group g in gs)
        {
            SelectListItem item = new SelectListItem();
            item.Text = g.leader;
            item.Value = g.leader;
            item.Selected = false;
            leads.Add(item);
        }
        ViewBag.Leaders = leads;
        return View(group);
}
```

以组员身份选报提交对应的控制器代码如下。

```csharp
[HttpPost]
[ValidateAntiForgeryToken]
public ActionResult ApplyForMember(Group group)
{
    User user = ((User)Session["user"]);
    if (user == null)
    {
        return RedirectToAction("Login","Home");
    }
    if (ModelState.IsValid)
    {
        string passwd = group.isFull;                        //isFull 为本组密码
        Topic t = db.TopicSet.Find(group.Topic.Id);
        string leader = group.leader;
        group = db.GroupSet.Where(g => g.leader == leader && g.Topic.Id ==
        t.Id &&g.isConfirm=="申请中").FirstOrDefault();
        //添加 Group 表
        if (passwd == group.password && group.isFull=="否")   //密码正确
        {
            int count = db.GroupStuSet.Where(gg => gg.Group.Id == group.Id).
                Count();
            if (count == (t.stusMax - 1))
            {
                group.isFull = "是";
            }
            else
            {
                group.isFull = "否";
            }
            db.SaveChanges();
            //添加 GroupStu 表
            GroupStu gs = new GroupStu();
            gs.Group = group;
            string name = user.name;
            Student student = db.StudentSet.Where(ss => ss.name == name).
```

```
                FirstOrDefault();
            gs.Student = db.StudentSet.Where(s => s.Id == student.Id).
                FirstOrDefault();
            db.GroupStuSet.Add(gs);
            db.SaveChanges();
            return RedirectToAction("MyApply");              //回到我的申报
        }
        else                                                  //密码错误
        {
            //弹出消息,跳转
            var info = string.Format("<script>alert('密码错误或本组已满！');" +
                "location.href='{0}'</script>", Url.Action("IndexStudent",
                    "Topics"));
            return Content(info, "text/html");
        }
    }
    return View(group);
}
```

2. 我的选报

通过"我的选报"可以查看历史记录,包括成功的选报。对应的视图文件内容如下。

```
@model PagedList.IPagedList<ExerciseManagement.Models.GroupVm>
@using PagedList.Mvc;
@{
    ViewBag.Title = "View";
    Layout = "~/Views/Shared/_LayoutPage.cshtml";
}
<div class="box">
    <div class="box-header">
        <div class="row">
            <div class="col-xs-2">
                <h3 class="box-title">课题列表</h3>
            </div>
        </div>
    </div>
    <div class="box-body">
        <table id="example1" class="table table-bordered table-striped">
            <thead>
                <tr>
                    <th>课题名称</th>
                    <th>指导老师</th>
                    <th>成员</th>
                    <th>状态</th>
                </tr>
            </thead>
            <tbody>
                @foreach (var item in Model)
                {
                    <tr>
                        <td>@Html.DisplayFor(modelItem => item.TopicName)</td>
                        <td>@Html.DisplayFor(modelItem => item.Teacher)</td>
                        <td>@Html.DisplayFor(modelItem => item.Members)</td>
```

```html
                        <td>@Html.DisplayFor(modelItem => item.IsConfirm)</td>
                    </tr>
                }
            </tbody>
            <tfoot>
                <tr>
                    <th>课题名称</th>
                    <th>指导老师</th>
                    <th>成员</th>
                    <th>状态</th>
                </tr>
            </tfoot>
        </table>
        @Html.PagedListPager(Model, page => Url.Action("Index", new { page }))
    </div>
</div>
```

对应的控制器代码如下。

```csharp
public ActionResult MyApply(int ? page)
{
    User user = ((User)Session["user"]);
    if (user == null)
    {
        return RedirectToAction("Login", "Home");
    }
    string name = user.name;
    Student student = db.StudentSet.Where(s => s.name == name).FirstOrDefault();
    List< GroupStu> listGS = db.GroupStuSet.Where(gss => gss.Student.Id == student.Id).OrderByDescending(g=>g.Id).ToList();
    if (listGS.Count >0)
    {
        List<GroupVm> listGV = new List<GroupVm>();
        foreach( var gs in listGS)
        {
            GroupVm vm = new GroupVm();
            vm.TopicName = gs.Group.Topic.name;
            vm.Teacher = gs.Group.Topic.TeacherInfo.userName;
            vm.IsConfirm = gs.Group.isConfirm;
            List<GroupStu> listGS2 = db.GroupStuSet.Where(gs3 =>
            gs3.Group.Id == gs.Group.Id).ToList();
            foreach (GroupStu gs2 in listGS2)
            {
                vm.Members += gs2.Student.userName + ";";
            }
            listGV.Add(vm);
        }
        var pageNumber = page ?? 1;
        ///每页显示项目数量
        var pageSize = 10;
        ///进行分页生成 model
        IPagedList<GroupVm> model = listGV.ToPagedList(pageNumber, pageSize);
        return View(model);
```

```
    }
    else
    {
        var info = string.Format("<script>alert('没有申报记录！');" +
            "location.href='{0}'</script>", Url.Action("IndexStudent",
"Topics"));
        return Content(info, "text/html");
    }
}
```

9.6 系统测试

本书只给出系统功能测试的用例描述。功能测试用例主要是根据系统需求文档中功能需求部分的内容进行设计，用到的测试方法主要是等价类划分、边界值分析、错误推测、场景法等，功能测试用例提供测试人员执行功能测试的依据，为测试报告中功能测试部分提供支撑。

在本书中，功能测试用例通过文档的形式进行展现，在实际过程中可以使用相关的支撑管理工具，从而更好地管理测试用例的更新、版本控制等工作。限于篇幅，本节只给出部分主要测试用例。

9.6.1 学生管理测试用例

1. 显示学生列表

显示学生列表的界面如图 9-26 所示。

学生列表		
账户	姓名	班级
zhangsan	张三	软工数192
xue1	学1	软工数192
xue2	学2	软工数192
xue3	学3	软工数192
xue4	学4	软工数192
teststu5	测试学生5	软工数192
lisi	李四	数科191
20192001003	王八	数科191
20211001002	李六	软工网212
账户	姓名	班级

图 9-26 显示学生列表

显示学生列表测试用例如表 9-18 所示。

表 9-18　显示学生列表测试用例

编　号	TC003		
功能描述	管理员查看系统中的学生列表		
用例目的	测试显示学生列表是否正常		
前提条件	管理员成功登录系统		
操作步骤	单击"学生管理"→"学生列表"		
测 试 项	输入数据/动作	预 期 结 果	实 际 结 果
显示效果	无	(1) 显示学生列表,包括账号、姓名、班级 (2) 分页显示	(1) 显示学生列表,包括账号、姓名、班级 (2) 分页显示

2．下载学生模板

下载学生模板测试用例如表 9-19 所示。

表 9-19　下载学生模板测试用例

编　号	TC004		
功能描述	管理员下载学生数据模板		
用例目的	测试模板文件下载是否正常		
前提条件	管理员成功登录系统		
操作步骤	单击"学生导入"→"下载模板"		
测 试 项	输入数据/动作	预 期 结 果	实 际 结 果
下载效果	无	下载 Excel 格式的模板文件	下载 Excel 格式的模板文件

3．导入学生信息

导入学生信息的界面如图 9-27 所示。

图 9-27　导入学生信息

导入学生信息测试用例如表 9-20 所示。

表 9-20 导入学生信息测试用例

编　　号	TC005		
功能描述	管理员导入学生数据		
用例目的	测试学生信息导入是否正常		
前提条件	管理员成功登录系统		
操作步骤	单击"学生管理"→"学生导入"		
测　试　项	输入数据/动作	预　期　结　果	实　际　结　果
正常的学生数据	(1) 编辑模板文件准备学生数据 (2) 单击"选择"按钮，选择编辑好的模板文件	提示导入成功	提示导入成功
部分重复数据	(1) 编辑模板文件准备学生数据，部分重复 (2) 单击"选择"按钮，选择编辑好的模板文件	提示导入成功	提示导入成功
空数据	(1) 编辑模板文件数据为空 (2) 单击"选择"按钮，选择编辑好的模板文件	数据为空，无须导入	数据为空，无须导入

9.6.2　题库管理测试用例

1. 教师创建题目

创建题目的界面如图 9-28 所示。

图 9-28　创建题目

创建题目的测试用例如表 9-21 所示。

表 9-21　创建题目测试用例

编　　号	TC006		
功能描述	教师创建个人题目		
用例目的	测试教师创建题目是否正常		
前提条件	教师成功登录系统		
操作步骤	单击"题库管理"→"创建题目"		
测 试 项	输入数据/动作	预 期 结 果	实 际 结 果
正常输入数据	(1) 题目：题目名称 (2) 题目描述：题目描述 (3) 题目备注：题目备注 (4) 单击"创建"按钮	提示创建成功	提示创建成功
异常输入数据	(1) 题目：空 (2) 题目描述：题目描述 (3) 题目备注：题目备注 (4) 单击"创建"按钮	提示创建失败	提示创建失败

2. 显示题库列表

显示题库列表的界面如图 9-29 所示。

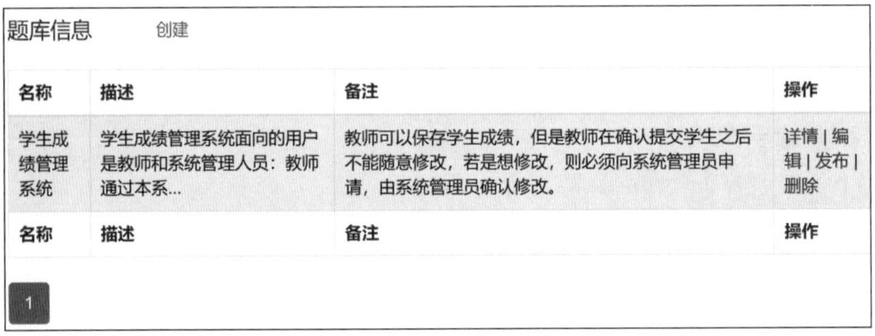

图 9-29　显示题库列表

显示题库列表的测试用例如表 9-22 所示。

表 9-22　显示题库列表测试用例

编　　号	TC007		
功能描述	显示教师个人的题库列表		
用例目的	测试显示教师个人题库是否正常		
前提条件	教师成功登录系统		
操作步骤	单击"我的题库"		
测 试 项	输入数据/动作	预 期 结 果	实 际 结 果
显示效果	无	(1) 显示个人的题目列表 (2) 每个题目显示操作入口 (3) 分页显示	(1) 显示个人的题目列表 (2) 每个题目显示操作入口 (3) 分页显示

3. 显示题目详情

显示题目详情的界面如图 9-30 所示。

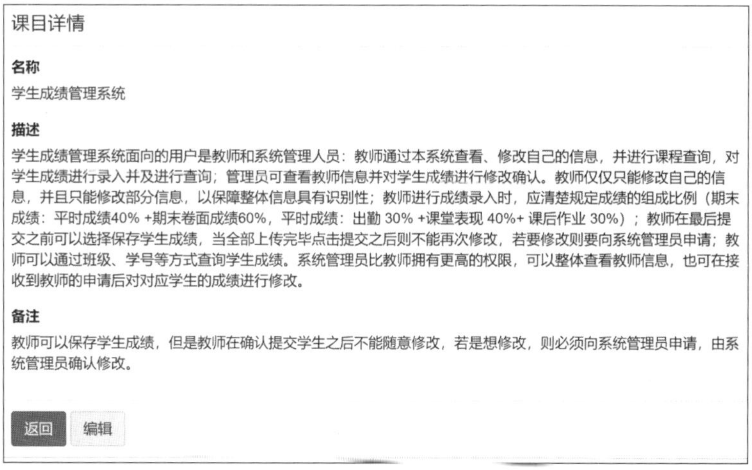

图 9-30　题目详情

显示题目详情的测试用例如表 9-23 所示。

表 9-23　显示题目详情测试用例

编　　号	TC008		
功能描述	显示教师题目的详情		
用例目的	测试显示教师题目详情是否显示正常		
前提条件	教师成功登录系统		
操作步骤	单击"我的题库"，针对想查看的题目，单击"详情"		
测 试 项	输入数据/动作	预 期 结 果	实 际 结 果
显示效果	无	显示题目详情	显示题目详情

4. 编辑题目信息

编辑题目信息的界面如图 9-31 所示。

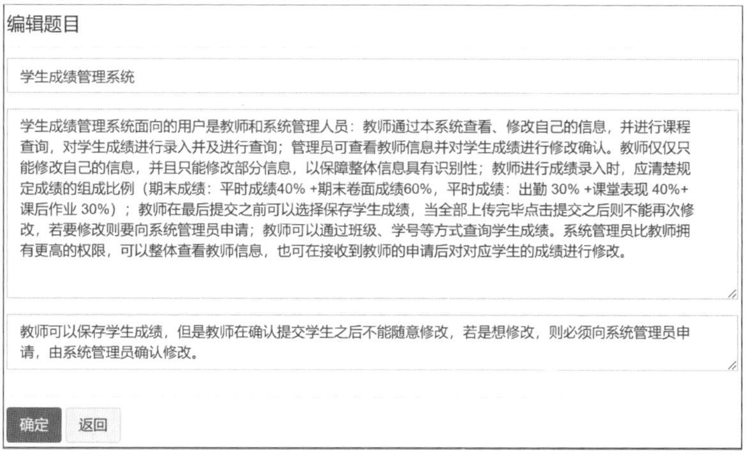

图 9-31　题目编辑

编辑题目信息的测试用例如表 9-24 所示。

表 9-24　编辑题目信息测试用例

编　号	TC009		
功能描述	编辑教师题目的信息		
用例目的	测试编辑教师题目信息是否正常		
前提条件	教师成功登录系统		
操作步骤	单击"我的题库",针对想查看的题目,单击"编辑"		
测　试　项	输入数据/动作	预　期　结　果	实　际　结　果
正常输入数据	(1) 题目:题目 (2) 题目描述:题目描述 (3) 题目备注:题目备注 (4) 单击"确定"按钮	(1) 提示修改成功 (2) 返回题库列表	(1) 提示修改成功 (2) 返回题库列表
异常输入数据	(1) 题目:空 (2) 题目描述:题目描述 (3) 题目备注:题目备注 (4) 单击"确定"按钮	(1) 提示修改失败 (2) 返回题库列表	(1) 提示修改失败 (2) 返回题库列表

5. 教师题目发布

教师题目发布的界面(部分)如图 9-32 所示。

图 9-32　题目发布

教师题目发布的测试用例如表9-25所示。

表9-25 教师题目发布测试用例

编　　号	TC010		
功能描述	教师发布个人题目		
用例目的	测试教师发布个人题目是否正常		
前提条件	教师成功登录系统		
操作步骤	单击"我的题库",针对想查看的题目,单击"发布"		
测　试　项	输入数据/动作	预　期　结　果	实　际　结　果
正常输入数据	(1) 最大组数：2 (2) 每组最多人数：3 (3) 课题密码：123 (4) 课题适用年级：2021 (5) 选择语言：Java、C# (6) 选择专业：软件工程 (7) 单击"提交"按钮	提示发布成功	提示发布成功
异常输入数据	(1) 最大组数：2 (2) 每组最多人数：3 (3) 课题密码：123 (4) 课题适用年级：没有选择 (5) 选择语言：没有选择 (6) 选择专业：没有选择 (7) 单击"提交"按钮	提示发布失败	提示发布失败

6. 教师删除题目

教师删除题目的测试用例如表9-26所示。

表9-26 教师删除题目测试用例

编　　号	TC011		
功能描述	教师删除个人题目		
用例目的	测试教师删除个人题目是否正常		
前提条件	教师成功登录系统		
操作步骤	单击"我的题库",针对想查看的题目,单击"删除"		
测　试　项	输入数据/动作	预　期　结　果	实　际　结　果
删除效果	无	(1) 提示删除成功 (2) 返回题库列表	(1) 提示删除成功 (2) 返回题库列表

9.6.3 课题选报测试用例

1. 查看课题列表

学生查看课题列表的界面如图9-33所示。

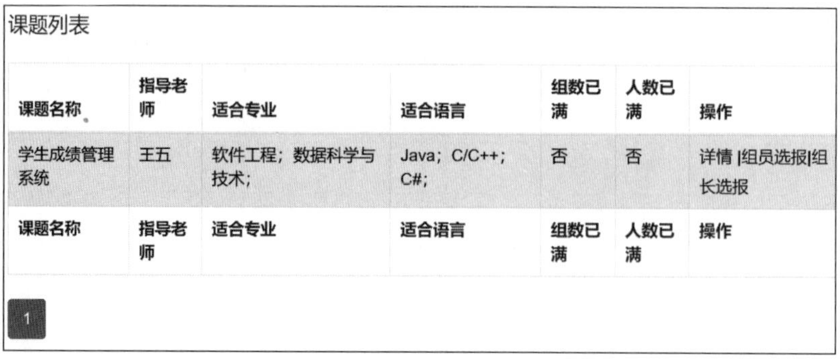

课题列表

课题名称	指导老师	适合专业	适合语言	组数已满	人数已满	操作
学生成绩管理系统	王五	软件工程；数据科学与技术；	Java；C/C++；C#；	否	否	详情|组员选报|组长选报
课题名称	指导老师	适合专业	适合语言	组数已满	人数已满	操作

1

图 9-33　查看课题列表

学生查看课题列表测试用例如表 9-27 所示。

表 9-27　学生查看课题列表测试用例

编　　号	TC012		
功能描述	学生查看可供选报的课题列表		
用例目的	测试学生查看可供选报的课题列表显示是否正常		
前提条件	学生成功登录系统		
操作步骤	单击"课题选报"→"课题查询"		
测 试 项	输入数据/动作	预 期 结 果	实 际 结 果
显示效果	无	（1）显示课题列表 （2）分页显示	（1）显示课题列表 （2）分页显示

2. 查看课题详情

学生查看课题详情的界面如图 9-34 所示。

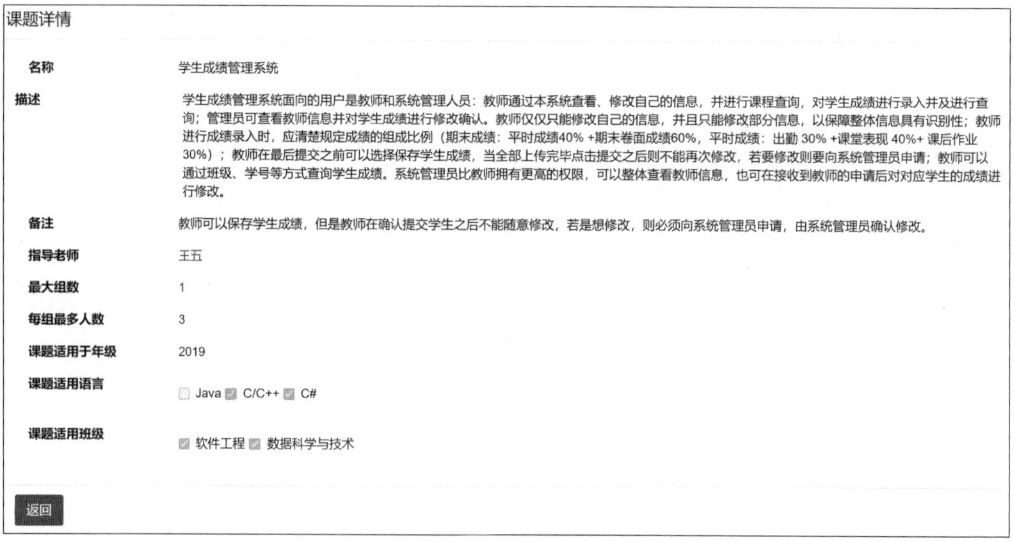

课题详情

名称	学生成绩管理系统
描述	学生成绩管理系统面向的用户是教师和系统管理人员：教师通过本系统查看、修改自己的信息，并进行课程查询，对学生成绩进行录入并及进行查询；管理员可查看教师信息并对学生成绩进行修改确认。教师仅仅只能修改自己的信息，并且只能修改部分信息，以保障整体信息具有识别性；教师进行成绩录入时，应清楚规定成绩的组成比例（期末成绩：平时成绩40% +期末卷面成绩60%，平时成绩：出勤 30% +课堂表现 40%+ 课后作业 30%）；教师在最后提交之前可以选择保存学生成绩，当全部上传完毕点击提交之后则不能再次修改，若要修改则要向系统管理员申请；教师可以通过班级、学号等方式查询学生成绩。系统管理员比教师拥有更高的权限，可以整体查看教师信息，也可在接收到教师的申请后对应学生的成绩进行修改。
备注	教师可以保存学生成绩，但是教师在确认提交学生之后不能随意修改，若是想修改，则必须向系统管理员申请，由系统管理员确认修改。
指导老师	王五
最大组数	1
每组最多人数	3
课题适用于年级	2019
课题适用语言	☐ Java ☑ C/C++ ☑ C#
课题适用班级	☑ 软件工程 ☑ 数据科学与技术

返回

图 9-34　查看课题详情

学生查看课题详情的测试用例如表 9-28 所示。

表 9-28 学生查看课题详情测试用例

编 号	TC013		
功能描述	学生查看课题详情		
用例目的	测试学生查看课题详情显示是否正常		
前提条件	学生成功登录系统		
操作步骤	单击"课题选报"→"课题查询",针对想查看的课题,单击"详情"		
测 试 项	输入数据/动作	预 期 结 果	实 际 结 果
显示效果	无	显示课题详情	显示课题详情

3. 作为组长选报

学生作为组长选报课题的界面如图 9-35 所示。

图 9-35 学生选报课题

学生作为组长选报课题的测试用例如表 9-29 所示。

表 9-29 学生作为组长选报课题测试用例

编 号	TC014		
功能描述	学生作为组长选报课题		
用例目的	测试学生作为组长选报课题是否正常		
前提条件	学生成功登录系统		
操作步骤	单击"课题选报"→"课题查询",针对想查看的课题,单击"组长选报"		
测 试 项	输入数据/动作	预 期 结 果	实 际 结 果
正常数据	(1) 输入课题密码:123 (2) 设置本组密码:456 (3) 单击"提交"按钮	(1) 提示选报成功 (2) 返回我的选报	(1) 提示选报成功 (2) 返回我的选报
错误密码	(1) 输入课题密码:空 (2) 设置本组密码:456 (3) 单击"提交"按钮	提示密码错误	提示密码错误

4. 作为组员选报

学生作为组员选报课题的界面如图 9-36 所示。

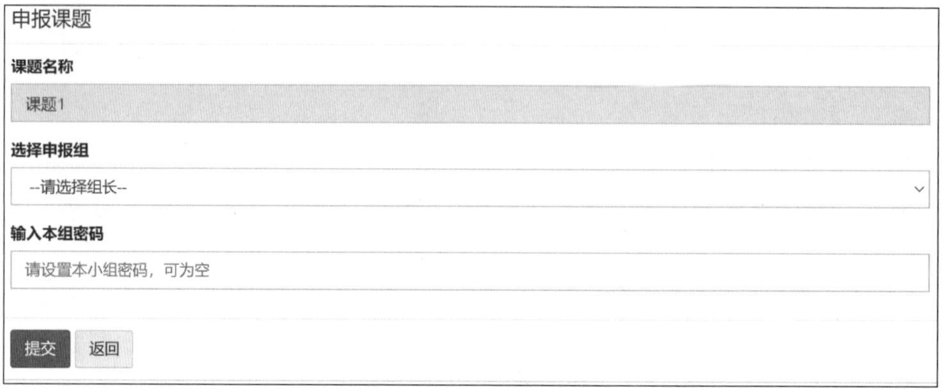

图 9-36 学生选报课题

学生作为组员选报课题的测试用例如表 9-30 所示。

表 9-30 学生作为组员选报课题测试用例

编　　号	TC014		
功能描述	学生作为组员选报课题		
用例目的	测试学生作为组员选报课题是否正常		
前提条件	学生成功登录系统		
操作步骤	单击"课题选报"→"课题查询",针对想查看的课题,单击"组员选报"		
测　试　项	输入数据/动作	预　期　结　果	实　际　结　果
正常数据	(1) 选择申报组：张三 (2) 输入本组密码：456 (3) 单击"提交"按钮	(1) 提示选报成功 (2) 返回我的选报	(1) 提示选报成功 (2) 返回我的选报
错误密码	(1) 选择申报组：张三 (2) 输入本组密码：123 (3) 单击"提交"按钮	提示密码错误	提示密码错误

5. "我的选报"记录

"我的选报"记录的界面如图 9-37 所示。

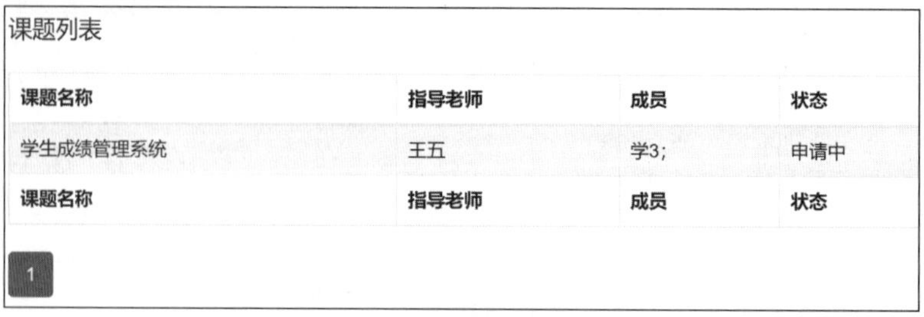

图 9-37 "我的选报"记录

"我的选报"记录的测试用例如表 9-31 所示。

表 9-31 "我的选报"记录测试用例

编　　号	TC015		
功能描述	学生查看"我的选报"记录		
用例目的	测试学生查看"我的选报"记录显示是否正常		
前提条件	学生成功登录系统		
操作步骤	单击"课题选报"→"我的选报"		
测　试　项	输入数据/动作	预　期　结　果	实　际　结　果
测试显示效果	无	(1) 显示我的选报记录 (2) 分页显示	(1) 显示我的选报记录 (2) 分页显示

9.7 技术经验总结

9.7.1 技术总结

本系统用到了以下技术及知识点。

(1) 本系统使用了 ASP.NET MVC 技术,使得系统结构更清晰、可维护性更强。

(2) 本系统在数据持久化上使用了 Entity Framework 6,使开发人员能够通过领域对象来处理数据,而无须关注存储此数据的基础数据库,与传统应用程序相比,可以使用更少的代码创建和维护面向数据的应用程序。

(3) 本系统使用 NPOI 库操作了 Excel 文件,实现了从 Excel 文件读取数据及导出数据至 Excel 的功能。

(4) 本系统前端使用了 AdminLTE 模板,它是建立在 Bootstrap 和 JQuery 之上的开源的模板,提供了一系列响应的、可重复使用的组件,并内置了多个模板页面;同时自适应多种屏幕分辨率。

9.7.2 经验总结

本章系统业务较复杂,所以在开始编写代码之前要进行细致、周密的需求分析及调研。从系统的三种用户的角度去分析,把握整个实践课题管理工作的业务流。与一般的管理信息系统不同,本系统各业务环节之间数据依赖性很强,如果前一个阶段的数据处理不准确,则会导致后面环节出现失误。因此本系统的分析及设计阶段是按照螺旋式开发方法进行的,即在设计过程中逐步验证需求分析阶段成果的正确性,反复修改及完善,最终实现需求分析与设计的一致性及正确性。

参 考 文 献

[1] 朱顺泉.管理信息系统理论与实务[M].3版.北京:人民邮电出版社,2008.
[2] 周贺来.管理信息系统理[M].北京:中国人民大学出版社,2012.
[3] 黄梯云.管理信息系统[M].4版.北京:高等教育出版社,2011.
[4] 张建华.管理信息系统理[M].北京:中国电力出版社,2008.